THE GREEK THEATER AND ITS DRAMA

FIG. 1

THE THEATER OF DIONYSUS ELEUTHEREUS AT ATHENS AS SEEN FROM THE ACROPOLIS

See p. 62, n. 2

THE GREEK THEATER AND ITS DRAMA

BY

ROY C. FLICKINGER, Ph.D.

THE UNIVERSITY OF CHICAGO PRESS

CHICAGO & LONDON

The University of Chicago Press, Chicago 60637
The University of Chicago Press, Ltd., London

© 1918, 1922, 1926, and 1936 by The University of Chicago
All rights reserved. Published 1918
Second Edition 1922. Third Edition 1926. Fourth Edition 1936
Chicago Reprint Series issue 1960. Fifth Impression 1973
Printed in the United States of America
International Standard Book Number: 0–226–25369–4
Library of Congress Catalog Card Number: 36–11686

PREFACE

Prior to the outbreak of the world-war in Europe it seemed that America was about to pass through a period of great popular interest in the drama. With the return of normal activities consequent upon the coming of peace it is to be hoped that this interest may be revived and may continue to grow. So far as such interest is hysterical or manifested by attempts at play-writing on the part of those without training, experience, or natural aptitude it has little to commend it. On the other hand, nothing can be more wholesome than a widespread comprehension of the origin, history, and basic principles of tragedy and comedy. Thus, we are deeply indebted to the successive scholars who have undertaken to analyze Elizabethan drama and assign to Seneca, the Latin comedians, Aristotle, the Greek playwrights, and the various mediaeval elements their respective shares of influence. But, as the ultimate source of all other dramatic art, the Greeks' contribution, whether in precept or example, must ever occupy a unique position. Accordingly, no effort, however humble, to make the theater and drama of the Greeks more widely known ought to require an apology.

In the following pages I have tried to do three things:

First, to elaborate the theory that the peculiarities and conventions of the Greek drama are largely explicable by its environment, in the broadest sense of that term. Some aspects of this fundamental proposition have already been developed by others. But, so far as results have been sought in the field of classical drama, it has been done less comprehensively than is here attempted; and the earlier work has been, for the most part, antiquated by the momentous accession of new information during the last twenty-five years.

Secondly, to emphasize the technical aspect of ancient drama. Technique has largely escaped the attention even of our playwrights, some of whom attempt to produce plays that will have

none. Most of our classical scholars, also, study and teach and
edit the ancient dramatists as if they, too, had been equally
slipshod. Our handbooks on scenic antiquities and the classical
drama have been written from the same point of view. Of late
years the Germans have awakened to the real situation, and
many of their recent monographs deal with various phases of
the subject. Nevertheless, so lately as 1911 a German dissertation began with these words:

> As yet not very many investigations into the technique of the Greek
> tragedians are available. In addition to the incidental hints that are
> scattered here and there, especially in the commentaries, two works in this
> field are above all to be mentioned and they are both very recent: Adolf
> Gross, *Die Stichomythie in der griechischen Tragödie und Komödie* (1905),
> and Friedrich Leo, *Der Monolog im Drama* (1908).[1]

In what terms, then, ought the indifference, not to say the
unawareness, of American scholars with regard to these matters
to be characterized? It is true that quite recently the German
publications have caused some attention to be devoted, in this
country, to the dramaturgy of the classical playwrights; but
as yet such researches have gained only scant recognition from
the generality of classical students.

Thirdly, to elucidate and freshen ancient practice by modern
and mediaeval parallels. This is an old and deeply worked mine,
and I am under heavy obligations to my predecessors; but the
vein is inexhaustible, and I have striven to keep the point in
mind more steadfastly than is sometimes the case. It is of a
piece with this to add that I have endeavored to treat the ancient
plays as if they were not dead and inert, belonging to a world
apart, but as if their authors were men as real as Ibsen or Galsworthy, who had real problems and met them in a real way.
The desirability of this point of view surely ought not to be a
matter of question; yet in fact it is exemplified with surprising
rareness. To many, Sophocles and Euripides seem to possess
scarcely more historicity than the heroes of Greek mythology.

---

[1] Cf. Hermann Deckinger, *Die Darstellung der persönlichen Motive bei Aischylos
und Sophokles* (1911), p. 1.

To a varying degree all these aims run afoul of a historic controversy among dramatic critics. In the *Poetics* Aristotle recognized the distinction between studying tragedy "by itself" and in reference also to the audience (or theater).[1] He included "spectacle" (ὄψις) or "the equipment of the spectacle" (ὁ τῆς ὄψεως κόσμος) among the six parts which every tragedy must have, but proceeded to declare that "this, though emotionally attractive, is least artistic of the parts and has least to do with the art of poetry, since the power of tragedy exists even apart from a public performance and actors and since, furthermore, it is the art of the costumer (or stage machinist) rather than that of the poet to secure spectacular effects." He granted that "fear and pity may be excited by the spectacle, but they may be excited also by the inner structure of the play, which is the preferable method and is typical of a better poet," etc. "The power of a tragedy," he thought, "may be made manifest by merely reading it." Finally, he pointed out that music and spectacle are just the accessories in which tragedy surpasses epic poetry and that they constitute no inconsiderable addition to its effect by rendering its pleasures most vivid. These citations suffice to show Aristotle's attitude, which was consistently maintained: he believed the spectacle to be one of the indispensable elements of drama, but that it ought also to be a comparatively subordinate element. This was an eminently sane position to take, and it would have been well if his successors had been equally judicious.

Dr. Spingarn has tried to break down the force of Aristotle's recognition of spectacular effects by saying that he could not "help thinking of plays in connection with their theatrical representation, any more than most of us can think of men and women without clothes. They belong together by long habit and use; they help each other to be what we commonly think them. But he does not make them identical or mutually

---

[1] Cf. Aristotle *Poetics* 1449a8. The other passages cited in this paragraph are *ibid.* 1449b33 and 1450a10, 1450b17–21, 1453b1–3, 1462a12, and 1462a14–17.

inclusive."[1] In other words, Aristotle had no acquaintance with
the "closet-drama," and so did not take it into account. But
there is an allowance to be made also on the other side. There
is some doubt as to just what Aristotle meant by "spectacle,"
whether merely "the visible appearance of the actors when got
up in character by the costumier" or "scenery, dresses—the
whole visible apparatus of the theater." Even if he had the
larger meaning in mind he could not have realized its full
significance. He knew but a single type of theatrical building,
which must therefore have seemed to him as integral a part of
dramatic performances as the Greek climate. He could not
look down the ages and contrast the simple arrangements of the
Greek theater with the varying lighting effects and scenic
splendor of modern and intervening types. He could not avoid,
then, underestimating the importance of this factor. Furthermore, when he states that of the six parts the spectacle has least
to do with the art of poetry and is more closely related to the art
of the costumer than to that of the poet, he means what he says
and no more. As its title indicates, his treatise was concerned
with the art of poetry, not with that of dramaturgy. Hence he
stressed the factors that dealt with the essence of tragedy rather
than those which influenced only its accidental features and
external form. Even so, he conceded to the latter elements no
negligible value. Considered from the dramaturgical standpoint
as well, he must have allowed them a much greater importance.

As it happens, Spingarn confines his examination of Aristotle's
views to the *Poetics*, but in the *Rhetoric* occurs the interesting
observation that "on the stage the actors are at present of more
importance than the poets."[2] Aristotle did not state that this
was the proper relationship, but as a practical man he simply
recognized the facts before his eyes. And these words utterly re-
pudiate Spingarn's attempt to subvert the obvious implication
of Aristotle's statements in the *Poetics*.

[1] Cf. his paper entitled "Dramatic Criticism and the Theatre" in *Creative
Criticism*, p. 56 (1917).

[2] Cf. Aristotle *Rhetoric* 1403b33 (Jebb's translation). This statement needs
to be interpreted in the light of pp. 190 f., below.

I have given so much space to Aristotle's opinions because Spingarn did. But, after all, it does not greatly matter. Times have changed since Roger Bacon placed the crown of infallibility on the Stagirite's brow with the words: "Aristotle hath the same authority in philosophy that the apostle Paul hath in divinity." The investigation of such questions no longer begins and ends with "the master of those that know."

Nevertheless I conceive Aristotle's position in the present matter to have been a sensible one, though it has oftentimes been sadly disregarded and even flouted. One school has ignored the spectacle as a factor in dramatic criticism. The other school has exalted it to the chief place. In my opinion both attitudes are erroneous. The former party is the older and more numerous. I fancy that most adherents of this view err unconsciously. It is particularly easy in dealing with the dramatic remains of bygone ages to ignore or minimize the effect which the manner of presentation must have exercised and practically to confine one's attention to literary criticism in the narrowest sense of the term. To this tendency classical scholars have been peculiarly prone. But there are many others who are quite aware of the full meaning of the position they occupy. One of these is Spingarn, who roundly declares: "A play is a creative work of the imagination, and must be considered as such always, *and as such only*."[1]

The opposing view seems to have been promulgated first by Castelvetro (1570) and enjoyed no particular popularity until recently. It was adopted by the Abbé d'Aubignac in the seventeenth century, by Diderot in the eighteenth century, by A. W. Schlegel during the first half of the nineteenth century, and by Francisque Sarcey during the latter half. There is no space here to trace the developments of the doctrine; for that the interested reader may consult Spingarn's article. But the general position of the school is as follows: "A play is a story (a) devised to be presented (b) by actors (c) on a stage (d) before an audience."[2]

---

[1] Cf. *op. cit.*, p. 56. The italics are mine.

[2] Cf. Clayton Hamilton, *The Theory of the Theatre* (1910), p. 3; and J. B. Matthews, *North American Review*, CLXXXVII (1908), 213 f.: "They believe that the playhouse has now, has had in the past, and must always have a monopoly

These are not merely important elements or essential elements; they are the prime elements. They outweigh all other considerations. It was Diderot's central idea that the essential part of a play was not created by the poet at all, but by the actor. The "closet-drama" they hold up to scorn as a contradiction in terms. The "psychology of the crowd," long before that name for it had been invented, was an integral part of this teaching. The inadequacy of this point of view is aptly expressed in Goethe's words concerning Schlegel: "His criticism is completely one-sided, because in all theatrical pieces he merely regards the skeleton of the plot and arrangement, and only points out small points of resemblance to great predecessors, without troubling himself in the least as to what the author brings forward of graceful life and the culture of a high soul."[1]

To me neither of these theories is satisfactory. I conceive the truth to lie between them. Etymologically the word "drama" means "action," and the practice of the Greek theater for centuries shows that an action carried on by living impersonators is involved. Action narrated on a printed page is not enough. I am willing to concede that by a natural extension of meaning a piece which was confessedly written for the closet and which does not and cannot succeed upon the stage may nevertheless deserve to be called a "drama." But despite its poetic charm and other merits such a drama *qua* drama is indeed a *vie manquée*. On the other hand, against the materialistic school I maintain the self-evident proposition that it is possible for a play to observe all the technical rules arising from the conditions of performance in a theater and before an audience and yet be so lacking in poetry, in truth to life, in inherent worth, as to be

---

of the dramatic form. They cannot recognize the legitimacy of a play which is not intended to be played. They know that the great dramatist of every period when the drama has flourished has always planned his plays for performance in the theater of his own time, by the actors of his own time, and before the spectators of his own time"; and *The Independent*, LXVIII (1910), 187: "In other words, the literary quality is something that may be added to a drama, but which is not essential to its value as a play in the theater itself."

[1] Cf. *Conversations with Eckermann*, March 28, 1827 (Oxenford's translation).

undeserving of the name of "drama." It is evident, then, that craftsmanship must be the medium of the playwright, not his sole possession. But, in truth, the issue here is more apparent than real. It does not confront us in practice. Both these extremes constitute a negligible fraction of our dramatic literature. Students of the drama in university seminars, dramatic reviewers in the theaters, and playwrights at their desks, at least those who aspire to an enduring fame, alike draw upon the same body of plays for their knowledge of dramatic lore—upon Shakespeare, Euripides, Molière, Lessing, Sophocles, Ibsen. All these masters had a close and practical knowledge of the theater for which they wrote. On the other hand, they were infinitely more than mere technicians.

But Spingarn would maintain that the aesthetic value of a play is entirely independent of theatrical conditions or the conventions arising therefrom. "For aesthetic criticism the theater simply does not exist" (cf. *op. cit.*, p. 89). Surely, if Sophocles were writing plays for the present-day public he would find it necessary to dispense with the choral odes which have been at once the delight and the despair of Greek students from his generation to this. Would not such an omission and the consequent readjustments affect the aesthetic value of his tragedies? Or if one of our dramatists could be set down in a Greek theater of some twenty-four hundred years ago, which was incapable of representing an interior scene and had never contained a box set, certainly his dramas would have to be turned literally inside out before they could be produced at all. Would this recasting in no wise affect their aesthetic criticism? Spingarn is anxious to protect Aristotle from the imputation of believing that plays and their theatrical representation are "mutually inclusive." But his own position makes them mutually *ex*clusive. Both theories are extreme and unwarranted. I have already quoted Spingarn's conception of a play. In my opinion, Mr. Galsworthy's putting of the matter is not only broader, but far preferable, for the reason that it duly recognizes, as Spingarn's dictum does not, the facts of existence. He writes:

"For what is Art but the perfected expression of self in contact with the world?"[1] While this definition takes full cognizance of aesthetic and spiritual values, it yet does not exclude such unmentioned but implicit factors as the medium of expression chosen by the artist, the circumstances under which his work is created and is to be exhibited, the past history and inherited conventions of the genre, etc. On the contrary, it is apparent that Galsworthy would not, after the fashion of the materialistic school, elevate these indispensable, though subordinate, matters to the exclusion of all else.

It thus appears that I array myself neither with the aesthetic nor with the materialistic school of critics, but occupy middle ground. Nevertheless, my book is devoted, in the main, to a consideration of the more materialistic and external factors in the development of Greek drama. These factors are different manifestations of Environment, which is a far broader term than Aristotle's Spectacle (ὄψις). I entertain no illusion as to the comparative importance of environment in the criticism of drama. It is distinctly of secondary importance. If it were possible to study Greek drama from but one point of view, perhaps this would not deserve to be that one. But since no such restriction obtains, it is my contention that a consideration of these factors, too, is not merely valuable, but essential to a complete survey of the field.

It will now be seen why I have no chapter on the "Influence of the Poet." He can hardly be considered a part of his own environment. But there were also other reasons for the omission. Partly it was because every chapter shows the master-mind of the dramatist adapting himself to the situation therein outlined, and partly because an adequate treatment of this topic would involve a presentation of the poets' ideas and teaching—a subject which is amply discussed in other treatises and which would swell this volume beyond the limits at my disposal. I am aware that to some the result will seem to give the uninitiated a lopsided view of the Greek drama. For example, a reviewer

[1] Cf. *The Inn of Tranquillity* (1912), p. 277.

of Signor Francesco Guglielmino's *Arte e Artifizio nel Dramma Greco* (Catania, 1912) maintains that "for the reader who is not technically a scholar" such a study of dramatic technique presents "a subtly distorted picture."[1] To this criticism my reply would be that the standard handbooks are guilty of much the same error in largely ignoring the phase of the subject which is here presented. But however that may be, for the language and style or for the political, moral, ethical, and religious ideas of ancient playwrights, I must recommend such invaluable works as Haigh's *Tragic Drama of the Greeks* (1896), Decharme's *Euripides and the Spirit of His Dramas*, Croiset's *Aristophanes and the Political Parties at Athens*, Legrand's *The New Greek Comedy* (the last three translated by Loeb, 1906, 1909, and 1917), Sheppard's *Greek Tragedy* (1911), Murray's *Euripides and His Age* (1913), etc. I must add, however, that to a certain extent these books treat also of the matters discussed in this volume and have freely been consulted.

In this connection I wish to comment upon another objection. Several of my articles which are incorporated in the present volume antedate Guglielmino's work, and my whole book was blocked out and large parts of it were written before his *Arte e Artifizio* came to my attention. Nevertheless my plan of treatment bears some points of resemblance to his. In particular, he employs the chauvinistic passages in Greek tragedy to show the poets striving for "immediate effects," i.e., deliberately exciting the patriotic sentiments of their audiences. It will be observed that I go a step farther and maintain that the winning of the prize was the ultimate object, to which the other motive was contributory (see pp. 213 ff., below). I believe that the tag at the end of Euripides' *Iphigenia among the Taurians, Orestes*, and *Phoenician Maids* and the parallels from Greek comedy confirm my interpretation. But the reviewer just cited declares it unfair to the dramatist and his art to forget that he and his audience were all Athenians together. . . . . When the Athenian dramatist, sharing the Athenian pride in their country's history or legend, makes a character

[1] Cf. *Classical Philology*, IX (1914), 96.

express a common patriotic emotion or belief, we cannot properly call that flattery of the audience, or an artifice for effect, even though the words were sure to call out rapturous applause. The bit of truth in such a view is so partial as to be false.

But, as Professor Murray says of the choral ode in the *Medea*, "They are not at all the conventional glories attributed by all patriots to their respective countries."[1] Moreover, these passages usually rest upon no popular belief, for the simple reason that they frequently corresponded neither to history nor to traditional mythology, but dealt with incidents that had been newly invented by the poet's fancy or had at least been invested by him with new details and setting.

At the beginning of the European conflagration in August, 1914, London managers hastened to bring out such plays as *Drake, Henry V*, and *An Englishman's Home*. Was this merely the prompting of genuinely patriotic fervor on their part, or a misdirected attempt to exploit the emotions of their countrymen? The fact that this class of plays was soon withdrawn after it became apparent that the public heard enough about the war elsewhere without being reminded of it also in the theaters favors the latter explanation. Now, that Aristophanes frankly angled for the suffrages of his audiences cannot be denied. When, then, we remember how Euripides began to write for the stage when he was only eighteen, how he had to wait for a chorus in the great contest until he was thirty and then gained only the last place, how his first victory was deferred until 441 B.C. when he was forty-four years of age, how few were the victories that he won, how he courted his public by seeking out unhackneyed themes, by inventing sensational episodes, by reverting to the mannerisms of Aeschylus, by introducing sex problems—when we remember all this, can it be doubted that his chauvinistic passages were part and parcel of the same policy and were deliberately written with the same motives as are revealed in the choice of plays by Sir Herbert Tree and the other London managers of today?

But perhaps it may be said that the psychology of managers is utterly unlike that of poets. In reply it would be possible

[1] Cf. *Euripides and His Age* (1913), p. 89. See p. 217, below.

and sufficient to cite the not infrequent concessions which
Shakespeare and many another have made to the groundlings
in their audiences, but I prefer to quote the words of a dramatist who has declared himself on the subject more explicitly.
Mr. Henry Arthur Jones has recently written:

A dramatist is often reproached for producing plays that are obviously
below the standard of his aspirations, and obviously below the level of his
best work. This assumes that the dramatist is, like the novelist, always
free to do his best work. There could not be a greater mistake. The dramatist is limited and curbed by a thousand conditions which are never suspected
by the public. The drama will always remain a popular art. . . . . The
dramatist who writes plays too far ahead, or too far away from the taste
and habits of thought of the general body of playgoers, finds the theatre
empty, his manager impoverished, and his own reputation and authority
diminished or lost. No sympathy should be given to dramatists, however
lofty their aims, who will not study to please the general body of playgoers
of their days. . . . . The question to be asked concerning a dramatist is—
"Does he desire to give the public the best they will accept from him, or
does he give them the readiest filth or nonsense that most quickly pays?"
He cannot always even give the public the best that they would accept from
him. In sitting down to write a play, he must first ask himself, "Can I get
a manager of repute to produce this, and in such a way and at such a theatre
that it can be seen to advantage? Can I get some leading actor or actress
to play this part for the benefit of the play as a whole? Can I get these
other individual types of character played in such a way that they will
appear to be something like the persons I have in my mind?" These and
a hundred other questions the dramatist has to ask himself before he decides
upon the play he will write. A mistake in the casting of a secondary character may ruin a play, so narrow is the margin of success. . . . . I hope I
may be forgiven for intruding this personal matter by way of excuse and
explanation. In no case do I blame or arraign the public, who, in the
theatre, will always remain my masters, and whose grateful and willing
servant I shall always remain.[1]

It should be recognized that my book is intended for two very
diverse types of readers, whose demands likewise are dissimilar:
First, for a general reading public which has little or no
acquaintance with the Greek and Latin classics in the original
but has a deep and abiding interest in the drama together with

[1] Cf. *The Theatre of Ideas* (1915), pp. 9 ff. (copyrighted by the George H. Doran
Company).

a desire to learn more of the prototypes and masterpieces of the genre. This situation has made necessary an amplitude of explanatory matter which, I fear, will at times prove irksome to my professional confrères. On the other hand, I have felt that intellectual honesty required me to treat the topics discussed in my Introduction and to meet the problems there raised at some length and without evasions. But to do so necessitated the interpretation of Greek texts and the presentation of much jejune material. Perhaps, therefore, some of my non-classical readers will prefer to omit the Introduction. By cross-references and slight repetitions I have endeavored to make the rest of the book intelligible without it. The English word "stage" is too convenient to be avoided in discussing theatrical matters, but those who omit the third section of the Introduction are to understand that its use in my text does not mean that I believe that the Greek theater of the fourth and fifth centuries B.C. had a raised stage for the exclusive use of actors.

Secondly, although much that I have written is necessarily well known to classicists, still, since I have striven to incorporate the results of the latest investigations and have arranged under one co-ordinating principle phenomena which are usually regarded as unrelated, and since I have combined points of interpretation which are scattered through scores of books and monographs, I venture to hope that my discussion will not be without interest even for specialists.

Inasmuch as the comedies of Plautus and Terence are but translations and adaptations of Greek originals, and since Seneca's tragedies are constructed upon the Greek model, I have not hesitated to cite these Latin plays whenever they seemed to afford better illustrations than purely Greek productions.

I must express my constant indebtedness to such invaluable storehouses of data as Müller's *Lehrbuch der griechischen Bühnen-alterthümer* (1886) and *Das attische Bühnenwesen*[2] (1916), Navarre's *Dionysos* (1895), and especially Haigh's *The Attic Theatre*,

third edition by Pickard-Cambridge (1907); also to Butcher's
Aristotle's Theory of Poetry and Fine Art, fourth edition with
corrections (1911), and Bywater's edition of Aristotle's *Poetics*
(1909).

I desire to thank the editors for permission, graciously
granted, to use material which I have already published in
Classical Philology, V (1910), VII (1912), and VIII (1913), the
Classical Weekly, III (1910), VIII (1915), X (1917), and XI
(1918), and the *Classical Journal,* VII (1911) and X (1914).
Needless to state, these papers have not been brought over into
the present volume verbatim, but have been curtailed, expanded,
revised, and rearranged according to need. Furthermore, fully
two-thirds of the book are entirely new.

Permission to quote from Mr. A. S. Way's translation of
Euripides in the "Loeb Classical Library," Dr. B. B. Rogers'
translation of Aristophanes, and Professor J. S. Blackie's translation of Aeschylus in "Everyman's Library" has been cour-
teously granted by William Heinemann, London (G. P. Putnam's
Sons, New York), G. Bell & Sons, and J. M. Dent & Sons,
respectively.

To my friends, Professor D. M. Robinson of Johns Hopkins
University and Dr. A. S. Cooley of Bethlehem, Pa., I am indebted
for having placed at my disposal their collections of photographs
of Greek theaters. My colleague, Professor M. R. Hammer of
the Northwestern University College of Engineering, has put
me under deep obligation by supervising the preparation of
several of the drawings.

In conclusion, my heartiest thanks are due to Professor
Edward Capps, who first introduced me to the study of scenic
antiquities. Several parts of this book, when originally published as articles, have enjoyed the benefit of his invaluable
suggestions and criticisms. It is unnecessary to add, however,
that he must not be held responsible for any part of them in their
present form.

ROY C. FLICKINGER

EVANSTON, ILL.

CONTENTS

LIST OF ILLUSTRATIONS

Some day a benefactor of his kind
may prove beyond cavil that the problem
of the origin of tragedy is as incapable of
solution as is that of squaring the circle.—
W. S BURRAGE.

INTRODUCTION

In undertaking to treat of a subject concerning hardly a detail of which can any statement be made without the possibility of dispute, the unfortunate necessity rests upon me of beginning with three topics which are the most controversial of all—the origin of tragedy, the origin of comedy, and the Greek theater. Instead of trying to conceal our ignorance on these matters by vague generalities, I shall set forth such data as are known, and attempt, clearly and frankly, to erect hypotheses to answer the questions that most naturally arise, even though this very striving for clearness and frankness will expose me to attack. I believe with Bacon that "truth emerges sooner from error than from confusion," or, as a recent writer has expressed it, that "the definitizing of error is often the beginning of its disappearance." Limits of space will require, at many points, a dogmatic statement of my views without stopping to examine the evidence from every angle. It must be understood, however, that no account of these subjects, whoever its author or however detailed his treatment, could find universal acceptance or anything approaching it.

The Origin of Tragedy.[1]—It is still the canonical doctrine, though its modern history goes back no farther than Welcker's

[1] Cf. Welcker, *Nachtrag zu der Schrift über die Aeschylische Trilogie nebst einer Abhandlung über das Satyrspiel* (1826); Furtwängler, "Der Satyr aus Pergamon," *Berliner Winckelmannsfest Programm*, XL (1880); U. von Wilamowitz-Möllendorff, *Einleitung in die griechische Tragödie* [Vol. I of his edition of Euripides' *Heracles* (1889)], pp. 43 ff. and *Neue Jahrbücher für das klassische Altertum*, XXIX (1912), 464 ff.; Bethe, *Prolegomena zur Geschichte des Theaters im Altherthum* (1896); G. Körte, "Satyrn und Böcke," in Bethe's *Prolegomena*, pp. 339 ff.; Wernicke, "Bockschöre und Satyrdrama," *Hermes*, XXXII (1897), 290 ff.; Schmid, *Zur Geschichte des gr. Dithyrambus* (1901); Reisch, "Zur Vorgeschichte der attischen Tragödie," in *Festschrift Theodor Gomperz* (1902), pp. 451 ff.; Crusius, *s.v.*

book on the *Satyrspiel* in 1826 and though no conclusive testimony for this view can be cited more ancient than Byzantine times, that satyric drama was the intermediate stage in the derivation of tragedy from the dithyramb. The argument runs somewhat as follows: The dithyramb was an improvisational song and dance in honor of Dionysus (Bacchus), the god of wine, and was performed by a band of men provided with goatlike horns, ears, hoofs, and tails and clad in a goatskin (or in a goat-hair loin-band) in imitation of Dionysus' attendant sprites, the satyrs; on account of this costume the choreutae (members of the chorus) were sometimes called *tragoi*, which is the Greek word for "goats"; in certain localities, as the dithyramb became quasi-literary and took on a dramatic element, its name was changed to satyric drama; still later, as these tendencies increased, especially through the addition of an actor, the satyr-play came to be called *tragoidia* ("goat-song"), derived from the nickname applied to the caprine choreutae; the chorus still consisted of satyrs and, since these were licentious, bestial creatures, the performance was yet crude and undignified; Aeschylus (525–456 B.C.) was possibly the first to abandon satyric choreutae and was certainly the first to raise tragedy to the rank of real literature; during the fifth century each poet was required to follow his group of three tragedies at the dramatic festival with a satyr-play as a concession to the satyric origin of the performance.

"Dithyrambos," in Pauly-Wissowa, *Real-Encyclopädie*, V, 1203 ff. (1903); Dieterich, "Die Entstehung der Tragödie," *Archiv für Religionswissenschaft*, XI (1908), 163 ff. [Kleine Schriften, pp. 414 ff.]; Farnell, *Cults of the Greek States*, V, 85 ff., and especially pp. 224 ff. (1909), and "The Megala Dionysia and the Origin of Tragedy," *Journal of Hellenic Studies*, XXIX (1909), xlvii; Ridgeway, *The Origin of Tragedy with Special Reference to the Greek Tragedians* (1910), and *The Dramas and Dramatic Dances of Non-European Races in Special Reference to the Origin of Greek Tragedy* (1915), reviewed by Flickinger in *Classical Weekly*, XI (1918), 107 ff.; Nilsson, "Der Ursprung der Tragödie," *Neue Jahrbücher für das klassische Altertum*, XXVII (1911), 609 ff. and 673 ff.; Jane Harrison, *Themis, a Study of the Social Origins of Greek Religion* (1912); Murray, "The Ritual Forms Preserved in Greek Tragedy," in Miss Harrison's *Themis*, pp. 341 ff.; Flickinger, "Tragedy and Satyric Drama," *Classical Philology*, VIII (1913), 261 ff.; and Cook, *Zeus, a Study in Ancient Religion*, I (1914), 665 ff. and 695 ff.

In recent years, essential supports of this doctrine have slowly crumbled away before searching investigation; at present, scarcely a single clause in the foregoing sketch would escape unchallenged by some scholar of deserved standing. An ever-increasing number of students believe that tragedy is not

FIG. 2.—Sketch Map of Attica and the Peloponnesus, Showing Early Centers of Dramatic Activities in Greece.

the child of the satyr-play, but that the two are separate in their origin. Unfortunately, however, these dissenters, including such men as Dr. Emil Reisch of Vienna, Mr. Pickard-Cambridge of Oxford, Professor Wilhelm Schmid of Tübingen, and Professor William Ridgeway of Cambridge, though they are unanimous in rejecting Welcker's hypothesis, cannot agree among themselves as to a constructive policy. My own view is that tragedy and satyric drama are independent offshoots of the same literary type, the Peloponnesian dithyramb. The former came to Athens from Corinth and Sicyon by way of Icaria. Somewhat later the latter was introduced directly from Phlius by Pratinas, a native of that place. My reasons for these opinions will develop in the course of the discussion.

Very recently, notable efforts have been put forth to interpret the religious practices of the Greeks, partly in the light of anthropology and partly in accordance with the new psychological method which inquires, not what the god is, but what are the social activities and the social organization of his devotees. Whatever may be said for these avenues of approach in other respects, in practice those who employ them have shown more eagerness to assemble data which might be considered confirmatory of their theories than to reach an unprejudiced interpretation of the whole body of ancient evidence. Thus, much has been made of present-day carnivals in Thessaly, Thrace, and Scyrus,[1] and these ceremonies are employed as if they were assured survivals of the primitive rites from which Greek drama developed and as if their evidence were of greater value than the most firmly established data in the ancient tradition. Now the a priori possibility that these carnivals should retain their essential features unchanged through two and a half millenniums amid all the vicissitudes which have come upon these regions must be pronounced infinitesimal. And an examination of the details confirms this impression. Certain parts of the ceremonies are parodies of the Christian rites of marriage and burial. Not only an Arab but also a Frank appear in the cast of characters. Though Phrynichus is said to have been the first to represent female rôles,[2] such rôles abound in these modern plays. Yet there is another defect in this assumption which is still more serious. If there is one well-authenticated fact in the history of Greek drama, expressly stated in ancient notices and fully substantiated by the extant

---

[1] Cf. Lawson, *Annual of British School at Athens*, VI (1900), 125 ff.; Dawkins, *ibid.*, XI (1905), 72 ff.; and Wace, *ibid.*, XVI (1910), 232 ff.

[2] Cf. Suidas, *s.v.* "Phrynichus."

plays, it is that tragedy arose from a choral performance and only gradually acquired its histrionic features. On the contrary, these carnivals are predominantly histrionic; there is either no chorus or its rôle is distinctly secondary. Had Aristotle been guilty of such a *faux pas*, we can easily imagine the derisive comments in which modern investigators would have indulged at his expense.

Of course, our evidence is far from being as complete as we could wish, and must therefore be supplemented at many points by conjecture pure and simple; but this fact does not justify us in throwing all our data overboard and in beginning *de novo*. In this matter we have been too prone to follow a practice which the late Professor Verrall characterized, in a different connection, as follows: "We are perhaps too apt, in speculations of this kind, to help a theory by the convenient hypothesis of a wondrous simpleton, who did the mangling, blundering, or whatever it is that we require."[1] Now, whatever may be true in other cases, Aristotle at least was no "simpleton," competent only to mangle his sources of information; and furthermore, apart from certain ethnographic parallels which are of only secondary importance after all,[2] our fund of knowledge in this field is in no wise comparable with his. In fact, except for the extant plays our information is almost confined to what we derive, directly or indirectly, from him. Since this is so, what can be more absurd than to reject his conclusions and have recourse to unhampered conjecture?

But if we are to hold fast to Aristotle, one precaution is necessary—we must be sure that we do not make him say more or less than he does say. He wrote for a very different audience from that which now reads his words and with a very different purpose from that to which his book is now put. And these factors often render him enigmatical. This resulted also from his frequently assuming a familiarity with things which now

[1] Cf. *Euripides the Rationalist*, p. 243.

[2] Cf. von Wilamowitz, *Neue Jahrbücher f. kl. Altertum*, XXIX (1912), 474, and Cook, *Zeus*, I, xiii f.

cannot always be taken for granted. As Professor Bywater expressed it: "It is clear from Aristotle's confession of ignorance as to comedy that he knows more of the history of tragedy than he actually tells us, and that he is not aware of there being any serious lacuna in it."[1] Thus, Aristotle says that tragedy was "improvisational by origin" and, more specifically, was derived "from the leaders of the dithyramb."[2] Though this expression unhappily is somewhat lacking in precision, the main item, that the dithyramb is the parent of tragedy, emerges from any interpretation. Ridgeway may proceed to dissociate the dithyramb from Dionysus and to derive it from ceremonies at the tombs of heroes if he choose; however unwarranted, that is at least logical. But to ignore this statement of Aristotle's and to seek, as many do, to trace tragedy back to δρώμενα ("ritual acts") of various kinds by another line of development transgresses good philological practice.

There is an unfortunate facility in such attempts. Tragedy embraced many diverse elements in its material and technique. Accordingly, whatever anyone sets out to find, he can be almost certain of discovering there. Thus, Dieterich with his theory of the development of tragedy from funeral dirges, the Eleusinian mysteries, and various aetiological sources; Ridgeway with his tomb theory; Miss Harrison with her "Year Spirit" (the Eniautos-Daimon) and sympathetic magic; and Murray with his attempt to reconcile and expand the Dieterich-Harrison theories, all find confirmation for their views in the same body of dramatic literature. The very facility of such analyzing is its undoing.

Moreover, despite numerous attempts to the contrary, the real nature of the primitive dithyramb can scarcely be a matter of doubt. Plato, who was also no "simpleton," defined it as a

---

[1] Cf. his *Aristotle on the Art of Poetry*, p. 135. This opinion is confirmed by the fact that men of such importance as Thespis and Phrynichus are not so much as mentioned in the *Poetics*.

[2] Cf. *Poetics* 1449a9–11: γενομένη <δ'> ἀπ' ἀρχῆς αὐτοσχεδιαστική, ... καὶ ἡ μὲν ἀπὸ τῶν ἐξαρχόντων τὸν διθύραμβον.

song in celebration of the birth of Dionysus.[1] Now since the dithyramb is known to have been opened up to a wider range of themes considerably before Plato's time, his definition must apply to the original meaning of the term. This interpretation does not remain unsupported. Thus, the first extant instance of the word occurs in a fragment of Archilochus (*ca.* 680–640 B.C.), who declares that he "knows how, when his heart is crazed with wine, to lead lord Dionysus' dithyramb."[2] It should be observed that Archilochus does not say that he knows how to write a dithyramb, but how to take part in one as a drunken ἐξάρχων ("leader")· Such a performance was doubtless, as Aristotle said, largely improvisational, being perhaps coupled with the rendition of some ritual chant (καλὸν μέλος). Dionysus is characterized as θριαμβο-διθύραμβος ("celebrated in dithyrambs") by Pratinas,[3] and addressed as διθύραμβος by Euripides in his *Bacchanals*, vs. 526. In an ode in honor of the victories which were won by Xenophon of Corinth in 464 B.C. Pindar inquires, "Whence appeared the charms of Dionysus in connection with the ox-driving dithyramb?"[4] Here, also, the author is not referring to the Corinthian dithyramb of his own day but to the period when

---

[1] Cf. *Laws* 700 B: καὶ ἄλλο (sc. εἶδος ῷδῆς) Διονύσου γένεσις, οἶμαι, διθύραμβος λεγόμενος.

[2] Cf. Bergk, *Poetae Lyrici Graeci*⁴, II, 404, fr. 77:
ὡς Διονύσοι' ἄνακτος καλὸν ἐξάρξαι μέλος
οἶδα διθύραμβον, οἴνῳ συγκεραυνωθεὶς φρένας.

[3] Cf. *ibid.*, III, 559, fr. 1, vs. 16.

[4] Cf. *Olymp.* XIII, 18 f.: ταὶ Διονύσου πόθεν ἐξέφανεν
σὺν βοηλάτᾳ χάριτες διθυράμβῳ;
Βοηλάτᾳ is usually explained by reference to the ox prize, cf. schol. Plato, *Republic*, 394C: εὑρεθῆναι μὲν τὸν διθύραμβον ἐν Κορίνθῳ ὑπὸ Ἀρίονός φασι. τῶν δὲ ποιητῶν τῷ μὲν πρώτῳ βοῦς ἔπαθλον ἦν, τῷ δὲ δευτέρῳ ἀμφορεύς, τῷ δὲ τρίτῳ τράγος, ὃν τρυγὶ κεχρισμένον ἀπῆγον. Kern, Crusius, and Ridgeway, however, refer it to the practice of an Arcadian community, the Cynaethaens, of whom Pausanias (viii. 19. 1) speaks as follows: "And as to the things most worthy of mention there is a shrine of Dionysus there, and in the winter season they celebrate a festival, in which men who have anointed themselves with oil lift up a bull from the herd, whatever one the god himself puts in their minds to lift, and carry it to the shrine. Such was their manner of sacrifice." Cf. Pauly-Wissowa, V, 1041 and 1206, and *Origin of Tragedy*, p. 6.

it was put upon a quasi-literary level by Arion (see below). Finally, Epicharmus went so far as to declare that "when you drink water, it isn't a dithyramb,"[1] showing that the more primitive meaning of the term was not crowded out by later developments. These passages are sufficient to show that the dithyramb was at all times intimately associated with Dionysus and at the beginning belonged to him exclusively; their force is not invalidated by the acknowledged fact that at an early period (see p. 11, below) the restriction was broken down.

It was not until after the middle of the seventh century that the dithyramb became "poetized." This step was taken by Arion of Methymna in Lesbos, then resident in Corinth. His connection with the dithyramb and early tragedy is vouched for by irrefutable evidence. Solon of Athens (639–559 B.C.) is said in a recently discovered notice[2] to have declared in his *Elegies* that "Arion introduced the first drama of tragedy." The question immediately arises as to exactly what language Solon had employed. The words τῆς τραγῳδίας πρῶτον δρᾶμα are, of course, only a paraphrase, for no form of the word τραγῳδία can be used in elegiac verse. This objection does not lie against the word δρᾶμα, however, and it will be remembered that the Dorians based their claims to tragedy partly upon this non-Attic term.[3] Thus, we obtain an explanation of the cumbersome circumlocution "the first drama of tragedy." In Solon's *Elegies* the author of this notice (or his source) found only the ambiguous term δρᾶμα. A desire to retain the terminology of the original prevented his frankly substituting τραγῳδία. Accordingly, he kept δρᾶμα but inserted the qualifying genitive τῆς τραγῳδίας. I do not understand that Aristotle either indorses or rejects the

---

[1] Cf. Kaibel, *Comicorum Graecorum Fragmenta*, p. 115, fr. 132;

οὐκ ἔστι διθύραμβος ὄκχ' ὕδωρ πίῃς.

[2] Published by Rabe in *Rheinisches Museum für Philologie*, LXIII (1908), 150.

[3] Cf. Aristotle's *Poetics* 1448b1: καὶ τὸ ποιεῖν αὐτοὶ [sc. οἱ Δωριεῖς] μὲν δρᾶν, Ἀθηναίους δὲ πράττειν προσαγοσεύειν. In referring to this passage von Wilamowitz says: "So viel wahr ist, dass δρᾶμα in der Tat ein Fremdwort ist; man redet im Kultus nur von δρώμενα"; cf. *op. cit.*, p. 467, n. 3.

Dorian pretensions with respect to this word; but in view of our present evidence I am of the opinion that Arion called his performances "dramas" and was the first to use the word in this sense and that there is so much of justice in the Dorian claims. It is not necessary to believe, however, that they were ever called *satyric* dramas, see pp. 11 and 22, below.

Now, Dr. Nilsson has objected that Solon would have had no occasion to express his opinion upon a matter of this kind (*op. cit.*, p. 611, note). But the mention of the title of the work from which the citation purports to come goes far to substantiate its genuineness. Furthermore, Solon was incensed at Thespis (see pp. 17 f., below), and therefore it was only natural that he should take an interest in the matter, assign the distinction to another, and state his opinion in as public a manner as possible. The fact that he lived in the days before real (Aeschylean) tragedy and before the importance of Thespis' innovations was understood explains the error in his judgment. But at the very least, this notice proves that the tradition of Arion's connection with tragedy was current as early as the first half of the sixth century.

Pindar's reference to the development of the dithyramb at Corinth has already been mentioned. In the next generation Herodotus characterized Arion as follows: "Arion was second to none of the harpists of that time and was the first of the men known to us to compose (ποιήσαντα) a dithyramb and to give it a name (ὀνομάσαντα) and to represent it at Corinth" (I, 23). It is customary nowadays to seek to explain such notices as arising from the rival claims of jealous cities; but be it noted that here are two Attic sympathizers, Solon and Herodotus, granting full recognition to the literary achievements of a neighboring city. In fact, Herodotus is apparently too generous, for Arion could not have been the inventor of the dithyramb, broadly speaking. But ποιεῖν denotes not only "to compose" but also "to poetize," and the latter translation is in better accord with what else we know of Arion's contribution to the history of the dithyramb. On the other hand, ὀνομάσαντα probably means that in Herodotus' opinion Arion was the first to give names (titles) to his performances.[1]

A Byzantine writer repeats and amplifies Herodotus' statements but adds one interesting clause to the effect that Arion "introduced satyrs speaking in meter."[2]   In this there is nothing surprising.   In the Peloponnesus caprine satyrs were regular attendants upon Dionysus, and in consequence the dithyrambic choreutae must usually have been thought of as satyrs.   Their improvisations, also, must always have engaged the speaking as well as the singing voice.   This fact, however, did not at this time involve histrionic impersonation ($\mu\iota\mu\eta\sigma\iota\varsigma$) for the reason that they would not attempt to say what was appropriate to satyrs but to themselves *in propria persona* as revelers and worshipers.   The word $\check{\epsilon}\mu\mu\epsilon\tau\rho\alpha$ ("in meter"), therefore, is the important one.   The use of meter marked the coming of artistic finish and the passing of a performance largely extemporaneous. Some idea of the technique of Arion's productions may be drawn from a dithyramb by Bacchylides (first half of the fifth century) in honor of Theseus.   This is in the form of a lyric dialogue and was doubtless influenced somewhat by contemporaneous tragedy. The chorus of Athenians, addressing Aegeus, king of Athens, inquires why a call to arms has been sounded (vss. 1–15), and the *coryphaeus* ("chorus-leader") replies that a herald has just arrived and summarizes his message (vss. 16–30).   The chorus asks for further details (vss. 31–45), and once more the king's reply is borrowed from the herald (vss. 46–60).   Here Theseus, not Dionysus, is the theme of the poem; the choreutae do not

---

[1] Cf. Haigh, *The Tragic Drama of the Greeks* (1896), p. 17, n. 1, and Pickard-Cambridge in *Classical Review*, XXVI (1912), 54.   It is also possible that Arion's employment of a new generic term ($\delta\rho\dot{\alpha}\mu\alpha\tau\alpha$) for his dithyrambs is alluded to. Herodotus may have taken it as a matter of course that everyone knew what this new name was and consequently failed to mention it, thus leaving the passage ambiguous.

[2] Cf. Suidas, *s.v.* "Arion": λέγεται καὶ τραγικοῦ τρόπου εὑρετὴς γενέσθαι καὶ πρῶτος χορὸν στῆσαι <κύκλιον> καὶ διθίραμβον ᾆσαι καὶ ὀνομάσαι τὸ ᾀδόμενον ὑπὸ τοῦ χοροῦ καὶ σατύρους εἰσενεγκεῖν ἔμμετρα λέγοντας.   I cannot agree with Reisch, *op. cit.*, p. 471, and Pickard-Cambridge, *op. cit.*, p. 54, in thinking that this notice refers to three separate types of performances instead of one.

represent satyrs, but appear in their true character as plain citizens of Athens; and the coryphaeus is given a dramatic character, that of Aegeus. These are all developments later than the time of Arion; nevertheless, the general effect must have been much the same.

Before the close of the sixth century the dithyramb had become a regular form of literature—a chorus of fifty, dancing and singing formal compositions. In 508 B.C. a contest of dithyrambic choruses of men was made a standing feature of the program at the City Dionysia in Athens. Simonides (556–467 B.C.) is known to have composed a dithyramb entitled *Memnon*, the exclusively Dionysiac character of the genre being then, if not earlier, abandoned. But it is important to remember that originally the dithyramb was extemporaneous and confined to the worship and exaltation of Dionysus.

In the new notice concerning Solon and Arion, von Wilamowitz finds "die Bestätigung dass die τραγῳδοί vor Thespis bestanden" (cf. *op. cit.*, p. 470). This development could scarcely have taken place at Corinth in Arion's time, for there was no need of coining a new word to designate the performers so long as they appeared as satyrs. And if a term had then been derived from the choreutae to designate their performance, it must have been *σατυρῳδία and not τραγῳδία. Neither could the new term have been derived at this period from the *prize*, for then the goat was only the third award.[1] Let us therefore turn to Sicyon.

In a well-known passage (v. 67) Herodotus tells how the Sicyonians used to honor their former king, Adrastus, in other ways, and in particular celebrated his sorrows with "tragic" (or "goat") choruses (τραγικοῖσι χοροῖσι) and how their tyrant Clisthenes in anger at Adrastus assigned these choruses to Dionysus and the other features of the rites to Melanippus. Melanippus in his lifetime had killed Adrastus' brother and son-in-law, and Clisthenes had brought his bones from Thebes and transferred to him part of the honors which had previously

[1] See p. 7, n. 4, above.

been paid to Adrastus, in order to insult the latter as outrageously as possible. The superimposition of the worship of Dionysus upon that of the local hero and the reference to tragic choruses have furnished Ridgeway a foundation upon which to rear his theory that tragedy developed from ceremonies at the tombs of heroes. In this passage the meaning of the word τραγικοῖσι has provoked much discussion. I believe that Herodotus meant τραγικός here in the sense current in his own day, viz., tragic, but I do not believe that he stopped to consider whether these Sicyonian dances "were sufficiently like the choruses in the tragedies of his contemporaries to be called 'tragic.'"[1] I think he employed that adjective simply because τραγικοὶ χοροί was the Sicyonians' own designation for their performances. If so, whatever τραγικοῖσι χοροῖσι connoted to Herodotus, or even to contemporaneous Sicyonians, originally τραγικός in this phrase must have meant "goat," and these choruses must originally have been, for whatever reason, "goat" choruses.

Some considered Epigenes of Sicyon the first tragic poet, Thespis being second (or as others thought, sixteenth) in the list.[2] In connection with Epigenes another tradition must be mentioned. Several explanations are preserved of the proverb οὐδὲν πρὸς τὸν Διόνυσον ("nothing to do with Dionysus"). These are somewhat vague in details and need not be taken too seriously; but at least they are valuable as showing the general periods in which their authors thought that the proper situation for the rise of such a proverb had existed. According to one account, this expression was uttered "when Epigenes had composed a tragedy in honor of Dionysus."[3] In just what particular Epigenes' performance seemed alien to the worship of Dionysus the retailers of the anecdote do not specify. Ridgeway supposes

[1] Cf. Pickard-Cambridge, *op. cit.*, p. 55.

[2] Cf. Suidas, *s.v.* "Thespis": Θέσπις Ἰκαρίου πόλεως Ἀττικῆς, τραγικὸς ἐκκαιδέκατος ἀπὸ τοῦ πρώτου γενομένου τραγῳδιοποιοῦ Ἐπιγένους τοῦ Σικυωνίου τιθέμενος, ὡς δέ τινες, δεύτερος μετὰ Ἐπιγένην· ἄλλοι δὲ αὐτὸν πρῶτον τραγικὸν γενέσθαι φασί.

[3] Cf. Suidas, *s.v.*, Photius, *s.v.*, and Apostolius xiii. 42: Ἐπιγένου τοῦ Σικυωνίου τραγῳδίαν εἰς τὸν Διόνυσον ποιήσαντος, ἐπεφώνησάν τινες τοῦτο· ὅθεν ἡ παροιμία.

that Epigenes "did not confine himself to Dionysiac subjects."[1]
But surely that development came much later. In my opinion,
the explanation is simpler. We have no information as to the
costume which the choreutae wore in honoring the sorrows of
Adrastus. There was, of course, no reason for their appearing
as satyrs. But were satyric choreutae introduced at the same
time that the dances were given over to Dionysus? If we answer
this question in the negative, the situation becomes clear. The
audience, or part of it, was sufficiently acquainted with the
performances instituted by Arion at Corinth to expect a chorus
of satyrs in the Sicyonian dances after they were transferred to
Dionysus. And when Epigenes brought on his choreutae in the
same (non-satyric) costume as had previously been employed,
they naturally manifested their surprise with the ejaculation:
οὐδὲν πρὸς τὸν Διόνυσον. By this they meant: "Why, these
choreutae are just what we have had all the time; there is
nothing of the satyrs about them. They have nothing to do
with Dionysus."

Practically everyone is convinced that τραγῳδία means
"goat-song." The only difficulty consists in explaining how
this name came to be applied. We have already noted (see
p. 2, above) that Welcker explained it on the basis of costume,
and this is now the prevailing view. But though the choreutae
at Corinth were satyrs, there were good reasons why no new term
should be coined there to designate them (see p. 11, above), and
in fact, τραγῳδία, τραγῳδός ("goat-singer"), and τραγικός (in a
technical sense) apparently did not originate there. On the
other hand, in Sicyon (where at least the expression τραγικοὶ
χοροί, if not the others, seems to have been in use at an early
day) the costume of the choreutae was assuredly not caprine
before the dances were transferred from Adrastus to Dionysus
and probably was not thereafter. Consequently, Welcker's
explanation must be rejected.

But the earliest and favorite explanation of these terms in
antiquity derived them from the fact that a goat was given to the

[1] Cf. *The Origin of Tragedy*, p. 58.

victorious poet as a prize.[1] Knowledge and approval of this interpretation can be traced almost uninterruptedly from the high authority of the *Parian Chronicle*[2] in the third century B.C. onward, and there is no cogent reason for doubting its truth. The other suggestion that the name was derived from the goat which was offered in sacrifice in connection with the performances will be seen not to conflict with this view when it is remembered that in the later dithyrambic contests the prize (a tripod) was not regarded as the personal possession of the victor but was customarily consecrated in some temple or other public place. In my opinion, these explanations have been most unwarrantably abandoned in modern times, and I think a reaction in their favor has set in. They are spoken of respectfully by Dr. Reisch,[3] and Mr. Pickard-Cambridge mentions them exclusively.[4]

Now the transfer of the Sicyonian dances from Adrastus to Dionysus would probably happen early in the reign of Clisthenes (*ca.* 595–560 B.C.), and for this very period Eusebius preserves a notice to the effect that "a goat was given to contestants among the Greeks, and from this fact they were called τραγικοί."[5] I therefore believe that Herodotus, Eusebius (Jerome), and Suidas all refer to the same event: that Clisthenes of Sicyon established the goat prize about 590 B.C. when he surrendered to Dionysus

[1] About a dozen explanations in addition to those discussed in the text are listed and criticized in *Classical Philology*, VIII (1913), 269 ff.

[2] Cf. Jacoby, *Das Marmor Parium*, p. 14: ἀφ' οὗ Θέσπις ὁ ποιητὴς [ὑπεκρίνα]το πρῶτος, ὃς ἐδίδαξε [δρ]ᾶ[μα ἐν ἄ]στ[ει καὶ ἆθλον ἐ]τέθη ὁ [τ]ράγος, ἔτη ΗΗ℞[ΔΔ·], ἄρχοντος 'Αθ[ήνησι] . . . ναιου τοῦ προτέρου.

[3] Cf. *op. cit.*, p. 468: "An der Tatsache, dass in älterer Zeit dem Tragödenchor ein Bock als Preis (der als Opferthier und Opferschmaus dienen sollte), gegeben wurde, wie dem Dithyrambenchor zu gliechem Zwecke ein Stier, daran ist zu zweifeln ist kein Grund."

[4] Cf. *op. cit.*, p. 59: "Since the interpretation of τραγῳδία as the 'song of the men in goat-costume' must be given up, the word can be interpreted as the 'song around' or 'for the goat'—whether the goat be sacrifice or prize."

[5] Cf. Eusebius' *Chronica*, Ol. 47, 2 (591–590 B.C.; Armenian version, Cl. 48, 1): τοῖς ἀγωνιζομένοις παρ' Ἕλλησι τράγος ἐδίδοτο, ἀφ' οὗ καὶ τραγικοὶ ἐκλήθησαν. Jerome's Latin version reads: "his temporibus certantibus in agone (de voce *add.* R) tragus, id est hircus, in praemio dabatur. Unde aiunt tragoedos nuncupatos."

the dances which had previously been performed in honor of Adrastus,[1] that Epigenes was the poet whom Clisthenes employed to initiate this innovation, and that non-satyric choreutae and the terms τραγικός, τραγῳδός, etc., arose in this manner, time, and place. The neatness with which these notices fit together to produce this result renders them comparatively secure from the critical assault which might more successfully be directed against them individually. In any case, it is incumbent upon any skeptic, not merely to reject the later authorities, but also to provide a more satisfactory explanation of Herodotus.

If this series of conclusions is accepted, we have an answer to the question under consideration—the occasion of the term τραγῳδοί. We must conclude that honoring Adrastus with choruses either did not involve the giving of a prize or that the prize was other than a goat. With the transfer to Dionysus, a goat (for some reason) was chosen as the object of competition, and was doubtless immediately consumed in a sacrificial feast. We have seen that at Corinth, where the choreutae were satyrs, there was no reason to coin a new term to designate them. But at Sicyon the situation was different. What more natural than that from the new prize should be derived new names (τραγικοὶ χοροί and τραγῳδοί respectively) for the new-old performances and their choreutae.[2] It is not enough to pass this tradition of Sicyonian tragedy by in silence or to brand it as aetiological or as arising from the partisanship of rival cities. It must first be shown to be inconsistent, either with itself or with other established facts.

Hitherto we have dealt with the Peloponnesus, which was inhabited by the Dorian branch of the Greek stock; at this point we pass to Attica, which was Ionic. We are indebted to the

[1] Contrary to Herodotus, these choruses were τραγικοί only after the transfer, not before—a negligible error.

[2] Of course, it is possible to argue that goats may have been sacrificed to Adrastus and that τραγικός and τραγῳδός were consequently older terms than is maintained in the text; this would also explain why the goat was continued as a prize after the sacrifice proper had been given over to Melanippus. Cf., however, Farnell, *Cults of the Greek States*, V, 233 and note *d*.

late Professor Furtwängler (*op. cit.*, pp. 22 ff.) for having pointed out that among the Dorians the attendant sprites of Dionysus were caprine satyrs, but that among the Ionians he was attended by sileni, creatures with equine ears, hoofs, and tails. Caprine satyrs do not appear upon Attic vases until about 450 B.C. (see p. 24, below). Although the sort of dances from which tragedy developed had existed in Attica from time immemorial,[1] yet they did not emerge into prominence and literary importance until the age of Thespis and in Icaria. Evidently Thespis' innovations were partly borrowed from the Peloponnesus and partly his own. Included among the former would be the dropping of improvisation, the use of meter, the goat prize, and such terms as δρᾶμα and τραγῳδός. Most distinctive among the latter was his invention of the first actor. In early choral performances it was customary for the poet himself to serve as coryphaeus, and in Bacchylides' dithyramb we have seen how the coryphaeus was set apart from the other choreutae, answering the questions which they propounded. It was inevitable that to someone should come the happy thought of developing this rôle still further and of promoting the coryphaeus to a position independent of the chorus. It is significant that the verb which was first used to designate the actor's function was ἀποκρίνεσθαι ("to answer"), and that until the time of Sophocles all playwrights were actors in their own productions. We are now in a position to realize the true inwardness of Aristotle's phrase: he does not say merely that tragedy was derived from the dithyramb but from the "leaders" of the dithyramb.

We have noted that the early dithyramb did not require impersonation (see p. 10, above). Even at an advanced stage it was probably much like a sacred oratorio of modern times in which the performers may sing words which are appropriate to characters and yet make no attempt by costume, gestures, or actions to represent those characters. Thespis changed all this.

---

[1] Cf. Plato *Minos* 321A: ἡ δὲ τραγῳδία ἐστὶ παλαιὸν ἐνθάδε, οὐχ ὡς οἴονται ἀπὸ Θέσπιδος ἀρξαμένη οὐδ' ἀπὸ Φρυνίχου, ἀλλ' εἰ θέλεις ἐννοῆσαι, πάνυ παλαιὸν αὐτὸ εὑρήσεις ὂν τῆσδε τῆς πόλεως εὕρημα.

Since he assumed an actor's rôle himself, first of all probably that of Dionysus, the choreutae could no longer conduct themselves as worshipers in disguise, but must now not merely look like real attendants of Dionysus but also behave as such. This is a fundamental matter. Only after this step had been taken could real drama in the modern sense become possible. Neither honoring the sorrows of Adrastus nor the "fore-doing" of imitative magic, not even the primitive δρώμενα at Eleusis or elsewhere demanded or presupposed actual impersonation. This development took place at Icaria and by the agency of Thespis. I cannot do better than to quote certain sentences of Miss Harrison's:

We are apt to forget that from the *epos*, the narrative, to the *drama*, the enactment, is a momentous step, one, so far as we know, not taken in Greece till after centuries of epic achievement, and then taken suddenly, almost in the dark, and irrevocably. All we really know of this momentous step is that it was taken sometime in the sixth century B.C. and taken in connection with the worship of Dionysus. Surely it is at least possible that the real impulse to the drama lay not wholly in "goat-songs" and "circular dancing places" but also in the cardinal, the essentially dramatic, conviction of the religion of Dionysus, that the worshipper can not only worship, but can become, can *be*, his god. Athene and Zeus and Poseidon have no drama, because no one, in his wildest moments, believed he could become and be Athene or Zeus or Poseidon. It is indeed only in the orgiastic religions that these splendid moments of conviction could come, and, for Greece at least, only in an orgiastic religion did the drama take its rise.[1]

Thespis' invention of impersonation probably provides the clue for understanding the clash between him and Solon:

Thespis was already beginning to develop tragedy, and on account of its novelty the matter was engaging general attention but had not yet been

[1] Cf. *Prolegomena to the Study of Greek Religion*[2] (1908), p. 568. Of course, I do not mean to deny that impersonation was subsequently borrowed from true drama by rites of various kinds which had not contained it at first. This situation probably obtained with reference to the Eleusinian mysteries in their later forms.

The indebtedness of tragedy to epic poetry for subject matter, dignity of treatment and of diction, and development of plot, including such technical devices as recognition (ἀναγνώρισις) and reversal of situation (περιπέτεια) is too well established to require argument. Aeschylus is said to have declared that his tragedies were "slices from Homer's bountiful banquets" (Athenaeus, p. 347E). The pertinent passages from Aristotle's *Poetics* have been conveniently assembled by Throop, "Epic and Dramatic," *Washington University Studies*, V (1917), 1 ff.

brought into a public contest. Now Solon, who by nature was fond of
hearing and learning, to a still greater extent in old age gave himself up to
leisurely amusement and even to conviviality and music. Therefore, he
went to see Thespis himself act, as was customary for the earlier poets.
And when the spectacle was over, Solon addressed him and inquired if he
had no sense of shame to lie so egregiously before so many. Moreover,
when Thespis said that it was no crime to say and enact such things in
sport, Solon struck the ground violently with his staff and said: "Yet if
we praise and honor this 'sport' under these circumstances, it will not be
long before we discover it in our contracts."[1]

To so straightforward a man as Solon such a facile abandonment
of one's own personality might well seem like barefaced lying,
and to augur and even encourage similar shuffling prevarications
in the more serious affairs of life.

To Ridgeway, however, all this appears in a different light.
In the first place, after citing Diogenes Laertius to the effect that
"in ancient times the chorus at first carried on the action in
tragedy alone, but later Thespis invented an actor in order to
allow the chorus intervals of relief,"[2] he declares flatly: "But
this cannot mean, as is commonly held, that Thespis first separated in some degree the coryphaeus from the chorus and made
him interrupt the dithyramb with epic recitations, for, as we
have seen above, before his time the poet or coryphaeus used to
mount a table and hold a dialogue with the chorus."[3]   In the
cross-reference Ridgeway had quoted Pollux iv. 123: "The ἐλεός
was a table in the olden days upon which in the period before
Thespis some one mounted and made answer to the choreutae,"
and *Etymologicum Magnum, s.v.* "θυμέλη": "It was a table upon
which they stood and sang in the country when tragedy had not
yet assumed definite form." These late notices are manifestly
vague and inexact references to rudimentary histrionicism among
the choreutae themselves or between them and their coryphaeus.

---

[1] Cf. Plutarch *Solon* xxix.   If Thespis treated the traditional myths with some
freedom, that may have added to Solon's anger.

[2] Cf. Diogenes Laertius iii. 56: τὸ παλαιὸν ἐν τῇ τραγῳδίᾳ πρότερον μὲν μόνος ὁ
χορὸς διεδραμάτιζεν, ὕστερον δὲ Θέσπις ἕνα ὑποκριτὴν ἐξεῦρεν ὑπὲρ τοῦ διαναπαύεσθαι
τὸν χορόν.

[3] Cf. *The Origin of Tragedy*, p. 60.

The first of them is probably due to a false inference from a scene in some comedy.[1] It is true that the invention of the first actor is expressly attributed to Thespis only by Diogenes, yet it may be inferred in several other connections. Evidently the matter is largely one of definition. Ridgeway himself concedes all that is important, when he continues: "There seems no reason to doubt that Thespis in some way defined more exactly the position of the actor, especially by the introduction of a simple form of mask."

In the second place, Ridgeway considers that Thespis made the "grand step" in the evolution of tragedy when he

detached his chorus and dithyramb from some particular shrine, probably at Icaria, his native place, and taking his company with him on wagons gave his performances on his extemporised stage when and where he could find an audience, not for religious purposes but for a pastime. Thus not merely by defining more accurately the rôle of the actor but also by lifting tragedy from being a mere piece of religious ritual tied to a particular spot into a great form of literature, he was the true founder of the tragic art. This view offers a reasonable explanation of Solon's anger on first seeing Thespis act. A performance which he would have regarded as fit and proper when enacted in some shrine of the gods or at a hero's tomb, not unnaturally roused his indignation when the exhibition was merely "for sport," as Thespis himself said (and doubtless also for profit), and not at some hallowed spot, but in any profane place where an audience might conveniently be collected [*op. cit.*, p. 61].

Not only does such an interpretation find no support in Plutarch's anecdote but it is highly improbable as well. It may be granted that after long neglect Thespis' "wagon"[2] seems to be enjoying a recrudescence of favor. Dieterich and von Wilamowitz have referred to it in all seriousness.[3] There is nothing improbable about the tradition nor any compelling reason for supposing it borrowed from the history of early comedy. It is natural to suppose that Thespis did not restrict his activities to Icaria, but

---

[1] Cf. Hiller, *Rheinisches Museum für Philologie*, XXXIX (1884), 329.

[2] Cf. Horace *Ars Poetica*, vs. 276:
        dicitur et plaustris vexisse poemata Thespis.

[3] Cf. *Kleine Schriften*, p. 422, and *Neue Jahrbücher für das klassische Altertum*, XXIX (1912), 474.

extended them to such other demes as were interested or found them appropriate to their festivals. In that case, means of transportation for performers and accessories became imperative. The use of such a vehicle in the *Prometheus Bound* of Aeschylus shows that it need not necessarily have served also as a stage, as has sometimes been thought. Now, as a matter of fact, several Attic vases, dating from the close of the sixth century B.C., represent the "wagon-ship" of Dionysus (Fig. 65). Just what relationship subsisted between primitive drama and the scenes depicted upon these vases has yet to be definitely established. Dr. Frickenhaus would associate them with the preliminary procession at the City Dionysia (see p. 121, below). But at least, until such time as any connection with Thespis' wagon has been shown to be impossible, the suggestion can scarcely be laughed out of court as utterly ridiculous. On the other hand, to suppose that Thespis entirely dissociated his performances from shrines and festivals not only rests upon no evidence but is so out of harmony with other data as to be incredible.

Whether the innovation of treating non-Dionysiac themes in tragedy must also be credited to Thespis before he brought his career to a close must remain a matter of doubt, though personally I am inclined to suppose so. Suidas[1] reports *Phorbas or the Prizes of Pelias*, *Priests*, *Youths*, and *Pentheus* as the titles of four of his plays. Of these the last is clearly Dionysiac, the first probably is not, and the other two are noncommittal. This evidence, however, cannot be relied upon, for the reason that Aristoxenus is said to have declared that Heraclides Ponticus wrote tragedies and attributed them to Thespis.[2]

But as we are not told that these plays bore the same titles as those ascribed to Thespis by Suidas, it does not by any means follow that the latter are spurious. But even if the titles were the same, it is not unlikely that Heraclides would have chosen as titles for his spurious compositions

---

[1] Cf. Suidas, *s.v.* "Thespis": μνημονεύεται δὲ τῶν δραμάτων αὐτοῦ ᾿Αθλα Πελίου ἢ Φόρβας, ᾿Ιερεῖς, ᾿Ηίθεοι, Πενθεύς.

[2] Cf. Diogenes Laertius v. 92. Both Aristoxenus and Heraclides were pupils of Aristotle.

names declared by tradition to be those of genuine works of the Father of Attic Tragedy. The titles as they have reached us indicate that the ancients most certainly did not believe that Thespis confined himself to Dionysiac subjects.[1]

In any case, this development could not have been long deferred after 534 B.C. To the more conservative it is said to have given offense; according to some authorities, the expression "Nothing to do with Dionysus" took its rise at this juncture.[2] Simultaneously, or at least only a little subsequently, the tragic choreutae were no longer dressed to represent sileni but whatever the needs of the individual play demanded, often plain citizens of Athens, Corinth, Thebes, etc.

Even after all that Thespis did for it tragedy must still have been a crude, coarse, only semi-literary affair. Nevertheless, in 534 B.C., when Pisistratus, tyrant of Athens, established a new festival called the City Dionysia, in honor of Dionysus Eleuthereus,[3] he made a contest in tragedy the chief feature of its program. As was but fitting, Thespis won the first goat prize ever awarded in this Athenian festival.[4] It is unnecessary to enlarge upon this recognition except to protest against a not uncommon tendency to assume that terms like τραγῳδία and τραγῳδός were not in use before this date. Of course, the matter can not be definitely proved, but the evolution which I have been tracing at Sicyon and Icaria distinctly favors the other view.

We have seen that Aristotle's statements ought not to be ignored or lightly rejected. On the other hand, it is no less important to read nothing into his language which does not belong there. Thus, when he declares: "Discarding short

[1] Cf. Ridgeway, *op. cit.*, p. 69.

[2] Cf. Suidas, *s.v.* οὐδὲν πρὸς τὸν Διόνυσον (quoted on p. 29, n. 2, below).

[3] The cognomen was due to the belief that the image and cult were derived from Eleutherae. At Eleutherae itself, however, his cognomen would naturally be different. There he was known as Διόνυσος Μελάναιγις, "Dionysus of the Black-Goat-Skin." From this fact an abortive attempt has recently been made to derive a new explanation for tragic performances being denominated "goat-songs"; cf. *Classical Philology*, VIII (1913), 270.

[4] Cf. *Marmor Parium* (quoted on p. 14, n. 2, above).

stories and a ludicrous diction, through its passing out of its satyric stage, tragedy assumed, though only at a late point in its progress, a tone of dignity,"[1] the phrase διὰ τὸ ἐκ σατυρικοῦ μεταβαλεῖν ὀψὲ ἀπεσεμνύνθη has generally been taken to mean that tragedy developed out of a form like the satyric dramas known to us, in the next century, from Sophocles' *Trackers* and Euripides' *Cyclops*. For such a historical development no other testimony can be cited until Byzantine times (see p. 29 and n. 2, below). Now this interpretation of Aristotle's phrase has always involved certain difficulties and has been pronounced inconsistent with his other statement that tragedy developed "from the leaders of the dithyramb." But in my opinion we must accept Reisch's interpretation: "We are certainly not warranted in translating ἐκ σατυρικοῦ baldly as 'from the satyr-play.' On the contrary, Aristotle is speaking only of the 'satyr-play-like origin' and of the 'satyr-like poetry' (as Theodor Gomperz suitably renders it in his translation); and from this, first of all, only a family relationship between primitive tragedy and the satyr-play, not an identity, may be inferred."[2] The same thought recurs in Aristotle's next sentence, when he says: "The iambic measure then replaced the trochaic tetrameter, which was originally employed *when the poetry was of the satyric order*, and had greater affinities with dancing."[3] In other words, though early Attic tragedy never received the name of "satyric drama," and though its choreutae were probably sileni and not satyrs, nevertheless, since the Thespian and pre-Thespian performances, by reason of their obscenities, grotesque language, ludicrous and

---

[1] Cf. *Poetics* 1449a19 ff., Bywater's translation.

[2] Cf. *op. cit.*, p. 472. This exegesis has now been commended by Pickard-Cambridge; cf. *Classical Review*, XXVI (1912), 53. Cornford has expressed the same view by means of a neat paraphrase: ἐκ σατυρικοῦ εἰς σεμνὸν μετέβαλεν, cf. *The Origin of Attic Comedy* (1914), p. 214, n. 1. Gomperz' translation (1897) reads as follows: "Was das Wachstum ihrer Grossartigkeit anlangt, so hat sich das Trauerspiel im Gegensatze zur ursprünglichen Kleinheit der Fabeln und der zum Possenhaften neigenden Artung der Diction ihres satyrspielartigen Ursprungs wegen erst spät zu höherer Würde erhoben. . . . . Ursprünglich hatte man sich nämlich, da die Dichtung satyrhaft und mehr balletartig war, des trochäischen Tetrameters bedient."

[3] Cf. *Poetics* 1449a22 f., Butcher's translation.

undignified tone, the predominance of choral odes, etc., bore a
certain resemblance to the contemporaneous exhibitions of
satyrs in the Peloponnesus and to Pratinas' satyric drama in
Athens at a later period, it can truthfully be said that tragedy
had passed through a "satyric stage" and had had a "satyric"
tinge which it was slow to lose.

What, then, was the origin of the performance which in the
fifth century constituted the final member of tetralogies? Such
tetralogies cannot be made out for any playwright before
Aeschylus; and the number of plays attributed to Pratinas,
eighteen tragedies and thirty-two satyric dramas, throws
additional doubt upon the probability that the early poets were
required to present four plays together.[1] We have thus far
considered three types of performances: the improvisational
dithyramb, which was still continued in rural and primitive
districts; the improved dithyramb (in 508 B.C. dithyrambic
choruses of men were added to the program of the City Dionysia
at Athens), and tragedy. The last two had by this time become
semi-literary types. Now we are expressly told, and there is no
reason to discredit the information, that Pratinas of Phlius in
the Peloponnesus was "the first to write satyr-plays."[2] The
general situation is clear. After tragedy had lost its exclusively
Bacchic themes and had considerably departed from its original
character, Pratinas endeavored to satisfy religious conservatism
by introducing a new manner of production, which came to be

[1] In 467 B.C. Aristias concluded his tragedies with the *Palaestae*, "a satyric
drama of his father Pratinas" (cf. arg. Aesch. *Seven against Thebes*). It is generally
supposed that this was a posthumous piece. But Professor Capps suggests that
Pratinas may frequently have provided a satyr-play for someone's else trilogy,
and thus explains the disproportionate number of satyric dramas in Pratinas' list
and of tragedies in other poets' lists.

[2] Cf. Suidas, *s.v.* "Pratinas": . . . . Φλιάσιος, ποιητὴς τραγῳδίας, ἀντηγωνίζετο
Αἰσχύλῳ τε καὶ Χοιρίλῳ, ἐπὶ τῆς ἑβδομηκοστῆς Ὀλυμπιάδος, καὶ πρῶτος ἔγραψε
Σατύρους . . . . καὶ δράματα μὲν ἐπεδείξατο ν΄, ὧν Σατυρικὰ λβ΄. ἐνίκησε δὲ ἅπαξ.
Note that the earliest name was simply Σάτυροι, "satyrs." Murray has proposed
another interpretation of Suidas' phrase: "I take this to mean that Pratinas was
the first person to write words for the revelling masquers to learn by heart. Thespis, like many early Elizabethans, had been content with a general direction:
'Enter Satyrs, in revel, saying anything'" (incorporated in Miss Harrison's *Themis*,
p. 344). Nevertheless, he adds that he "does not wish to combat" the other view.

called satyric drama.   This was a combination of the dramatic
dithyramb of his native Phlius, which of course had developed
somewhat since the days of Arion and Epigenes, and of contemporary Attic tragedy; and it had the merit of continuing,
at least for a while, the Dionysiac subjects which were so appropriate to the god's festival.   It appears that at first satyr-plays
were brought out independently of tragedy and in greater
numbers, comparatively, than was afterward the case.   But
about 501 B.C. the City Dionysia was reorganized: the goat
prize was abandoned; κῶμοι, i.e., the volunteer performances
from which comedy was later to develop, were added to the
program; and, in particular, the regulation was established that
each tragic poet must present three tragedies and one satyr-play
in a series.   Pratinas is known to have competed against Aeschylus about 499 B.C.   His innovation doubtless fell somewhere
between the institution of the tragic contest in 534 B.C. and the
reorganization of the festival program in 501 B.C., possibly about
515 B.C.

There remains the difficult problem as to the appearance of
the choreutae in the satyric drama at different periods in Athens.
Fortunately the aspect of non-dramatic sileni and satyrs is fairly
certain.   Already on the François vase, a crater signed by
Clitias and Ergotimus and belonging to about 600–550 B.C.,
there are representations of three ithyphallic creatures with
equine ears, hoofs, and tails (Fig. 3).[1]   An inscription ⳞIΛΕΝOI
leaves no doubt as to the identity of the figures.   Mr. A. B. Cook
lists six other vases from Attica which bear the same identifying
inscription.[2]   None of these seven vases, however, betrays any
relationship to the theater.

On the other hand, a list[3] of fifteen Attic vases has been drawn
up on which goat-men appear.   None of these antedates 450 B.C.,

[1] Fig. 3 is taken from Furtwängler and Reichhold, *Griechische Vasenmalarei*,
first series, II, Pls. 11–12.   The *membrum virile* has been omitted in the reproduction.

[2] Cf. *op. cit.*, I, 696 f.

[3] This was originally assembled by Hartwig in *Römische Mittheilungen*, XII
(1897), 89 ff. and Wernicke, *op. cit.*   It is now conveniently summarized by Cook,
op. cit., pp. 697 ff.

FIG. 3.—Caprine Sileni upon the Francois Vase, 600–550 B.C.
See p. 24, n. 1

FIG. 5.—View of a Satyr-Play from a Dinos in Athens
See p. 25, n. 2

so that it is clear that such figures did not go back to a remote period in Athenian history. In fact, they can hardly be conceived of as preceding Pratinas' introduction of the satyric drama toward the close of the sixth century. Unfortunately none of these vases is inscribed with the name of the creatures depicted, but the caprine ears, hoofs, horns, and tails scarcely leave room for doubt that these creatures, like similar figures of Hellenistic and Roman times, were known as satyrs. With one possible exception (Fig. 9), which will be discussed presently,

FIG. 4.—Preparations for a Satyric Drama from a Naples Crater of About 400 B.C.

See p. 25, n. 1

these representations also have no direct relationship to the theater. It would thus appear that from first to last a clear distinction was drawn, outside the sphere of theatrical influence, between the equine sileni and the caprine satyrs.

Of the vases which may certainly be regarded as representing scenes from satyric drama the best known and most pretentious is a crater in Naples (Fig. 4).[1] This and a crater at Deepdene were painted about 400 B.C. Somewhat earlier are another crater at Deepdene, a dinos at Athens (Figs. 5 and 6), and fragments of two dinoi at Bonn (Fig. 7).[2] The last three are derived

[1] Fig. 4 is taken from Baumeister, *Denkmäler*, Fig. 422. The two craters at Deepdene are illustrated in Cook, *op. cit.*, Pl. XXXIX, Figs. 1–2.

[2] The three dinoi are discussed by Miss Bieber in *Athenische Mitteilungen*, XXXVI (1911), 269 ff. and Pl. XIII, Figs. 1–3 and Pl. XIV, Figs. 1–5. My Figs. 5–7 are taken from her publication, corresponding to Pl. XIII, Fig. 1, Pl. XIV, Fig. 4,

from the same original. On the Naples crater preparations for a satyr-play are being made in the presence of Dionysus and Ariadne, who are seen in an affectionate embrace in the center of the top row. The names of the figures are made known by inscriptions in most cases but are not always significant. Just beyond Ariadne, Love ("Ιμερος) hovers above an uninscribed actor in women's costume, whose mask is provided with a Scythian cap. The next figure is Heracles (inscribed) and the next is thought to be Silenus. Beyond Dionysus is an uninscribed actor in royal costume. Except Love, all these figures carry masks and constitute the histrionic personages in the drama. It has been claimed with great plausibility that the play dealt with Heracles' exploits at Troy.[1] In that case the king is Laomedon and the maiden is Hesione, his daughter, who was rescued from the sea monster by Heracles. To the right of the dancing choreutes in the lower row is the flute-player (Pronomus), who will furnish the accompaniment for the lyrical portions of the play; to the left is Demetrius with a roll in his hand, probably the poet. The remaining twelve figures are probably choreutae and bear more directly upon our present investigation. Most of them carry masks, and they have human feet and no horns. They resemble sileni in having long equine tails. The sole resemblance to satyrs is found in the fact that nine of them wear a shaggy covering about the loins, supposedly a goatskin. The waistband upon the choreutes in the extreme upper left-hand corner, however, resembles cloth trunks more than a skin. Yet this divergence is probably to be explained as due to carelessness or a whim on the part of the draftsman instead of to an essential difference in material. This appears plainly from a

and Pl. XIV, Figs. 1 and 2 respectively. Cook maintains that all six vases are descended from a fresco by Polygnotus, *op. cit.*, pp. 700 f.; but this suggestion seems improbable.

[1] Cf. De Prott, "De Amphora Neapolitana Fabulae Satyricae Apparatum Scaenicum Repraesentante," in *Schedae Philologicae Hermanno Usener Oblatae* (Bonn, 1891), pp. 47 ff. It seems strange that De Prott should mar his own interpretation by supposing the figure whom I have called Hesione to be a Muse. The Scythian cap ought to be decisive.

study of the other vases in this series, on which the loin-bands
resemble the trunks of the last-mentioned choreutes on the
Naples crater rather than the skins of his nine companions.
None the less, a multitude of short dashes on the waistbands in
one of the Bonn dinoi (Fig. 7) is plainly intended to characterize
them as skins, and the bands on the Deepdene craters are
"patterned in such a way as to suggest a fringed or shaggy edge."
An illuminating side light upon the freedom which the painter
exercised is afforded by a comparison of the left-hand choreutae
in Figs. 6 and 7. These are identical figures in different copies
of the same original; yet the shagginess of the loin-band is
clearly indicated in the one and entirely omitted in the other.
Moreover, the choreutes on the other dinos at Bonn seems to
wear no waistband at all![1] In conclusion, it will be observed
that, except for variations in the representation of the conventionalized goatskin, the choreutae upon all these vases are
exactly alike:[2] they all have human feet, no horns, and equine
tails. It is evident that by 400 B.C. or a little earlier this type
had become standardized for theatrical purposes. That it
suffered no material modification thereafter appears from a
Pompeian mosaic (Fig. 8).[3]

It is plain that this was the type of satyr which the unknown
source of the notice in *Etymologicum Magnum* had in mind when
attempting to explain the etymology of τραγῳδία: ". . . . or
because the choruses generally consisted of satyrs whom they
called 'goats' in jest either *on account of the shagginess of their
bodies* or on account of their lasciviousness, for the animal is of
such a sort; or because the choreutae plaited their hair, imitating

[1] Cf. Miss Bieber, *op. cit.*, Pl. XIV, Fig. 3.

[2] Except the eleventh and twelfth choreutae on the Naples crater (Fig. 4),
viz., the figure with a lyre near the middle of the lower row and the fully clad figure
next to the last on the right. If De Prott is correct in considering these figures
choreutae, they must be regarded (I suppose) as having not yet completed their
make-up.

[3] Fig. 8 is taken from Baumeister, *Denkmäler*, Fig. 424. The choreutae in this
scene are not to be understood as having no tails; their position does not permit
this feature to be seen, cf. Haigh, *The Attic Theatre*[3], p. 293, note.

the form of goats.''[1]   This passage has been used to support the canonical doctrine that tragedy was the child of satyric drama (see pp. 2 and 22 f., above), but is far from adequate for that purpose.   The words after δασύτητα ("shagginess") are often ignored or even omitted.   But it is necessary to interpret the

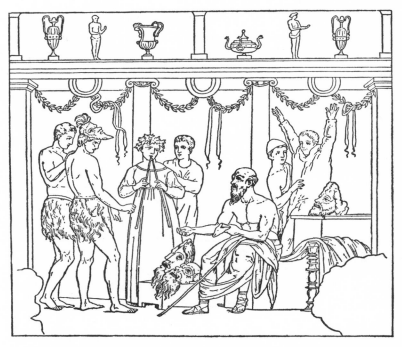

FIG. 8.—Poet and Choreutae of a Satyric Drama from a Pompeian Mosaic
See p. 27, n. 3

final phrase, "imitating the form of goats," in terms of the details stated in the context.   So far as we are now concerned, the only point of resemblance mentioned is their "shagginess." This and Horace's expression about the tragic poet "stripping

[1] Cf. *Etymologicum Magnum, s.v.* τραγῳδία: . . . . ἢ ὅτι τὰ πολλὰ οἱ χοροὶ ἐκ σατύρων συνίσταντο, οὓς ἐκάλουν τράγους σκώπτοντες ἢ διὰ τὴν τοῦ σώματος δασύτητα ἢ διὰ τὴν περὶ τὰ ἀφροδίσια σπουδήν · τοιοῦτον γὰρ τὸ ζῷον. ἢ ὅτι οἱ χορευταὶ τὰς κόμας ἀνέπλεκον, σχῆμα τράγων μιμούμενοι.

FIG. 6.—View of a Satyr-Play from a Dinos in Athens

See p. 25, n. 2

FIG. 7.—Views of a Satyr-Play from a Dinos in Bonn

See p. 25, n. 2

FIG. 10

A BRITISH MUSEUM PSYKTER BY DURIS OF ABOUT 480 B.C., PROBABLY SHOWING INFLUENCE OF CONTEMPORANEOUS SATYRIC DRAMA

See p. 31, n. 3

his satyrs" for the satyr-play[1] would be entirely suitable in describing the choreutae on the Naples crater. Furthermore, it will be noted that this explanation occurs only in a late Byzantine notice and that no earlier source is mentioned. The only way in which a respectable antiquity can be claimed, by means of literary evidence, for this interpretation consists in maintaining that it is implicit in Aristotle's phrase ἐκ σατυρικοῦ μετέβαλεν. But we have already seen (see p. 22, above), that this expression need not, and probably does not, support this view. The only other passage which can be cited in this connection occurs in three other Byzantine writers.[2] The conclusion is irresistible that both the goat-men explanation of the word τραγῳδία and the supposed development of tragedy from satyric drama are due to "reconstructions" of literary history at an extremely late period.

Evidently this standard type of theatrical satyr took its genesis from an amalgamation of the caprine satyrs and the equine sileni. It is significant that in Euripides' *Cyclops* and Sophocles' *Trackers* Silenus is one of the characters and *is the father of the chorus*. These satyr-plays were brought out in the vicinity of 440 B.C.[3] The question now arises: Was this conventional type the invention of Pratinas or did it develop later? It will be remembered that in the list of fifteen fifth-century vases from Attica on which representations of goat-men occur (see p. 25, above), one was mentioned as having a possible connection

[1] Cf. Horace *Ars Poetica*, vss. 220 f:
>carmine qui tragico vilem certavit ob hircum,
>mox etiam agrestis Satyros nudavit, etc.

[2] Cf. Suidas and Photius, *s.v.* οὐδὲν πρὸς τὸν Διόνυσον and Apostolius xiii. 42. After giving the explanation of this phrase already cited on p. 12, n. 3, above, they continue: βέλτιον δὲ οὕτως, τὸ πρόσθεν εἰς τὸν Διόνυσον γράφοντες τούτοις ἠγωνί-ζοντο, ἅπερ καὶ Σατυρικὰ ἐλέγετο· ὕστερον δὲ μεταβάντες εἰς τὸ τραγῳδίας γράφειν, κατὰ μικρὸν εἰς μύθους καὶ ἱστορίας ἐτράπησαν, μηκέτι τοῦ Διονύσου μνημονεύοντες, ὅθεν τοῦτο καὶ ἐπεφώνησαν. καὶ Χαμαιλέων ἐν τῷ Περὶ Θέσπιδος τὰ παραπλήσια ἱστορεῖ. The word παραπλήσια leaves it doubtful for how much of this notice Chamaeleon (Aristotle's pupil) should be held responsible. But at the most his accountability cannot extend beyond explaining the introduction of non-Dionysiac themes; the side remarks are Byzantine.

[3] Cf. von Wilamowitz, *N. Jahrbücher f. kl. Altertum*, XXIX (1912), 461, and Tanner, *Transactions American Philological Association*, XLVI (1915), 173 ff.

with the theater.   The single exception is a crater in the British
Museum of about 450 B.C. (Fig. 9).[1]   The upper design on the
same side of the vase represents the decking of Pandora, and it is
commonly thought that the two scenes belong together and are
derived from a satyr-play dealing with Pandora.   However
that may be, the presence of a flute-player would seem to indicate that at least Fig. 9 is theatrical.   If so, the choreutae are
not of the type which we have been studying, but true satyrs
with caprine hoofs, horns, and tails.[2]   About their loins they
wear trunks, which in three cases are painted black (to represent
a goatskin?) but in one case are left unpainted.   Now from

FIG. 9.—Satyrs on a British Museum Crater of About 450 B.C.

See p. 30, n. 1

Aeschylus' satyric drama entitled *Prometheus the Fire-Kindler*
is preserved a line "O goat, you will mourn (lose) your beard,"
which was addressed by Prometheus to a satyr who wished to
kiss a flame and which has been used as proof that the choreutae
were caprine in appearance.[3]   Again, in Sophocles' *Trackers*
occur the words: "For though you are young with a flourishing

[1] Fig. 9 is taken from the *Journal of Hellenic Studies*, XI (1890), Pl. XI, and is
reproduced by permission of the Council of the Hellenic Society.

[2] Reisch, *op. cit.*, pp. 456 f., considers the goat-men Pans, or choreutae in some
such comedy as Eupolis' Αἶγες.

[3] Cf. Nauck, *Tragicorum Graecorum Fragmenta*, p. 69, fr. 207:

τράγος γένειον ἆρα πενθήσεις σύ γε.

The use of the nominative τράγος instead of a vocative is harsh, and Shorey,
Classical Philology, IV (1909), 433 ff., interprets the line as an abbreviated
comparison with ὡς omitted: " <If you kiss that fire>, you'll be the goat (in the
proverb) who mourned his beard."   Of course, this play must have been written
considerably before 456 B.C., the year of Aeschylus' decease.

FIG. 11.—A Satyr upon a Würzburg Cylix of About 500 B.C.
See p. 31, n. 6

FIG. 12.—A Comus upon a Berlin Amphora
See p. 38, n. 2

beard, you revel as a goat in the thistles."[1] Finally, in Euripides' *Cyclops* the chorus speak of wandering about "with this poor goatskin cloak."[2] Although these passages do not constitute proof that the dramatic satyrs were of caprine appearance, they gain considerably in point if we may suppose that they were, and to that extent they confirm the evidence of the British Museum crater.

Such, then, is the penultimate stage in the evolution of the satyric chorus, and many authorities are content to stop here. But there remains evidence for a still earlier stage. A British Museum psykter by Duris (Fig. 10)[3] represents ten "choreutae" and a herald, and a British Museum cylix by Brygus contains two scenes, in one of which three "choreutae" are attacking Iris before Dionysus and his altar and in the other Hermes and Heracles are protecting Hera from four "choreutae."[4] These vases belong to about 480 B.C., and the "choreutae" upon them have human feet, no horns, no loin-bands, and equine ears and tails. Reisch is undoubtedly correct in recognizing in these scenes at least the indirect influence of the satyr-play.[5] Furthermore, a similar figure appears upon a Würzburg cylix of about 500 B.C. (Fig. 11).[6] This bears the inscription ϾATPYBϾ, a

----

[1] Cf. *Oxyrhynchus Papyri*, IX (1912), 59:

> νέος γὰρ ὢν ἀνὴρ
> πώγωνι θάλλων ὡς τράγος κνήκῳ χλιδᾷς.

[2] Cf. Euripides' *Cyclops*, vss. 79 f.:

> δοῦλος ἀλαίνων
> σὺν τᾷδε τράγου χλαίνᾳ μελέᾳ.

Reisch thinks the goatskin characterized the chorus as shepherds; cf. *op. cit.*, p. 458, note; Ridgeway considers it "the meanest form of apparel that could be worn by a slave"; cf. *Origin of Tragedy*, p. 87.

[3] Fig. 10 is taken from Höber, *Griechische Vasen*, Fig. 57 (1909).

[4] Cf. Reinach, *Repertoire des Vases Peints*, I, 193, or Baumeister, *Denkmäler*, Supplementtafel, Fig. 7.

[5] Cf. *op. cit.*, p. 459. The possibility of direct borrowing had already been denied by Wernicke, *op. cit.*, pp. 302–6. Wernicke's objections are not altogether convincing.

[6] Fig. 11 is taken from a photograph for which I am indebted to Professor Heinrich Bulle. He was also kind enough to express the following judgment with

manifest mistake for σάτυρος. Here we have the earliest representation of a satyr (identified by inscription) in Attica. And though it does not belong to a theatrical scene, its divergence from contemporaneous satyrs of the Peloponnesus and from Attic satyrs of a later period can be explained only on the basis of the appearance of the choreutae in contemporaneous satyr-plays. The Duris psykter and the Brygus cylix show that this type did not at once disappear.

To my mind the meaning of all this is fairly clear. When Pratinas attempted to restore the Dionysiac element to contemporaneous drama at Athens, he kept the Peloponnesian name but did not venture to shock conservatives still further by disclosing to their eyes creatures so foreign and strange as the Dorian goat-men would have been. Accordingly, he transformed his satyrs so as to approximate the sileni of native tragedy.[1] After fifty or sixty years, however, satyric drama had become so thoroughly at home in Athens that the experiment was tried of imposing the Peloponnesian type unchanged upon the Attic choruses. But the reaction could not and did not endure. In two or three decades the final type had emerged, such as we see it in the Naples crater. Except for the goatskin about the loins, which is often highly conventionalized, the native sileni are at every point victorious.

The Greeks were inordinately fond of associating every invention or new literary genre with some one's name as discoverer (εὑρετής). In the case of tragedy the problem was unusually complicated. In later years Arion, Epigenes, and

---

regard to the inscription: "Ich kann nicht mit Ch. Fränkel, *Satyr- und Bakchennamen auf Vasenbildern* (1912), S. 35, der Lesung von Schulze (*Göttinger gel. Anz.* 1896, S. 254) ⵣIBYPTAⵣ zustimmen; denn die Inschrift ist ja rechtsläufig. Man kann übrigens auch deutlich an dem Kleinerwerden der Buchstaben sehen, dass der Zeichner von links nach rechts geschrieben hat. Ich glaube mit Urlichs, (*Verzeichniss d. Antikensammlung d. Univ. Würzburgs*, I, S. 50), dass es eine einfache Verschreibung aus ΣΑΤΥΡΟΣ ist." The *membrum virile* has been omitted in the reproduction.

[1] Cf. the contemporaneous sileni in connection with the "wagon-ship" of Dionysus; see Fig. 65 and p. 121, below.

Thespis all had their partisans. The last named is the one most frequently mentioned, and strictly speaking this view is correct. But more broadly considered, the question largely depends upon the stage of development to which one is willing to apply the word "tragedy." To many moderns, with almost two and a half millenniums of dramatic history as a background, Aeschylus will seem the first tragic playwright. At least, in his hands tragedy became for the first time real literature.

The foregoing treatment will show that I do not believe a study of the origin of religion to be indispensable for a discussion of the origin of Greek tragedy. Prior to Arion and Epigenes there was nothing which the most fanciful could recognize as akin to modern tragedy. After the work of Thespis and Aeschylus no one can fail to note its presence. To trace, so far as we may, the gradual unfolding of the new genre from a state of nonexistence to a period of vigorous growth seems to me a concrete problem and distinctly worth while. The songs and dances from which tragedy and the satyr-play developed were associated, *at the period when they became truly dramatic*, with the worship of Dionysus, and *at that same period* Dionysus was as truly a "god" (as distinct from a "hero") as any that the Greeks ever knew. To abandon these plain facts and others like them in favor of vague theorizing on religious origins will never bring us satisfactory results. Now, in his *Origin of Tragedy* Ridgeway, who may serve as a protagonist of this method, recognized only the satyr-play as Dionysiac in origin, and attempted to dissociate tragedy and the dithyramb from that deity and to derive them from ceremonies at the tombs of heroes, i.e., from ancestor worship. I cannot conceive that many classical scholars will believe him to have succeeded in this attempt. Ridgeway evidently foresaw this and tried to forestall it by saying that "as Dionysus himself had almost certainly once been only a Thracian hero, even if it were true that Tragedy had risen from his cult, its real ultimate origin would still be in the worship of the dead" (*op. cit.*, p. 93). What, then, was the point in his

conceding that satyric drama was Dionysiac in origin ?   In that
case the ultimate origins of tragedy and satyric drama must,
after all, have been identical, and the differences in their origins
must have consisted only of the minor divergencies in the final
stage of their development.   In practice, how does this result
differ from the more usual procedure, which ignores the ultimate
sources and concentrates attention upon the last stage of development ?   So far as I can see, it would differ only to the extent
that the underlying religion of both genres would now be understood to be ancestor worship.   But this distinction loses all
meaning, for the reason that in his last volume Ridgeway maintains that "Vegetation, Corn, and Tree spirits, as well as those
of rocks, mountains, and rivers, and what are collectively termed
Totemistic beliefs," fertility-rites, initiation-rites, mana, "the
worship of Demeter and almost[1] all other Greek deities" are
"not primary phenomena but merely secondary and dependent
on the primary belief in the immortality and durability of the
soul," and consequently that tragedy and serious drama (being
everywhere associated with some form of religion) not only in
Greece but "wherever they are found under the sun have their
roots in the world-wide belief in the continued existence of the
soul after the death of the body."[2]   How much of truth there
may be in Ridgeway's contention that ancestor worship is prior
to and the ultimate source of other forms of religion I shall not
stop to discuss.   But the practical value of so universal a generalization has been well expressed by another: "Even if it can be
shown that your far-off ancestor was an ape, it does not follow
that your father was an ape."[3]   In other words, in spite of any
resemblance which may have obtained between the ultimate
forms of Dionysiac worship and the true veneration of heroes, *at
the time when tragedy actually came into being* the existing differ-

---

[1] Why "almost" is inserted here does not appear.   Many Greek divinities are
mentioned on Ridgeway's pages, but none is recognized as "totally independent"
of the cult of the dead.

[2] Cf. his *Dramas and Dramatic Dances*, etc., pp. 63, 337, 385, and *passim*.

[3] Cf. Marrett, *Classical Review*, XXX (1916), 159.

ences between them were of much greater significance than any
alleged identity of origin in the far-distant past could have been.
If it were possible for Ridgeway to substantiate his first position,
viz., that tragedy arose *directly* from the worship of the hero
Adrastus at Sicyon, or the like, there would be some meaning in
his work.   But his doctrine of *ultimate* derivation loses itself in
primeval darkness.

The Origin of Comedy.[1]—The difficulty of this problem was
recognized as early as Aristotle:

Now the successive changes in tragedy and the persons who were
instrumental thereto have not passed into oblivion, but comedy did suffer
oblivion for the reason that it was not at first taken seriously.   And a proof
of this is found in the fact that it was relatively late [viz., 486 B.C.] before
the archon granted a chorus of comic performers; they used to be volunteers.
And comedy already had certain forms when the aforementioned comic
poets [i.e., Chionides and Magnes, the first comedians after official recognition was granted] appear in the records.   Who furnished it with "characters" (πρόσωπα)[2] or prologues or number of actors and the like remains
unknown.   Developing a regular plot was a Sicilian invention, but of the
Athenians the first to abandon the "iambic" or lampooning form and to
begin to fashion comprehensive themes and plots was Crates.[3]

[1] Cf. Zieliński, *Die Gliederung der altattischen Komödie* (1885); Humphreys,
"The Agon of the Old Comedy," *American Journal of Philology*, VIII (1887),
179 ff.; Poppelreuter, *De Comoediae Atticae Primordiis* (1893); A. Körte, "Archäo-
logische Studien zur alten Komödie," *Jahrbuch d. archäologischen Instituts*, VIII
(1893), 61 ff.; Loeschcke, *Athenische Mittheilungen*, XIX (1894), 518, note; Bethe,
Prolegomena zur Geschichte des Theaters im Alterthum (1896), pp. 48 ff.; Mazon,
Essai sur la Composition des Comédies d' Aristophane (1904); Capps, "The Intro-
duction of Comedy into the City Dionysia," *University of Chicago Decennial
Publications*, VI (1904), 266 ff., and in Columbia University lectures on *Greek
Literature* (1912), pp. 124 ff.; Navarre, "Les origines et la structure technique de
la comédie ancienne," *Revue des Études anciennes*, XIII (1911), 245 ff.; White,
The Verse of Greek Comedy (1912); Cornford, *The Origin of Attic Comedy* (1914),
reviewed by Flickinger in *Classical Weekly*, VIII (1915), 221 ff.; and Ridgeway,
*The Dramas and Dramatic Dances of Non-European Races with an Appendix on the
Origin of Greek Comedy* (1915), reviewed by Flickinger, *Classical Weekly*, XI
(1918), 109 f.

[2] I am indebted to Professor Capps for this translation; the word is generally
taken to mean "masks" here.

[3] Cf. Aristotle's *Poetics* 1449a37–b9.

But whatever uncertainties may obscure the various stages
in the history of comedy, fortunately there is little doubt as to
the source from which it came.   Aristotle states that "comedy
also sprang from improvisations, originating with the leaders of
the phallic ceremonies,[1] which still survive as institutions in
many of our cities."[2]   Mr. Cornford (*op. cit.*, pp. 37 ff.) finds
the best illustration of these ceremonies in the well-known
passage in Aristophanes' *Acharnians*, vss. 237 ff.   Dicaeopolis
has just concluded a private peace with Sparta and prepares to
celebrate a festival of Dionysus on his country estate.   He
marshals his meager procession as if it contained a multitude,
his daughter carries upon her head a sacred basket with the
implements of sacrifice, two slaves hold aloft a pole which is
surmounted by the phallic symbol, and Dicaeopolis himself
brings up the rear with a large pot in his arms, while the wife
and mother constitutes the watching throng.   At vss. 246 ff. a
sacrifice is offered to the accompaniment of an invocation to
Dionysus.   Finally Dicaeopolis re-forms his procession with
various coarse remarks and starts up a phallic ballad of an
obscene nature in honor of Phales, "mate of Dionysus and fellow-
reveller" (ξύγκωμε).   The proceedings thus consist of a procession to the place of sacrifice, the sacrifice itself, and the phallic
song or *comus* (κῶμος).   The last is important for our present
purpose because comedy (κωμῳδία) etymologically means "comus-
song" (κῶμος+ᾠδή).   Κῶμος denotes both a revel and the band of
masqueraders participating therein.   The comus was the particular type of phallic ceremony from which comedy developed.

The comus in Aristophanes' *Acharnians* is sung by Dicaeopolis
alone for the reason that the lack of suitable helpers compelled
him to act as both priest and congregation.   But Cornford is
right (*op. cit.*, pp. 38 ff.) in recognizing this song as belonging to a
widely spread type in which the improvisations of one or more
leaders (ἐξάρχοντες) are interrupted at more or less regular
intervals by a recurrent chantey on the part of the chorus.   In

---

[1] The phallus was a representation of the *membrum virile*, and such ceremonies
were primarily intended to secure fertility.

[2] Cf. Aristotle's *Poetics* 1449*a*9–13.

this instance the song is not continued to a length natural to the
type, but is cut short by the real chorus of the play which has
been hiding but now bursts forth and stops proceedings with a
shower of stones.   From the standpoint of contents Cornford
detects two elements in the comus: an invocation to the god to
attend his worshipers in their rites, and an improvisational
"iambic" element of obscene ribaldry, which often took the form
of satire directed against individuals by name (*ibid.*, p. 41).
These two elements exactly correspond to the double object of
all phallic ceremonies, which were both a "positive agent of
fertilization" and a "negative charm against evil spirits."   The
former result was obtained by the invocation of friendly powers;
as to the latter,

the simplest of all methods of expelling such malign influences of any kind
is to abuse them with the most violent language.   No distinction is drawn
between this and the custom of abusing, and even beating, the persons or
things which are to be rid of them, as a carpet is beaten for no fault of its
own, but to get the dust out of it. . . . . There can be no doubt that the
element of invective and personal satire which distinguishes the Old Comedy
is directly descended from the magical abuse of the phallic procession, just
as its obscenity is due to the sexual magic; and it is likely that this ritual
justification was well known to an audience familiar with the phallic ceremony itself [*ibid.*, pp. 49 f.].

It is possible to cite many examples of ritualistic scurrility
among the Greeks, such as that indulged in by the Eleusinian
procession as it approached "the bridge," that of the riders upon
the carts on the Day of Pots (χόες) at the Anthesteria, that at the
Stenia festival, and many others.   Sometimes these involved
physical violence as well as mere abuse, and this element (or the
threat of it) frequently recurs in Old Comedy.   Perhaps the
most interesting parallel is afforded by Herodotus v. 82 f.   In
the sixth century B.C., in order to avert a famine, the Epidaurians
set up wooden statues of Damia and Auxesia, goddesses of
fertility.[1]   Somewhat later, the Aeginetans stole these images

---

[1] The second is, of course, the personification of Increase; the first is not so
obvious.   Some connect it with Demeter; it has also been proposed to interpret it
as the Cretan form of ζημία, "damage."   The one would therefore represent the
productive and the other the destructive powers; cf. Macan's edition *ad loc.*
This would accord very neatly with Cornford's positive and negative charms.

and set them up in their own country; "they used to appease them with sacrifices and female satiric choruses, appointing ten men to furnish the choruses for each goddess; the choruses abused no man but only the women of the country; the Epidaurians also had the same rites."

The comus frequently took the form of a company marching from house to house to the music of a flute-player and rendering a program of singing and dancing at every dwelling.   From what has already been said it will be understood that the improvisations of the comus leaders would rarely redound to the credit of the householders.   These scurrilous attacks upon their neighbors combined with other motives to induce the comus revelers to assume disguises, which varied from year to year.   Now, according to the *Parian Chronicle*, comic choruses were the invention of Susarion and were first performed at Icaria.   This doubtless means that Susarion transformed the ceremonies of an old ritual procession in the country into a "stationary" performance in an orchestra.   The same authority informs us that this innovation was introduced into Athens between 580 and 560 B.C.[1] This notice must refer to the Lenaean festival, since the program of the City Dionysia did not receive this addition until about 501 B.C.   At both festivals the performances still continued for some time to be called comuses (κῶμοι), comedy being a name of later date, and were produced by "volunteers."   Five Attic vase paintings of *ca.* 540–490 B.C. depict comus revelers as cocks, birds, or as riding upon horses, dolphins, or ostriches (Figs. 12–16).[2] The state did not assume official supervision of comedy until 486 B.C. at the City Dionysia and about 442 B.C. at the Lenaea.[3]

---

[1] Cf. Jacoby, *Das Marmor Parium*, p. 13: ἀφ' οὗ ἐν 'Αθ[ήν]αις κωμω[ιδῶν χο]ρ[ὸς ἐτ]έθη, [στη]σάν[των πρώ]των 'Ικαριέων, εὑρόντος Σουσαρίωνος, καὶ ἆθλον ἐτέθη πρῶτον ἰσχάδω[ν] ἀρσιχο[s] καὶ οἴνου με[τ]ρητής, [ἔτη . . . . The exact date is not determinable but is limited to a period of twenty years by other entries just before and after this one.

[2] Figs. 12 and 13 are taken, by permission of the Council of the Hellenic Society, from the *Journal of Hellenic Studies*, II (1881), Pl. XIV, A1 and B1; Fig. 14 from Poppelreuter, *op. cit.*, p. 8; and Figs. 15 and 16 from Robinson, *Boston Museum Catalogue of Greek, Etruscan, and Roman Vases* (1893), p. 136.

[3] Cf. Capps, *University of Chicago Decennial Publications*, VI, 286, and *American Journal of Philology*, XXVIII (1907), 186 f.

Fig. 13

A COMUS UPON A BRITISH MUSEUM OENOCHOE

See p. 38. n. 2

Before we can proceed further, it will be necessary to consider the nature of ancient comedy. In the time of Hadrian the history of literary comedy at Athens was divided into three periods, called Old, Middle, and New Comedy, respectively. Old Comedy came to a close shortly after the beginning of the fourth century B.C. Politics and scurrilous attacks upon contemporaneous personages made up the bulk of its subject-matter. Living men, such as Pericles, Socrates, Euripides, and

FIG. 14.—A Comus upon a Berlin Amphora
See p. 38, n. 2

Cleon were represented by actors on the stage and were lampooned with the utmost virulence. Sometimes their identity was thinly disguised under a transparent pseudonym, but oftentimes the very name of the victim was retained along with the other marks of identification. Middle Comedy was a transitional period of about half a century's duration between Old and New. It renounced the political and personal themes of its forerunner and was largely given up to literary criticism, parodies, and mythological travesty. New Comedy, in turn, abandoned such subjects for the most part and devoted itself to motives drawn from everyday life. Except for the occasional presence of the chorus, it does not greatly differ in structure, theme, or technique from the comedy of manners today, *mutatis mutandis*.

For the study of origins, however, we must turn back to the earliest type, Old Comedy, which is entirely unlike any present-day genre. We are fortunate in possessing eleven complete plays of Aristophanes, the chief poet of Old Comedy; and though no two of them are exactly alike in the details of their

FIG. 15

FIG. 16

FIGS. 15–16.—Comus Scenes upon a Boston Skyphos
See p. 38, n. 2

structure, yet the general outline is clear.   The leading features are as follows:[1]

1. The *prologue* (πρόλογος) spoken by the actors and serving both as an exposition and to set the action of the play in motion.

2. The *parodus* (πάροδος), or entrance song of the chorus. Originally this division must have been exclusively choral, but by Aristophanes' time it has been developed so as sometimes to include lines spoken by actors.

[1] The divisions of tragedy are discussed on pp. 192 f., below. Five of the terms applied to the divisions of comedy appear also in tragedy, viz., prologue, parodus, episode, stasimum, and exodus; several, if not all, of the five seem to have originated in tragedy.

3. The *agon* (ἀγών, "contest"), a "dramatized debate" or verbal duel between two actors, each supported by a semi-chorus; see p. 43, below.

4. The *parabasis* (from παραβαίνω, to "come forward"), a "choral agon" in which the chorus, the actors being off stage, march forward to address the audience. When complete, the parabasis consists of seven parts which fall into two groups: the first group contains three single parts, which were probably rendered by the first coryphaeus. Dropping all dramatic illusion and all connection with the preceding events of the play, he sets forth the poet's views concerning his own merits and claims upon the public, ridicules the rival playwrights, announces his opinions on civic questions, etc. The second group contains four parts in the form of an epirrhematic syzygy, i.e., a *song* (ᾠδή) and *epirrheme* (ἐπίρρημα, "speech") by one semi-chorus and its leader, respectively, are counterbalanced by an *antode* (ἀντῳδή) and an *antepirrheme* (ἀντεπίρρημα) by the other semi-chorus and its leader; here the chorus usually sing in character once more, the knights praising their "horses," the birds their manner of life as compared with men's, etc.[1]

5. There follows a series of *episodes* (ἐπεισόδια), histrionic scenes separated (6) by brief *choral odes* (στάσιμα or χορικά). The episodes portray the consequences of the victory won in the agon (3). For example, in the *Acharnians* the subject of controversy is whether Dicaeopolis shall be punished for the alleged treason of having made a private peace with Sparta, and part (5) represents him, in a succession of burlesque scenes, as enjoying the fruits of that peace.

7. The *exodus* (ἔξοδος), or recessional of the chorus. Properly speaking, this should contain only the final, retiring song

[1] From this second half of the parabasis comedy developed another epirrhematic division to which Zieliński also gave the name of syzygy. This was not exclusively choral, however, stood at no definite point in the play, and differed in still other respects from the epirrhematic syzygy of the parabasis. Three syzygies appear in Aristophanes' *Acharnians* and *Birds*, none in his *Lysistrata, Women in Council,* and *Plutus.* Cf. White, *op. cit.*, § 677. Since it is apparent that such syzygies are not primary in origin, they have been ignored in the foregoing discussion.

of the chorus (the ἐξόδιον), but the term came to include the histrionic passage just preceding it, also.

This is a very incomplete sketch of a highly complicated subject, but it will suffice for present purposes.

Now in the scurrility of the primitive (non-literary) comus Professor Navarre (op. cit., p. 248) would recognize three stages. In the first, the ribaldry of the comus received no answer from the crowd of spectators. This is doubtless to be explained by supposing that all who were competent to participate were already members of the comus; the spectators consisted only of women and children, who frequently had no more right of speech in religious ritual than in law. So Dicaeopolis' wife is present but speechless in Aristophanes' Acharnians (see p. 36, above). In the second stage, the bystanders retorted to the assaults of the comus revelers. This probably indicates that membership in the comus has been restricted in some way, leaving others free to retaliate in kind from the crowd. The third stage was reached when this new element was formally recognized and brought within the comus itself, which was thus divided into antagonistic halves for mutual recrimination. Thus may be explained a peculiar feature of Old Comedy. Its chorus was a double chorus of twenty-four members, always divided into two semi-choruses, which often were hostile during a large portion of the play. Sometimes this division between them was shown by their masks or costumes, as when the chorus represented men and women, horses and their riders, etc. But sometimes the division was one of sentiment—one semi-chorus, for example, favoring peace and the other being opposed to it. The result of this division of the early comus revelers into semi-choruses is a parallelism of structure in certain parts of comedy, ode being matched by antode, and the epirrheme of one chorus leader by the antepirrheme of the other. It is clear that all the divisions which show this duality of arrangement descend from the comus.[1]

One of these divisions is the parabasis (4). Though one of the most ancient features of Old Comedy, it was also one of the

[1] Or at least reflect its influence; cf. the syzygies mentioned in the last note.

first to decay: complete in Aristophanes' earlier plays, it is always mutilated in some way during his middle period and in his last two comedies has disappeared entirely. We have seen (p. 37, above) that the essential characteristics of the phallic ceremonies were the induction of the good influences by invocation and the aversion of the bad by vituperation. Now in the epirrhematic syzygy which constituted the second half of the parabasis, even as late as Aristophanes, when it naturally must have changed considerably in function, "the ode and antode normally contain an invocation, either of a muse or of gods, who are invited to be present at the dance, the divine personages being always selected with reference to the character of the chorus. The epirrheme and antepirrheme often contain the other element of satire or some milder form of advice and exhortation."[1]

Another division of Old Comedy which was carefully balanced and which ought, therefore, to be a derivative of the comus is the agon (3). Normally this division was epirrhematic in structure and fell into nine parts, as follows: First comes the ode sung by one half-chorus, then the *cataceleusmus* (κατακελευσμός, "encouragement") in which their leader exhorts one of the actor contestants, thirdly this actor delivers his speech (epirrheme), concluding with a peroration (πνῖγος, "choke," so called because it was all to be delivered in one breath and left the performer speechless). Next came the antode, anticataceleusmus, antepirrheme, and antipnigus rendered by the other half-chorus, their leader, and the second actor, respectively. Finally, in the *sphragis* (σφραγίς, "seal") is given the unanimous verdict of the whole chorus. At first glance it would seem that too important a rôle is here played by actors for the agon ever to have been derived from the comus, which was purely choral. The comus consisted of an undifferentiated band of revelers and its choreutae assumed no distinct parts. In fact, there is no reason to suppose that their performances involved dramatic impersonation (μίμησις) at all. They might be dressed to represent birds or animals, but with few or no exceptions they

[1] Cf. Cornford, *op. cit.*, p. 46.

sang and spoke and conducted themselves as would be appropriate for men engaged in such a rite to do. As we have already
seen (p. 38, above) their costumes were for disguise.

Nevertheless, the situation is not so impossible as it seems.
The fact that the masks and costumes of the choreutae were all
alike, or at most of two types to correspond to the two semi-
choruses, did not prevent each member of the chorus from
speaking, or singing, apart from the rest. This was sometimes
done even in fully developed tragedy, where the line of distinction
between chorus and actors was usually a sharp one. Thus, in
Aeschylus' *Agamemnon*, vss. 1348 ff., each of the choreutae in
turn pronounces two iambic lines. In particular, the rôles of
the two chorus leaders must have been developed in the comus
and early comedy so as partly to compensate for the lack of
actors. Note that Aristotle does not state merely that comedy
sprang from phallic ceremonies but from the *leaders* (ἐξάρχοντες)
of the phallic ceremonies. An illustration of what may result
from participation in the action on the part of individual choreutae is afforded by Aristophanes' *Women in Council*. I believe
that the "First Woman" and the "Second Woman" who appear
in our editions as uttering brief remarks at the beginning of this
play are not actors but the leaders of the two half-choruses.[1]
In function they are not at first distinguishable from Praxagora.
Indeed, it does not transpire until later that Praxagora herself
is an actor, not the coryphaeus. The fact is that in all his
plays Aristophanes seems to have assigned his two chorus leaders
more extensive participation both in lyrics and in recitative than
has been generally recognized (cf. White, *op. cit.*, *passim*). In
my opinion this sort of thing was even more common at an
earlier period, and in this way it was possible for the comus
to have a quasi-agon from which the later histrionic agon could
easily develop. Of course, the chorus leaders could not appear
in individualized rôles, as the actors did in the Aristophanic
agon, for characters had not yet been introduced into comedy;

[1] Cf. White, "An Unrecognized Actor in Greek Comedy," *Harvard Studies*,
XVII (1906), 124 f.

but they could engage in a contest of perfectly general, deperson-
alized billingsgate or, at a later period, speak as the poet's
mouthpiece for the pros or cons of any question. Thus, they
would not represent individual men, with an individual's name
and characterization, but *any* men. Their sentiments would
have been equally appropriate in the mouths of any of the other
choreutae.

The agon and parabasis must necessarily have been flanked
on either side by a processional and a recessional. In their
simplest form, these need not have involved more than silent
marching in and out again; but probably the flute accompaniment was always present, and singing would soon be added.
Even when words and singing were employed, there was no
necessity of these being newly composed for each occasion or
even original at all. It will be remembered that in Aristophanes'
earliest and latest plays he did not write special exodia but borrowed from earlier poets any popular airs that suited his purpose.[1]
Moreover, Aristophanes' exodi lack the balanced structure which
is characteristic of all divisions which descend directly from
the primitive comus; but in this instance that fact has no significance, for the reason that by the end of a comedy (or comus)
the two half-choruses would always be reconciled and go
marching off together. Nevertheless, the intrusion of the histrionic element, the comparative rarity of the earliest dramatic
meter (the trochaic tetrameter), and the absence of a canonical
structure make it plain that the recessional of the primitive
comus never developed into a regular division—in other words,
that the exodus of Aristophanic comedy was the product of a
later period.

On the other hand, the Aristophanic parodus resembles the
agon and the parabasis in making a large use of the tetrameter
(*op. cit.*, p. 185). Moreover, it contains distinct survivals of
epirrhematic composition (*ibid.*, pp. 159 and 366), so that, in
spite of its histrionic elements and the absence of a canonical
form, the parodus ought to be considered as having been

[1] Cf. Zieliński, *op. cit.*, p. 190.

exclusively choral by origin and as having developed out of the simple processional before the comus became histrionic.

The theatrical comus, then, must have been something as follows: first a choral parodus, next a semi-histrionic agon, then a parabasis, and finally a recessional which ultimately developed into an exodus. A late notice,[1] if correctly emended, informs us that at one time comedies contained no more than three hundred verses. I am of the opinion that this is the type of performance alluded to and that comedy did not, in essence, greatly depart therefrom until actors, as distinct from the chorus, were added.

How did this addition come to be made? It is impossible that the comic playwrights, with the actors of tragedy ever before them, should never have thought of taking this step. Nevertheless, the main impulse seems to have come from another direction. We have seen (p. 36, above) that in the non-theatrical comus the phallus was borne on a pole in the ritual procession with which the comus was originally associated; it was not worn. Neither is it worn by the comus choreutae as represented on Attic vase paintings (Figs. 12–16). But in Old Comedy it is clear that at least some of the characters wore the phallic emblem. That this was in fact the general practice appears from the language in which Aristophanes boasts of the modesty of his *Clouds:*

> And observe how pure her morals: who, to notice first her dress,
> Enters not with filthy symbols on her modest garments hung,
> Jeering bald-heads, dancing ballets, for the laughter of the young.[2]

And Dr. Körte (*op. cit.*, pp. 66 ff.) has collected ten passages in other plays of our poet which indicate that Aristophanes was not always so puritanical as he claims to be here. These conclusions are confirmed also by numerous representations, of

---

[1] Published by Usener in *Rheinisches Museum f. Philologie*, XXVIII (1873), 418.

[2] Cf. Aristophanes' *Clouds*, vss. 537 ff. (Rogers' translation). The original of "filthy symbols" is σκίτινον καθειμένον. It has therefore been suggested, especially since there seems to be an allusion to a phallus even in the *Clouds* (vs. 734), that Aristophanes is not to be understood as discontinuing the use of the phallus altogether in this play, but merely as abandoning the φαλλὸς καθειμένος in favor of the less indecent φαλλὸς ἀναδεδεμένος. Both types are seen in Fig. 17.

Attic workmanship, which are plausibly thought to depict actors in Old and Middle Comedy (Figs. 17–19).[1] By the time of New Comedy, on the contrary, the phallus was apparently no longer worn, and the characters were garbed in the dress of everyday life. Now the Dorian mime or farce was widely cultivated in the Peloponnesus and Magna Graecia. The performers were individualized actors, not welded into a chorus. They wore the phallus, had their bodies stuffed out grotesquely both in front and behind by means of copious padding, and in general bear a very close resemblance to the comic actors at

FIG. 17.—Comic Actors and Flute-Players upon an Attic Vase in Petrograd
See p. 47, n. 1

Athens (Figs. 20 and 21).[2] Their performances were loosely connected, burlesque scenes, abounding in stock characters and enlivened by obscenity and ribald jests. Most authorities agree that the burlesque episodes (5) of Old Comedy are derived from this source. According to Aristotle,[3] the Megarians claimed that comedy originated with them about 600 B.C. when a democracy with its resultant freedom of speech was established among them. It was even asserted that Susarion, the reputed founder of Attic comedy (see p. 38, above), came from Megara, but this claim is

[1] Figs. 17–19 are taken from Körte, *op. cit.*, p. 69 (Fig. 1), p. 78 (Fig. 3), and p. 80 (Fig. 5), respectively. In Fig. 17 there are only three actors; the end figures are flute-players. Körte believes this scene to be taken from Middle Comedy. In Fig. 19 the phallus has been omitted.

[2] Figs. 20 and 21 are taken from Körte, *op. cit.*, p. 91 (Fig. 8), and Baumeister's *Denkmäler*, Fig. 2099, respectively. The phallus has been omitted from some of the actors.

[3] Cf. Aristotle's *Poetics* 1448a31 f.

apparently unwarranted.[1] The fact remains, however, that
Aristophanes and his confrères often speak of stupid, vulgar
scenes or jokes as being "stolen from Megara."[2] Though these
words have been otherwise explained,[3] I believe that Megara,
which is the nearest Dorian city to Attica, had something to do
with the introduction of the histrionic element into Attic comedy.
Of course, this does not mean that Megara is to be regarded as

FIG. 18.—An Attic Terra Cotta in
Berlin Representing a Comic Actor.
See p. 47, n. 1

FIG. 19.—An Attic Terra
Cotta in Munich Representing a
Comic Actor.
See p. 47, n. 1

the inventor of Athenian comedy, for the comus was indigenous
and received its development on Attic soil and the type of performance which came into being after the introduction of actors
was quite unlike anything in Megara or any other part of the
Dorian world.

[1] Those who admit this claim rest under the necessity of placing the introduction of actors at this early date. This would mean that comedy had actors
before tragedy did! On the other hand, the reader needs to be warned that I
place the introduction of comic actors later than most writers.

[2] Cf. Aristophanes' *Wasps*, vs. 57, and Kock, *Comicorum Graecorum Fragmenta*, I, 9 f., fr. 2 (Ecphantides), and I, 323, fr. 244 (Eupolis).

[3] Von Wilamowitz' skepticism with regard to Megarian comedy, however,
has not gained many converts; cf. "Die megarische Komödie," *Hermes*, IX
(1875), 319 ff.

With actors, impersonation became possible for the first time
in Attic comedy. Besides the nondescript chorus and chorus
leaders, there were now performers who could assume the identity
of real or imaginary characters and carry a rôle or, by a change of
mask, several rôles through the play. The importance of all
this is too obvious to require amplification. It marked the
birth of dramatic comedy at Athens. Through the introduction
of actors, comedy became amenable to several other influences.
Tragedy could at once make itself felt. A histrionic prologue
could now be added, the comic prologue corresponding in length

FIG. 20.—Actors of Dorian Comedy upon a Corinthian Crater in Paris
See p. 47, n. 2

and function to the tragic prologue and first episode combined.[1]
A real agon of actors now became possible, whatever use may have
been made previously of the chorus leaders for this purpose.
Furthermore, the new Megarian burlesque episodes (5) would
naturally be separated by stasima (6) in imitation of tragedy.
It would also be possible to insert an episode[2] between the parodus
and the agon, as is done in Aristophanes' *Plutus*, vss. 322–486;
or between the agon and the parabasis, as in Aristophanes'

[1] Cf. Navarre, *op. cit.*, p. 268. The same fact is brought out more graphically
in the lithographic table at the close of Zieliński's book.

[2] The episodes referred to in this sentence are more properly termed "mediat-
ing scenes" in contradistinction to the true episodes (5) which follow the parabasis (cf. White, *The Verse of Greek Comedy*, §§ 679 f.). Twenty-six connecting
links of this sort occur in Aristophanes, twenty of them just before an agon or
parabasis. Syzygies are also employed to extend the length of the play, especially
in the first half (cf. p. 41, n. 1, above).

Knights, vss. 461–97; or to compose a second parabasis and
to insert an additional episode between them, as in Aristophanes'
Peace, vss. 1039–1126, etc.   In addition to all this, tragedy
would exert a constant influence in elevating and standardizing
all parts of comedy alike.

But the restricted and even disconnected method of elaboration employed in earlier comedy, with its invective, lampoons,

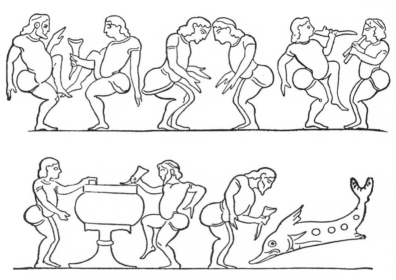

FIG. 21.—Actors of Dorian Comedy upon a Corinthian Vase
See p. 47, n. 2

and obscene jests, would not suffice to fill so ample a framework.
Therefore, it became necessary to broaden and deepen the
plots; in fact, now for the first time in Attic comedy was it
possible to have a plot worthy of the name.   All this is implied
in the words which have already been quoted from Aristotle
(p. 35, above): "Developing a regular plot was a Sicilian invention, but of the Athenians the first to abandon the 'iambic' or
lampooning form and to begin to fashion comprehensive themes
and plots (καθόλου ποιεῖν λόγους καὶ μύθους) was Crates."   The
reference in the first half of this sentence is to Epicharmus, whose

name actually appears in Aristotle's text at this point but without grammatical construction. Epicharmus was a resident of Megara Hyblaea in Sicily, whence he migrated to Syracuse about 485 B.C. Like the Megarians on the Greek mainland, also the Sicilian Megarians laid claim to the honor of having invented comedy.[1] They based their pretensions on the fact that Epicharmus flourished and won his reputation before 486 B.C., which was the *terminus post quem* for the beginning of the official careers of Magnes and Chionides, who were the first poets of state-supported (as opposed to volunteer) comedy, at the City Dionysia in Athens. Epicharmus raised the Dorian mime in Sicily to literary importance, and seems to have improved upon the detached or but loosely connected scenes of his predecessors by stringing them together upon the thread of a common plot-interest. His plays had no chorus and did not touch upon his contemporaries or politics. Now Aristotle's words concerning Crates must certainly be understood as indicating a resemblance between him and Epicharmus in at least some of these particulars. The expression which I have translated "to fashion comprehensive themes and plots" has been rendered "generalized his themes and plots" by Butcher, "to frame stories of a general and non-personal nature, in other words, Fables or Plots" by Bywater, and "composed plots or fables of a 'universal' character" by Cornford (*op. cit.*, p. 217). Whatever other meaning may inhere in this phrase, I think that it must be taken to mean, first of all, that Crates, like Epicharmus, made all or, at least, most of the parts of his plays subservient to one connecting idea or plot; and it seems to me that the previous clause which refers to his abandonment of the "iambic" or lampooning form looks in the same direction. In my opinion, the invective of his predecessors had been episodic and unrelated to its context by any sequence of thought, often being expressed in passages like the following:

> Shall we all a merry joke
> At Archedemus poke,
> Who has not cut his guildsmen yet, though seven years old;

[1] Cf. Aristotle's *Poetics* 1448a32–4.

Yet up among the dead
He is demagogue and head,
And contrives the topmost place of the rascaldom to hold?
And Clisthenes, they say,
Is among the tombs all day,
Bewailing for his lover with a lamentable whine.
And Callias, I'm told,
Has become a sailor bold,
And casts a lion's hide o'er his members feminine.[1]

Here this abuse is dragged in apropos of nothing, and the three citizens who are assailed within a score of lines have no connection with the main theme of the play. It was this sort of thing, I venture to believe, that Crates discontinued; and Aristotle's language does not require us to conclude that he relinquished scurrility altogether. It is usually thought, however, that Crates made no assaults of any kind upon his contemporaries but "generalized" his plots by treating imaginary, "ideal" characters in his plays. In other words, he is supposed to have anticipated to some extent the manner and material of New Comedy. I have no desire to combat this view, which simply advances a step beyond my own. The main fact, that of Crates' having invented plot sequence in Attic comedy, can hardly be made a matter of dispute.

We are indebted to a late authority, Tzetzes, for the following statements:

But also Old Comedy differs from itself [i.e., falls into two types], for those who first established the institution of comedy in Attica (and they were Susarion and his successors) used to bring on the characters (πρόσωπα) in an undifferentiated crowd (ἀτάκτως), and laughter alone was the object sought. But Cratinus [a contemporary of Crates], succeeding them, put a stop to the confusion (ἀταξίαν) and set the characters (πρόσωπα) in comedy for the first time at three; and he added profit to the pleasure of comedy, lampooning the evildoers and chastising them with comedy as with a public scourge. But even he still shared in the archaic qualities and, slightly, in the confusion (ἀταξίας).[2]

[1] Cf. Aristophanes' *Frogs*, vss. 416–30, Rogers' translation. The original is more vulgar than would be tolerable in an English translation.

[2] Cf. Kaibel, *Comicorum Graecorum Fragmenta*, p. 18.

Whatever the ultimate source of this notice, it contains much of value. In the first place, a distinction is correctly drawn between primitive comedy (Susarion to Cratinus; *ca.* 565 to *ca.* 450 B.C.) and Old Comedy (450 to *ca.* 385 B.C.). The earlier period is marked by ἀταξία, which I refer to the practice of having characterless choreutae take part singly as if they were actors (see p. 44, above). Though still occasionally guilty of this practice, as even Aristophanes sometimes was, Cratinus regularly withdrew his choreutae from participation in the dialogue and reduced the performers to three. These three, however, were now real actors, as distinct from the chorus and chorus leaders, and played individualized rôles which demanded dramatic impersonation. The number three was doubtless due to contemporaneous tragedy in which the number of actors had recently been increased by Sophocles from two to three (see p. 167, below).[1]

A second difference between primitive comedy and Old Comedy is found in the use which was made of invective. If this development had not taken place, Old Comedy would not occupy the unique place which it now holds in the dramatic literature of the world. As we have just seen, the lampooning of primitive comedy was probably episodic and detached from the context, like that in Aristophanes' *Frogs*, vss. 416-30; a

---

[1] Some would interpret this passage as meaning that Cratinus was the first to observe the aesthetic law that not more than three persons should participate in the same conversation (cf. Rees, *The So-called Rule of Three Actors in the Classical Greek Drama*, p. 9, n. 1). When the only speakers were the individual choreutae, who were twenty-four in number, such a restriction must have been unheard of. On the other hand, if it should prove true that Megarian actors were brought in before the time of Cratinus, then we must suppose that their number was at first in excess of three and was reduced to three by him. Of course, the use of but three actors in the tragedy and comedy of this period would automatically result in not more than three persons participating in a conversation and so in the observance of the aesthetic law. This statement, however, is subject to the qualification that the chorus leaders continued to have speaking parts both in comedy (see p. 44, above), and in tragedy (cf. pp. 164 f. and 169, below), and that a fourth actor was occasionally employed (cf. pp. 171 and 182, below). In any case I am of the opinion that conscious formulation of the aesthetic law was not made until Hellenistic times (see pp. 187 f., below).

whole play was not devoted to one person, and no citizen was impersonated by an actor. Its object was merely to cause a laugh and it rarely served any useful purpose, certainly none for the public interests of the state. It was a natural outgrowth of the magical abuse of the old phallic processions. Now Old Comedy, on the whole, was just the reverse of this, and Cratinus seems to have been the innovator who, "generalizing" his plots by giving them a single theme, after the fashion set by Crates, devoted them solely or mainly to political and social questions and dragged his victims in person upon his stage.

When did these changes take place? First let it be noted how they mutually depend one upon another: neither tragedy nor the Sicilian mime could greatly influence early Attic comedy until actors, as distinct from a chorus, were introduced, nor could their influence be long delayed after the actors came. I think that these factors came to fruition not long before 450 B.C.

a) Reverting to Aristotle's words (quoted on p. 35, above), when are we to suppose that the Athenians began to "treat comedy seriously"? The most obvious answer would be, "486 B.C., when comedy first received official recognition." Chionides and Magnes are the poets of this period, and there is no reason to believe that they improved upon their immediate predecessors of the "volunteer" comedy otherwise than in a more worthy literary treatment of their plays. Aristophanes describes Magnes' efforts in the following terms:

> All voices he uttered, all forms he assumed, the Lydian, the fig-
> piercing Fly,
> The Harp with its strings, the Bird with its wings, the Frog with
> its yellow-green dye.[1]

It is plain that these words refer to plays by Magnes which were called *The Lydians*, *The Gall-Flies*, *The Harpists*, *The Birds*, and *The Frogs*. These titles at once remind us of the animal masks which were so common in the comus (Figs. 12–16). Of course, state supervision implies a certain amount of serious attention. Nevertheless I think that in this passage Aristotle had a later period in mind.

[1] Cf. Aristophanes' *Knights*, vss. 522 f., Rogers' translation.

It was long ago pointed out that Attic comedies were not published before the time of Cratinus. The fact of publication shows that comedy was at last being treated with true seriousness and helps to explain the ignorance, in later times, with respect to certain points. Though the state records gave the names of comic victors from 486 B.C. on, they did not include information upon matters of mere technique. For knowledge of this sort Aristotle (the ultimate source of Tzetzes) and all other ancient investigators were almost entirely dependent upon what they could glean from the editions of Cratinus, Crates, and their successors. Now the earliest texts available revealed the use of characters, prologues, and three actors as well as of the parodus, agon, parabasis, and exodus. Why did Aristotle specifically name the first group and not the second?

In my opinion, Professor Capps[1] has provided the correct answer. He maintains that Aristotle distinguished two kinds of ignorance concerning the history of comedy. In the first place, there was the Egyptian darkness which covered the period previous to 486 B.C. For example, when Aristotle declared that comedy "already had certain forms" ($\sigma\chi\dot{\eta}\mu\alpha\tau\dot{\alpha}\ \tau\iota\nu\alpha$) at this time, he could not have specified what these forms were; he was merely surmising that the fact of state supervision presupposed more or less definiteness of form. In the second place, there was the period of semi-darkness immediately after 486 B.C. Tradition must have placed in this period the introduction of characters, prologues, and three actors, and so Aristotle singled them out for mention. But tradition had not handed down also the names of the innovators, and in the absence of texts it was impossible to probe the matter further. Needless to state, the situation regarding the other innovations, whether of this period or earlier, was much worse.

b) Though Thespis is said to have invented the prologue in tragedy, this statement is justly discredited (see p. 298, below); and no tragedy is actually known to have had one before

---

[1] Cf. "The Introduction of Comedy into the City Dionysia," *University of Chicago Decennial Publications*, VI, 266 ff.

Phrynichus' *Phoenician Women* (476 B.C.). Aeschylus' *Suppliants* (about 490 B.C.) and *Persians* (472 B.C.) have none. It is
most unlikely that comedy should have anticipated tragedy in
this feature.

c) Capps[1] has plausibly suggested that knowledge of Epicharmus' achievements in comedy was brought to Athens by
Aeschylus, who is known to have been in Sicily *ca.* 476 B.C.,
shortly after 472 B.C., and for about two years before his death
there in 456 B.C.

d) The third actor was introduced into tragedy between
about 468 and 458 B.C., and it is more probable that the use of
three actors in comedy was borrowed from tragedy than vice
versa.

e) Cratinus won his first victory at the City Dionysia of
452 B.C. and (*f*) Crates at that of 450 B.C.   Doubtless the activity
of both men began somewhat earlier.

g) It is incredible that the state should have postponed
official control of comedy at the Lenaean festival until about
442 B.C., if the developments which we have been sketching had
taken place long before.

h) The earliest comedian to refer to Megarian comedy is
Ecphantides, whose first victory was won between 457 and 453
B.C.   Whenever Aristophanes "names any writers of 'vulgar
comedy' who used the stale antics which he repudiates, these
writers are his own predecessors and contemporaries of the
Attic stage."[2]   This implies that the borrowing was a fairly
recent occurrence.

i) Finally, Megara was actually under the sway of Athens
during 460/59–446/45 B.C.   The opportunity for the exchange of
ideas between Megara and Athens would naturally be most
favorable at that time.

In view of the preceding considerations, I am of the opinion
that actors were introduced into Athenian comedy shortly
before 450 B.C.

[1] Cf. Columbia University Lectures on *Greek Literature*, p. 130.

[2] Cf. Cornford, *op. cit.*, pp. 179 and 193, n. 1; see p. 48, above.

The Greek Theater.[1]—Since, as we have seen, both tragedy and comedy among the Greeks were choral by origin, the center of their theaters was a circular "dancing place" called an *orchestra*[2] (ὀρχήστρα), in the middle of which stood a *thymele* (θυμέλη) or "altar" (Figs. 22 f.).[3] When an actor was added to the tragic

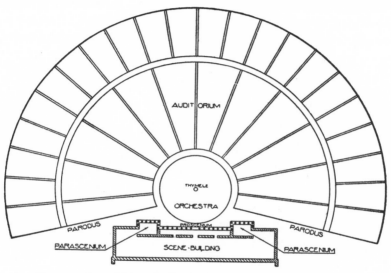

FIG. 22.—Ground Plan of a Greek Theater with Names of Its Parts
See p. 57, n. 3

choreutae, it became necessary to provide a dressing-room where he might change his mask and costume. This temporary structure was called a σκηνή ("hut": our English word "scene"), and

[1] It is unfortunate that there is at present no satisfactory book dealing with the Greek theater on the structural side. English readers are practically restricted to Haigh's *The Attic Theatre*, revised by Pickard-Cambridge in 1907, which devotes nearly one hundred pages to a summary and criticism of the different views. But this work has already been off the press for a decade and on the main issue, viz., (Footnote 1 continued on p. 58)

[2] For a slight variability in the application of the word orchestra see p. 83 and nn. 1 and 2, below; see also p. 72, n. 3.

[3] Fig. 22 is specially drawn and does not exactly reproduce any single theatrical structure. Fig. 23 is taken, simplified and slightly altered, from Dörpfeld-Reisch, *Das griechische Theater*, Pl. VIII (a).

at first stood outside the spectators' range of vision.   Afterward
it was brought immediately behind the orchestral circle and then
served also as a background in front of which the dramatic action
was performed.   Its face was pierced by doors, usually three but
sometimes only one, which were conventionally thought of as
leading into as many different houses.   The scene-building often
had two projecting side wings called *parascenia* (παρά, "beside"+
σκηνή).   The front of the scene-building and of the parascenia

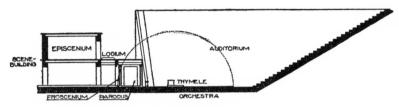

FIG. 23.—Cross-Section of a Greek Theater with Names of Its Parts
See p. 57, n. 3

came to be decorated with a row of columns, the *proscenium*
(πρό, "before"+σκηνή).   The top of this proscenium was used
by actors when they had occasion to speak from the housetop
or were thought of as standing upon some elevation.   In the

as to whether the Greek theater of the classical period was provided with a raised
stage for actors, makes too many concessions to the traditional view.   For German
readers, on the other hand, the situation is not a great deal better.   Dörpfeld's
book has been before the public since 1896, and in the interim his opinions have
necessarily changed on many points.   He has promised a thoroughly revised second
edition, which is demanded also by the excavation of additional theaters and by the
publication of numerous special articles.   But it is hardly likely that this promise
will ever be redeemed.   The only comfort is to be derived from the fact that, as
works of major importance have appeared, Dörpfeld has promptly published
critiques which have often been of such length as to furnish convenient restatements
of his views.   These more recent works in German, however, have attempted
merely to force a modification of certain details in Dörpfeld's position; they are in
no wise calculated to serve as independent presentations of the whole matter or as a
means of orientation for the uninitiated.

From the extensive bibliographical material which is available it is manifestly
impossible to cite more than a fraction here.   The outstanding books are Dörpfeld-
Reisch, *Das griechische Theater* (1896), defended against reviewers and partially
modified in "Das griechische Theater Vitruvs," *Athenische Mittheilungen*, XXII

course of time it was employed also for divinities, especially in epiphanies at the close of tragedies (see p. 292, below). Since this spot was never invaded by the singing or dancing of the chorus and was the only place reserved for actors exclusively, it came to be called the *logium* (λογεῖον, from λέγειν to "speak") or "speaking place."[1] Behind the logium was the second story of the scene-building, known as the *episcenium* (ἐπισκήνιον; ἐπί, "upon"+σκηνή); its front wall was pierced by one or more large doorways. Past each parascenium a "side entrance" or *parodus* (πάροδος; παρά, "beside"+ὁδός, "passage") led into the orchestra. These entrances were used by the audience before and after the play, and during it by the actors (who could use also the

---

(1897), 439 ff., and XXIII (1898), 326 ff.; Puchstein, *Die griechische Bühne* (1901), answered by Dörpfeld in *Athenische Mittheilungen*, XXVIII (1903), 383 ff.; and Fiechter, *Die baugeschichtliche Entwicklung des antiken Theaters* (1914), summarized by its author and criticized by Dörpfeld in *Jahrbuch d. arch. Instituts, Anzeiger*, XXX (1915), 93 ff. and 96 ff., respectively. Other important publications are von Wilamowitz-Möllendorff, "Die Bühne des Aischylos," *Hermes*, XXI (1886), 597 ff.; Todt, "Noch Einmal die Bühne des Aeschylos," *Philologus*, XLVIII (1889), 505 ff.; Capps, "Vitruvius and the Greek Stage," *University of Chicago Studies in Classical Philology*, I (1893), 3 ff.; Bethe, *Prolegomena zur Geschichte des Theaters im Alterthum* (1896), and "Die hellenistischen Bühnen und ihre Decorationen," *Jahrbuch d. arch. Instituts*, XV (1900), 59 ff. (answered by Dörpfeld in "Die vermeintliche Bühne des hellenistischen Theaters," *ibid.*, XVI [1901], 22 ff.); Petersen, "Nachlese in Athen: Das Theater des Dionysos," *ibid.*, XXIII (1908), 33 ff.; and Versakis, "Das Skenengebäude d. Dionysos-Theaters," *ibid.*, XXIV (1909), 194 ff., answered by Dörpfeld, *ibid.*, pp. 224 ff. Still other titles will be cited as they are needed in the discussion. See also p. 221, below. For reports on the excavations of various theaters the reader should consult the bibliographical references given by Dörpfeld-Reisch and Fiechter in their footnotes.

[1] Dörpfeld claims that the name was given because the speakers stood there in addressing the public assemblies and that the same place was known as the *theologium* when used by divinities; cf. *Athenische Mittheilungen*, XXIII (1898), 348 f., and XXVIII (1903), 395, and *Jahrbuch d. arch. Instituts, Anzeiger*, XXX (1915), 98. Reisch thought that logium was the name of some kind of special structure in the orchestra; cf. *Das griechische Theater*, p. 302. Inscriptions prove the presence of a logium in the Delian theater in 279 B.C. (εἰς τὸ λογεῖον τῆς σκηνῆς) and 180 B.C. (τὴν κατασκευὴν τῶν πινάκων τῶν ἐπὶ τὸ λογεῖον); cf. Homolle, *Bulletin de Correspondance Hellénique*, XVIII (1894), 162 and 165, and Robinson, *American Journal of Philology*, XXV (1904), 191; but they do not make its nature clear. Personally I am of the opinion that at Athens speakers always stood in the orchestra to address the public assemblies until the building of the Nero stage about 67 A.D.;

doors in the scene-building) and the chorus. The parodi were often framed by beautiful gateways (Figs. 51 f.). The remainder of the orchestral circle was surrounded by the auditorium, the "theater" proper.[1] Chorus and actors stood on the same level in the orchestra or in the space between it and the scene-building. There was no stage in the Greek theaters until about the beginning of the Christian era.

But when the Greek theaters came under Roman influence and were provided with a stage, these technical terms naturally acquired a somewhat different significance (Figs. 24, 24a, 59, 62–64).[2] The proscenium was still the columned wall in front of the scene-building, but it now stood upon the stage (at the rear), and the stage itself was the logium. Whenever theophanies required a still higher level, this was furnished by the top of the proscenium,[3] which was called the *theologium* (θεολογεῖον; θεός, "god"+ λογεῖον) or "speaking place of divinities."[4] The space beneath

---

cf. Flickinger, *Plutarch as a Source of Information on the Greek Theater* (1904), p. 55, and see p. 102, below. My present view, therefore, is that logium suffered a change of meaning, being first applied to the top of the proscenium and being used for elevated action of various kinds, as explained in the text, and afterward being applied to the stage as the place of actors and public speakers. In either case, it referred to the same general part of the theater, viz., an elevated platform in front of the scene-building. But the original application of this term is one of the most perplexing problems in connection with scenic antiquities, and it is earnestly to be hoped that additional evidence may be brought to light which will unmistakably reveal its earlier history. The word does not appear in literature until Roman times (thrice in Plutarch), but then indisputably means "stage." See next paragraph in text.

[1] "Theater" (θέατρον) is derived from θεᾶσθαι, to "see," and was originally applied to the space occupied by the spectators. The wider meaning was a natural but later development. It is customary to employ the Latin term *cavea* ("an excavated place") to express the narrower meaning.

[2] Fig. 24 is taken from Wilberg's drawing, simplified by the omission of numerous details, in *Forschungen in Ephesos*, II, Fig. 96. I am responsible for the addition of the names.

[3] That this platform (or rather its equivalent in purely Roman theaters) might be conventionally regarded as the roof of the scene-building appears from Seneca *Medea*, vs. 973 (Medea speaking): "excelsa nostrae tecta conscendam domus," and vs. 995 (Jason speaking): "en ipsa tecti parte praecipiti imminet."

[4] The word occurs only in Pollux, *Onomasticon*, IV, § 127.

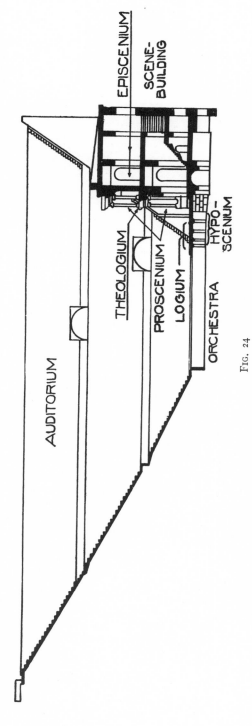

EPISCENIUM

SCENE-BUILDING

THEOLOGIUM

PROSCENIUM

LOGIUM

HYPO-SCENIUM

ORCHESTRA

AUDITORIUM

Fig. 24

CROSS-SECTION OF THE GRAECO-ROMAN THEATER AT EPHESUS WITH NAMES OF ITS PARTS

See p. 60, n. 2

the stage, or its front wall alone, was known as the *hyposcenium*
(ὑποσκήνιον; ὑπό, "beneath"+σκηνή).[1] There were now two
sets of parodi, leading upon the
stage and into the orchestra respectively. These two paragraphs
are meant for purposes of orientation and are written from the
standpoint of one who believes
with Dörpfeld that in Greek
theaters of the classical period
actors and chorus normally moved
upon the same level.[2]

A Greek town could hardly be
so small or so remote as not to
have its own theater and dramatic festival (Figs. 25 and 70 f.).[3]

[1] Dörpfeld applies the term to the first
story of the purely Greek (stageless) theater
(see p. 100, below).

[2] For a discussion of the technical
terms from the traditional standpoint cf.
A. Müller, "Untersuchungen zu den
Bühnenalterthümern," *Philologus*, Supplementband, VII (1899), 3 ff. Many of the
terms, notably σκηνή, have numerous
secondary meanings; cf. Flickinger, *Plutarch
as a Source of Information on the Greek
Theater*, pp. 23 ff., and Scherling, *De Vocis
Σκηνή, Quantum ad Theatrum Graecum
Pertinet, Significatione et Usu* (1906).
Thymele is sometimes extended in application so as to denote the whole orchestra;
hence θυμελικός was sometimes applied to
purely orchestral performers (or their performances) in contradistinction to those
who came into more immediate relationship
with the scene-building and who were in
consequence known as σκηνικοί (see pp. 96
f., below).

FIG. 24a.—Cross-Section of the
Proscenium (*Bühnenfassade*) of the
Graeco-Roman Theater at Ephesus
according to Hörmann.
See p. 61, n. 3.

[3] Fig. 24a is taken from Hörmann, "Die römische Bühnenfront zu Ephesos,"
Jahrbuch d. arch. Instituts, xxxviii–xxxix (1923–24; actually 1925), Beilage VII;
and Fig. 25 from a photograph by Professor D. M. Robinson.

The Greek theaters were regularly built upon a hillside and often commanded an outlook over a scene of great natural beauty and picturesqueness (Figs. 26–28).[1] So far as such structures have come down to us, the oldest is the theater of Dionysus Eleuthereus at Athens, and this is also the one of greatest interest to us, for the reason that in it were produced practically all the masterpieces of the greatest Greek dramatists (Figs. 1 and 31–41).[2] It seems strange that this building should not have remained continuously known to men from ancient times until

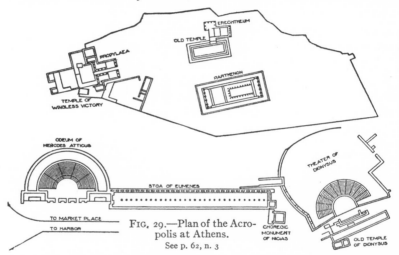

FIG. 29.—Plan of the Acropolis at Athens.
See p. 62, n. 3

the present hour, but in fact its very location passed into oblivion for centuries. During mediaeval times and until well into the modern era it was thought that the theater or odeum of Herodes Atticus, a Roman structure of the second century A.D. and situated at the opposite end of the Acropolis, represented the Dionysiac theater of the classical period (Fig. 29).[3] The correct site was first pointed out by R. Chandler in 1765, and is clearly indicated by a bronze coin of imperial times which shows the relation subsisting between the theater of Dionysus and the

[1] Figs. 26 f. are taken from photographs by Dr. A. S. Cooley; Fig. 28 from one by Professor D. M. Robinson.

[2] Fig. 1 is taken from a photograph furnished by Professor D. M. Robinson.

[3] Fig. 29 is specially drawn and is based upon several different drawings.

FIG. 25.—Theater at Oeniadae in Acarnania

See p. 61, n. 3

FIG. 26.—Theater and Temple of Apollo at Delphi

See p. 62, n. 1

FIG. 27.—Theater at Megalopolis in Arcadia

See p. 62, n. 1

FIG. 28.—Theater at Pergamum in Asia Minor

See p. 62, n. 1

Parthenon (Figs. 30 f.).[1] Excavations were conducted desultorily from time to time, beginning in 1841, but were not completed until the work under Dörpfeld's direction in 1886, 1889, and 1895.

The oldest structure in the precinct of Dionysus Eleuthereus is the earlier temple (Fig. 32).[2] This was built in the sixth century B.C., possibly in 534 B.C., when Pisistratus established the tragic contest. Here was housed the cult image of Dionysus which had been brought from Eleutherae.

Somewhat later are the remains of the early orchestra. According to late notices,[3] the original place of holding theatrical performances in Athens was an orchestra in the old market place, the location of which has not yet been determined. At that period the audience sat upon "wooden bleachers" (ἴκρια), which are said[4] to have collapsed on the occasion of a contest between Aeschylus, Pratinas, and Choerilus in the seventieth

FIG. 30.—Athenian Coin in the British Museum Showing the Parthenon and Outline of the Theater of Dionysus Eleuthereus.

See p. 63, n. 1

[1] Fig. 30 is taken from Wieseler's *Theatergebäude und Denkmäler d. Bühnenwesens bei den Griechern und Römern*, Pl. I, Fig. 1, and is magnified two diameters as compared with the original coin. See also the medallion on the outside cover, which is reproduced from the *British Museum Catalogue of Greek Coins, Attica, Megaris, Aegina*, Pl. XIX, Fig. 8. Fig. 31 is from a photograph by Dr. A. S. Cooley.

[2] Fig. 32 is redrawn, with slight alterations, from Dörpfeld-Reisch, *Das griechische Theater*, Pl. II. The age of the different remains is indicated in colors in *ibid.*, Pl. I.

[3] Cf. Photius, *s.v.* ἴκρια· τὰ ἐν τῇ ἀγορᾷ, ἀφ' ὧν ἐθεῶντο τοὺς Διονυσιακοὺς ἀγῶνας πρὶν ἢ κατασκευασθῆναι τὸ ἐν Διονύσου θέατρον; likewise *s.v.* ληναῖον and ὀρχήστρα.

[4] Cf. Suidas, *s.v.* Πρατίνας . . . . ἀντηγωνίζετο δὲ Αἰσχύλῳ τε καὶ Χοιρίλῳ, ἐπὶ τῆς ἑβδομηκοστῆς Ὀλυμπιάδος, ... ἐπιδεικνυμένου δὲ τούτου συνέβη τὰ ἴκρια, ἐφ' ὧν ἑστήκεσαν οἱ θεαταί, πεσεῖν. καὶ ἐκ τούτου θέατρον ᾠκοδομήθη Ἀθηναίοις. It is also possible that the orchestra in the precinct of Dionysus is somewhat earlier than is maintained in the text, possibly going back to the vicinity of 534 B.C., and that it was the earlier and less substantial seats near it which collapsed *ca.* 499 B.C.

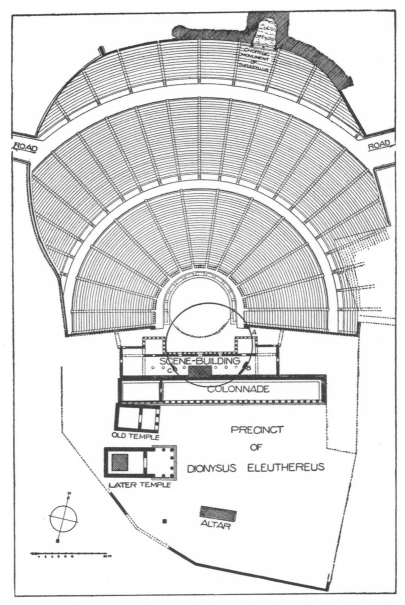

FIG. 32.—Precinct of Dionysus Eleuthereus in Athens, Showing Dörpfeld's Restoration of the Early Orchestra and of the Lycurgus Theater.

See p. 63, n. 2

FIG. 31.—Parthenon and Theater of Dionysus; in Foreground Altar in Precinct of Dionysus Eleuthereus.

See p. 63, n. 1

FIG. 33.—East Fragment of Wall Belonging to the Early Orchestra in Athens.

See p. 65, n. 1

FIG. 34.—West Fragment of Wall Belonging to the Early Orchestra in Athens.

See p. 65, n. 1

Olympiad (about 499 B.C.). In consequence, a new theater was constructed in the precinct of Dionysus, where the seats, though still of wood, could be supported in part by the south slope of the Acropolis. When the stone theater on this site was first brought to light, it was erroneously supposed that this was the structure which had been erected as a result of the accident just mentioned. As a matter of fact, practically all that remains of the first theater are certain fragments of the orchestra (Figs. 33 f.).[1] These are sufficient to indicate that this orchestra was about eighty-eight feet in diameter and extended some fifty feet farther south than the later orchestra (Figs. 32a and 81).[2] As it receded

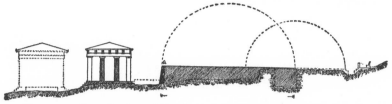

FIG. 32a.—Cross-Section of Precinct of Dionysus Eleuthereus in Athens, Showing Later and Early Temples and Early Terrace and Later Orchestra.
See p. 65, n. 2

from the Acropolis it was banked up to a maximum of about six and a half feet, leaving a declivity immediately behind it. The extant plays of this period show that for about thirty years no background of any kind stood in this declivity (see p. 226, below). Theatrical properties, such as a tomb, might be temporarily built at the center or to one side of the orchestra. If dressing-rooms were then provided for the actors and chorus they must have stood some distance away. In the absence of a back scene, the performers could enter only at the sides. These same entrances were used also by the spectators in assembling. The

[1] Figs. 33 f. are taken from photographs by Dr. A. S. Cooley. The position of these stones is marked by B and C respectively in Fig. 32. Another arc of the same orchestral circle is indicated by a cutting in the native rock near the east parodus, A in Fig. 32.

[2] Fig. 32a is taken from F. Noack, Σκηνὴ Τραγική, eine Studie über die scenischen Anlagen auf der Orchestra des Aischylos und der anderen Tragiker (1915), p. 3.

seats, being of wood until the fourth century, have left no trace; but there can, of course, be no doubt of their position on the slope.   Well up the side an ancient road cut the auditorium into an upper and lower section[1] and permitted ingress and egress for the audience at two additional points.   The Athenian theater was somewhat unusual in having these upper entrances.

About 465 B.C., as the plays indicate,[2] a wooden scene-building was set up behind the orchestra, where the declivity had been.[3]   The front of this was probably pierced by three doors, which might be conventionally thought of as leading to as many different buildings, and thus the number of entrances available for the actors' use was more than doubled.   This seemingly simple alteration produced profound changes in dramatic technique (see pp. 228–31, below).   The scene-building of this period must be thought of as quite unpretentious: its material was wood; it probably consisted of but a single story, with parascenia but no columned proscenium (Fig. 74; see pp. 235 and 339 ff., below).   Its construction was flimsy enough for it to be capable of being easily rebuilt or remodeled to meet the scenic requirements of each drama, for of course it was not until long after the introduction of a scenic background that the plays were uniformly laid before a palace or temple.   According to Aristotle, Sophocles was the inventor of scene-painting, and this is also said to have been invented during the lifetime of Aeschylus.[4]   If these notices are correct, we must suppose that scene-painting was invented in the decade ending in 458 B.C. and so under theatrical conditions such as have just been described. This would mean that at first the scenery must have been attached directly to the scene-building itself and not inserted between the intercolumniations of the proscenium columns.

[1] Possibly the seats did not go back of this road at this period; they certainly did in the fourth century (Fig. 32 and *J* in Fig. 81).

[2] Cf. Dignan, *The Idle Actor in Aeschylus* (1905), p. 13, n. 14.

[3] Preferably, in the south margin of the old orchestra-terrace and behind it; see Fig. 82 and pp. 339 ff., below.

[4] Cf. Aristotle's *Poetics* 1449a18, and Vitruvius, *De Architectura*, VII, praefatio, § 11.

The next building in the precinct seems to have been the later temple, slightly south of the earlier one (Fig. 32). Its substructure was of breccia (conglomerate), and its erection must be assigned to about the last quarter of the fifth century B.C.[1] An image of Dionysus by Alcamenes found its home here.

Of the same material are the foundations of the parascenia and of the front and back walls of the scene-building (Fig. 35),[2] and perhaps they are to be assigned to the same period as the temple which has just been mentioned.[3] The superstructure

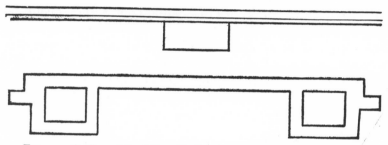

FIG. 35.—Outline of the Oldest Walls of the Scene-Building in Athens
See p. 67, n. 2

was still of wood, since the wide variation of scenic setting called for a background which could readily be adapted to changing needs. It is likely that the ten square holes in the rear foundation wall (Fig. 38) were intended to receive the supporting beams of such an adjustable structure.[4] Probably the scene-building now rose to a second story, a supposition which is confirmed by the

[1] Dörpfeld, following Reisch, is willing to accept a date as early as 421–415 B.C., cf. *Das griechische Theater*, pp. 21 f.

[2] Fig. 35 is taken from Fiechter, *op. cit.*, Fig. 14.

[3] So Furtwängler, "Zum Dionysostheater in Athen," *Sitzungsberichte d. bayer. Akademie der Wissenschaften zu München, philosophisch-philologische u. historische Classe*, 1901, p. 411; Puchstein, *op. cit.*, pp. 137 ff.; E. A. Gardner, *Ancient Athens*, pp. 435 f. and 448; and Fiechter, *op. cit.*, p. 11. Dörpfeld, on the contrary, would attribute these foundations to the Lycurgus theater in the next century; cf. *Das griechische Theater*, pp. 59 ff.

[4] Cf. Dörpfeld, "Das griechische Theater zu Pergamon," *Athenische Mittheilungen*, XXXII (1907), 231; but differently in *Das griechische Theater*, pp. 61 ff.

use of the crane or μηχανή ("machine") in the extant plays of this
period (see pp. 289 and 292 f., below).   At about the same time
a proscenium (also of wood) was erected before the parascenia
and the intermediate front of the scene-building (see pp. 235 f.,
below), and painted panels of scenery could be fastened between
its intercolumniations.   In my opinion, we must suppose that
such a proscenium stood far enough removed from the front of
the scene-building[1] so that, when there was no occasion to fill the
intercolumniations with panels, a porch or portico was automatically produced (its floor probably raised a step or two above
the orchestra level), in which semi-interior scenes might be
enacted (see pp. 238 f., below).   It has even been maintained
that a projecting vestibule was sometimes built out from the
center of the proscenium in order to provide additional space of a
semi-private sort (see pp. 236 f., below and Fig. 73).   Of course,
no foundations for such a structure are found either at this period
or subsequently, for the reason that permanent foundations for
something which was only occasionally employed would have
been unsightly and in the way for the greater part of the time.
No fragments belonging to the orchestra of this period have been
discovered (see next paragraph and p. 73).   Moreover, the seating arrangements belong to the Lycurgus theater of the next
century.   Fortunately, however, there can be no doubt as to the
relative position of these parts: it is apparent that the whole
theater has been pushed about thirty-five feet north and west
(Fig. 81), and the causes of this alteration are not hard to guess.
In the first place, room was thus secured for the scene-building
without occupying the space immediately in front of the earlier
temple of Dionysus.   In the second place, the slope of the
Acropolis could now be employed more extensively as a support
for the seats of the spectators, see Fig. 81.   There is now some
reason for believing that this slight change in site was made at
this period, see pp. 343 and 346, below.

Slight as may seem the theater remains which have been
discussed up to this point, it must be noted before proceeding

[1] As in the Hellenistic theater (Fig. 38).

Fig. 36

THEATER OF DIONYSUS IN ATHENS, LOOKING NORTH; CHOREGIC
MONUMENT OF THRASYLLUS IN THE BACKGROUND

FIG. 37

THEATER OF DIONYSUS IN ATHENS, LOOKING NORTH AND WEST

that they entirely exhaust the field. There is not a stone outside
of Athens which can be assigned to any Greek theater before
400 B.C.[1] Yet all the plays of Aeschylus, Sophocles, and Euripides, and all the extant comedies of Aristophanes, except two,
were performed before this date! In the latter half of the fourth
century Lycurgus, who was finance minister of Athens between
338 and 326 B.C., "completed"[2] the theater which is reproduced
so clearly in Dörpfeld's plan (Fig. 32) that it is unnecessary to
describe it at length. Most of the stone remains now upon the
site belong to this structure. So far as the auditorium is preserved, its arrangements and furnishings are almost entirely
those of Lycurgus' time. Most of the inclosing walls, the stone
thrones in the front row for the use of dignitaries, and the stone
seats for the rest of the audience all belong to this period
(Fig. 36). The only part of the present orchestra which goes
back to the fourth century is the gutter just inside the balustrade
(Fig. 37), but this is sufficient to show that the Lycurgus orchestra
was sixty-four feet and four inches in diameter or exactly sixty
Greek feet. This figure is significant as showing that the orchestra was the starting-point in the measurements and not incidentally derived from some other part of the theater. Behind the
orchestra and upon the old foundations was now erected a
scene-building of stone, one hundred and fifty-two feet in breadth
and twenty-one feet deep at its shallowest part. About its
parascenia stood a row of stone columns, from which it can be
estimated that the first story was about thirteen feet in height.
But the stone connecting columns which Dörpfeld restored before
the central part of the scene-building (Fig. 32) have been assailed
on every hand and have now been relinquished by their sponsor.[3]
This part of the proscenium was still of wood, for though the
scenic requirements by this time were fairly standardized for
each genre, the conventional setting for tragedy was quite

[1] Except possibly at Thoricus (see p. 103, below).

[2] Cf. pseudo-Plutarch X Oratorum Vitae, 841D and 852C.

[3] Cf. Dörpfeld, "Das Theater von Ephesos," Jahrbuch d. arch. Instituts,
Anzeiger, XXVIII (1913), 38.

different from that for comedy or satyric drama. Furthermore, the Greeks seem to have been slow to lose the notion that a wooden background was necessary in order to secure the best acoustic results.[1] This wooden proscenium probably did not stand so close to the scene-building as the drawing would indicate, but formed a portico as in the Hellenistic theater (Fig. 38). At the same time, or possibly at the close of the fifth century, a colonnade was built just behind the scene-building as a place of refuge from heat and sudden showers. There are two considerations which make the Lycurgus theater highly important to us: in the first place, here were produced the plays of the Greek New Comedy which furnished the originals of Plautus' and Terence's Latin plays and which has partially been restored to us by the recent discovery of large fragments of Menander's comedies; and in the second place this fourth-century structure probably reproduced in stone the main outlines of the earlier theater in which the later tragedies of Sophocles and Euripides and all the plays of Aristophanes were performed (pp. 339 ff.). This supposition is strengthened by the fact that the extant fifth-century dramas could readily be "staged" in the Lycurgus theater.

Further alterations were made in the Athenian theater during the first or second century B.C. (Fig. 38).[2] So far as can now be established, this Hellenistic theater differed from its immediate predecessor only in two particulars. The front of the parascenia was moved back about six and a quarter feet,[3] the parodi being thereby enlarged to the same extent. What advantage was gained by this alteration has not yet been discovered. The other change consisted in the erection, at last, of a stone proscenium, about thirteen feet in height, between the parascenia and about six and a half feet in front of the central fore wall of the scene-building. At Epidaurus, Oropus, Delos, etc., the supports of the proscenium were only half-

Dörpfeld, "Das Theater von Ephesos," Jahrbuch d. arch. Instituts, Anzeiger, XXVIII (1913), 40 f.

[2] Fig. 38 is taken from Dörpfeld-Reisch, *Das griechische Theater*, Fig. 26.

[3] Cf. *ibid.*, p. 63. This shift has been disputed by many but is defended by Fiechter, *op. cit.*, pp. 9 ff.

columns, and sometimes they had grooves or rims running verti-
cally along their sides or had the rear half of the column cut into
an oblong for the purpose of providing a firmer fastening for the
painted panels (πίνακες) in the intercolumniations (Fig. 72).

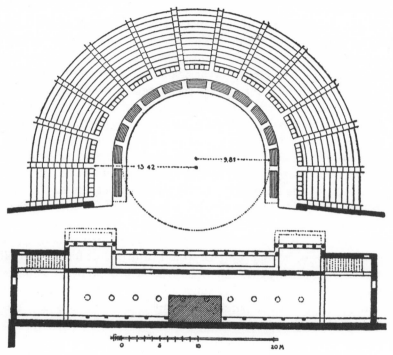

FIG. 38.—Ground Plan of the Hellenistic Theater in Athens According to
Dörpfeld.

See p. 70, n. 2

But at Athens the proscenium columns were whole and were not
equipped with any of these devices.

We have already passed far beyond the time when masterpieces of Greek drama were receiving their premier performances
in the Athenian theater; after the third century the dramatic
productions in Attica were no longer of consequence. Yet for
the sake of completeness it will be necessary to record briefly
two later periods in the history of this structure.

The result of the earlier of these remodelments is commonly known as Nero's theater, for the reason that its façade originally bore an inscription of dedication to Dionysus and Nero. The motive for the alteration and dedication is doubtless to be found in the Emperor's visit to Greece and "artistic" triumphs there in 67 A.D. Under the circumstances it is not surprising that two features of Roman theaters were now for the first time introduced into Athens: a stage was built before the scene-building, and the hitherto full orb of the orchestral circle was thereby infringed upon. At the back of the stage rose a new proscenium, probably no longer in the form of a straight and simple colonnade but an elaborate facade with projecting and receding members, such as was common in the Roman and Graeco-Roman theaters (Figs. 40 and 59). The depth of the stage cannot be exactly determined,[1] but its front wall is usually thought to have coincided with that of the stage now standing, which belongs to the next period. But we shall presently find reasons for believing that, though the Nero stage was deeper than the Hellenistic proscenium, it was shallower than the later (Phaedrus) stage (see pp. 75 and 99, below). Space would thus be left for the parodi still to lead directly into the orchestra. Dörpfeld first estimated the height of the Neronian stage at about four feet nine and a half inches (see next paragraph), but is now inclined to think that it belonged to the high Graeco-Roman type.[2] In my judgment, however, his earlier position is to be preferred. I consider it probable that stone steps led from the orchestra to the center of the stage, as in the Phaedrus theater (Fig. 40). Just outside the gutter of the Lycurgus theater was erected a marble balustrade (Fig. 39),[3] which stood about three and a half

[1] Cf. Dörpfeld, *Das griechische Theater*, p. 89.

[2] Cf. *ibid.*, p. 89; *Athenische Mittheilungen*, XXII (1897), 459; XXIII (1898), 330 and 347; and XXVIII (1903), 414. For the Graeco-Roman stage see pp. 80 ff. and 110 f., below.

[3] Fig. 39 is from a photograph taken by Dr. Lewis L. Forman and furnished by Dr. A. S. Cooley. Owing to its change of function, in Roman times the orchestra was sometimes known as the κονίστρα (= the Latin *arena*); owing to its change of shape, it was sometimes called σῖγμα from its resemblance to the semicircular form of the Greek letter Ϲ.

Fig. 39.—Nero Balustrade and Pavement, and Phaedrus Stage of the Theater in Athens.

See p. 72, n. 3

Fig. 41.—Frieze of the Phaedrus Stage in Athens

See p. 74, n. 2

feet above the orchestra level and protected the spectators from accident when gladiatorial combats (another Roman institution) or the like were being exhibited in the orchestra. In order to compensate for the curtailment of the orchestra by the stage, the gutter, which had been left open except opposite the vertical

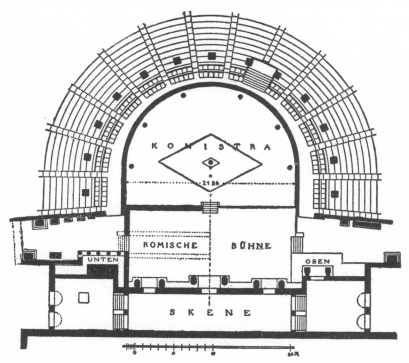

Fig. 40.—Plan of the Romanized Theater in Athens According to Dörpfeld
See p. 74, n. 1

aisles of the auditorium, was covered over, except for occasional rosette-shaped openings. Up to this time the orchestra seems to have had no covering but hard-pressed earth, but it was now paved with marble slabs. In the middle of the pavement is a rhomboid design (Fig. 40), and in its central block is a depression about twenty inches in diameter, by means of which an altar of Dionysus (the thymele) was doubtless held in place.

The final alterations in the Athenian theater (Fig. 40)[1] were made in the third or fourth century A.D. by Phaedrus, governor of Attica ('Aτθίδος ἀρχός), who dedicated the "platform of the theater" (βῆμα θεήτρου) to Dionysus in an inscription which still stands on the uppermost of the stone steps leading from the orchestra to the stage. The gutter was now filled up with earth and refuse, and the rosette-shaped openings in its covering were carefully closed. Plaster was used as needed, and the balustrade and the front wall of the stage (the hyposcenium) were reinforced and made water-tight by supporting walls. The intention was plainly to enable the orchestra to be flooded for the representation of mimic sea fights. The stage was partially rebuilt and was lowered. The hyposcenium was adorned with a frieze (Figs. 39 and 41),[2] the extant portion of which is interrupted at three points by as many niches or recesses, one of which is filled by a kneeling Silenus. It is clear that the frieze had been used before and that its slabs had originally been placed in immediate juxtaposition. Moreover, the heads of the figures have been cut away, so that the frieze, when complete, must have been about half a foot higher than at present. The Phaedrus stage is four feet three and a half inches high; and as Dörpfeld was originally inclined to believe that this same frieze had at first stood before the Neronian stage, he estimated the height of the latter at about four feet nine and a half inches. In my opinion, this estimate ought to be retained. But though Dörpfeld now considers the Nero stage to have been higher than this, he has not indicated whether he still believes its front wall to have been the original position of the frieze.

It has been suggested that after the lapse of two centuries or more the Neronian stage was perhaps in need of repair or renewal and that the changes for which Phaedrus was responsible are thus to be explained. However that may be, other influences

---

[1] Fig. 40 is taken from Dörpfeld-Reisch, *Das griechische Theater*, Fig. 32.

[2] Fig. 41 is from a photograph belonging to Northwestern University; the stone steps at the left and another slab at the right do not appear in this view (see Fig. 39). For the latest interpretation and drawing of the frieze, cf. Cook, *Zeus*, I, 708 ff., and the pocket at end of his volume.

were plainly at work. I think that at this period the Athenian theater was at last thoroughly Romanized. That is to say, I think that the Nero stage did not project so far into the orchestra (see p. 72, above), but was now enlarged so as to accommodate all the performances, and that at the same time the Roman custom of placing seats in the orchestra was for the first time introduced into Athens. But in order that the orchestra might find occasional continuance of its function as a place of exhibition, or possibly because of interest in the sport per se, all openings were closed up and the old dancing place was made capable of being flooded. It follows that the parodi no longer debouched into the orchestra but led to steps at either side of the stage, as shown in Fig. 40. The participants in the mimic sea fights and gladiatorial combats and the spectators at other performances could enter the orchestra only by passing over the stage and down the front steps. Of course, the presence of spectators so close to the performers would permit no type of stage except one of moderate height; evidently even the low Nero stage was a little too high under these conditions.

The foregoing account of the Athenian theater is founded, in the main, upon Dörpfeld's conclusions, but the reader needs to be warned that not all of his conclusions are acceptable to everyone. Until about half a century ago our information concerning Greek theaters was largely restricted to literary tradition. There was no theater of the earlier Greek types above ground, and even the exact location of the Athenian theater had been, during many centuries, forgotten. The literary tradition was mainly derived from Vitruvius, a Roman architect at the beginning of the Christian era, who devoted two chapters of Book V in his work *On Architecture* to a description of Greek and Roman theaters. According to him, the front and back walls of the Roman stage were determined by the diameter of the orchestral circle and one side of an inscribed equilateral triangle; in other words, its depth would be one-half the radius of the orchestra (Fig. 42).[1] Its height was not to exceed five

---

[1] Fig. 42 is taken from *Athenische Mittheilungen*, XXII (1897), 452.

feet,[1] since all the performers stood on the stage and the unelevated front half of the orchestral circle was reserved for the seats of senators. In the Greek theater, on the other hand, Vitruvius asserted that the front wall of the stage was marked by one side of an inscribed square, and its back wall, which he calls the

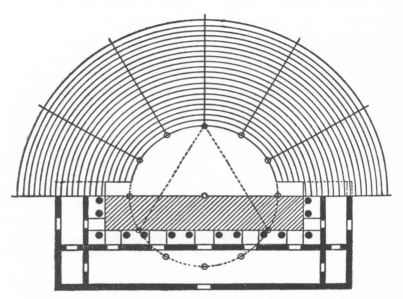

FIG. 42.—Vitruvius' *Theatrum Latinum* According to Dörpfeld
See p. 75, n. 1

scaenae frons, by the parallel tangent, its depth being thus about three-tenths of the radius (Fig. 43).[2] Its height was to range between ten and twelve feet. Vitruvius expressly states that this stage in the Greek theater was called a logium, that the

[1] Vitruvius, of course, speaks of Roman feet, which are equal to 11.65 English inches.

[2] Fig. 43 is taken from *Athenische Mittheilungen*, XXII (1897), 453. This drawing differs somewhat from that given in *Das griechische Theater*, Fig. 66, which was prepared while Dörpfeld was still of the opinion that Vitruvius was describing the Hellenistic theater and had misapprehended the function of its proscenium (see p. 81, below). He now includes the proscenium at the back of the stage in the *scaenae frons*.

tragic and comic actors performed *in scaena*[1] and the "other artists" *per orchestram,* and that for this reason the Greeks drew a distinction between the adjectives "scenic" and "thymelic" as applied to performances and performers.[2] The differences between the two types of structure are obvious: (1) the

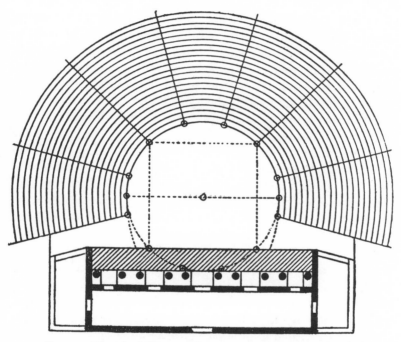

Fig. 43.—Vitruvius' *Theatrum Graecorum* According to Dörpfeld
See p. 76, n. 2

auditorium and orchestra in Vitruvius' Roman theater occupied exactly a semicircumference, in his Greek theater distinctly more than this; (2) the Roman stage was deep and low, the Greek high and comparatively shallow; (3) in the Greek theater both orchestra and stage were employed (separately) by

[1] Whatever *scaena* may mean in Latin, *in scaena* in this context is at least equivalent to "on the stage."

[2] Cf. p. 61, n. 2, above and pp. 96 f., below.

different forms of entertainment; in the Roman theater all performers stood on the stage and the semicircular orchestra was
occupied by the seats of senators.

Moreover, Pollux (second century A.D.) states that in the
Greek theater "the σκηνή belongs to the actors and the orchestra
to the chorus."[1] Everyone used to think (and some still do)
that σκηνή here signified "stage" and that Vitruvius' reference to
scaenici and *thymelici* was to be interpreted in a similar fashion.
Accordingly, it was supposed that Greek actors performed
(and had always performed) upon a ten- or twelve-foot Vitruvian
stage and the dramatic chorus in the orchestra below. Confirmation was found for this theory in Pollux' further mention of
ladders rising from the orchestra to the σκηνή.[2] The use of both
orchestra and stage is mentioned a few times also in scholia
(ancient commentaries) upon the Greek plays. The possibility
of other interpretations of these passages will be considered
later (see pp. 97 ff., below). For the present this should be said:
We are interested in the Greek theater mainly because of Aeschylus, Sophocles, Euripides, and Aristophanes, all of whom lived
in the fifth century B.C., and Pollux and Vitruvius, who flourished
many centuries later, nowhere assert that they are attempting
to describe the theater of this earlier period. Nevertheless, this
initial assumption used tacitly to be taken for granted, and these
Procrustean conditions were arbitrarily imposed upon the extant
Greek dramas by all editors and commentators alike. As a
matter of fact, such a difference of level between orchestra and
stage, chorus and actors, with no convenient connection between
the two, presented an insuperable obstacle to the (imaginary)
"staging" of the fifth-century plays. Various expedients were
proposed to evade the difficulty. One of the most popular was
that of G. Hermann, who in 1833 suggested that the Greek
orchestra was covered with a wooden platform to within a few

---

[1] Cf. Pollux *Onomasticon* iv, § 123: καὶ σκηνὴ μὲν ὑποκριτῶν ἴδιον, ἡ δὲ ὀρχήστρα τοῦ χοροῦ.

[2] Cf. *ibid.*, iv, § 127: εἰσελθόντες δὲ κατὰ τὴν ὀρχήστραν ἐπὶ τὴν σκηνὴν ἀναβαί-
νουσι διὰ κλιμάκων.

feet of the stage level and that thus a more intimate connection between the two was established, and Wieseler (1847) proposed to identify this platform with the thymele. Nonsensical as this suggestion appears to everyone without exception now, it enjoyed a tremendous vogue for some time. In the eighties the news began to seep through to Western Europe and this country that Dörpfeld had evolved a new theory, to the effect that actors and chorus had performed in the orchestra on the same level until Roman times.[1] Again, Mr. A. E. Haigh (1889) maintained that a low stage was employed uninterruptedly until the fourth century B.C., when a high Vitruvian stage was introduced. Dr. Bethe (1896) contends that at first actors and chorus performed in the orchestra but that about 427 B.C. a low stage was introduced, which in the fourth century was raised to the Vitruvian level. On the other hand, Dr. Puchstein (1901), who stated in his Preface that he ignored the literary evidence, argued for a Vitruvian stage already in the fifth century. And now Professor Fiechter (1914) has given his adherence to Bethe's hypothesis that a low stage at the end of the fifth century was raised to a high one in the fourth. It will be seen that all authorities are in substantial agreement that the Greek theater had a stage, even a high Vitruvian stage, but they are hopelessly divided with regard to the important detail as to when this stage was introduced—at the very first, at the close of the fifth century, in the time of Lycurgus, in the Hellenistic period, or in the reign of Nero.

But before taking up the question of the stage in the Greek theater, it will first be necessary to determine Vitruvius' relationship to the matter. The Roman architect's description of the Roman theater does not coincide precisely with any extant Roman theater. Nevertheless, there has never been any doubt as to the general type of structure which he had in mind. It is

---

[1] Dörpfeld's views were first given general publicity in the Appendix to Müller's *Lehrbuch der griechischen Bühnenalterthümer* (1886), pp. 415 f., but were not published in full until 1896. They have suffered modification in several material points since then.

evident, however, that he is describing no particular, actually existent, theater but is giving directions for an ideal structure. Indeed, he declares: "Whoever wishes to use these directions will render the perfect qualities of theaters faultless."[1]   There is, therefore, no reason to expect that his directions for Greek theaters would agree any more closely with any extant Greek theater, and in fact they do not.   During the last two decades of the nineteenth century the ancient theaters at Epidaurus, Oropus, Thoricus, Eretria, Sicyon, Megalopolis, Delos, Assus, Pergamum, etc., were unearthed.   The first result of this activity was to show that no two of these structures were entirely alike and that none exactly corresponded to Vitruvius' directions. Furthermore, it has become evident that all ancient theaters are no longer to be classified under the two general Vitruvian types, "Greek" and "Roman," but rather under a larger number of categories according to time, place, and conditions of use. But the question which one of these types Vitruvius had in mind still remains, and unfortunately the answer has not been so clear as to compel everyone's acceptance.   In Vitruvius' day many Hellenistic, stageless theaters were still standing, and the modern attempt to identify these with Vitruvius' Greek type and to force them into conformity with his prescriptions has wrought great confusion in the field of scenic antiquities.   But Vitruvius nowhere professes to be writing a *history* of Greek theaters nor had he any intention of presenting antiquarian lore. His book was planned for distinctly practical purposes.   Now in his day only two kinds of new theaters were being erected, the Roman and what Dörpfeld has christened the Graeco-Roman.[2] Dörpfeld supposes the latter type to have originated with the theater which Pompey had built in Rome in 55 B.C.   This is said to have been modeled upon the Greek theater at Mitylene

---

[1] Cf. *De Architectura* v. 8, 2: "ita his praescriptionibus qui voluerit uti, emendatas efficiet theatrorum perfectiones."

[2] This is now Dörpfeld's name for what he at first called the Asia Minor type; cf. *Athenische Mittheilungen*, XXVIII (1903), 389 and 414.   The latter term was unfortunate as suggesting a geographical restriction which had no basis in fact.

in the island of Lesbos,[1] and Dörpfeld supposes that the orchestra
of Pompey's theater was kept free of seats, after the Greek
fashion, and devoted to thymelic performances, but that the
top of the proscenium, despite its height and narrowness, was
converted into a stage, to which, according to Roman practice,
the comic and tragic actors were now elevated. However this
may be, the fact remains that from about this time theaters of
this type were so extensively built or created by a remodeling
of Hellenistic theaters that they became the only rivals of purely
Roman structures. Such theaters are found in the Nero theater
at Athens (according to Dörpfeld's present but questionable
view), Pompeii, Segesta, Syracuse, Taormina, and extensively
in Asia Minor. Early in the nineteenth century Schönborn and
Wieseler correctly recognized buildings of this type as representing Vitruvius' Greek theater.[2] But later on, when the earlier
Greek theaters were revealed by new excavations at Athens and
elsewhere, an attempt was made to identify these with Vitruvius'
Greek type. Dörpfeld himself fell into this error and in *Das
griechische Theater* maintained that Vitruvius had misunderstood
the function of the Hellenistic proscenium, interpreting as a
stage what in fact was only a background. But though Dörpfeld thus incurred a large share of blame for confusing the
situation, he soon came to recognize his error and frankly
recanted.[3] Unhappily the pro-stage writers still persist in it.

It might be supposed that Vitruvius' Greek theater could
readily be identified by comparing his directions for the height
and depth of the stage with the actual measurements of various
Greek theaters. Dörpfeld and Fiechter have both attempted
this but without any great success.[4] For the sake of convenience

[1] Cf. Plutarch *Life of Pompey*, c. xlii.

[2] It is significant that Vitruvius seems to have depended upon Asia Minor
rather than the Greek mainland for his knowledge of Greek architecture; cf.
Noack, "Das Proscenion in der Theaterfrage," *Philologus*, LVIII (1899), 16 ff.

[3] Cf. *Athenische Mittheilungen*, XXII (1897), 439 ff.

[4] Cf. *Athenische Mittheilungen*, XXII (1897), 443, 449 f., and 454, and Fiechter,
op. cit., pp. 59 ff.

and clearness I have drawn up their figures in the form of tables. Dörpfeld cited six Graeco-Roman structures as affirmative arguments and two Hellenistic buildings as negative arguments. Of course, the figures for the Hellenistic theaters refer to the

TABLE I (Dörpfeld)

Buildings	Radius of Orchestra	Three-tenths of Radius	Depth of Stage or Proscenium	Height of Stage or Proscenium
Graeco-Roman:				
Termessus.......	11.00 m.	3.30 m.	about 4.00 m.	2.45 m.
Sagalassus.......	12.75 m.	3.80 m.	5.70 m.	2.77 m.
Patara..........	11.85 m.	3.55 m.	3.50 m.	2.50 m.
Myra..........	17.50 m.	5.20 m.	3.50 m.	....
Tralles..........	....	....	....	about 3.00 m.
Magnesia (rebuilt)	....	....	....	at least 2.30 m.
Hellenistic:				
Eretria..........	....	....	2.40 m.	....
Oropus..........	....	....	1.95 m.	....

TABLE II (Fiechter)

Buildings	Radius of Orchestra	From Center of Orchestra to *Scaenae Frons*	Three-tenths of Radius	Depth of Stage or Proscenium	Height of Stage or Proscenium
Hellenistic:					
Priene..........	9.32 m.	9.31 m.	2.79 m.	2.74 m.	2.72 m.
Ephesus........	12.33 m.	12.25 m.	3.69 m.	....	2.62 m.
Delos..........	about 10.55 m.	10.60 m.	3.16 m.	3.60 m.	3.00 m.
Magnesia.......	....	....	....	....	more than 2.30 m.
Graeco-Roman:					
Termessus......	9.90 m.	12.60 m.	2.97 m.	4.00–5.5 m.	....
Sagalassus......	12.73 m.	17.94 m.	3.80 m.	7.54 m.	2.77 m.
Patara.........	11.85 m.	14.50 m.	3.55 m.	6.00 m.	2.50 m.
Tralles.........	13.20 m.	....	3.96 m.	6.50 m.	at least 2.50 m.
Magnesia (re-built)	10.65 m.	....	3.20 m.	6.00 m.	more than 2.30 m.
Ephesus (rebuilt)	14.47 m.	12.50 m.	4.34 m.	6.00–9.00 m.	2.62 m.

proscenium, in which some would recognize a stage. The problem, therefore, is not merely as to what type of Greek theater Vitruvius was describing, but the function of the proscenium in Hellenistic theaters is also involved. On the other hand, Fiechter, whose object is diametrically opposed to Dörpfeld's, cites four Hellenistic and six Graeco-Roman theaters as positive and negative arguments respectively.

It will be observed that five theaters appear in both tables, and that for three of them the figures do not altogether agree. This is to be explained as due to differences in the manner of taking the measurements. Thus, for Termessus, Fiechter gives for the depth 4 m. (Dörpfeld's figure) and 5.5 m. Similarly, for Ephesus he gives 6 m. and 9 m., and explains that the former does not include the socle projections. Evidently Fiechter still believes that the *scaenae frons* in Vitruvius' description of the Greek theater ran behind the proscenium and did not include it (see p. 76, n. 2, above). The same difference of interpretation probably accounts for 6 m. (Fiechter) and 3.50 m. (Dörpfeld) being reported as the depth of the stage at Patara.

A similar opportunity for variance of measurement occurs also in connection with the orchestra. In my opinion, Vitruvius used this term in its broadest sense, viz., as including all the space between the lowest tier of seats[1] (Fig. 43). Fiechter's measurement of the Hellenistic orchestra at Priene is given on this basis. Sometimes, however, the term is used with reference to the space bounded by the gutter.[2] Fiechter states that this was his method in measuring the Hellenistic orchestras at Ephesus and Delos. The discrepancy in the reports concerning the orchestra at Termessus (9.90 m. and 11 m.) is also to be explained thus.

But whatever allowance may be made for variations of this sort, I think that whoever impartially examines these figures with the expectation of obtaining a clear answer to the problem

[1] It is easy to see why he should do so. When Hellenistic theaters were made over into Graeco-Roman structures, several rows of seats were often removed, resulting in a drop of several feet between the auditorium and the orchestra (see p. 116, below, and Fig. 24). So distinct a line of demarcation could scarcely be ignored in favor of any less clearly marked boundary. In fact, the orchestra in the narrowest sense (see next note) was sometimes not indicated at all in the Graeco-Roman theaters.

[2] The word is applied also to a still more restricted space which in some Graeco-Roman and most earlier theaters is marked off by a circular boundary.

involved will be doomed to disappointment. Vitruvius' Greek stage should range between ten and twelve feet (Roman) in height, or 2.959 m. and 3.55 m., respectively. Only one Graeco-Roman stage and one Hellenistic proscenium in both tables fall within these limits.[1] On the other hand, though Dörpfeld is clearly right in maintaining that the proscenia at Eretria and Oropus are too shallow to accommodate the entire histrionic action of a play, Fiechter makes it appear that Vitruvius' rule that the stage of the Greek theater should be about three-tenths of the orchestra radius in depth is satisfied more closely by the Hellenistic proscenium than by the Graeco-Roman stage. It should be emphasized, however, that he obtains this result only by shifting the value of the word "orchestra," taking it now in the largest and now in a narrower sense.

Fiechter has tried to utilize Vitruvius' diagram still further by pointing out that in Vitruvius' Greek theater the distance from the center of the orchestra to the front wall of the stage (the hyposcenium) plus the depth of the stage, i.e., the distance from the center of the orchestra to the *scaenae frons*, ought to equal one radius (Fig. 43). The figures in the first two columns of his table apparently show that this condition is met by the Hellenistic theaters and is not met by the Graeco-Roman theaters. But here again we encounter a variable quantity caused by a dispute as to whether the proscenium is to be counted a part of the *scaenae frons* (see above). In the Patara theater the distance from the center of the orchestra to the hyposcenium is 8.50 m. (14.50 m. − 6.00 m., Fiechter's figures), and the depth of the stage according to Dörpfeld, who measures from the proscenium, is 3.50 m. Therefore, the total distance is 12 m. as against a radius of 11.85 m. Again, in the Termessus theater

---

[1] Of course, Dörpfeld and Fiechter cite only a fraction of the instances available (others are given in Puchstein's table, *op. cit.*, p. 7), but it is to be inferred that they bring forward those which are most favorable to their own position and most difficult for their opponents to explain. For example, the proscenium of the Hellenistic theater in Athens was about thirteen feet (English) high, which exceeds Vitruvius' maximum. Consequently Fiechter says nothing about it. In general, the Hellenistic proscenia were higher than the Graeco-Roman stages.

the distance from the center of the orchestra to the hyposcenium is 7.10 m. (12.60 m.— 5.50 m., Fiechter's figures), and the depth of the stage is 4 m. according to Dörpfeld, measuring as before. Therefore, the total distance is 11.10 m. as against a radius of 11 m. according to the largest (Vitruvian) measure of the orchestra. These correspondences are close enough so as not to be unworthy of comparison with those obtained by Fiechter.

In my opinion, the net result of the above must be the frank recognition that such data concerning the Greek theaters as are at present known to us do not afford convincing proof as to the type which Vitruvius was describing. Nor need this conclusion surprise us, if we accept Dörpfeld's theory that Pompey's theater was the first example of the Graeco-Roman type. We have no information concerning the Mitylene theater, upon which Pompey's building was modeled, nor concerning the number or extent of its departures from that model. But any theater in Asia Minor at that time must have belonged to the Hellenistic type. Consequently, a certain resemblance between Hellenistic and Graeco-Roman theaters was inevitable. If Vitruvius was describing an old type, viz., the Hellenistic, its variations in regard to the particulars just discussed must have been too great for him to be able to find any single formula which would comprehend them all, and he had to content himself with recording a theoretical ideal. Or if he was describing a contemporaneous but developing type, viz., the Graeco-Roman, we must suppose that his authority was not sufficient to secure the adoption of his rules by later architects.

Are we, then, unable to determine which type of Greek theater was the subject of Vitruvius' discussion? I think that we can, but that we must depend upon other arguments. I mention a few of the many which have been advanced: (a) In the Hellenistic and earlier Greek theaters the orchestra, in the narrowest sense (see p. 83, n. 2, above), usually formed a complete circle, or at least, if its boundary was not actually continued into a complete circle, there was room for one without infringing upon the proscenium. Examples of this are found at

Epidaurus (Fig. 46), Athens (Fig. 38), Eretria (Fig. 53), Oropus (Fig. 56), Magnesia, Piraeus, etc.   Fiechter denies this (*op. cit.*, p. 65), but only because he chooses to understand the word "orchestra" in a larger sense.   Now though Vitruvius used the term in the largest sense (measured from the lowest seats, see p. 83, above) he nowhere informs us what relative size the most restricted orchestra should or might have as compared with the largest space passing under that name.[1]   But his directions require the stage to intrude so far upon his orchestra that it is apparent that, if the same proportions were to be observed as in the Hellenistic theaters, there could be no such full orchestra with a smaller diameter.   This is also true of Graeco-Roman structures, and in this important respect they resemble Vitruvius' Greek theater and the Hellenistic theaters do not.

b) The logium of Graeco-Roman theaters is never supported by columns along its front wall.   The only exception to this statement is found at Priene (Figs. 63 f.), where the columns of the Hellenistic proscenium were left standing when the theater was remodeled.   The reason why columns were not set in this place is obvious—the floor of the Graeco-Roman stage naturally was thought of as representing earth or a street and it was manifestly improper for either to be supported on columns.[2]   On the contrary, so fundamental an aesthetic principle would have been violated if the actors had regularly appeared upon the top of the Hellenistic proscenium.   But there is no doubt that Vitruvius' Greek theater had a stage for actors.   It is, therefore, more likely that this corresponds to the Graeco-Roman logium than to the colonnade-like proscenium of the Hellenistic theaters. Moreover, the columns of the Hellenistic proscenia were in some cases unmistakably equipped to hold painted panels.   But if the actors had stood on top of the Hellenistic proscenium, this scenery would have been beneath their feet and not behind them!

[1] Doubtless for the reason that in the pitlike Graeco-Roman orchestra the smaller circle really was not needed and often was not indicated (see p. 83, n. 1).

[2] Cf. Dörpfeld, *Athenische Mittheilungen*, XXVIII (1903), 403 and 405.

c) Vitruvius discussed the *theatrum Latinum* in chapter 6 of his fifth book and his *theatrum Graecorum* in chapter 7. The former chapter is longer than the latter by more than a half, and the latter begins with these words: "In the theaters of the Greeks not all things are to be done in the same way" (as in the Roman theaters). The implication is plain that some of the directions in chapter 6 are to be understood as applying also to the Greek theater of chapter 7, and of course the particulars involved would be those which are not modified by the discussion in chapter 7. One of these is the injunction that, for acoustic reasons, the roof of the portico at the top of the auditorium shall be of the same height as the scene-building (v. 6. 4). The scene-building is never built so high as this in Hellenistic theaters, but the rule is often observed in Graeco-Roman and purely Roman theaters.[1]

Dörpfeld has advanced several other arguments bearing upon this problem,[2] but in my opinion those just mentioned are sufficient. Now if Vitruvius' Greek theater is to be identified with the Graeco-Roman structures dating from just before the beginning of the Christian era, it becomes impossible to cite Vitruvius in support of a stage or the use of the proscenium as a stage in Greek theaters of Hellenistic or earlier times. It will be necessary, therefore, to turn back to the fifth century and examine without prejudice the conflicting claims with reference to the presence or absence of a stage at that period. Our discussion of the extant theatrical remains of that century has already made it plain that there is nothing in them which can be employed to prove that there was a stage for the exclusive use of actors. But fortunately the paucity of such evidence is compensated for by the preservation of forty-odd tragedies and comedies of this period. A leading by-product of the stage

[1] Cf. Bethe, *Jahrbuch d. arch. Instituts*, XV (1900), 71 f., and Dörpfeld, *ibid.*, XVI (1901), 35 f.

[2] Cf. *Athenische Mittheilungen*, XXVIII (1903), 424 ff. The arguments advanced in this article are reaffirmed as still valid in *Jahrbuch d. arch. Instituts, Anzeiger*, XXX (1915), 99 ff.

controversy has been the recognition of the fact that these plays are not only to be taken into consideration together with other evidence but that they must be the final test of all theories based on evidence drawn from other sources. If a given theory will not permit these plays to be "staged" easily and naturally, that theory *ipso facto* falls to the ground. As von Wilamowitz wrote: "Von dem, was in den Stücken selbst steht, lässt sich nichts abdingen."[1] Whatever judgment may ultimately be formulated with respect to Dörpfeld's contributions to scenic antiquities, one of his principal achievements must ever be recognized as the minute, searching, and unprejudiced re-examination of the plays themselves which he provoked.

An illuminating exemplification of the use that may be made of the plays in the study of such problems has been given by Professor Edward Capps.[2] He showed that if chorus and actors be thought of as separated by a clearly marked line such as the edge of a ten-foot stage would afford, the action of the forty-four extant dramas requires the chorus alone to pass over this boundary at least sixty-eight times, the chorus and actors together nine times, and the actors alone thirty-nine times. Actors and chorus are repeatedly brought into the closest possible contact. For example, in Euripides' *Iphigenia among the Taurians*, vss. 1068–70, Iphigenia appeals to each member of the chorus in turn, touching the hand of one and the chin and knees of another, begging for their help.

Again, the incidents of many plays come into harmony with theatrical conditions only if we suppose that there was no stage. Perhaps the best and clearest illustration of this is afforded by Aristophanes' *Frogs* (405 B.C.). Xanthias and Dionysus, engaged in conversation, enter the orchestra at one of the side entrances (Fig. 44*A*). At vs. 35 the latter calls attention to the nearest of the three doors in the proscenium, saying: "I am

[1] Cf. *Hermes*, XXI (1886), 603.

[2] Cf. "The Greek Stage According to the Extant Dramas," *Transactions of the American Philological Association*, XXII (1891), 5 ff. Similar results were obtained by White, "The 'Stage' in Aristophanes," *Harvard Studies*, II (1891), 159 ff.

already near this door where I must turn in." It transpires that this is the house of Heracles (Fig. 44*B*), and Dionysus' knock brings his brother in person to the door. From him they receive directions for their trip to the lower world—that first

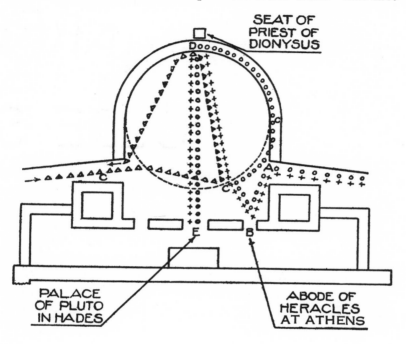

++++ COURSE OF DIONYSUS
oooo COURSE OF XANTHIAS
▲▲▲▲ COURSE OF CHARON

FIG. 44.—Movements of the Actors in Aristophanes' *Frogs*, vss. 1–460

they will come to a large lake which they must cross in a tiny boat, then they will see perjurers, thieves, and criminals of the deepest dye, and finally will be received by happy bands of initiates (the chorus), who "dwell alongside the very road at the doors of Pluto" (vss. 162 f.). Scarcely have they left Heracles' door when they behold a trundle-boat pushed from the opposite parodus into the orchestra (*CC'*) and hear Charon's "Yo-heigh, Yo-ho" (vs. 180). He approaches the edge of the orchestra where they now stand, but when they prepare to embark Charon refuses to receive a slave on board and poor Xanthias is ordered to run around the lake (*C'C"D;* vs. 193). Meanwhile Dionysus and Charon direct their boat across the orchestra (*C'D*) to where, in the center of the front row of seats, the priest of Dionysus and other functionaries always sat (Fig. 45);[1] and from behind the scenes, to accompany their rowing, the choreutae sing a "frog" chorus as if from the bottom of the lake (vss. 209–69). Upon disembarking (at *D*) Dionysus calls for his slave and catches his faint reply as he comes into sight (!) from his "arduous" trip around the orchestra's semicircumference. Xanthias now points out to his master the perjurers, etc., in the nearby audience (vs. 275). Presently they are badly frightened and Dionysus appeals to his priest, who is within arm's length of him, to protect him (vs. 297). Now the sound of flutes is heard and the chorus of initiates enter. Dionysus and Xanthias crouch down, where they are, to listen (vs. 315). Immediately the orchestra, which has just been a subterranean lake, is changed to the imagination into a flowery meadow (vss. 326, 351, etc.). At vs. 431 Dionysus starts up from his lurking-place and inquires of the chorus, "Could you tell us where Pluto dwells hereabouts?" and the coryphaeus promptly replies: "Know that you have come to the very door" (vs. 436). Dionysus orders his slave to pick up the baggage, walks across the orchestra (*DE*), and raps at the central door (*E*), which represents the palace of Pluto (vss. 460 ff.). We need continue no further, for the remainder of the play contains nothing that is noteworthy for our present purpose; but it is already evident how closely the successive situations of the comedy correspond to the physical conditions and arrangements of a stageless theater. To those who would apply Vitruvius' account to the

[1] Fig. 45 is from a photograph belonging to the University of Chicago. The inscription beneath the seat reads: "Of the priest of Dionysus Eleuthereus." P. 344.

Fig. 45

STONE CHAIR OF THE PRIEST OF DIONYSUS OPPOSITE THE CENTER
OF THE ORCHESTRA IN ATHENS

See p. 90, n. 1

fifth-century theater, this play presents ineluctable difficulties; there is insufficient room for Charon's boat on a Vitruvian or any other kind of a Greek stage, Dionysus must appeal to his priest who is some ninety feet away,[1] Xanthias has no lake to run around, and Dîonysus must inquire the way to Pluto's palace when he would be standing considerably nearer to it than the chorus.

It was a convention in the earlier fifth-century plays that if the chorus and one actor were before the audience, an incoming actor should speak first to the chorus and ignore the other actor for the time being (see pp. 165 f., below). This convention was oftentimes extremely awkward and unnatural; but if both actors had stood on a stage several feet above the chorus it surely would have been altogether impossible.[2]

The only tangible argument for a stage of any height in the fifth century is afforded by the occurrence of the words ἀναβαίνειν ("to ascend") in Aristophanes' *Acharnians* (vs. 732), *Knights* (vs. 149), and *Wasps* (vs. 1342), and καταβαίνειν ("to descend") in his *Wasps* (vs. 1514) and *Women in Council* (vs. 1152). All of these plays, except the last, were performed prior to Aristophanes' *Frogs*, which we have already seen to be incapable of presentation in a staged theater. In my opinion, then, these words are best explained on the basis of the slight difference in level between the orchestra and the floor of the proscenium colonnade, which was probably elevated a step or two above the orchestra and was often used by the dramatic performers (see p. 68, above, and pp. 238 f., below).[3] Since the *Acharnians* was produced in 425 B.C., the appearance of ἀναβαίνειν in that

[1] Cf. scholium on vs. 299 of the *Frogs*: ἀποροῦσι δέ τινες πῶς ἀπὸ τοῦ λογείου περιελθὼν καὶ κρυφθεὶς ὄπισθεν τοῦ ἱερέως τοῦτο λέγει. φαίνονται δὲ οὐκ εἶναι ἐπὶ τοῦ λογείου ἀλλ' ἐπὶ τῆς ὀρχήστρας.

[2] Cf. Graeber, *De Poetarum Atticorum Arte Scaenica* (1911), p. 4.

[3] Cf. Rees, "The Function of the Πρόθυρον in the Production of Greek Plays," *Classical Philology*, X (1915), 128 and n. 2. For other interpretations consistent with a stageless theater, cf. White, *Harvard Studies*, II (1891), 164 ff., and Capps, *Transactions of the American Philological Association*, XXII (1891), 64 ff. A convenient summary from the pro-stage point of view may be found in Haigh, *The Attic Theatre²*, pp. 166 f. See p. 344, below.

play is valuable as affording a *terminus ante quem* for the introduction of a wooden proscenium at Athens.

The chorus of the fifth-century plays is fatal to any suggestion
of a Vitruvian stage, and except Puchstein, who frankly ignored
the literary evidence, no recent writer has advocated a high stage
for the theater of that period. The advocates of a high stage
have clearly seen that they can make headway only by the
sacrifice of the dramatic chorus. They are assisted in this
attempt by the fact that only three complete plays of the
fourth century are extant, the pseudo-Euripidean *Rhesus* and
two comedies of Aristophanes, and that the rôle of the chorus
in the latter happens to be curtailed. Aristotle,[1] also, speaks
of irrelevant *embolima* in the work of Agathon, who won his
first victory in 416 B.C. From these facts it has been declared
that at the close of the fifth century or early in the fourth the
chorus was either given up altogether or "its functions were
merely those of the modern band" or "of mere interlude-singers."
Accordingly, it has been argued that the actors at the end of the
fifth century stood upon a low stage (which for the kind of plays
then exhibited was only less impracticable than a Vitruvian
stage) and that they were suddenly elevated to the full height
of the proscenium before the close of the fourth century. It
must be added that even among those who accept Dörpfeld's
theory for the fifth century there is a tendency to go over to
Vitruvius for the period represented by the Lycurgus theater at
Athens and by the theater at Epidaurus—the last quarter of
the fourth century.[2] So far as Vitruvius himself is involved in
this, the matter has already been disposed of. The alleged
disappearance or waning of the chorus, however, furnishes no
better ground of support for pro-stage writers. To trace the
history of the chorus in detail will not be feasible at this point.[3]

[1] Cf. Aristotle's *Poetics* 1456a29, and see pp. 144 ff., below.

[2] Cf. White, *op. cit.*, p. 167, note, and Robert, "Zur Theaterfrage," *Hermes*,
XXXII (1897), 447.

[3] See pp. 99, 116 f., 134 f., and 144–49, below. Cf. Capps, "The Chorus in the
Later Greek Drama," *American Journal of Archaeology*, X (1895), 287 ff.; Körte,

It will be sufficient to state that there is no reason to believe that the tragic chorus failed to participate in the action or to bear a respectable share of the spoken lines until Roman times. Even in New Comedy, in which the chorus is now known to have appeared only for the *entr' actes*, its on-coming is often used to motivate the withdrawal of the actors. Such a motivation could scarcely have become common if the actors stood so far above the choreutae as to be safe from their drunken words and acts.[1]

Another argument in favor of a stage has been drawn from the phrases ἐπὶ τῆς σκηνῆς and ἀπὸ τῆς σκηνῆς, which occur in two fourth-century authors, Aristotle and Demosthenes.[2] It has been claimed that ἐπί "naturally means 'on' and implies elevation" and that σκηνή means "stage." If this exegesis were correct, there could be no doubt as to the presence of a stage in the fourth-century theater; but as a matter of fact neither claim is warranted. Everyone would concede that the primary, untechnical meaning of σκηνή is "hut" or "tent," and that the word was applied to the scene-building, which was erected back of the orchestra and which came to be increasingly substantial in construction. Though the term acquired a variety of other theatrical meanings, I agree with those who maintain that at

---

"Das Fortleben des Chors im griechischen Drama," *N. Jahrbücher f. kl. Altertum,* V (1900), 81 ff.; Flickinger, "ΧΟΡΟΥ in Terence's *Heauton* and Agathon's ΕΜΒΟ-ΛΙΜΑ," *Classical Philology,* VII (1912), 24 ff.; and Duckett, *Studies in Ennius* (1915), pp. 53 ff.

[1] See p. 147, below, and cf. Graf, *Szenische Untersuchungen zu Menander* (1914), p. 14. The same motive appears also in the fifth century, in Euripides' *Phoenician Maids,* vss. 192 ff., and *Phaethon* (Nauck, *Tragicorum Graecorum Fragmenta,* p. 602, fr. 773, vss. 10 ff.); cf. Fraenkel, *De Media et Nova Comoedia* (1912), p. 71, and Harms, *De Introitu Personarum in Euripidis et Novae Comoediae Fabulis* (1914), p. 60; see p. 282, below.

[2] The former phrase occurs in Aristotle's *Poetics* 1453a27, 1455a28, 1459b25, and 1460a15, and Demosthenes xix, p. 449, § 337; the latter in Aristotle's (?) *Poetics* 1452b18 and 25, Aristotle's *Problems* 918b26, 920a9, and 922b17, and Demosthenes xviii, p. 288, § 180. Cf. Richards, *Classical Review,* V (1891), 97, and XVIII (1904), 179, and Flickinger, "The Meaning of ἐπὶ τῆς σκηνῆς in Writers of the Fourth Century," *University of Chicago Decennial Publications,* VI (1902), 11 ff., and "Scaenica," *Transactions of the American Philological Association,* XL (1909), 109 ff.

no period did it mean "stage" in classical Greek. It is manifestly impossible to discuss the matter here, but I shall presently have occasion to show that even in Pollux, who lived in the second century A.D., it had not gained this meaning (see p. 98, below). If σκηνή does not mean "stage," it is unnecessary to argue that ἐπί does not mean "on," for actors could speak from the porch or from between the columns of the proscenium, and so could be said to speak "from the scene-building" (ἀπὸ τῆς σκηνῆς) or to be standing "on the scene-building" (ἐπὶ τῆς σκηνῆς) without being "on top of the scene-building." Just so the teachings of the Stoic philosophers are referred to as οἱ ἀπὸ τῆς στοᾶς λόγοι[1] without any implication that the Stoics spoke from a platform, let alone from the top of the stoa. Nevertheless, it is a fact that ἐπί does not always mean "on." For example, Diodorus and Plutarch both employ ἐπὶ σκηνῆς in a non-technical sense with reference to an occurrence "before" or "at the quarters" of a commander. And Lucian's metamorphosed ass was mortified at being shown to be a thief and glutton "before his master" (ἐπὶ τοῦ δεσπότου)[2]—surely there was no superposition there. Such passages, however, come from later Greek, when the prepositions were less clear-cut in meaning, and it is better, as Professor Gildersleeve has suggested,[3] to "repose quietly on the phraseological use of ἐπί; 'on the playhouse side' is all the Dörpfeld theory demands."

This being the theoretical situation with regard to the original meaning of ἐπὶ τῆς σκηνῆς, it is important to observe that already in its fourth-century usage the phrase was employed vaguely, often meaning little more than "in the theater" or "in a play." In fact, in one Aristotelian passage, as frequently in later writers, it clearly includes both chorus and actors within its scope. "We ought, therefore, to represent the marvelous in tragedy, but in epic there is greater room for the improbable (by which the

---

[1] Cf. Athenaeus, p. 211 B.

[2] Cf. Diodorus Siculus xi. 10, Plutarch *Life of Brutus*, c. xlv, and *Life of Demetrius*, c. xxxii, and Lucian (?), *Lucius sive Asinus*, §47.

[3] Cf. *American Journal of Philology*, XVIII (1897), 120.

marvelous is most often brought to pass) on account of our not actually beholding the characters. For example, Achilles' pursuit of Hector, if enacted in a play (ἐπὶ τῆς σκηνῆς), would appear absurd—the Greeks (οἱ μὲν) standing still instead of joining in the pursuit and Achilles (ὁ δ') motioning them back— but in epic verse the absurdity escapes notice."[1] It is evident that Aristotle was thinking of Homer's *Iliad* xxii, vss. 205 f.: "But Achilles shook his head to the people in refusal and did not permit them to cast their sharp weapons at Hector," and was trying to show why a scene that was excellent in an epic could not be dramatized with success. In Homer there are two groups of characters: (*a*) Achilles and Hector, and (*b*) the Greek army. In Aristotle's imaginary dramatization of the incident these groups are represented by the actors (ὁ δέ) and the chorus (οἱ μέν), respectively. Consequently, if σκηνή here means an elevated stage, chorus as well as actors must have stood thereon. Nor did the incongruity consist in the mere position of the chorus inactive in the orchestra and the actors running on the stage, but in the action itself, since the action is equally irrational in the epic (where orchestra and stage assuredly play no part) but is there more tolerable because the scene is not distinctly visualized. I do not insist upon σκηνή here meaning "play" or "perform- ance," though that is a frequent use and gives the indefinite sense required; but at least until this passage can be shown capable of another interpretation, believers in a stage cannot fairly cite Aristotle's use of ἐπὶ τῆς σκηνῆς in support of their opinion.

But though ἐπὶ (ἀπὸ) τῆς σκηνῆς was broad enough to comprise both chorus and actors, it naturally did not always include them both. Particularly, if it were desired to distinguish between the two kinds of dramatic performers, since οἱ ἐπὶ (ἀπὸ) τῆς θυμέλης could be used of the dithyrambic choruses and other "thymelic" (i.e., orchestral) performers, and could not possibly be applied to the actors, that phrase would naturally be used to designate the dramatic chorus as well, and οἱ ἐπὶ (ἀπὸ) τῆς σκηνῆς would be

[1] Cf. Aristotle's *Poetics* 1460a11–17.

used in the restricted sense for the actors alone, even in opposition to the dramatic chorus. This was especially common in the case of οἱ ἀπὸ σκηνῆς, doubtless because the scene-building was thought of as the home of the characters "from" which they came, as the choreutae, whether dramatic or dithyrambic, did not. Thus, a lyrical duet between the dramatic chorus and the actors (a *commus*—κομμός) is defined as a "dirge shared by the χοροῦ καὶ <τῶν> ἀπὸ σκηνῆς."[1] But neither the original meaning of ἐπὶ (ἀπὸ) τῆς σκηνῆς nor this secondary development which brought it into opposition to the thymelic performers and even to the dramatic choreutae presupposes a raised stage for the exclusive use of actors, still less requires that σκηνή should have meant "stage."

Now οἱ ἐπὶ (ἀπὸ) τῆς σκηνῆς and οἱ ἐπὶ (ἀπὸ) τῆς θυμέλης are exactly equivalent to the more common expressions οἱ σκηνικοί and οἱ θυμελικοί. For example, Euripides is called both ὁ ἐπὶ τῆς σκηνῆς φιλόσοφος and *philosophus scaenicus*.[2] The relationship is an obvious one, but is worth noting because one of Bethe's pupils has made σκηνικός and θυμελικός the basis of an attempt to prove the existence of a stage in the fourth-century theater at Athens. But since the earlier expressions ἐπὶ (ἀπὸ) τῆς σκηνῆς and ἐπὶ (ἀπὸ) τῆς θυμέλης were used with the same distinctions of meaning but without presupposing a stage, there is obviously no need of one to explain the later expressions. Moreover, Dr. Frei is guilty of an egregious *petitio principii:* he first accepts Bethe's hypothesis that the Lycurgus theater had a stage and consequently concludes that the distinction between σκηνικός and θυμελικός must be explained on the basis of difference in the place of performance there, and then uses these conclusions to prove a stage at that period.[3] All attempts to forge a pro-stage

[1] Cf. Aristotle (?) *Poetics* 1452b24 f.

[2] Cf. Clemens Alexandrinus (Potter), p. 688, and Vitruvius viii, praefatio §1. Incidentally it may be remarked that Euripides' philosophizing and personal views are found in his choral odes no less than in the histrionic parts of his plays (see p. 140, below).

[3] Cf. Frei, *De Certaminibus Thymelicis* (1900), pp. 14 and 15. The dissertation provoked a controversy between Bethe and Dörpfeld; cf. Bethe, "Thymeliker und Skeniker," *Hermes*, XXXVI (1901), 597 ff., and Dörpfeld, "Thymele und Skene," *ibid.*, XXXVII (1902), 249 ff. and 483 ff.

argument out of any of these expressions must be pronounced a failure. But of course in the Roman era, after most Greek theaters had been provided with a raised stage, the differentiation between ἐπὶ (ἀπὸ) τῆς σκηνῆς and σκηνικός, on the one hand, and ἐπὶ (ἀπὸ) τῆς θυμέλης and θυμελικός, on the other, became doubly appropriate, because the difference in levels now reinforced a distinction which had already existed without it.

Vitruvius, of course, made no philological or archaeological study of the two adjectives but explained them in terms of the theater which was known to him (see pp. 76f., above). It should be noted, however, that Vitruvius mentions only the tragic and comic actors under the term *scaenici* and includes under *thymelici* "the other artists" who perform in the orchestra. Does the dramatic chorus belong among the latter? Or is it simply ignored here? The answer is far from certain. If we were dealing only with new plays, it is conceivable that the choruses were so detached from the histrionic action as to be able to stand ten or twelve feet below the actors. But it is well known that some of the fifth-century tragedies were still popular and frequently acted; and as we have already seen, they were not amenable to any such method of staging. In revivals of early masterpieces, then, did all the performers, actors and chorus alike, appear in the orchestra, as in the old Greek theaters? Or was the chorus so reduced in size, and its manner of performance so altered, that it could stand with the actors on the high and narrow Graeco-Roman stage, as they all certainly did on the low and broad Roman stage? It is impossible to determine. All that can truthfully be said is that Vitruvius does not clearly indicate the place of the dramatic chorus in the Graeco-Roman theater. My own opinion is that he is speaking of two distinct types of performance and is ignoring the dramatic chorus.

The same question arises in connection with Pollux. He catalogues eleven parts of a theater. Of these, only six concern us at present: σκηνή, orchestra, logium, proscenium, parascenia, and hyposcenium (IV, 123). Dörpfeld thinks that Pollux is describing the Greek Hellenistic theater,[1] but Pollux was for

[1] Cf. *Athenische Mittheilungen*, XXVIII (1903), 420 f.

many years a professor at Athens and dedicated his work to the
emperor Commodus (161–92 A.D.).   Unless his language prevents it, it is more natural to suppose that he had the Athenian
structure of his own day in mind, and this would be the Nero
theater.   In that case, every term falls into place.   For the
Nero theater logium could refer to the stage alone; and as there
would be no sense in Pollux mentioning two words for stage, and
since no other term for scene-building as a whole (including
logium, proscenium, and parascenia) appears in his list, σκηνή
must still mean scene-building and not stage.   Pollux then
proceeds to say that "the scene-building belongs to the actors
and the orchestra to the chorus," and a little later that "entering
at the orchestra they mount to the scene-building on steps
(κλιμάκων)."[1]   Believing that Pollux is describing the Hellenistic
theater, Dörpfeld interprets the first of these passages much as
Aristotle's use of ἐπὶ (ἀπὸ) τῆς σκηνῆς has just been explained.
The second passage he considers a reference to some such
unusual incident as occurs in Aristophanes' *Clouds*, where an
actor is bidden to climb (from the orchestra) by means of a
ladder to the housetop (i.e., to the top of the scene-building) and
destroy the roof.[2]   There is much merit in this explanation, and
it is not necessarily inconsistent with a belief that Pollux is in
general dealing with the contemporaneous theater; such learned
digressions occur not infrequently in his text.   Nevertheless,
since stone steps leading from the orchestra to the stage of the
scene-building are a part of the Phaedrus theater at Athens, it
is not improbable that they belonged also to the Nero stage, if,
as Dörpfeld first thought, this was only about six inches higher
than the present stage (see p. 74, above).   On the other hand,
the pro-stage writers boldly cite these passages in support of
their views and as if they pertained to the earlier periods of the
theater's history.   But though Pollux is probably discussing a
theater with a stage, σκηνή does not mean stage in these two

[1] The Greek text has already been quoted on p. 78, nn. 1 and 2.

[2] Cf. *Clouds*, vss. 1486 ff.   A somewhat similar use of ladders is mentioned in
Euripides' *Bacchanals*, vss. 1212 ff.

sentences any more than in his catalogue of theater parts; and his testimony, however it is to be interpreted, should not be applied to fifth- and fourth-century conditions unless confirmatory evidence for so doing can be produced from these periods. Now the last of these sentences from Pollux concludes a discussion of the conventional significance of the parodi in the ancient theater (see p. 233, below). In my opinion, the Nero stage, though much deeper than the Hellenistic proscenium, was shallow enough so that the parodi still led directly into the orchestra. In that case, when the characters entered by either parodus, as they would when they were thought of as coming from the market place, harbor, or country, they would have to pass through the orchestra first and mount from there upon the stage by means of the steps, exactly as Pollux says. Furthermore, if actors could traverse this route it must have been available also for the chorus. In other words, although at this period the orchestra was the exclusive sphere of the dithyrambic choruses and other thymelic performers and was the normal place for the dramatic chorus, and though the actors regularly stood upon the stage, yet both the actors and the dramatic chorus appeared in either orchestra or stage according to the requirements of the plays. It must be understood, however, that this manner of staging was confined to the Nero theater at Athens; the stage of the Graeco-Roman theaters and the proscenium of the Hellenistic theaters were too high to make it feasible, and in the purely Roman theaters all performers appeared upon the stage. But why is it permissible to accept a low stage for the Nero theater and reject it for the fifth century? In the first place, the stage in Roman times is attested by incontrovertible evidence, both literary and archaeological, but for the fifth century it rests upon pure hypothesis. In the second place, there is no reason to believe that the Athenian chorus in Roman times was brought into actual contact with the tragic actors or had to pass to their place of action so frequently as in fifth-century drama (see p. 88, above).

There is still another sentence in Pollux which needs to be discussed. He declares that "the hyposcenium is adorned with columns and sculptured figures turned toward the audience, and it lies beneath (ὑπό) the logium."[1] There is no doubt as to the general position of the hyposcenium—it is the room[2] immediately behind the orchestra and on the same level—but there is a division of opinion as to the type of theater which had one and as to its function. In accordance with his belief that Pollux is describing the Hellenistic theater, Dörpfeld understands it as the first story of the scene-building in a theater of this type.[3] The columns and statuary would then refer to the proscenium just in front of it and to the figures which were sometimes placed in the intercolumniations thereof. In Hellenistic theaters Dörpfeld believes the top of the proscenium to have been used by speakers in the public assemblies and for that reason to have been known as a logium (see p. 59, n. 1, above); the hyposcenium, of course, lay on a lower level. Pollux' statement could not refer to a theater with a stage because the wall beneath the front of the stage was not decorated with columns or statuary (see p. 86, above), the proscenium now being raised one story and appearing at the back of the stage. On the contrary, the pro-stage writers maintain that Pollux refers to the space under a stage. In this instance I agree with them as against Dörpfeld, though I would not look upon Pollux' statement as applying to the theaters before his own day. Accepting Dörpfeld's opinion that the Hellenistic theaters had no stage, I think that the first story of their scene-buildings had no special name and that the term "hyposcenium" had not yet come into use; Pollux, however, is referring to the space under the stage in the Nero theater. The front of this was probably adorned with the same frieze as now stands before the Phaedrus stage, and we may not dogmatically

---

[1] Cf. Pollux iv. 124: τὸ δὲ ὑποσκήνιον κίοσι καὶ ἀγαλματίοις κεκόσμηται πρὸς τὸ θέατρον τετραμμένοις, ὑπὸ τὸ λογεῖον κείμενον.

[2] Also, the front wall of this room, just as σκηνή is not only the scene-building as a whole but also its front wall; cf. Flickinger, *Plutarch as a Source of Information on the Greek Theater*, pp. 43 f.

[3] Cf. *Athenische Mittheilungen*, XXVIII (1903), 418 ff.

assert that no columns stood there as well.[1]   The Athens theater
was inclined to be *sui generis* at all periods, and these would not
be the only particulars in which the Nero theater differed from
the Graeco-Roman type.

There remains for discussion a passage in Plutarch.   It
concerns an episode in the career of Demetrius Poliorcetes
(337–283 B.C.) and has been thought to refer to the theater of his
day.   But a study has been made of Plutarch's practice in such
matters and it has been found that many times he deliberately
sought vividness of presentation by modernizing his accounts
and picturing his scenes amid the familiar surroundings of
contemporaneous life;   in other words, the references to the
theater in connection with his anecdotes never presuppose any
other type of building than the stage-equipped buildings of his
own day, and in several instances this method resulted in patent
anachronisms.   One example will suffice.[2]   Plutarch declares
that Lycurgus, the Spartan lawgiver of about the ninth century
B.C., believed that the minds of assemblymen were distracted
by "statues and paintings or the proscenia of theaters or the
extravagantly wrought roofs of council chambers," and so caused
the Spartans to hold their assemblies in an open space.   The
author has here modernized his account in two particulars:
he speaks as if Lycurgus were familiar with a fully developed
theater building and as if it had already come to be used, elsewhere in Greece, as a place of meeting for the popular assembly.
Of course, Lycurgus antedated the Greek drama and all but the
crudest forms of choral performances by centuries, and this fact
was as well known to Plutarch as it is to us.

Now Plutarch says[3] that "Demetrius came into the city
(Athens) and ordered the entire population to be assembled into

[1] Robert would emend the text so that the statement would explain the
proscenium instead of the hyposcenium; cf. *Hermes*, XXXII (1897), 448.   In
that case ὑπό must mean "behind," a possible meaning, and Pollux would be
speaking of the proscenium in a theater with a stage.   Pollux includes the proscenium in his catalogue of theater parts (see pp. 97 f., above), but does not define it.

[2] Cf. Plutarch *Life of Lycurgus*, c. vi, and Flickinger, *Plutarch as a Source of
Information on the Greek Theater* (1904), p. 52.

[3] Cf. Plutarch *Life of Demetrius*, c. xxxiv.

the theater and hedged in the scene-building (σκηνήν) on every side with troops and surrounded the stage (λογεῖον) with guards, and himself descending (καταβάς), like the tragic actors, through the upper parodi (διὰ τῶν ἄνω παρόδων) he ended their fears with his very first words." In my opinion, the word καταβάς ("descending") clearly shows that λογεῖον means "stage." The

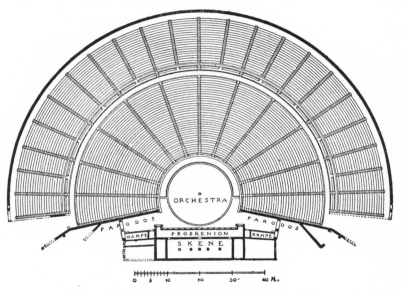

FIG. 46.—Plan of the Theater at Epidaurus in Argolis
See p. 104, n. 1

"upper parodi," then, must be the passages opening upon the logium from the parascenia. As Plutarch visualized the scene and wished his readers to do so, Demetrius came out upon the stage from one of the side entrances but did not address the people from there, as an orator of Plutarch's own day would have done.[1] Instead, in his desire to show the Athenians his goodwill he passed on down the central steps, as Plutarch had often seen the actors do in that theater (see p. 99, above), and addressed the assemblage from the orchestra. Since he could have passed

[1] Cf. Plutarch *Praecepta Gerendae Reipublicae* 823B, and see p. 59. n. 1, above.

through only one side entrance, the plural (παρόδων) must be due to a sort of zeugma, to imply that he came through one upper parodus and one upper entrance, viz., the central steps. The pro-stage writers who seek to apply Plutarch's words to the Lycurgus theater in which the incident really happened, and who use them as an argument for a stage at that period, are forced to ignore the word καταβάς, for they cannot allow that "tragic actors" regularly descended from the Lycurgus proscenium into the orchestra. If we go back of Plutarch's words and inquire what Demetrius actually did in the Lycurgus theater, the answer is plain: he simply advanced from the scene-building into the orchestra, and expressions consistent with this must have appeared in the source from which Plutarch derived his account. In fact, in describing a similar scene at Corinth, Plutarch retained words which are vague enough to be applicable to either type of theater.[1] He has simply modernized one account and brought over the other unchanged.

The zenith of Attic drama had passed by, entirely for tragedy and almost so for comedy, before the remains of theaters outside of Athens become frequent.[2] Nevertheless, these sometimes aid materially in reconstructing or interpreting the Athenian theater, and it will be necessary to dwell briefly upon a few of them. Perhaps the earliest and most primitive is found at Thoricus in southern Attica (Figs. 70 f.). This was built in the fifth or fourth century B.C. and was subsequently enlarged somewhat. The orchestra is oblong rather than circular, being bounded at one side by a temple, at the other side by a greenroom or storage chamber, and at the rear by a retaining wall. There is no reason to believe that a permanent scene-building was ever erected behind the orchestra. It is apparent that this structure has

---

[1] Cf. Plutarch's *Life of Aratus*, c. xxiii: ἐπιστήσας δὲ ταῖς παρόδοις τοὺς Ἀχαιοὺς αὐτὸς ἀπὸ τῆς σκηνῆς εἰς τὸ μέσον προῆλθε. For other interpretations, cf. Robert, *Hermes*, XXXII (1897), 448 ff.; Müller, *Philologus*, Supplementband, VII (1899), 52 f. and 90 f.; Dörpfeld, *Athenische Mittheilungen*, XXVIII (1903), 421 ff., etc.

[2] A convenient chronological table of the extant theaters is given by Fiechter, *op. cit.*, pp. 24–27.

several points of resemblance to the Athenian theater of the period between *ca.* 499 B.C. and *ca.* 465 B.C. (see pp. 65f., above).

The most symmetrical of all the Greek theaters and one of the best preserved is that at Epidaurus (Figs. 46–52 and 72, 2).[1] Its architect was the younger Polyclitus, and it was built toward the close of the fourth century B.C. If we are right in believing that the proscenium was not used as a stage, then the Epidaurus theater never had a stage. At any rate, it was not rebuilt and provided with one in Roman times. In the center of the orchestra stands a block of stone with a circular cavity, doubtless the foundation of the thymele. There is not only space for the full circle of the orchestra (in the narrowest sense; see p. 83, n. 2) but the bounding stones are actually continued for the full distance. The stone proscenium, containing half-columns (Fig. 72, 2) of the Ionic order and once eleven feet seven inches or about twelve Roman feet in height, was erected in the second or third century B.C. and replaced a wooden proscenium. The parascenia were rebuilt at the same time and seem originally to have been broader and to have projected farther from the scene-building. In either parodus stood a handsome double gateway (Figs. 49 and 51 f.), one door of which led into the orchestra and the other opened upon a ramp, somewhat sharply inclined, which debouched on the top of the proscenium. Ramps are found also in the Sicyon theater.

The theater at Eretria, on the west coast of Euboea, is not only one of the earliest but also presents several unusual features (Figs. 53–55 and 72).[2] It falls into three periods. The old scene-building was erected early in the fourth century B.C. A later scene-building was erected in front of the other about 300 B.C. The white marble proscenium belongs to the first century B.C. or later. The precinct of Dionysus at Eretria was situated on level ground, and this fact necessitated different arrangements than were

---

[1] Fig. 46 is taken from Dörpfeld-Reisch, *Das griechische Theater*, Fig. 50. Figs. 47–52 are from photographs by Dr. A. S. Cooley.

[2] Figs. 53–54 are redrawn from Dörpfeld-Reisch, *Das griechische Theater*, Figs. 44–45, respectively; Fig. 55 is from a photograph by Dr. A. S. Cooley.

FIG. 47.—The Auditorium from the North

FIG. 48.—Orchestra and Scene-Building from the South

THE THEATER AT EPIDAURUS

See p. 104, n. 1

FIG. 49.—The West Parodus

FIG. 50.—The East Parodus
THE THEATER AT EPIDAURUS
See p. 104, n. 1

FIG. 51.—The Gateway in the West Parodus

FIG. 52.—Looking through the West Parodus

THE THEATER AT EPIDAURUS

See p. 104, n. 1

feasible on the usual hillside site. The highest ground in Fig. 55 shows the original level on which the first scene-building, orchestra, and auditorium were erected (Fig. 54). This scene-building was of the common type with projecting parascenia between

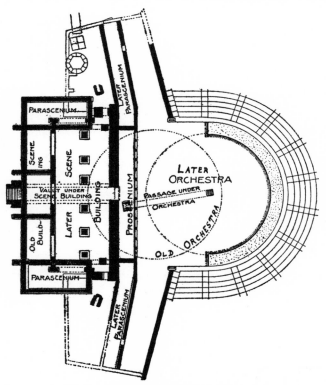

FIG. 53.—Ground Plan of the Theater at Eretria in Euboea

See p. 104, n. 2

which the proscenium must have been constructed of wood. The seats at this period apparently were wooden bleachers like the ἴκρια of the primitive orchestra in the old market place at Athens (see pp. 63 f., above); and when they proved unsatisfactory, it seemed easier to excavate the center of the area than to throw up a mound around it. Accordingly, earth to a depth of ten and a half feet was removed to form a new orchestra somewhat north of the old one.   In order that the old scene-building might not have to be taken down or lose its serviceability, the earth just in front of it was left standing and was held in place by a retaining wall.   Over this space was built a new scene-building, really only an episcenium.   Communication between the old level and the new was secured by means of a vaulted passageway and stone steps.   Before the retaining wall stood a wooden proscenium, the top of which doubtless continued the floor of the scene-buildings at the original ground level.   The boundary of

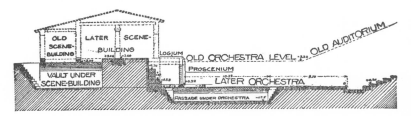

FIG. 54.—Cross-Section of the Theater at Eretria
See p. 104, n. 2

the orchestra (in the narrowest sense) stopped at the semi-circumference, but there was sufficient room before the proscenium for the complete circle.   A tunnel, six and a half feet high and three feet wide and with stone steps at either end, led from behind the proscenium to the center of the orchestra. Such an arrangement is probably what Pollux referred to as "Charon's steps"[1] and was convenient when an actor was to make an appearance from the earth or, like the ghost of Darius in Aeschylus' *Persians*, from some structure which might temporarily be erected in the orchestra.   Somewhat similar passages have been found in several other theaters, including Athens, but because of their size or other considerations seem not to have been used by actors.   The downward pitch of the parodus, owing to the excavations, is clearly seen in Fig. 55. The marble proscenium is thought to have been about eleven

[1] Cf. Pollux *Onomasticon* iv, § 132: αἱ Χαρώνιοι κλίμακες.

FIG. 55.—The Theater at Eretria as Seen from the Northwest

See p. 104, n. 2

FIG. 57.—The Scene-Building of the Theater at Oropus

See p. 108, n. 1

and a half feet high and was supported by rimmed columns (Fig. 72, 1b). The parascenia did not project from this but merely continued the line of the proscenium, as in many of the Asia Minor theaters. Traces of tracks for the wheels of an eccyclema (see pp. 284 ff., below) are said to have been found in this theater on a level with the logium,[1] but the stones have now disappeared and their purpose is not free from doubt.

Inscriptions in the island of Delos[2] show that contractors received payment for a scene-building and proscenium in 290 B.C. Panels (πίνακες) for the proscenium are mentioned in 282 B.C. Wood for the "logium of the scene-building" was paid for in 279 B.C. Extensive repairs and improvements seem to have been carried through in 274 B.C. Stone was provided for the parascenium in 269 B.C. Wood was used for "panels for the logium" in 180 B.C. These were probably used to close large openings in the episcenium (see the θυρώματα at Oropus on p. 109, below). Most of these entries refer to wooden construction and antedate the extant remains in stone. There is no orchestra in the more restricted sense, but a gutter extends for about two-thirds of a circumference. If prolonged, this would just reach the front wall of the scene-building but would have a large segment subtended by the proscenium. The scene-building is an oblong with three doors in front and one in the rear. It is bounded on all four sides by a portico about nine and a third feet high. The front of this formed the proscenium, and it is clear that what was an ornament and certainly not a stage on the other three sides was primarily an ornament and certainly not a stage also on the fourth side. The oblong pillars, which were left plain on the other three sides of the building, on this side have their front surfaces rounded off into half-columns, and a vertical rim expedited the insertion of panels (Fig. 72, 3). There were no parascenia in the stone theater except as these were provided

---

[1] Cf. Fossum in *American Journal of Archaeology*, II (1898), 187 ff. and Pl. **IV**; see p. 288, n. 2, below.

[2] A convenient series of excerpts from the Delian inscriptions is given by Haigh, *The Attic Theatre*[3], pp. 379 ff.

by the ends of the side porticos. The inscriptions, however, would seem to indicate that the situation had previously been different. From the front corners of the colonnade slanting doorways extended across the parodi. In the orchestra several bases stand in front of the proscenium, probably for the erection of statues or votive offerings.

There are theaters also at Delphi (Fig. 26), Megalopolis (Figs. 27 and 72, 1a), and Sicyon, but it is not possible to discuss every theater on the Greek mainland. We must not, however, pass by the small theater at Oropus in northern Attica (Figs. 56 f. and 72, 4).[1] It stood in the precinct of Amphiaraus and dates from the first and second centuries B.C. The auditorium is almost completely destroyed; evidently the seats were always wooden bleachers. Five marble thrones, however, stand within the orchestra, an unusual arrangement which recurs at Priene (see p. 113, below). Another peculiarity is that no orchestra, in the narrowest sense, is marked out, either in whole or in part. But if a circle is drawn through the seats of honor, as has been done in Fig. 56, it falls just outside the proscenium. On the contrary, a circle as determined by the lowest row of seats cuts into the proscenium slightly. The parodi have been banked up so that their outer entrances are on a level with the top of the proscenium. The chief merit of this theater consists in the fact that the superior preservation of its scene-building and the presence of two inscriptions enable us to form a fairly clear picture of how a proscenium and an episcenium looked at this period. The front wall of the scene-building is pierced by one door; the side walls are continued so as to frame the proscenium but themselves turn sharply back along the parodi without forming projecting parascenia. The proscenium consisted of Doric half-columns and was eight and a quarter feet high. Its central intercolumniation was intended to be filled by a door, but the four on either side were so made as to be readily filled in with painted panels (Fig. 72, 4). Across the architrave ran an inscrip-

---

[1] Fig. 56 is taken from Dörpfeld-Reisch, *Das griechische Theater*, Fig. 35; and Fig. 57 is from a photograph of the German Archaeological Institute at Athens.

tion: " . . . . having been agonothete, dedicated the proscenium and the panels." Another inscription ran along the top of the episcenium: " . . . . having been priest, dedicated the scene-building and the doors."[1] The last item refers to five (or three)

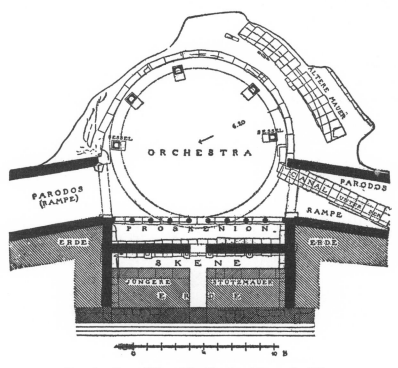

FIG. 56.—Ground Plan of the Theater at Oropus in Attica
See p. 108, n. 1

large openings in the front wall of the episcenium. Similar doors are found at Ephesus, and they were doubtless used in connection with the crane (μηχανή, see pp. 67 f., above, and p. 289,

[1] . . . . ἀ]γωνοθετήσας τὸ προσκήνιον καὶ τοὺς πίν[ακας, and . . . . ἱερεὺ]ς γενό-μενος ——— τὴν σκηνὴν καὶ τὰ θυρώμ[ατα τῷ Ἀμ]φιαράῳ. For the functions of an agonothete, see pp. 271 f., below. For the θυρώματα, cf. Dörpfeld in *Athenische Mittheilungen*, XXVIII (1903), 394, and *Jahrbuch d. arch. Instituts, Anzeiger*, XXX (1915), 102; wrongly interpreted in *Das griechische Theater*, p. 109.

below).   All in all, Oropus contributes very materially to our knowledge of the ancient theater.

Beginning with the first century B.C. the only kind of Greek theater which was newly built was what Dörpfeld calls the Graeco-Roman type, cf. the theaters at Termessus (Fig. 58)[1]

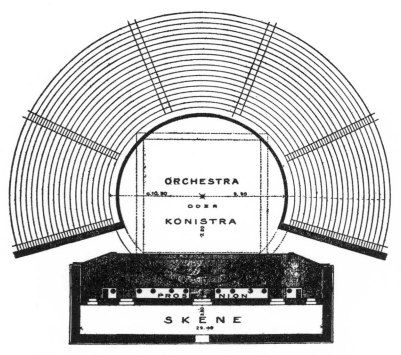

FIG. 58.—Ground Plan of the Graeco-Roman Theater at Termessus
See p. 110, n. 1

and Aspendus in Asia Minor.   During this period several Hellenistic theaters (e.g., those at Priene, Magnesia, Tralles, Pergamum [Fig. 28], Athens [?], Syracuse, Pompeii, etc.) were remodeled to the Graeco-Roman type.   That this is a Greek and not a Roman form of theater is proved by the fact that its orchestra, though no longer a complete circle, yet exceeded a semicircum-

[1] Fig. 58 is taken from *Athenische Mittheilungen*, XXII (1897), Pl. X.

FIG. 59.—The Proscenium of the Graeco-Roman Theater at Ephesus

See p. 111, n. 2

FIG. 64.—The Theater at Priene as Seen from the Southeast

See p. 113, n. 1

ference (see p. 77, above). These theaters had a stage varying from eight to ten feet in height and from eleven and a half to twenty in depth. The scene-buildings were of three stories— hyposcenium, logium, and theologium (Fig. 24). The first presented to the spectator an undecorated wall with doors leading into the orchestra; the second was terminated by a proscenium with columns and statues. The proscenium was seldom so simple as in the earlier theaters but was an ornamental façade with projections and recesses (Fig. 59), which added materially to the area of the stage.

Hellenistic theaters could be remodeled either (a) by building a new (undecorated) wall in front of the old proscenium and roofing the two over to form a stage or (b) by moving back the front wall of the scene-building slightly and constructing a stage between this and the old proscenium.[1] In either case, a new (decorated) proscenium would be erected at the back of the stage. In the latter case, the columns of the old proscenium would either be removed and a blank surface built in their stead or they would be walled up. As already explained (see p. 86, above) this was done because the floor of the stage was thought of as representing earth or a street. At Priene (Fig. 64) the Hellenistic columns were left standing, but this is the sole instance of a Graeco-Roman hyposcenium having columns.

Method (a) is illustrated at Ephesus (Figs. 24 and 59–62),[2] where the first permanent scene-building was built about 300 B.C. (Fig. 60). The dotted lines show the position of the stone proscenium, eight and a half feet high and nine feet ten inches deep, which was erected in the first century B.C. (Fig. 61). There were no parascenia. The seven openings (θυρώματα) in the episcenium furnish an interesting parallel to the five at Oropus (see p. 109, above). In the last half of the first century A.D. this

[1] Cf. Dörpfeld in *Athenische Mittheilungen*, XXII (1897), 458, and XXVIII (1903), 429.

[2] Fig. 59 is taken from Niemann's drawing in *Forschungen in Ephesos*, II, Pl. VIII: and Figs. 60–62 are from drawings by Wilberg, *ibid.*, Figs. 5, 56, and 57, respectively. Cf. also Dörpfeld, "Das Theater von Ephesos," *Jahrbuch d. arch. Instituts, Anzeiger*, XXVIII (1913), 37 ff.

structure was converted into a Graeco-Roman type (Figs. 24
and 62). The new logium was left of the same height as the
old proscenium, but was made nearly twenty feet deep; and at

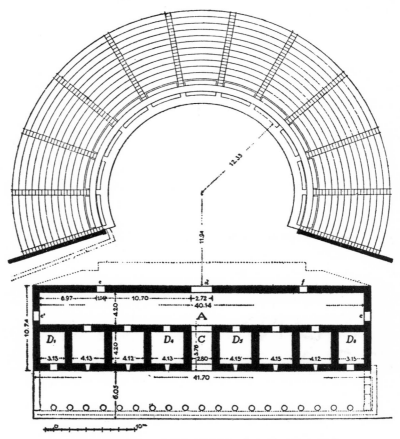

Fig. 60.—Ground Plan of the Early Hellenistic Theater at Ephesus
See p. 111, n. 2

certain points this depth received a considerable accession from
the recesses of the new proscenium (Fig. 59). These changes
were made at the expense of the orchestra, which derived some
compensation from the fact that several rows of the lowest seats

were removed; as a result the orchestra became a sort of pit (Fig. 24). The hyposcenium was plain and was pierced by three doors leading into the orchestra. The top story of the proscenium in Fig. 59 was not added until the third century A.D.

Method (*b*) was employed at Priene (Figs. 63 f.).[1] This theater enjoys the distinction of being the only one in which an altar was found, and this was not situated in the center of the orchestra, as the foundations at Athens and Epidaurus would

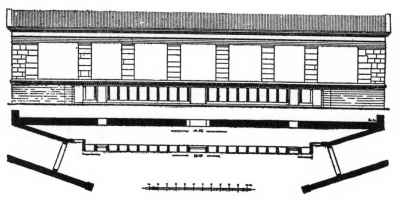

FIG. 61.—The Later Hellenistic Theater at Ephesus: Above, Elevation of Proscenium and Episcenium; Below, Ground Plan of Proscenium and Parodi.
See p. 111, n. 2

seem to indicate was the case there, but on its circumference. Seats of honor were placed in the orchestra, as at Oropus (see p. 108, above); but in Roman times new seats for dignitaries were erected in the center of the fifth row of seats (Fig. 63). The proscenium was of the same age as the scene-building and belongs to the third century B.C. At the Graeco-Roman rebuilding the columns of this proscenium were left standing, but the inter-columniations, except the three which served as doors, were walled up. The front wall of the Hellenistic episcenium was torn

[1] Fig. 63 is redrawn from *Athenische Mittheilungen*, XXIII (1898), Pl. XI; the cross-hatched walls belong to the Graeco-Roman rebuilding. Fig. 64 is from a photograph taken by Professor C. P. Bill and furnished by Dr. A. S. Cooley.

down and a new proscenium was built about six and a half feet farther back (see cross-hatched wall in Fig. 63).

The height of the Graeco-Roman stage as compared with the low Roman stage was partly due to convenience in remodeling

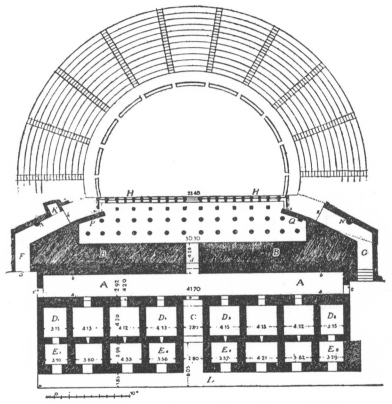

FIG. 62.—Ground Plan of the Graeco-Roman Theater at Ephesus

See p. 111, n. 2

when it was kept at the same figure as the earlier proscenium, but mostly to the conditions of exhibition.[1]   The Greeks did not, like the Romans, sit in their orchestras.   Choral and musical competitions still were held there, as well as such Roman sports

[1] Cf. Dörpfeld, in *Athenische Mittheilungen*, XXII (1897), 456 ff.

as gladiatorial and animal combats.   It was necessary, therefore, that the orchestra should be accessible from the hyposcenium, and

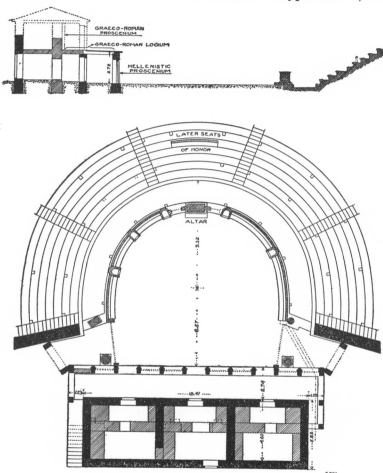

FIG. 63.—Ground Plan and Cross-Section of the Theater at Priene

See p. 113, n. 1

the doors could scarcely be lower than six and a half or seven feet. Accordingly, the stage could hardly be less than eight feet high.

But the seats of honor in Greek theaters had always been in the lowest tier (nearest the orchestra), and from there the view of dramatic performances, when presented upon an eight- or ten-foot stage, would be seriously obstructed.[1]   Usually when such theaters were remodeled, as at Ephesus, Assus, Pergamum, and Delphi, enough tiers were removed so that the lowest seats would be only about five feet below the stage level.   The orchestra thus became like a pit and was inclosed with vertical walls (Fig. 24).   At Side the space from which seats had been removed was built over with a six-foot wall, which was especially suitable in view of the gladiatorial and animal fights of Roman times.   Where the auditorium was not altered, as at Priene and Magnesia, it is supposed that the lowest seats were unoccupied at dramatic performances, but were put to use, as the best places, at orchestral sports and contests.

As to the function of the dramatic chorus in the period of the Graeco-Roman theaters, especially in Asia Minor, we have little information.   Nevertheless, it is necessary to consider the question.   Already in Hellenistic (New) Comedy the chorus appeared only between acts (see p. 147, below).   It is possible that by this time it had disappeared entirely or that it was so detached that, though the comic actors stood on a stage, the *entr' actes* could be given in the orchestra, or that its numbers were so reduced (see p. 135, below) that it could perform upon a Graeco-Roman stage—in any case, the chorus in contemporaneous comedy is negligible.   The number of the tragic choreutae had probably been reduced also (see p. 134, below).   But what is still more significant is that, if the fragments of Roman drama are any criterion[2], the tragic choruses had abandoned the strophic responsions of the old Greek tragedy, and this means the abandonment of the complicated evolutions which had carried the chorus over the full expanse of the ancient orchestra.   It was quite feasible for a small chorus which sang astrophic odes, spoke

[1] Cf. Dörpfeld, *ibid.*, XXII (1897), 458 f.; XXIII (1898), 337; and XXVIII (1903), 426.

[2] Cf. Duckett, *Studies in Ennius* (1915), p. 70.

through its coryphaeus, and danced in a restricted fashion to appear upon a Graeco-Roman stage with the actors, to be closely connected with the plot, and even to participate in the action. As to the reproduction of old plays, the situation was not especially different. Fifth-century comedies were probably never repeated at this period. New Comedy, as we have just seen, would present little difficulty. As to old tragedies, the choral parts could be excised *ad libitum* or sung on the stage by a reduced chorus without dancing (or at least without evolutions). It will be remembered that I do not accept Dörpfeld's opinion that the Nero stage at Athens was of the Graeco-Roman type. Accordingly, I believe that different physical conditions and the glory of their traditions kept up a livelier interest in the dramatic chorus at Athens than elsewhere and still retained the Athenian orchestra as the normal place of activity for the dramatic choreutae (see p. 99, above).

The foregoing account shows that there are many points of dispute with regard to the Greek theater and many points concerning which no one can do aught but guess. In closing, let me repeat that we are interested in the Greek theater mainly because of the Greek drama and that the extant pieces belong almost exclusively to the fifth century B.C. Now for that century the irreducible minimum, as shown by the plays themselves, is that there can have been no place, elevated much or little, which was reserved exclusively for the actors.

In the case of the drama the religious origin and the persisting religious meaning are self-evident. Performed at a festival of Dionysus, beside his temple, in the presence of his altar and his priest, tragedy and comedy are the natural response to that Greek demand for the enrichment of worship by art.—ARTHUR FAIRBANKS.

CHAPTER I

THE INFLUENCE OF RELIGIOUS ORIGIN[1]

If a modern theatergoer could be suddenly set down in ancient Athens, perhaps one of the first things to surprise him would be the discovery that he could not have recourse to his favorite recreation any day that he might choose. Of course, this situation resulted from the fact that ancient drama was connected with religion, was part of some god's worship, and as such could be presented only at the time of his festivals. This patron deity was uniformly Dionysus (Bacchus), god of wine, for the reason that tragedy and satyric drama were offshoots of the Dionysiac dithyramb (see pp. 2–4 and 6 f., above) and that the *comus* (κῶμος), from which comedy had developed (see p. 36, above) had a meaning and function similar to those of certain rites of Dionysus and in the course of time was brought into connection with his worship. At Athens, Dionysus had several festivals, but only two at which plays were performed, viz., the City Dionysia and the Lenaea. Thanks to the labors of many scholars and the finding of additional inscriptional evidence our information concerning these occasions, though still far from complete, is somewhat less scanty than it has been.[2] At the City Dionysia tragedy dated from 534 B.C., while comedy was not given official recognition there until 486 B.C. Though the Lenaea was the older festival, its dramatic features were later, comedy being added about 442 B.C. and tragedy about 433 B.C. It ought to be stated, however, that at both festivals there had been volunteer, unofficial performances of primitive comedy (κῶμοι) prior to the dates just given, when the state took them

[1] Cf. the works mentioned on pp. xvii and xx f., above. There is no special literature on this subject.

[2] Cf. chaps. iv and ix and the bibliographies on pp. 196 and 318, below.

119

under its formal protection. The comus was introduced into the Lenaean festival between 580 B.C. and 560 B.C., and into the program of the City Dionysia about 501 B.C. (see p. 24).

Now if our imaginary modern visitor to ancient Athens chanced to be somewhat acquainted with the history of mediaeval drama, he would probably surmise that the close connection between Greek drama and religious festivals would result in the plays being performed in temples, just as mysteries and miracle plays were originally presented in the churches. But in this he would be much mistaken. There is a fundamental difference in function between a Greek temple and a Christian church. The latter is primarily intended as a place for congregational worship, and its size and interior arrangements are chosen accordingly. On the other hand, the temple was pre-eminently thought of as the earthly abode of some divinity; it was, therefore, uniformly too small to accommodate any considerable crowd, neither was its interior well adapted for that purpose. In the second place, the worshipers at an ancient shrine were not more or less rigidly restricted to a list of members with their more intimate relatives, neighbors, and friends, as is the case with a Protestant church today. In most cases, any free-born citizen would feel as free to worship at any particular temple or to take part in its festivals as could any other citizen, and on no infrequent occasions practically the whole body of citizens was present. In fact, so important was it deemed that everyone should attend the dramatic festivals that toward the end of the fifth century it was provided that whoever felt unable to pay the daily admission fee of two obols[1] should, upon application, receive a grant for this purpose from the state. "The whole city kept holiday, and gave itself up to pleasure, and to the worship of the wine-god. Business was abandoned; the law-courts were closed; distraints for debt were forbidden during the continuance of the festival; even prisoners were released from jail, to enable them to share in the common festivities."[2] Boys

---

[1] A drachma contained six obols and was worth about eighteen cents without making allowance for the greater purchase value of money in antiquity.

[2] Cf. Haigh, *The Attic Theatre* (3d ed. by Pickard-Cambridge, 1907), p. 1.

Fig. 65

A "WAGON-SHIP" OF DIONYSUS AND PROCESSIONAL UPON AN ATTIC SKYPHOS IN BOLOGNA OF ABOUT 500 B.C.

See p. 121, n. 2

and slaves were admitted, if their fathers or their masters were willing to pay their way. It seems, though the evidence is inconclusive,[1] that despite the oriental-like seclusion of Greek households even women and girls might attend. They certainly participated in the ceremonies of the first day. Plato and Aristotle favored restricting the attendance, but their views seem to have had no effect. Thus, children and respectable women who would have invited divorce by being present at real scenes of that character were allowed to witness the indecencies of satyric drama and Old Comedy and to listen to the broadest of jokes. Such is the power of religious conservatism.

From these considerations it follows that the attendance upon the dramatic performances was enormous, and that the use of temples to accommodate the spectators was entirely out of the question. Therefore it became necessary to provide a separate structure, which in fourth-century Athens could seat as many as seventeen thousand. From this fact arose the further necessity for an annual procession, in order to escort the statue of Dionysus from his temple to his theater. Since the two buildings were situated in the same precinct on the south slope of the Acropolis and within a few feet of each other (Figs. 29 and 32), there was no need of the processional ceremony being other than a very simple one. As a matter of fact, from the spectacular standpoint this was one of the most splendid features of the festival and consumed the whole first day. It has been claimed that several Attic vases, dating from the close of the sixth century B.C. and depicting the "wagon-ship" of Dionysus, give a hint as to the character of this part of the City Dionysia (Fig 65).[2] The car is drawn by two men representing attendant sprites of Dionysus. The tip of the long equine tail

---

[1] The affirmative side of the question is presented by Haigh, *op. cit.*, pp. 324 ff.; the negative by Rogers, Introduction to Aristophanes' *Women in Council* (1902), pp. xxix ff.

[2] Cf. Frickenhaus, "Der Schiffskarren des Dionysos in Athen," *Jahrbuch d. arch. Instituts*, XXVII (1912), 61 ff. Fig. 65 originally appeared as Beilage I, Fig. 3, in connection with this article. It is taken from a drawing by Signor G. Gatti, a photograph of which was furnished me through the courtesy of Professor Ghisardini, Director of the Museo Civico at Bologna.

of one of them is clearly indicated.   In the car are two other
sprites, whether sileni or satyrs, playing on flutes, and the god
himself is seated between them.   Alongside of the sacrificial bull
are two citizens standing.   Farther forward are two youths with
branches (θαλλοφόροι), then a youth with a censer, another with
a basket (κανηφόρος), and finally, at the head of the procession,
a boy who is perhaps to be regarded as a trumpeter.   Whatever
relationship may subsist between such vase paintings and contemporaneous drama (see p. 20, above) the entire free population,
from the chief magistrate of the city (the archon eponymus)
down, participated in the procession at the City Dionysia and took
the god's statue by stages from his temple to a point near the
Academy on the road to Eleutherae (Fig. 2).   This direction was
chosen because. as the Athenian god's cognomen of Eleuthereus
shows, this image and its cult were supposed to have been
introduced from this town on Attica's northern border (see p. 21
and n. 3, above) and because the return of the processional was
intended to imitate the final portion of the original entry.
After the remainder of the day had been spent in rites and
festivities the procession escorted the sacred relic back to its
precinct by torchlight and placed it near the orchestra in the
theater, where it remained during the rest of the festival.   Thus
the god was supposed to have witnessed every play presented at
the City Dionysia from 534 B.C. on, and it is as a connoisseur and
critic of wide experience that he is appointed to judge between
the rival claims of Aeschylus and Euripides in Aristophanes'
Frogs, vss. 810 f.   Our English and Protestant ideas concerning
the nature of a religious ceremony are only too likely to give us a
misleading conception of the whole festival and especially of its
first day.   The *festa* of some popular saint in Southern Europe,
who demands the veneration of his people and yet is broad-
minded enough to enter into the spirit of the occasion and is not
offended even by being made the subject of rollicking jests,
would afford a far better parallel, and even this falls short.
Drunkenness combined with the darkness at the close of the
day's proceedings to intensify the license natural on such an

occasion. Children born as the result of chance meetings at these annually recurring processions are frequently mentioned in New Comedy and often motivate the action.[1]

Nevertheless, the religious character of these festivals and of the dramatic exhibitions connected with them was a very real thing to the Greeks, and everyone in attendance would fully realize that he was present at no secular proceeding. To a mediaeval spectator of miracle plays and mysteries this feeling would seem perfectly natural, but it would be another occasion of surprise to a modern visitor. Already in Elizabethan times Shakespeare could assure his audience: "Our true intent is all for your delight." So exclusively is this now the motive of theatrical performances that we seldom think of the theater as a place for the inculcation of religious truths or for teaching the facts of religious history. It follows that the subject-matter of Greek drama was drawn from their mythology as inevitably and uniformly as the text of a modern sermon is drawn from the Bible. In fact, freedom of choice was originally still more restricted. Whether tragedy was derived from satyric drama and satyric drama from the dithyramb or whether, as I believe, both tragedy and satyric drama were independent offshoots of the dithyramb (see pp. 2–4), this remains true—the early dithyramb was exclusively devoted to the exaltation of Dionysus, and in consequence the themes of tragedy and of satyric drama were likewise, at the beginning, entirely Dionysiac. By the time of Thespis or soon thereafter (see pp. 20 f., above) tragedy broadened out so as to treat any mythological theme. Of the thirty-two extant Greek tragedies Dionysus appears in only one,

---

[1] Cf. Plautus' *The Casket*, vss. 89 f.:

> per Dionysia
> mater pompam me spectatum duxit,

and vss. 156 ff.:

> fuere Sicyoni iam diu Dionysia.
> mercator venit huc ad ludos Lemnius,
> isque hic compressit virginem, adulescentulus,
> <vi>, vinulentus, multa nocte, in via.

For the differences between Old Comedy, Middle Comedy, and New Comedy, see p. 39, above.

Euripides' *Bacchanals,* and even in that he is disguised during most of the play. But the playwrights were not content to stop at this point. Phrynichus, who was a pupil of Thespis and won his first victory in 511 B.C., introduced the innovation of dramatizing contemporaneous history. In 494 B.C. the Persians captured and destroyed the Ionic city of Miletus. Shortly thereafter Phrynichus treated this subject in a tragedy. Though it moved the Athenians to tears, they were so indignant at being reminded of the misfortunes of their kinsmen that they fined the poet one thousand drachmae. Undeterred by this rebuff, however, in 476 B.C. Phrynichus brought out his *Phoenician Women,* dealing with the Persian invasion of Greece in 480–479 B.C. This play served as a model for Aeschylus' *Persians* (472 B.C.) on the same subject. But by laying the scenes of these plays in Asia Minor or Persia the dramatists gained remoteness of place instead of the usual remoteness of time. As Racine[1] wrote on a similar occasion: "The general public makes hardly any distinction between that which is removed from them by a thousand years or by a thousand leagues." A still further innovation was made toward the close of the fifth century by Agathon, in whose *Antheus* both incidents and character names were entirely fictitious. A very similar development can be traced in mediaeval times. Originally the gospel story was the theme, then subordinate incidents of Scripture, then the lives of saints since Bible times, then allegorical tales, etc.

But in practice Greek tragedians did not avail themselves of their liberty. Agathon's innovation was not followed up; and though the Greeks did not sharply differentiate mythology and history,[2] they did not take kindly to the treatment of contemporary events in tragedy. The three plays above mentioned exhaust the instances at Athens. Even in mythological subjects experimentation soon led them to confine themselves to the stories of a few houses—to the misfortunes of Oedipus, Orestes, Meleager, Thyestes, etc. This tendency is illustrated by the

[1] Cf. his Preface to *Bajazet.*
[2] Cf. Ribbeck, *Rheinisches Museum,* XXX (1875), 145.

fact that three of the extant tragedies, Aeschylus' *Libation-Bearers*, Sophocles' *Electra*, and Euripides' play of the same name, ring the changes upon the same topic. Since almost every playwright of consequence would turn his hand to these oft-tried themes, the only chance of success necessarily lay in improving upon the dramatic technique and the elaboration of character and plot already displayed by one's rivals. As Aristotle wrote,[1] each poet was expected "to surpass that which was the strong point of each of his predecessors." We are therefore not surprised to learn from the same source that in his day the finest tragedies were based upon these hackneyed subjects. Furthermore, the practice is commended by so high a modern authority as Goethe: "If I were to begin my artistic life over again, I should never deal with a new story. I should always invest the old stories with new and more vital meanings."

The poets' choice of tragic themes from traditional mythology does not mean that their material was rigid and intractable. They enjoyed entire freedom to revamp the old tales, by invention, alteration, or suppression, in order to suit their own purposes. Here again the practice of the mediaeval playwrights, though more restricted to minor matters, affords the best clue. On the other hand, the fact that most spectators knew at least the general outline of his plot in advance allowed the ancient dramatist to introduce numerous subtleties that are quite beyond the reach of modern playwrights (see pp. 315 f., below). It is true, as Aristotle[2] warns us, that "even the known stories were known only to a few." Nevertheless, the more intelligent in the audience would always be well informed, and of the oft-repeated tragic themes even the most stupid could hardly remain in ignorance.

In the case of satyric drama the situation was naturally somewhat different. Whatever the relationship between the dithyramb, satyr-play, and tragedy, the fact remains that the satyr-play was placed in the program of the City Dionysia

[1] Cf. Aristotle's *Poetics* 1456a6 and 1453a19.

[2] Cf. *ibid.*, 1451b25.

largely as a concession to the Dionysiac element. Consequently, Bacchic themes were retained in the satyric drama long after they had been abandoned by tragedy. Even so, it did not take long to develop a secondary stage in which the Dionysiac element is practically restricted to the appearance of Bacchus' attendant sprites, the chorus of satyrs, who are harshly superimposed upon some non-Dionysiac subject. Until recently our direct information concerning the satyr-play was derived solely from Euripides' *Cyclops*, the only extant representative of this genre, but now the major portion of another, *The Trackers* (*Ichneutae*) by Sophocles, has been revealed to us.[1] Both in the *Cyclops* and now in the *Trackers* the Bacchic element is restricted to Silenus and the chorus of satyrs, and Dionysus himself figures only as he is appealed to or mentioned in the choral odes or episodes. How generally Bacchus was omitted from his own special brand of play we have no means of knowing, but it was inevitable that this should not be a rare occurrence. The myths in which the wine-god could appropriately appear in person must soon have been exhausted; and the playwrights, more concerned in producing an interesting performance than in maintaining an outworn custom, would yearn to exercise in this field the same freedom that they had already won for themselves in the composition of tragedies. Even in the two plays now before us the new wine is fairly bursting the seams of the old wineskins. In the *Cyclops*, Silenus and his children are joined to the story of Odysseus' adventures in Polyphemus' cave, in which neither earlier mythology nor rhyme or adequate reason had vouchsafed them a place. Their presence is explained by the statement that they had set sail in search of Dionysus, after learning that he had been seized by pirates, were shipwrecked near Mt. Aetna, and enslaved by the Cyclops (vss. 11 ff.). The situation in the *Trackers* is still more forced. The play deals with the theft of Apollo's cattle by the infant Hermes. Upon the offer of a reward, the satyrs turn detectives in order to track down the stolen beasts. Thus it will be seen that in both plays the

[1] Cf. *Oxyrhynchus Papyri*, IX (1912), 30 ff.

Dionysiac element is a mechanical, extraneous feature in the plot. It is not surprising that the dramatic poets should chafe under the limitations of so clumsy a compromise.[1]

Yet again, in the case of comedy the situation was still different. The embryonic form of comedy, the comus, was originally intended by a sort of sympathetic magic to superinduce friendly powers and to expel malign spirits, and involved neither plot, unity of theme, nor fiction. When these features were introduced, they were influenced by mature tragedy and by the Sicilian mime, which had already reached a high stage of development (see pp. 36 f. and 46–52, above). As a result, though comedy had become as much a part of Dionysiac worship as was tragedy or satyric drama, it did not go through a stage of Bacchic or semi-Bacchic themes, but passed at once to fictitious subjects. The difference between tragedy and comedy in this regard is clearly indicated by Antiphanes, a poet of Middle Comedy:[2]

Tragedy is a happy creation in every respect, since the audience knows the plot before ever a word has been spoken. The tragic poet needs only to awaken their memories. If I barely mention Oedipus, they know all the rest: that his father is Laius, his mother Jocaste, who are his sons and daughters, what he has done, and what will befall him. . . . . This is not possible for us, but we must invent everything: new names, preceding events, the present circumstances, the catastrophe, and the exposition.

Furthermore, the Sicilian mime seems to have been unassociated with religious worship, and perhaps this fact has a share in explaining the irreverent, almost atheistic, tendency which Attic comedy manifested. Though it was part of divine worship, it treated the divinities with the utmost disrespect. Even Dionysus himself, the patron deity of the festivals, is represented in Aristophanes' *Frogs* as cowardly, lecherous, and foolish, beaten with many stripes before the eyes of his worshipers.

The Greek theater suffered no scene of bloodshed to be enacted before its audience. When the plot of the play, as was

---

[1] For still further developments in the history of satyric drama see pp. 198 f., below.

[2] Cf. Kock, *Comicorum Atticorum Fragmenta*, II, 90, fr. 191.

not infrequently the case, required such an incident, the harrowing details were narrated by a messenger who had witnessed the event.   In Aeschylus' *Persians* the combats between Greeks and Asiatics are all narrated.   In Aeschylus' *Seven against Thebes* and Euripides' *Phoenician Maids* the fatal duel between the brothers occurs off-stage.   Similarly, in Euripides' *Bacchanals* the report is brought to Thebes that Pentheus has been torn to pieces on Mt. Cithaeron.   In these and numerous other cases the incidents related took place at some distance from the imaginary scene.   When it is remembered that the action of Greek plays is usually laid before a palace or temple, it will at once occur to everyone how conveniently located such a structure was for violence nearer the scene of action.   Thus, in Aeschylus' *Libation-Bearers* (vs. 904) Orestes drives his mother indoors to dispatch her, and in Sophocles' *Electra* he is lucky enough to enter the palace and find her there alone and off her guard. This situation recurred again and again, and a further refinement lay close at hand.   The hearts of the spectators were often thrilled with tragic fear or pity by hearing from behind the scenes the screams of the dying, their cries for help, even their death rattle.   So Agamemnon dies in Aeschylus' play of that name (vss. 1343–45); so Clytemnestra in Sophocles' *Electra* (vss. 1404 ff.) and Euripides' play of the same title (vss. 1165–67); so Lycus in Euripides' *Madness of Heracles* (vss. 749 and 754); and so many another.   The murder of Duncan in *Macbeth* shows that such scenes must have been far more effective than any attempt at a realistic representation could possibly have been.   An additional effect is sometimes secured by flinging open the back scene and disclosing the dead forms within; cf. the slaughtered children of Heracles (Euripides' *Madness of Heracles*, vss. 1029 ff.), Eurydice (Sophocles' *Antigone*, vs. 1293), etc.   Sometimes death-cries and the opened scene are combined, as in Aeschylus' *Agamemnon*, vss. 1343–45, 1372 ff.   Still another artifice for avoiding seen violence is found in Euripides' *Children of Heracles*, which ends by Alcmene and her attendants dragging Eurystheus off to his doom.

The rule of Greek dramaturgy which has just been described is liable to one notable exception—the dramatic characters may not commit murder before the eyes of the spectators but they may commit suicide there. Not, of course, that all suicides must take place within the audience's vision; most of them, like all cases of manslaughter, are reported. But the important fact remains that at least in some instances suicide is enacted before the spectators' very eyes. So, in Sophocles' *Ajax* that hero falls upon his sword (vs. 865), and in Euripides' *Suppliants* (vs. 1071) Evadne flings herself from the rocks upon her husband's funeral pyre. It thus appears that it is neither the bare fact of death nor yet its mere hideousness which was obnoxious to ancient taste. The first conclusion is confirmed by the fact that the life-strength of Alcestis is allowed to ebb away upon the stage (Euripides' *Alcestis*, vs. 391), and the second by the sight of Heracles racked by agonizing tortures in Sophocles' *Maidens of Trachis*, vss. 983 ff. The distinction between what is permissible and what is forbidden seems to hinge upon a trivial matter, viz., whether only one character is involved or several.

Passing now to the *raison d'être* of this practice I will first mention some minor considerations. The paucity of actors in Greek drama (see p. 182, below) made any representation of mass effects, such as a battle, quite impossible. The lack of complicated stage machinery prevented the melodramatic actualism that modern audiences love so well. Being thus unaccustomed to the more difficult feats of realism, the ancients had not learned to demand it in lesser matters. Without a sigh they dispensed with that which everyone knew to be incapable of actual enactment before their eyes. Furthermore, in the absence of a drop curtain (see pp. 243 f., below) it would have been necessary for characters slain upon the stage either to rise and walk casually off, as in the Chinese theaters of today, or to be carried off. The first alternative is unthinkable in ancient Greece and the second would have been too monotonous.

It has also been claimed[1] that the use of masks, each with its own unchanging features, would have been an insuperable obstacle to scenes of violence, as normally presupposing great and rapid changes in the facial expressions of the characters. But in connection with other scenes the Greeks frequently ignored and frequently evaded the difficulties caused by the immobility of their masks (see pp. 222 f., below); so there is no reason to believe that the use of masks would by itself have driven incidents of this nature from the Greek stage.

Ludovico Castelvetro (1570) alleged that the high and narrow stage of the Greek theater was too cramped for the dignified representation of violence.   Whatever plausibility this suggestion may previously have enjoyed has been lost since Dörpfeld has shown that the fifth-century theater at Athens had no raised platform for the exclusive use of actors and that actors and chorus stood alike in the broad expanse of the orchestra (see pp. 79 and 117, above) (Figs. 22 f.).

It is customary to explain the Greek avoidance of violence upon aesthetic grounds; to assert that the susceptibilities of the Greeks were so refined as to have been offended by scenes of bloodshed.   That which would be disagreeable or painful to see in real life should never be presented to an audience.   This is the French position.   In the first place the French took over the Greek practice on faith.   It was only when they were called upon to explain it that they proceeded to evolve this justification. Then the logic of their argument carried them beyond their models.   "A character in <French> tragedy could be permitted to kill himself, whether he did it by poison or steel: what he was not suffered to do was to kill someone else.   And while nothing was to be shown on the stage which could offend the feelings through the medium of the eyes, *equally was nothing to be narrated with the accompaniment of any adjuncts that could possibly arouse disagreeable sensations in the mind.*"[2]   They were

[1] Cf. Freytag s *Technique of the Drama*[2], translated by MacEwan, p. 75, and Hense, *Die Modificirung der Maske in der griechischen Tragödie*[2] (1905), pp. 2 f.

[2] Cf. Lounsbury, *Shakespeare as a Dramatic Artist* (1902), p. 175 (italics mine).

therefore under the necessity of attempting to paint the lily—
"they took exception to the way in which Philoctetes speaks of
the plasters and rags which he applied to his sores; and equally
so to the description which Tiresias gives in the *Antigone* of the
filth of the ill-omened birds which had fed on the carcass of
Polynices."[1] I would not be understood as altogether rejecting
this aesthetic explanation; doubtless the practice of the Greek
playwrights created, if it did not find ready made, such taste
concerning these matters. It certainly applies to cases of
blinding, which, whether self-imposed (Sophocles' *Oedipus the
King*) or wrought by others (Euripides' *Hecabe*), always take
place off-scene—the later sight of the bloody masks and ghastly
eyes is harrowing enough and to spare. Nevertheless, however
strong a case may be made out for it, the aesthetic interpretation cannot, because of one cogent objection, provide the real,
ultimate reason for the convention. Is suicide so much less
revolting than homicide that the same taste can consistently
shrink from the sight of one but tolerate the other?

The same objection lies against another suggestion, viz.,
that the theater precinct was sacred ground which would be
polluted by murder, though done in mimicry. To those who
remember the taint which the Greeks thought to be brought upon
a land by manslaughter, this theory will not, at first, seem lacking in plausibility. But unfortunately, accidental homicide and
suicide were thought to involve pollution no less than did murder.
Even a natural death, in the Greeks' opinion, brought a taint.
Consequently, this suggestion fails to explain how suicides and
natural deaths could occur on the Greek stage.

My own interpretation of the phenomena under consideration
is somewhat similar to that just mentioned. Not only was the
theater sacred ground but all who were connected with the
dramatic performances—those who bore the expenses (the
choregi; see p. 270, below), poets, actors, and chorus—"were
looked upon as ministers of religion, and their persons were

[1] Cf. *ibid.*, p. 204. The passages referred to are Sophocles' *Philoctetes*, vss.
38 f., 649 f., and 696–99, and *Antigone*, vss. 1016–22 and 1080–83. The expressions
employed in the Greek could be seriously objected to only by the most fastidious.

sacred and inviolable."[1] Even the audience shared in this immunity. Any outrage at such a time and in such a place was not viewed in its usual light but was visited with severe penalties as an act of desecration. Thus, when Demosthenes acted as choregus for a dithyrambic chorus in 350 B.C. and was assaulted by Midias, he wished the latter to be punished, not merely for assault (ὕβρις) but for sacrilege (ἀσέβεια).[2] In the speech which he prepared for this suit Demosthenes cited some of the precedents (§§ 178–80). He reminded his auditors how Ctesicles had been put to death for striking a personal enemy with a whip during the procession and how in 363 B.C. the archon's own father had only by a natural death avoided punishment for having violently ejected a spectator from a seat which he had unwarrantably occupied. In like manner the person of an actor was for the time being sacrosanct. Of course, the Greeks were not fools; they knew that a single blow in genuine anger was a greater outrage than murder itself in make-believe. Convention allowed the audience to express their disapproval of actors or of their performances by pelting them with figs, olives, or even stones. Custom had dulled their sanctity to this extent. Nevertheless, the taboo which had been derived from ancient ritual prevented one actor from murdering another upon the stage. But this taboo did not protect an actor against himself or against the assaults of nature or of the gods. Hence suicides and natural deaths were permissible within the audience's sight, though homicides were not.

In comedy the influences which tended to prevent the enacting of scenes of violence were partly nullified by the fact that one of the purposes of the comus and other fertility rites had been the expulsion of malign powers by violence, not only of language but also of conduct (see p. 37, above). Of course the comic playwrights rarely had occasion to treat of death or murder. But scenes of physical violence and horseplay, such as the lashes administered to Xanthias and Dionysus (at his own festival!) in Aristophanes' *Frogs*, vss. 644 ff., are common.

[1] Cf. Haigh, *The Attic Theatre*[3], p. 2.
[2] Cf. argument, Demosthenes' *Against Midias* §§ 2 f.

That most wonderful of Greek dramatic instruments, the chorus.—GILBERT
MURRAY.

A really great artist can always trans-
form the limitations of his art into valuable qualities.—OSCAR WILDE.

CHAPTER II

THE INFLUENCE OF CHORAL ORIGIN[1]

Tragedy and satyric drama were derived from the dithyramb;
comedy from the comus (see pp. 6, 23 f., 36, and 43 f., above).
Now both the dithyramb and the comus were entirely choral.
Consequently early tragedy and comedy were also choral. No
other fact in the history of Greek drama is better authenticated,
both by literary tradition and the extant plays, than this.[2] The
dithyrambic chorus consisted of fifty dancers, and this seems to
have been the size of the chorus also in early tragedy. So the
chorus in Aeschylus' *Suppliants* (between 500 and 490 B.C.)
was made up of the fifty daughters of Danaus. Whether this
was still the regular practice or a reversion, on this occasion, to
the earlier number cannot now be determined. At least by
487 B.C. the tragic chorus had been reduced to twelve. It is
supposed that this came about as follows: During the fifth
century each tragic poet was required to present four plays at a
time in the annual competition at the City Dionysia, three
tragedies and one satyric drama. This grouping of plays cannot
be proven for any poet before Aeschylus (525–456 B.C.) and
probably was introduced at a rearrangement of the festival
program which took place about 501 B.C. The members of the

[1] In addition to the works mentioned on pp. xvii and xx f., above, cf. Decharme,
Euripides and the Spirit of His Dramas (1892), translated by Loeb (1906); Capps,
"The Chorus in the Later Greek Drama," *American Journal of Archaeology*, X
(1895), 287 ff.; Helmreich, *Der Chor bei Sophokles und Euripides* (1905); A. Körte,
"Das Fortleben des Chors im gr. Drama," *N. Jahrb. f. d. kl. Altertum*, V (1900),
81 ff.; Flickinger, "ΧΟΡΟΥ in Terence's *Heauton*, The Shifting of Choral Rôles
in Menander, and Agathon's 'ΕΜΒΟΛΙΜΑ," *Classical Philology*, VII (1912),
24 ff.; Stephenson, *Some Aspects of the Dramatic Art of Aeschylus* (1913); Fries,
De Conexu Chori Personae cum Fabulae Actione (1913); Duckett, *Studies in Ennius*
(1915); and Helmreich, *Der Chor im Drama des Äschylus* (1915).

[2] Nevertheless, it has been ignored by certain recent writers on the origin of
tragedy, cf. *Classical Philology*, VIII (1913), 283.

chorus (the choreutae) must have found it irksome to memorize
the words, music, dance steps, and stage business for so many
plays.   To relieve this burden Aeschylus or a contemporary
divided the choreutae at his disposal into four groups of twelve
each, assigning one group as a chorus for each of his four plays.
Whether the dramatist continued to be provided with forty-
eight or fifty choreutae or whether, as the rôle of the chorus lost
its bulk and importance, a single group of twelve choreutae
appeared in all four pieces is unknown.   In the former case, the
three groups of choreutae that would normally be idle during any
one play could be conveniently employed as a supplementary
chorus, mute attendants, etc.   But however this may be, twelve
was the size of the chorus in the three extant tragedies of Aeschylus which followed the *Suppliants;* and it continued to be such
until the middle of the fifth century, when Sophocles raised the
number to fifteen.[1]   This innovation enabled the chorus to enter
the orchestra in three files of five men each and to retain this
formation for their dance movements.   This gave better results
than to draw them up, as was previously necessary, in two files
of six men each or three files of four each.   Furthermore, the
chorus leader (the *coryphaeus*) could now stand to one side
occasionally without spoiling the symmetry of the two half-
choruses, each of which had a sub-leader of its own.   Aeschylus
probably adopted Sophocles' innovation in the three plays which
he brought out in 458 B.C.   One of the test passages is *Agamemnon*, vss. 1344-71, where a single tetrameter line seems to be
assigned to each of three choreutae and an iambic couplet to each
of the remaining twelve.   There is no reason to believe that the
number was altered again for a long time; but further information of a change is lacking until Roman times—at Cyrene a wall-
painting of a tragic chorus represents but seven choreutae.

It is unlikely that the chorus in the early comus consisted of
any fixed number.   Toward the end of the fifth century the
comic chorus contained twenty-four choreutae.   Probably this

[1] Whether the satyric chorus was increased at the same time is unknown.   In
Fig. 4, which represents a satyric drama of about 400 B.C., not more than twelve
choreutae are represented.

number was chosen at the time that comedy was granted the official recognition of the state, 486 B.C. If such was the case the comic chorus was just twice as large as the tragic chorus of that period. The reason for doubling the number is found in the hostility which frequently rent the chorus of ancient comedy and in the parallelism which is an outstanding feature of its choral odes (cf. p. 42, above). About the close of the fourth century, when the functions of the comic chorus had been greatly curtailed, it is likely that its size was also reduced. At any rate, the chorus at the Soteric festival at Delphi from 272 to 269 B.C. contained but seven or eight choreutae and at Delos in the next century only four.

The chorus of Greek comedy was Protean in the forms that it assumed. In accordance with the animal disguises which were so popular in the early comus (see p. 54, above), we hear of choruses representing wasps, birds, frogs, goats, snakes, bees, gall-insects, fishes, ants, storks, etc. A suggestion as to the appearance of such choruses is afforded by five Attic vase paintings of *ca.* 540–490 B.C. (Figs. 12–16). Still more fantastic were choruses of clouds, dreams, cities, seasons, islands, laws, ships, sirens, centaurs, sphinxes, dramas, etc. Less grotesque would be choruses of Persians, knights, graces, athletes, poets, etc. These lists convey but a slight hint of the diversity which the fancy of the poets provided for the choruses of Old and Middle Comedy. The choreutae, of course, were always men, but some or all of them might be dressed to represent women. Thus, the clouds in Aristophanes' play are thought of as women, and in his *Frogs* the chorus of initiates comprises both men and women. At the beginning of Aristophanes' *Women in Council* the choreutae are men dressed to represent women who have tried to disguise themselves as men! By the time of New Comedy the chorus had sunk to a position of comparative insignificance and had become more conventional, usually consisting of men engaged in a carousal (κῶμος). In the earliest form of Attic tragedy the chorus was invariably composed of sileni.[1] But when its themes

---

[1] For the differences between sileni and satyrs and for their appearance on the stage, see pp. 24–32.

were no longer exclusively Dionysiac (see p. 123, above), the choruses became more sedate, generally consisting simply of men or women.   In most cases these are citizens of the imagined scene of action.   In addition to sex it was customary to indicate whether they were thought of as being young or old.   Sometimes they are characterized as foreigners.   For example, the scene of Euripides' *Phoenician Maids* is laid in Thebes; but dress, accent, and the habit of oriental prostration mark the women in the chorus as non-Hellenic.   The staid character of tragic choruses is abandoned in the unique furies of Aeschylus' *Eumenides*.   According to tradition their black garments, bloody faces, and snaky locks produced so frightful an impression that boys fainted and women miscarried.   In satyric drama the chorus always consisted of satyrs (see pp. 125 f., above).

One of the first problems that confronted the Greek dramatist was the choice of such a character for his chorus as would make it an integral part of the play's action.   The never-changing character of the chorus in the satyr-plays prevented, for the most part, anything but the loosest of connections between chorus and actors there, as we have already noted (pp. 126 f., above). In tragedy the task was somewhat easier, yet still most difficult. In the earliest Greek tragedy extant, Aeschylus' *Suppliants*, the chorus, the fifty daughters of Danaus who have fled from Egypt to Argos in order to escape marriage with their fifty cousins, are themselves the story.   The actors are of secondary importance.   From the standpoint of dramatic interest Danaus himself, the king of Argos, and the suitors' herald do not compare with the girls themselves.   In the *Persians* and the *Seven against Thebes*, Aeschylus has been nearly as successful.   In these plays the fate of the chorus, though not the prime object of interest, is almost inextricably bound up with that of the other dramatic characters.   In the former the Persian elders, for patriotic as well as personal motives, are no less concerned than the queen mother (Atossa) or King Xerxes himself in the fate of the army invading Greece.   Similarly, in the *Seven against Thebes* the possibility of the city's being captured has as vital a meaning to the chorus of Theban girls as to the others, and frightens them more. Here we find a new note; for whereas in the first part of the play the thought of the danger threatening themselves and the city swallows up all else, in the last part their hearts are torn with fear for Eteocles as he fares forth to single combat with his brother. This latter motivation, viz., that the chorus should be moved by a more or less sentimental interest in some actor rather than by a vital fear for itself, or for others and itself, was destined to play a prominent part in the history of the dramatic chorus. It recurs in Aeschylus' *Prometheus Bound, Agamemnon,* and *Libation-Bearers* (not to mention the plays of Sophocles and Euripides), in all of which the interest of the chorus in the action is more or less adventitious. Even in such cases, however, it was the practice of Greek playwrights, if possible, to bind the chorus more intimately to the hero in the final catastrophe. Thus, in *Prometheus Bound* the daughters of Oceanus, who constitute the chorus, bear no real relationship to the leading character; nevertheless, at the close (vs. 1067) they declare their wish to share his fate, mount the crag where he is fastened, and with him are hurled to Tartarus. A final refinement is found in Aeschylus' *Eumenides.* Here the chorus of furies, so far from fearing for or sympathizing with one of the characters, is set in deadly opposition to Orestes and is bent upon tracking the guilty man down. Inasmuch as this was the especial duty of furies the chorus is raised once more to a point of primary importance. Thus it appears that from the standpoint of choral technique Aeschylus' earliest play, the *Suppliants,* and his last play, the *Eumenides,* are the most successful.

In general, the chorus in Sophocles and Euripides is less intimately related to the plot than in Aeschylus. Yet there are notable exceptions to this statement. Thus, the chorus of Euripides' *Suppliants* consists of Argive women together with their handmaids—the mothers of the seven chieftains who fell in the attack upon Thebes. They implore the aid of Theseus to force the Thebans to surrender the bodies of their sons for burial. According to ancient thought this was a matter of paramount importance and the whole play is occupied with it. The mothers are in fact the chief personages of the drama; the other characters speak and act only in their behalf. Not even the Danaids of Aeschylus' *Suppliants* are more indispensable to the mechanism of the piece. On the other hand, the connection between chorus and plot in Euripides' *Phoenician Maids* is of the flimsiest. This tragedy deals with the same subject as Aeschylus' *Seven against Thebes*. But the Aeschylean chorus consists, as we have observed, of Theban girls who are vitally concerned in the outcome of the battle. Euripides' chorus is made up of Tyrian virgins on their way to Delphi. They have no personal interest in the possible capture of Thebes or in the fratricidal strife of Eteocles and Polynices.

The same sort of thing occurs also in Old Comedy. Dr. Fries (*op. cit.*, p. 35) correctly points out that the knights in Aristophanes' play of that name are present rather to listen than to act. In Aristophanes' *Clouds* and *Frogs* the connection between chorus and action is of the slightest and entirely artificial. In general it can be said that the character of comic choruses is chosen rather to fit into some fantastic situation, and may be largely ignored toward the end of the play. Thus, in Aristophanes' *Women at the Thesmophoria* the women of Athens assemble to contrive a punishment for Euripides, who has been maligning their sex. Euripides' father-in-law, made up as a woman, tries to defend him but is detected. During vss. 871–1160 Euripides under various disguises attempts to rescue his relative, but each time is frustrated. But the chorus of Euripides-haters assist in balking him neither by word nor deed. Their original character, if retained throughout these lines, would have too effectually thwarted the humor of his stratagems.

It is possible, however, to detect more subtle effects in the relations between chorus and actors. Since the chorus is usually friendly to the principal character, the bond of sympathy is often strengthened by having the chorus of the same sex and of about the same age as that character. So, in Aeschylus' *Libation-Bearers* the choreutae are Trojan slave women who are cognizant of conditions in the palace and fully share Electra's eagerness to avenge her father's murder. In Sophocles' *Maidens of Trachis* the chorus of girls is in thorough accord with the gentle, unsophisticated Deianira. Furthermore, men or older women might have warned her against sending to her husband a robe dipped in the centaur's blood, an act which is so essential to the plot; but such innocence is made to seem entirely plausible by reason of the youth and inexperience of the chorus. On the contrary, sometimes the run of the plot requires an effect precisely the opposite. In Sophocles' *Antigone*, for example, the isolation of the heroine is intensified by a chorus, not only of men but of old men, who would be least sympathetic with her violation of a public edict. In Aeschylus' *Prometheus Bound* the defiant Titan would have scorned the overtures of a group of men, whoever they might be, but the feminine tact and sympathy of the Oceanides reach his heart at once. Such a chorus, moreover, is an effective foil the better to emphasize the hero's indomitable strength and will-power. In Aeschylus' *Persians* the chorus of Persian elders is not only natural in itself, but such experienced men's fear for the army and their grief at its misfortunes produce an impression of utter collapse beyond the power of any chorus of women to effect. In Aristophanes' *Knights* the chorus, in spite of criticisms, was appropriately constituted, since it represented a body of men who are said to have entertained a special grudge against Cleon. It would be easy to extend this topic to a great length. Suffice it to state that both the extant plays and the ancient commentaries upon them[1] prove that the Greek poets expended no little thought upon this detail of their dramaturgy.

Having once selected his chorus, the necessity rested upon the poet of composing choral odes appropriate to the character chosen. In this they were not always successful. In Euripides' *Electra* the chorus consists of virgins from the Argive countryside. At vss. 434–78 they give an elaborate description of Achilles'

---

[1] Cf. the scholia to Sophocles' *Ajax*, vs. 134, to Euripides' *Phoenician Maids*, vs. 202, etc.

armor. Such women would have had no opportunity of seeing Achilles at Troy themselves, and hearsay would scarcely have been so circumstantial. Again, in Euripides' *Phoenician Maids*, vss. 638–75, 801–27, and 1019–67, the Tyrian girls unroll the scroll of Theban history like antiquarians. Their knowledge is not justified by the fact that Thebes had been founded, some five generations before, by a Phoenician prince. Again, in Euripides' *Hippolytus*, vss. 1102–19, women of Troezen, the intimates of a local washerwoman (!), discourse upon the conflict between faith and reality! Still again, in Euripides' *Iphigenia at Aulis*, vss. 794–800, a band of unassuming women from Chalcis throw doubt upon the mythological tradition that Zeus had appeared unto Leda in the form of a swan. The first two examples are somewhat different from the last two. The former arise simply from failure to find a satisfactory solution for the problem under consideration. But the latter reveal the poet dropping his mask and using the chorus as a mouthpiece for his own philosophizing and skepticism.

Lest anyone suppose that I exaggerate the difficulty or attribute to Greek playwrights a perplexity which they did not experience, let me point out the confessed failure of a modern poet. Concerning the close of Act III in the second part of *Faust*, Goethe said: "You have observed the character of the chorus is quite destroyed by the mourning song: until this time it has remained thoroughly antique, or has never belied its girlish nature; but here of a sudden it becomes nobly reflecting, and says things such as it has never thought or could think." And to this Eckermann, uncontradicted, replied: "These little inconsistencies are of no consequence, if by their means a higher degree of beauty is obtained. The song had to be sung, somehow or other; and as there was no other chorus present, the girls were forced to sing it."[1] That Euripides was equally conscious of what he was doing is proven by the fact that in some cases he makes only too patent an attempt to gloss over the difficulty. Thus, he makes the chorus in the *Electra* explain that they had

[1] *Conversations with Eckermann*, July 5, 1827 (Oxenford's translation).

heard of Achilles' shield in the nearby harbor of Nauplia "from one who had fared from Troy" (vss. 452–55); and the Tyrian maidens justify their knowledge of Theban history by saying that they "had received an account at home in an alien tongue" (*Phoenician Maids*, vs. 819). A curious self-consciousness seems to obsess dramatic poets and force them to call to the hearer's attention the very difficulty that they are striving to avoid. Like some scientists who think they have explained a phenomenon if they have provided a name for it, playwrights sometimes act as if they had justified an incongruity if they mention it. An excellent modern illustration of this occurs in *Twelfth Night*, II, 5. In order to extract the full humor from the scene it is necessary that Malvolio read aloud the forged letter which he has just found. Therefore, Shakespeare makes Sir Toby say: "The spirit of humours intimate reading aloud to him!" Since these words are uttered in an aside, they can have no real effect. Nevertheless, the dramatist eased his conscience by inserting them.

Sometimes the difficulty of finding motifs suitable for the rôle of the chorus caused the playwrights to introduce a second chorus of a different type. Phrynichus seems to have done this in 476 B.C., bringing on a chorus of elders as well as one of Phoenician women.[1] Likewise, in Euripides' *Hippolytus* that hero's comrades in the chase appear and sing a short ode (vss. 61–72) before the arrival of the regular chorus. Several other instances are known of in Euripides' lost plays. In Seneca's *Agamemnon* there is a chorus of Mycenaean women and another of Trojan captives. In the same writer's *Hercules on Mt. Oeta*, Dr. Fries (*op. cit.*, p. 49) maintains that three choruses are introduced, one of Oechalian captives at vs. 104, another of Deianira's companions at vs. 583, and a third of Hercules' comrades at vs. 1031. The same sort of thing occurs also in comedy. Thus, from Terence's *Self-Tormentor*, which is a Latin translation of Menander's play of the same name, it would appear that in the Greek original a chorus of banqueting companions performed at vs. 171 and another chorus of maidservants

[1] Cf. Graeber, *De Poetarum Atticorum Arte Scaenica* (1911), pp. 56 ff.

at vss. 409 and 748.[1] Occasionally, before making its appearance, the chorus sings, from behind the scenes, in a different character from that which it later assumes. Aristophanes' *Frogs*, for example, derives its name from a chorus which never is seen. At vs. 209 the chorus, from behind the scenes, delivers a batrachian strain as an accompaniment to Dionysus and Charon when they row across the subterranean lake (see p. 90, above). It is not until after vs. 315 that this chorus actually appears and reveals its true character, that of men and women who had, when on earth, been initiated into the mysteries. This method of procedure gained one of two results—it obviated the necessity either of a lightning change of costume on the part of the chorus or that of hiring extra choreutae. As to the latter alternative, whatever may have been true of the tragic poets (see p. 134, above), there is no reason to suppose that the comic poets always had spare choreutae at their disposal.

But not only should choral odes be appropriate to the dramatic character of the chorus; they ought also to be closely connected with the theme of the play. And this requirement is no less difficult than the other. The ode on the inventive spirit of man in Sophocles' *Antigone*, vss. 334–75, is so vague that an audience might well be in doubt as to which one of the dramatic characters it was intended for. Verses 1115–52 in the same play, a hymn to Dionysus, is quite irrelevant, except in so far as that divinity was the patron of the dramatic festival. Other instances are found in Euripides. Verses 1301–68 of *Helen* deal with Demeter's search for her lost daughter and are so alien to the subject of the tragedy that many have considered them an interpolation. An adventitious connection is sought, at the close, by the suggestion that Helen's misfortunes are due to her neglect of Demeter's worship (vss. 1355–57). Again, the chorus' eulogy of Apollo in *Iphigenia among the Taurians*, vss. 1234–83, is so disconnected with the story that Professor Decharme (*op. cit.*, pp. 312 f.) could defend it only by saying: "If, therefore, the chorus wishes not to rouse the suspicion of Thoas, it

[1] Cf. Flickinger, *op. cit.*, pp. 28 ff.

must speak of something else than that which really engrosses its attention. Hence the eulogy of Apollo that compromises nobody, whose purport Thoas would not understand were he to appear suddenly, but which the spectator comprehends, provided he reflects." The description of Achilles' armor in Euripides' *Electra*, vss. 434–78, has already been mentioned (pp. 139 f., above). It is as little connected with the plot as it is appropriate to the chorus of that play. Nevertheless, Euripides brought the ode back to the theme with a jerk by saying: "The lord of such warriors didst thou slay, O Clytemnestra" (vss. 479 f.). There are but two things that can be said to palliate this offense. The first is to indicate the difficulty of the problem; the other, to point out that the ingenuity of the ancient playwrights fell short in only a few plays and seldom more than once in any one piece.

There are certain ways, however, in which the lack of an organic relationship between chorus and actors or the failure of the odes to spring naturally from the dramatic situation may be compensated for or glossed over. One is by giving the choreutae an active participation in the action. The scene of Euripides' *Helen* is laid in Egypt and the chorus consists of Greek slaves, who assist the heroine in her deception mainly because she is a fellow-Greek and her victim a barbarian. Their connection, therefore, is only moderately close and, as we have seen (p. 142, above), one of their odes is by some considered an interpolation. Yet, apart from their choral songs, they take an active and important part in the play. It is they who persuade Helen not to believe Teucer's announcement of her husband's death but to consult the seeress Theonoe concerning the matter (vss. 306 and 317). Again, it is they who, when the Egyptian king avows his intention of murdering Theonoe for abetting his deceivers, grasp his garments and declare: "We are your slaves and you can slay us, but slay us you must ere you can kill Theonoe" (vss. 1629 ff.). Similarly, in Euripides' *Orestes* the chorus of Argive women is friendly toward Electra and her brother but does not share the danger which threatens them. Yet when Helen is being murdered behind the scenes, at Electra's request, in order to guard against surprise, it divides into semi-choruses, which picket the two roads leading before the palace (vss. 1251 ff). A little later they attempt to make noise enough to prevent the tumult from within the palace attracting the notice of the Argive citizens (vss. 1353 ff.). Thus, a chorus may actively participate in a plot to which it is but loosely joined. In fact, Professor Capps has boldly declared: "In every play whose chorus has been criticized for the irrelevancy of its songs, whether the criticisms have been just or not, are found indications of direct participation in the action" (op. cit., p. 295).

In this connection certain words of Aristotle[1] are usually cited: "The chorus ought to be regarded as one of the actors; it ought to be an integral part of the whole and take a share in the action, in the manner, not of Euripides but of Sophocles. The choral songs of the successors of Euripides and Sophocles have no more to do with the subject of the piece than with that of some other tragedy. They are therefore sung as mere intercalary numbers (ἐμβόλιμα), a practice first begun by Agathon. Yet this is no more justifiable than to transfer a speech or a whole act from one tragedy to another." Aristotle's praise of Sophocles at the expense of Euripides probably refers to the choice and setting of Sophoclean choruses and to the relevancy of their songs—points in which Sophocles usually surpassed his rival. Aristotle failed to notice or did not value the other characteristic of Euripidean choruses, viz., that they have more effect upon the plot and come into more direct contact with the actors, that is to say, that they really "act" more, than is the case in Sophocles. In fact, it is Sophocles' use of the chorus which is mainly responsible for the modern notion that the Greek chorus was merely the "ideal spectator."

The precise meaning of the latter part of this passage from the Poetics has not until recently become clear. It is evident that Aristotle brings the same charge, that of irrelevancy, against the choruses of both Euripides and Agathon. But if the difference between them were merely one of degree, he would hardly

[1] Cf. Aristotle's Poetics, 1456a26 ff.

have said that Agathon "began" a practice which he had really borrowed from Euripides and only "developed" or "extended." Therefore, Aristotle must mean that Agathon was guilty of a different *kind* of irrelevancy than Euripides, and we are now in a position to see whereof this consisted. Recently discovered fragments of Menander show that often in New Comedy the chorus did not appear in the course of the action at all, but only between acts, and that the poets did not write down the words of these *entr'actes* but simply indicated where they should come by writing the word XOPOY ("of the chorus") at the places required. To the stage manager XOPOY in the manuscript would be simply a hint to use anything he chose or to refer to the poet or that he could rely upon the latter to provide the choreutae with a libretto, according to whatever arrangement they had between them on the subject. To the reader it was convenient, as marking off the divisions of the play. A parallel to this custom is found in Greene's *James the Fourth*, where at the beginning of Act IV the stage directions read "Enter certain huntsmen (if you please, singing)," and again at the close of the same act, "Enter a round, or some dance at pleasure." A passage in the ancient *Life of Aristophanes* had already mentioned this practice of the writers of New Comedy but had received scant consideration until substantiated by the Menander fragments.

Now, since embolimon means "something thrown in," it seems clear that the songs of the chorus in the intermissions marked by XOPOY (if songs not recorded in the text were sung) would be embolima in Aristotle's use of the term. I believe that this was the innovation which Agathon introduced. This conclusion will be strengthened if we ask ourselves what sort of evidence enabled Aristotle to attribute the invention of embolima to Agathon. It is fairly certain that he never saw one of Agathon's tragedies actually performed in the theater. Then his knowledge of Agathon's dramatic art must have depended upon the latter's published works. Therefore, if Agathon's choral numbers were notable rather for the music than for the libretto, or consisted of music and dancing without words, or were borrowed from other poets, or if for any reason whatsoever Agathon preferred not to copy them down with the rest of the text, but merely to mark their location by XOPOϒ or some other symbol, then we can understand how Aristotle could know that Agathon had inaugurated something new in dramatic technique. Whatever their defects of irrelevancy, Euripides' odes were not "thrown in" in this sense; they were right there in the text. But in Agathon's manuscripts, on the other hand, there were gaps indicated between acts. In actual performance suitable odes were "thrown in." A "thrown-in" ode then would be one not appearing in the text. It is self-evident that this interpretation throws a flood of light upon Aristotle's statements.

That XOPOϒ was so used in tragedy prior to the time of New Comedy is attested by its occurrence in a recent fragment of a fourth-century *Medea.*[1] Moreover, by inference its use can be safely traced still further back, even close to the period of Agathon. We have seen that tragedy exercised a profound influence upon Old Comedy (see pp. 49 f., above); and Professor Navarre[2] has correctly pointed out that the influence of tragedy was more quickly and strongly felt in the second half of a comedy (that after the parabasis or, when that is lacking, after the agon; see p. 41, above). Accordingly a strong reason for believing that this use of XOPOϒ originated in tragedy is found in the fact that XOPOϒ occurs in this part of Aristophanes' last two (extant) comedies; cf. *Women in Council,* vss. 729 and 876 (393-392 B.C.), and *Plutus,* vs. 770 (388 B.C.). It is significant that Aristophanes' use of embolima is still embryonic, has not yet been carried to the logical issue found in New Comedy. That is to say, the chorus of these two plays still figures in the action and converses with the actors. In the *Women in Council* it even has, in addition to embolima, several choral songs, the words of which are preserved. The fragments of the fourth-

[1] Cf. *Philologus,* LXX (1911), 497 f.

[2] Cf. *Revue des Études anciennes,* XIII (1911), 273.

century *Medea*, scanty as they are, nevertheless suffice to indicate that its author employed embolima and the chorus in the same fashion as Aristophanes.

But by the time of New Comedy a great change had taken place. In comedies of this period, or at least in many of them, the chorus appeared only to furnish entertainment between acts, withdrawing again at the end of its performance. It bore no speaking part and from the nature of the case could exercise no influence upon the plot. Occasionally it was brought into formal relationship with one of the actors. For example, in Menander's *Girl with the Shorn Locks* the chorus seems to consist of Polemon's boon companions, who took breakfast with him in the country and have now come to his house in the city to be on hand for the dinner in the evening. This is the most frequent type of chorus in New Comedy. The approach of these inter-mezzic choruses is often mentioned by the actors who thus motivate their own withdrawal from the scene during the choral *entr'acte*. For instance, in one case[1] XOPOΥ is prefaced by one character remarking to another: "Let us withdraw into Charisius' home, for a throng of tipsy youths is approaching whom it is inadvisable to provoke." Such an introduction occurs also in a fragment of Alexis, a poet of Middle Comedy,[2] but the quotation is not long enough to determine whether Alexis resembled Aristophanes or the New Comedy in his use of embolima and of the chorus. Racine's *Athalie*, which has been pronounced[3] the "one thoroughly satisfactory choric drama" that modern art has produced, presents several points of likeness to the later Greek chorus. The Levite maidens do not appear until just before the close of the first act and are withdrawn several times subsequently, being thus absent from the scene during long stretches of the dialogue. Their entrances, also, are sometimes alluded to by the actors. Their songs, however, are not em-bolima, but constituent parts of the text.

[1] In the Jernstedt fragment; cf. Capps, *Four Plays of Menander*, pp. 98 f.

[2] Cf. Kock, *Comicorum Atticorum Fragmenta*, II, 333 f., fr. 107.

[3] Cf. Verrall, *Euripides the Rationalist*, p. 219, note.

We have seen that with reference to the plot these intermezzic choruses of New Comedy are irrelevant. At times they must even have been disconcerting. Notwithstanding, in the light of modern dramatic theory they are not utterly defenseless. The principle is the same as that which is used to justify intermissions between acts. "It would be no gain but a loss, if a whole two hours' or three hours' action could be carried through in one continuous movement, with no relaxation of the strain upon the attention of the audience, and without a single point at which the spectator might review what was past and anticipate what was to come. The act division positively enhances the amount of pleasurable emotion through which the audience passes."[1]

A word of caution is necessary. We have seen that the use of embolima and of the sign XOPOT to indicate their position in the play originated in fifth-century tragedy (Agathon), that an actual instance of XOPOT in a fourth-century tragedy is preserved, and that Aristophanes brought this tragic innovation over into comedy, where it was greatly extended. Now despite the fourth-century *Medea* there is good reason for believing that this practice never had the vogue in later tragedy that it had in later comedy. The *Rhesus* has erroneously come down to us under the name of Euripides, but is generally regarded by scholars as the product of some fourth-century writer, the only complete tragedy of that century which is extant. It contains no embolima and is a natural continuation of the tradition of Aeschylus, Sophocles, and Euripides. The chorus is made up of the night watch in the Trojan camp. They go to Hector's tent and rouse him with the news that the Greek host is on the move. They take part in the dialogue, almost capture Odysseus, who has entered the camp as a spy, have a keen personal interest in the proceedings, and sing choral odes which, though short, are apposite. It is indisputable that from the beginnings of tragedy to the end the rôle and importance of the chorus steadily declined, but there is no reason to suppose that it ever fell so low as was

[1] Cf. Archer, *Play-making*, p. 142.

the case in New Comedy. This conclusion is confirmed by Seneca's Latin tragedies and by the fragments of earlier Roman tragedies. In the fragments of Ennius, Pacuvius, and Accius the chorus is shown to be connected, sometimes even intimately connected, with the plot and some of the characters. It still conversed with the actors and its odes were not embolima, but actually written in the text. There are only two signs of a choral decline. In the first place the odes are no longer characterized by the elaborate strophic responsion which was seldom lacking in the choral songs of fifth-century tragedy in Athens. This doubtless means that the chorus no longer engaged in the complicated, carefully balanced evolutions which had once carried the choreutae over the broad expanse of the Greek orchestra, but sang and danced without moving about so much or occupying so much space. In the second place there is no evidence that the chorus and actors were brought into actual physical contact so frequently as in the fifth-century drama (see p. 88, above). Of course, these changes were not due to physical conditions, since in the Roman theaters actors and chorus performed together on a broad, low stage (see p. 78, above). The Romans seem to have had less appreciation for choral performances than the Greeks, and the chorus in contemporary Greek tragedy ought to be thought of as playing even a larger part than appears from the fragments of Roman tragedy.

The difference between tragedy and comedy in their treatment of the chorus arises from the innermost nature of each, as has been well stated by Mr. Cornford: "The comic chorus has not, from the standpoint of art, the justification and utility which kept the chorus alive in tragedy to the last days of ancient drama. In tragedy it is needed for a high function, not to be so well fulfilled by any other means. It has to utter emotions that can be expressed only in lyric poetry, to say things which the audience longs to have said, but which cannot be said by any character on the stage. . . . . Their function, too, is integral and need never decay. Nothing of this applies to the comic chorus. The audience here can completely relieve their feelings in laughter; there are no thoughts or emotions stirred that lie too deep for stage dialogue, no remoter universal meaning to be caught only in the passionate images of lyric poetry."[1]

Playwrights experience considerable difficulty in plausibly motivating the entrances of their characters, and this was a more troublesome problem in ancient times than it is today. I shall revert to the matter later in connection with the actors (see pp. 229 f. and 239, below), but I wish to touch upon it now as regards the chorus. Of course the chorus was so inevitably present in every Greek drama that it might be thought needless to account for its presence at all. As Richter[2] said: "The chorus in Attic tragedy is so firmly established, so much a matter of course, that its entrance does not need to be motivated." Accordingly, in Aeschylus' *Suppliants*, Sophocles' *Philoctetes*, etc., the choral entrance is unmotived. In the *Suppliants*, however, the audience scarcely required to be explicitly told that the sacred precinct with its altars, which is what the orchestra represents in this play, was a natural place of retreat for refugees. Likewise it is quite unnecessary for Neoptolemus' sailors, in the *Philoctetes*, to give an excuse for following their prince and captain ashore. On the contrary, in Aeschylus' *Persians* there is no self-evident reason why the Persian elders should go to the tomb of Darius or why Atossa should expect to meet them there rather than at the palace or the council chamber, and Aeschylus apparently felt no necessity of inventing a pretext. Nevertheless, in most instances the Greek playwrights did motivate their choral entrances. In Aeschylus' *Seven against Thebes* the chorus of maidens, through fear of the invading host, has fled for protection to the images of the gods on the acropolis (vss. 214 and 240). In Aeschylus' *Prometheus Bound* the ocean nymphs have been drawn to the hero's side by the sound of the shackles being bolted upon him (vss. 133 f.). In the same writer's *Libation-Bearers* the maidservants are sent from the palace with offerings for the grave of Agamemnon

---

[1] Cf. *The Origin of Attic Comedy*, p. 107.

[2] Cf. *Zur Dramaturgie des Äschylus* (1892), p. 135.

(vss. 22 f.). In his *Eumenides* the furies sing their first song behind the scenes within the temple at Delphi, where they have been besetting the guilty Orestes; presently Apollo drives them from his sanctuary into the orchestra (vss. 179 ff.). Often the chorus enters in response to the cries of the tragic heroine,[1] or as the bearer of news,[2] or as the result of hearing a rumor;[3] still more often in reply to a summons.[4] "After going through some years of Dionysia it must have been hard not to smile, when the 'shrieks' were raised or the 'proclamation' issued."[5] In Aeschylus' *Eumenides*, vs. 244, Sophocles' *Oedipus at Colonus*, vss. 117 ff., and Aristophanes' *Acharnians*, vss. 280 ff., the chorus comes upon the stage on the track of a transgressor. Occasionally the pretext is extremely trivial, far-fetched, or improbable. In Euripides' *Ion*, vss. 234 f., Creusa's handmaidens have obtained their mistress' permission to view the sights at Delphi. The chorus in Euripides' *Phoenician Maids*, vss. 202 ff., are on their way from Tyre to Delphi to be consecrated to Apollo's service as a thank-offering and chance to be caught in Thebes at the time of the country's invasion. In Euripides' *Iphigenia at Aulis*, vss. 164 ff. and 187 f., Chalcidian women are constrained by curiosity to cross the strait and blushingly visit the Greek camp. In Euripides' *Electra*, vss. 168 ff., the choreutae come to invite Electra to participate with them in an Argive festival in honor of Hera, and when the princess replies that she has "nothing to wear," generously offer to lend her raiment from their store! Nothing more is heard of this motive during the remainder of the play. Finally, the same heroine in Sophocles' *Electra* intimates that the women of the chorus have come to soothe her woes (vss. 129 f.). Now when Aegisthus was home Electra was

[1] Cf. Euripides' *Helen*, vs. 184, and *Medea*, vss. 131 ff.

[2] Cf. Euripides' *Hecabe*, vs. 105, and *Electra*, vss. 168 ff.

[3] Cf. Sophocles' *Maidens of Trachis*, vs. 103, and *Ajax*, vs. 143, Euripides' *Hippolytus*, vss. 129 ff., etc.

[4] Cf. Sophocles' *Oedipus the King*, vs. 144, and *Antigone*, vss. 164 f., Euripides' *Trojan Women*, vss. 143-45, Aristophanes' *Clouds*, vs. 269, *Peace*, vss. 296 ff., *Birds*, vss. 310 f., and *Plutus*, vs. 255, etc.

[5] Cf. Verrall's edition of Euripides' *Ion* (1890), p. lx.

never permitted to leave the palace (cf. vss. 516 ff.). It is only the accident of his absence which allowed her to pass the doors on this occasion. But the choreutae were unaware of his absence (vss. 310 ff.). What reason, then, could they have had to expect that they would be able to meet Electra outside the house and comfort her? Sophocles supplies no answer to this question. Kaibel[1] seems entirely justified in writing: "Ihr Kommen ist durch nichts motivirt als dadurch, dass ein Chor nothwendig ist."

The history and traditions of the Greek theater required a chorus to appear in each drama. But they also required it to render several songs at intervals throughout the play. If we stop to analyze this convention it will surely appear ridiculous enough. How absurd that the subjects and well-wishers of kings and princes should resort to singing and dancing at the crises of their royal fortunes! Dennis[2] sought a *reductio ad absurdum* in the dramatization, *à la grecque*, of the Spanish invasion: "Suppose, then, that an express gives notice to Queen Elizabeth of the landing of the Spaniards upon our coast, and of great number of subjects revolting and running in to them. The Queen, upon the reception of this news, falls a lamenting her condition. . . . . But then, Sir, suppose as soon as the Queen has left off lamenting, the ladies about her, in their ruffs and farthingalls, fell a dancing a *Saraband* to a doleful ditty. Do you think, Sir, that if this had really happened at White-Hall, it would have been possible to have beheld it without laughing, though one had been never so much concerned for his country?" Nevertheless, despite the incongruity, these odes were so much a matter of course that usually not even a motivation was provided for them. Occasionally, however, this was done. For example, in Euripides' *Alcestis*, vss. 423 f., Admetus invites the chorus to "chant an antiphonal strain to the implacable god below," and to the balanced strophe and antistrophe of their song (vss. 435–76) the remains of his wife are borne into the palace.

[1] Cf. p. 89 of his edition (1896).
[2] Cf. John Dennis, *The Impartial Critick* (1693).

In Aeschylus' *Eumenides* the furies have tracked Orestes from Delphi to Athens and at last have overtaken him. But since he has invoked Athena's protection and is clasping her image, they cannot lay hands upon him. Therefore, they resort to a magic incantation to prevent his escaping them again: at vs. 306 they announce "you shall hear this spell to bind you," referring to and motivating the long ode (vss. 307–96) which follows. Again, in Euripides' *Cyclops*, Odysseus asks the chorus to accompany him and his comrades with a song of good cheer (see below).

Sometimes the noise of fifteen lusty choreutae lifting their voices in united song sadly interferes with the verisimilitude of the scene, especially when the dramatic situation imperatively demands silence. The stricken Orestes, in Euripides' play of that name, has at last fallen asleep, guarded by his devoted sister. Enter the chorus to inquire of his condition. Electra groans as she catches sight of them, well assured that they will waken Orestes (vss. 131 ff.). She begs them to be quiet, to stand far away from his bed, to drop their voices still lower. She inquires why they have come; warns them that they will be the death of him if they rouse him; beseeches them to depart, to cease their chanting. It is all in vain. The chorus enjoin quiet, declare that they are obeying her biddings, protest that their singing is but a murmur, invoke winged night to come upon him, etc. They needs must enter and needs must carry their part of the lyric dialogue with Electra, until finally (vs. 211) her fears are realized and Orestes' slumber is broken. Similarly, in Sophocles' *Philoctetes*, Neoptolemus suggests that they give Philoctetes an opportunity to sleep. But the chorus sings an invocation to slumber, which under like circumstances in real life could hardly have had a very soporific effect. Nevertheless, Philoctetes succumbs to it; whereupon the chorus advise Neoptolemus to execute his sinister designs, circumspectly enjoining that his reply to them should be couched in whispered tones! An especially striking instance occurs in Euripides' *Cyclops*. At vs. 601 Polyphemus, well filled with powerful wine, has just entered his cave; Odysseus prays that the liquor will close the monster's

eyelids in sleep and follows him in.   It is not a moment suitable
for any unnecessary noise, such as might tend to keep the
Cyclops awake.   But the satyrs, being alone upon the stage,
have no option but to chant an ode (vss. 608–23).   At its
conclusion Odysseus rushes in with an expostulation:

> Hush, you wild things, for Heaven's sake!—still as death!
> Shut your lips tight together!—not a breath!
> Don't wink, don't cough, for fear the beast should wake
> Ere we twist out his eye with that red stake.   [Way's translation]

Yet it is a foregone conclusion that as soon as he leaves the stage
they will be at it once more.   How can this difficulty be glossed
over ?   The poet makes two suggestions.   Odysseus wishes the
satyrs to pass in and help gouge out the Cyclops' eye, but that,
of course, was theatrically impossible; they prefer to sing an
incantation which will plunge the firebrand, of its own accord,
into their victim's brain (vss. 648 ff.).   We have just seen that
magic as a motive passed muster with Aeschylus, but it was
different with Euripides.   Odysseus indignantly ignores their
offer, and after a few words of reproach he actually requests them
to cheer on himself and his comrades at their dangerous task
(vs. 653).   A choral song in this tenor immediately follows
(vss. 655–62).   Thus, within the space of thirty lines, with no
essential change in the situation, Odysseus first commands the
chorus to be quiet and then urges them to sing!

The history and traditions of the Greek theater, the necessity
of delivering songs at frequent intervals, and the difficulty of
motivating the withdrawal of the chorus and its later return to
the scene almost demanded the uninterrupted presence of the
chorus upon the stage.   The some half-dozen exceptions that
are known to us outside of New Comedy will be discussed later
(see pp. 250 f., below).   How unnatural this convention would
be can be realized from Euripides' *Bacchanals*, in which Pentheus
arrested Dionysus and took active measures against the Bac-
chantes upon Mt. Cithaeron and yet allowed a chorus of the
new god's devotees (and foreigners at that) to remain practically
unmolested before his palace throughout the play.   What a

baneful effect so rigid and arbitrary a rule had upon any compli-
cation of plot can readily be imagined. The situation was racily
described by Gray:[1] "How could Macbeth and his wife have laid
the design for Duncan's murder? What could they have said
to each other in the hall at midnight, not only if a chorus, but
if a single mouse, had been stirring there? Could Hamlet have
met the ghost, or taken his mother to task in their company?
If Othello had said a harsh word to his wife before them, would
they not have danced to the window and called the watch?"
In the *Agamemnon*, Clytemnestra had to address to her returning
lord words of loyal greeting the falsity of which she knew the
chorus was well aware of. Aeschylus strove to surmount the
difficulty by having the queen turn first to the choreutae:
"Reverend citizens of Argos, I feel no shame to mention my
husband-loving ways before you, for as we mortals grow older
we lose such blushing fear" (vss. 855 ff.). We are to suppose
that her effrontery in this and other respects intimidated the
meticulous elders and prevented their denouncing her to Agamemnon. In Sophocles' *Oedipus the King*, Creon is bringing an
oracular response from Delphi and meets the king before the
Theban palace. In reply to Oedipus' eager question he lets his
eyes rest on the choreutae for a moment and says: "If you would
hear while these are near, I am ready to speak; or else to go
within." In real life the second alternative probably would have
been adopted; on the Greek stage it was impossible (cf. pp. 237-41,
below). Accordingly, Oedipus makes answer as follows: "Speak
before all, for I bear more sorrow for these than for my own life"
(vss. 91-94). In Sophocles' *Electra*, Orestes discovers himself
and his design to his sister in the presence of the chorus, "so
that he entrusts a secret, upon which his empire and life depends,
in the hands of sixteen women."[2] The implication is that a body
of women cannot keep a secret under any circumstances. Yet
Sophocles has done what he could. At vs. 1202 Orestes' identity is not yet revealed, but his sympathy has begun to make

[1] Cf. Tovey, *Letters of Thomas Gray*, II, 293 f.
[2] Cf. Dennis, *op. cit.*

Electra suspicious. She inquires: "Can it be that you are some unknown kinsman?" And when Orestes, glancing at the chorus, replies: "I would answer, if these as friends were present," she reassures him by saying: "But they are friends, so that you can speak without mistrust." This device was borrowed by Euripides in his *Orestes*, vss. 1103 f. Pylades says: "Silence now, for I put small trust in women," meaning the chorus; but Orestes replies: "Fear not, for these are friends to us."

In general, the constant presence of the chorus bore more heavily upon Euripides than upon either Aeschylus or Sophocles, since his plots were more complicated than theirs. Usually the Euripidean choruses are bound to secrecy by an oath or promise. But this is only to shift the problem, not to solve it. In real life groups of people do not take such oaths without an adequate reason. In his *Hippolytus*, vss. 710–14, the chorus swear by Artemis to conceal their knowledge of Phaedra's guilt, and they remain true to their oath, though by their so doing the innocent Hippolytus is brought to ruin and death before their eyes. But their willingness to take such an oath is without motive except as one is implied in their kindly feeling toward the heroine. In Euripides' *Iphigenia among the Taurians* and *Helen* the choruses consist of Greek slaves, who would naturally, because of racial ties, plot against their barbarian masters in order to help their fellow-countrywomen. Other reasons, however, are cited. In both plays the actors promise to rescue the chorus as well as themselves (vss. 1067 f. and 1387 ff., respectively). In the *Iphigenia* an additional motive for choral secrecy is found in an appeal to sex loyalty: "We are women," says Iphigenia, "a sex most staunch to one another, most trustworthy in keeping common counsel" (vss. 1061 f.). The same plea recurs, in an intensified form, in Euripides' *Medea*. Theatrical conditions compelled Medea to take the chorus into her confidence, and she bases her request for their silence not only upon the ground of their common womanhood but also upon the fact that she is alone, sadly wronged, and in distress (vss. 230–66). But this chorus consists of Corinthian women in whose sight Medea must be a foreigner, nay worse, a barbarian. It is so utterly improbable that womanly sympathy should cause Greek women to acquiesce in a barbarian's plans for the assassination of their sovereign and his daughter that Professor Verrall[1] supposed a chorus to have been mechanically added in a subsequent revision (our present text) to a play originally written for private presentation without a chorus. On the other hand, the chorus are occasionally permitted to act as real people would and communicate their secret. Thus, in Euripides' *Ion*, vss. 666 f., Xuthus threatens his wife's handmaidens with death if they betray to her the supposed fact that Ion is his son. Nevertheless, this is exactly what they do, declaring to her: "It shall be told, though I die twice over" (vs. 760); and thus they precipitate one of the most thrilling scenes in Greek tragedy. This is a characteristic product of Greek dexterity. Not content to surmount a troublesome obstacle, they actually derive an advantage from it.

We have seen that it was practically impossible for the chorus to leave the scene of action during the play. This convention was particularly awkward when circumstances arose which would naturally demand their presence elsewhere. Such a situation was most frequently brought about by a murder or suicide just behind the scenes. Up to some thirty years ago an explanation of the chorus' failure to pass through the back scene under such circumstances might be sought in the physical conditions, since until then it was supposed that the Greek actors had stood upon a stage ten or twelve feet above the chorus (see p. 78, above). This interpretation never had more than half a leg to stand upon, inasmuch as the extant plays prove conclusively that, whatever the physical conditions, intercourse between actors and chorus was quite feasible and was often resorted to (see p. 88, above); but it lost the slightest claim to acceptance after Dörpfeld's excavations and a re-examination of the evidence showed that during the classical period of Greek drama chorus and actors had stood upon the same level (see

[1] *Four Plays of Euripides* (1905), pp. 125–30.

p. 117, above). Moreover, it is illuminating to note that the chorus found it as difficult to leave the scene of action during the play by the side entrances as by the doors in the background. By vs. 1070 of Sophocles' *Philoctetes*, Odysseus and Neoptolemus have gained possession of Heracles' bow and are preparing to return to their ship. As the chorus consists of sailors, these would naturally leave with their commander. But the play was not to end at this point, and the poet wished the chorus to sing at vs. 1095. Accordingly, Philoctetes appeals to the chorus not to desert him (vss. 1070 f.), and upon their referring the request to Neoptolemus he replies, very improbably, that at the risk of his being considered soft-hearted they may tarry until the ship is ready to sail and that possibly by that time Philoctetes will have decided to accompany them to Troy (vss. 1074–79). No; the convention was derived from the fact that by origin the chorus was an integral part of Greek drama and had a rôle to play which required its continual presence; that is to say, leaving the stage is not, with rare exceptions, "the kind of action that a < Greek > chorus can ever perform."[1]

But as already intimated, the difficulty arose most frequently and most glaringly when murder was threatened or was actually being committed behind the scenes. In such a case "to say that convention prevented the chorus from entering the palace may be true; but such a convention was of little assistance to a great dramatist who keenly felt the force of cause and effect. Such an artist knows that even convention must be met in a natural way. Does convention prevent the entrance of the chorus into the palace? Then common sense and ordinary conduct must as well, else there is an unreality which is absent in a work of art" (Stephenson, *op. cit.*, p. 44). As successful a solution of the problem as any Greek dramatist ever devised occurs in Aeschylus' *Agamemnon*. The chorus consists of Argive elders, who must not be represented as cravenly betraying their lord. On the other hand, when Agamemnon's cry of agony is heard at vs. 1343, they cannot be allowed to rush in and prevent his mur-

[1] Cf. Murray, *Euripides and His Age* (1913), p. 238.

der. This would alter the whole course of the story and at the same time would cause an unparalleled lacuna in the action of the play by leaving the stage, for a considerable interval, absolutely bare of performers. As soon as Agamemnon's voice is heard, the choreutae fall into a wrangle, each declaring his opinion in turn (vss. 1346–71); but before they can reach a decision and act upon it, Clytemnestra and the bodies of her husband and of Cassandra are revealed.

Except that the debate is here so extended, the same device occurs again and again. In Euripides' *Hecabe*, Polymestor has been enticed within the tents, and cries out that he has been blinded and his children slain but that his enemies will not escape (vss. 1034–40). The chorus of Trojan captive women ask whether they ought not to rush in to help thwart this counter-stroke (vss. 1042 f.), but at once Hecabe appears and obviates the need of their entering (vs. 1044). Similarly, in Euripides' *Andromache*, vss. 815–19, Hermione's nurse declares that her strength has given out in trying to prevent her mistress' suicide, and beseeches the chorus to enter the palace and lend their aid. The slaves acknowledge that they hear the cries of servants from within, which confirm the nurse's story; but at this moment Hermione herself slips from the restraining clutches of her attendants and darts upon the stage. Less successful is the scene in Euripides' *Hippolytus*. At vss. 776 ff. a handmaid raises the cry that Phaedra has hanged herself, and begs someone to cut her down. One semi-chorus inquires whether they should not render this service, but the other rejoins that there are attendants nearer at hand to do so and that officious meddlers often endanger their own lives! Immediately thereafter a further cry announces that the queen is dead past recovery (vss. 786 f.). One more illustration will suffice. The failure of the chorus to rescue Medea's children is doubly motived: first, by the Colchian's threat to anyone that might interfere (Euripides' *Medea*, vss. 1053 f.), and secondly, by the fact that the palace doors are barred, so that Jason's servants have to break them down (vss. 1312 ff.). It has also been conjectured that the

chorus' description of Medea as iron-hearted and like a rock
(vss. 1279 ff.) is intended to suggest that they felt unable to cope
with so masterful and relentless a creature.   This explanation
finds some support in the undoubted fact that the necessity of
comparative inactivity on the part of the chorus had much to do
with the Greek tragedians' fondness for choruses of women and
old men.   In speaking of the elders in Aeschylus' *Agamemnon*
Cornford[1] says that they "cannot enter the palace; not because
the door is locked, nor yet because they are feeble old men.
Rather they are old men because an impassible barrier of convention is forming between chorus and actors, *and their age gives
colour to their powerlessness.*"   In concluding this paragraph I wish
to point out that the chorus's inability to enter the background
during the play existed quite independently of the threat of
murder.   In Euripides' *Ion* Creusa's maidservants, by the
express permission of their mistress, examine and admire the
sculpture on the outer walls of Apollo's temple at Delphi (vss.
183–218).   In real life it would be inevitable that a crowd bent
on sight-seeing should soon wish to pass inside and view the
omphalus and other objects of interest; and this, of course, the
poet cannot allow.   Accordingly, when the point is raised (vss.
219 ff.), Ion replies that it is forbidden to enter the inner fane
except after the offer of sacrifice.

Finally, even at the very end of the play the chorus could not
leave the stage except after the actors or in their company.
This convention arose from the same conditions as have already
been mentioned, but produced some incongruities of its own.
For example, in Euripides' *Iphigenia among the Taurians* and
Helen the Greek slaves in the choruses are promised, as a reward
for their silence and help, a return to Greece (see p. 156, above).
But since in the latter play Helen and Menelaus make their
final exit nearly five hundred lines before the end of the piece,
it is manifestly impossible for the chorus to be spared.   Consequently they are most unconscionably left in the lurch without
a single word being said of their rescue.   In the *Iphigenia* they

[1] *Thucydides Mythistoricus* (1907), p. 147 (italics mine)

fare no better up to the time when Orestes' ship is driven back to land; but in the final outcome Athena appears and includes the chorus among those whom King Thoas must allow to depart in peace (vss. 1467 f.).   Possibly a desire to keep this promise to the chorus was one of the considerations that induced the poet to have the ship forced back to shore and thus to make a divine apparition unavoidable.

So inextricably is the chorus interwoven with Greek drama that its influence may be detected almost anywhere.   I have traced some of the broader effects, however, and in subsequent chapters minor results will be mentioned in connection with other factors.

Ἐκεῖ (sc. ἐν τοῖς ἀγῶσι) μεῖζον δύνανται νῦν τῶν ποιητῶν οἱ ὑποκριταί.—ARISTOTLE.

CHAPTER III

THE INFLUENCE OF ACTORS[1]

The dithyramb and the comus, together with their derivatives, early tragedy and early comedy, were entirely choral. Actors were first developed in tragedy (see pp. 16 and 48, n. 1, above). Inasmuch as the early dithyramb and early tragedy were devoted to the worship of Dionysus and since their choreutae were his attendant sprites (satyrs or sileni), it followed that their songs would mostly take the form of prayers addressed to him, hymns in his honor, or odes descriptive of his adventures, sufferings, etc. A lyric duet between the coryphaeus and the other choreutae was also possible. Such performances bore much the same relationship to later tragedy that the modern oratorio bears to a sacred opera. That is to say, the choreutae were not differen-

[1] In addition to the works mentioned on pp. xvii and xx f., above, cf. Detscheff, *De Tragoediarum Graecarum Conformatione Scaenica ac Dramatica* (1904); Rees, "The Meaning of Parachoregema," *Classical Philology*, II (1907), 387 ff.; *The So-called Rule of Three Actors in the Classical Greek Drama* (1908); "The Number of the Dramatic Company in the Period of the Technitae," *American Journal of Philology*, XXXI (1910), 43 ff., and "The Three Actor Rule in Menander," *Classical Philology*, V (1910), 291 ff.; O'Connor, *Chapters in the History of Actors and Acting in Ancient Greece* (1908); Leo, *Der Monolog im Drama* (1908), and *Plautinische Forschungen*[2] (1912), pp. 226 ff.; Listmann, *Die Technik des Dreigesprächs in der griechischen Tragödie* (1910); Kaffenberger, *Das Dreischauspielergesetz in der griechischen Tragödie* (1911); Foster, *The Divisions in the Plays of Plautus and Terence* (1913); Stephenson, *Some Aspects of the Dramatic Art of Aeschylus* (1913); Graf, *Szenische Untersuchungen zu Menander* (1914); and Conrad, *The Technique of Continuous Action in Roman Comedy* (1915), reviewed by Flickinger in *Classical Weekly*, X (1917), 147 ff.

Fig. 66 is taken from Baumeister's *Denkmäler*, Fig. 1637, and belongs to the Roman period. The apparent height of the tragic actors is said to have been increased by means of the ὄγκος projecting above the head and of thick-soled boots (κόθορνοι), both represented in Fig. 66. The employment of such paraphernalia rests upon late evidence, however, and has been disputed for fifth-century tragedy; cf. for example Smith, "The Use of the High-soled Shoe or Buskin in Greek Tragedy of the Fifth or Fourth Centuries B.C.," *Harvard Studies*, XVI (1905), 123 ff. For the costumes of comic actors, see pp. 46 f., above.

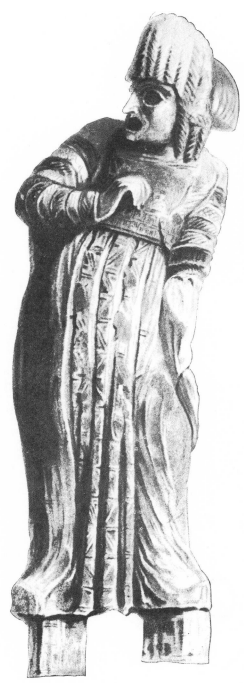

FIG. 66

IVORY STATUETTE OF A TRAGIC ACTOR

See p. 162, n. 1

tiated in character, and there was no dramatic impersonation (μίμησις); despite their costumes the chorus sang as human worshipers of Dionysus, not in accordance with their character as sileni. From the duet between the coryphaeus and the other choreutae it was only a step, but a highly important one, no longer to think of the coryphaeus as one silenus among his fellows but as Dionysus himself in the midst of his followers, and then to set him off by himself as an actor in contradistinction to the choreutae and their (new) coryphaeus. This innovation was the work of Thespis, and however long the name "tragedy" may already have been applied to the previous performances this step marked the first beginning of tragedy in the modern sense (see p. 16 f., above). Now that the new actor had to impersonate Dionysus, the necessity rested likewise upon the sileni in the chorus to live up to their own, previously neglected, character. It was not long until by a change of mask and costume the actor was enabled to represent other personages as well as Dionysus himself. This practice made possible a much more involved type of drama than the limited resources would at first glance seem to permit.

Aeschylus' earliest extant play, the *Suppliants*, belongs to the two-actor period, but employs the second actor so sparingly as to afford a very good idea of the possibilities of the one-actor play. Omitting the choral odes, the action runs as follows: The fifty daughters of Danaus (the chorus) seek sanctuary near Argos to escape the unwelcome suit of their cousins. At vs. 176 Danaus begins to admonish his daughters and a dialogue (vss. 204–33) ensues between them. At vs. 234 the king of Argos enters and engages with the chorus in a dialogue and a lyric duet (vss. 234–417). During this scene Danaus is present, silent, inactive, and all but unnoticed; cf. vs. 318. Of course in a one-actor play this character must have been removed so that the single actor might reappear as the king. But that could easily have been managed and would affect the present piece in no essential way. After an ode the dialogue between the king and the chorus is resumed (vss. 438–523), broken in upon only by a brief conversation between the king and Danaus (vss. 480–503). The former instructs Danaus how to supplicate the citizens in the town and, upon the latter's request for protection, orders attendants to accompany him. Here for the first time are the two actors simultaneously employed, but their words serve no more important purpose than to motivate the exit of one of them. At vs. 523 the king likewise withdraws. At vs. 600 Danaus reappears and with but a slight interruption on the part of his daughters (vss. 602–4) informs them that the Argives have decided to shield them (vss. 600 f., 605–24). At vs. 710 Danaus descries the suitors' fleet in the distance and declares, "I will return with helpers and defenders" (vs. 726). Nevertheless, the scene is continued until vs. 775, when Danaus departs to spread the alarm, incidentally releasing this actor to play the part of the suitors' herald. At vs. 836 the herald enters and to the accompaniment of a lyric duet between himself and the chorus tries to drag the Danaids away. At vs. 907 this attempt at violence is brought to a standstill by the king's return. The following altercation between the herald and the king (vss. 907–53) provides the only bit of genuine dramatic conflict, visually represented, in the play and the only instance of both actors being fully made use of together. In a one-actor play such a passage would have been impossible but could have been presented indirectly by means of a messenger's narrative. At vs. 953 the herald withdraws, discomforted, and the king turns to the chorus (vss. 954–65). In reply the chorus ask that their father be returned to them (vss. 966 ff.). The interval having been sufficient to enable the actor to shift from the mask and costume of the herald to those of Danaus, the latter re-enters at vs. 980 and converses with his daughters until the final ode. Of all the extant plays of Aeschylus the *Suppliants* probably makes the slightest appeal to the modern student. Its principal value for us lies in the fact that it could readily be revamped for presentation by one actor and in the light which it thus sheds upon the character of one-actor drama.

Several times in this play, as appears from the foregoing outline, an actor participates in a dialogue with the chorus. It was not the practice for the choral part in such dialogues to be spoken by all the choreutae in unison, but by the chorus leader alone. Thus, though a sharp distinction was drawn between actors and chorus, the former being furnished by the state and the latter by private means (cf. pp. 270 f., below), yet the coryphaeus served as a bond of connection between the two. We have seen how the first actor was developed from the chorus leader; doubtless the successive additions to the number of actors were suggested in each case by the advantages arising from this quasi-histrionic function of the coryphaeus. Thus in addition to the regular actors, at each stage of development the tragic poet always had at his disposal also one quasi-actor for carrying on his dialogues. And the comic poet always had two such quasi-actors, since the leaders of the two semi-choruses could be used in this way (see p. 44, above). In the one-actor period this quasi-histrionic function of the coryphaeus resulted in a convention which continued long after the necessity for it had passed away. It is obvious that at that juncture the single actor could converse with no one but the chorus. This practice became so stereotyped that in the two-actor period whenever a character came into the presence of the chorus and another actor he directed his remarks to the chorus before turning to the other character. Of course oftentimes this was the natural thing to do. But the force of tradition is seen in the fact that the principle was sometimes observed under unfavorable conditions. Thus, as we have already observed, in the *Suppliants* the king enters at vs. 234 and at once begins a dialogue with the chorus, ignoring their father until vs. 480. Greek respect for age and partiality for the masculine sex make this arrangement in a Greek play very unnatural. Again, in the *Persians* a messenger from Greece ignores his queen (vss. 249 ff.) and reports the Persian disaster to the chorus of elders. Not until vs. 290 does Atossa address him, and in typical Greek fashion Aeschylus strives to make her words gloss over the unreality of his characters' compliance with convention. "For a long time have I kept silence," she begins, "dumbfounded by catastrophe. This ill exceeds my power to tell or ask our woes." The same convention persisted even into the three-actor period.   Clytemnestra's husband has been gone ten years or more, yet she must excuse herself to the chorus (Aeschylus' *Agamemnon*, vss. 855–78) before greeting her lord (see p. 155, above).   Another instance occurs in Euripides' *Children of Heracles*, vss. 120 ff.   Moreover the coryphaeus sometimes exercises an important influence upon the plot.   For example, in Aeschylus' *Libation-Bearers*, vss. 766 ff., it is the coryphaeus who induces the servant to alter the wording of the summons with which she is sent to Aegisthus.   By this device he comes unescorted and falls an easy victim to the conspirators.

In view of the normal employment of the coryphaeus as a quasi-actor, Aeschylus took an easy and obvious step, or rather half-step, in advance when he introduced the second actor.   We have seen that the *deuteragonist* was already made use of, though sparingly, in the *Suppliants*.   Also the *Persians*, the *Seven against Thebes* (except possibly the closing scene; see p. 175, below), and the *Prometheus Bound* require but two actors for presentation.   The great advantage accruing from the second actor is manifest.   Instead of being compelled to resort to a messenger's report of an altercation or dialogue between two personages, the playwright was now enabled to bring the characters face to face in person upon his stage.   On the other hand, so limited a number of actors often seriously embarrassed the dramatist in the economy of his play.   Perhaps the best example of this is afforded by Aeschylus' *Prometheus*.   In the opening scene Cratos and Bia (Strength and Force) drag Prometheus to a remote spot in Scythia and Hephaestus nails him to a crag. How can these four characters be presented by two actors?   In the first place Bia has no speaking part, and mutes were freely employed in addition to the regular actors.   In the second place Prometheus was represented by a wooden figure.   This explains how it was possible for a nail to be driven right through his breast (vss. 64 f.).   It explains also why so great emphasis is laid upon the fastening process; first the hands are pinned down (vs. 55), then the arms (vs. 60), the breast (vs. 65) and sides (vs. 71), and finally the legs (vs. 74).   Thus the immobility and lifelessness of the supposed Prometheus are accounted for. Neither Hephaestus' sympathy nor Cratos' insults elicit a single word of reply from his lips. Although this silence arises naturally from the Titan's unyielding disposition, yet the real reason lies in the use of a dummy. At vs. 81 Hephaestus retires, and after six lines of further insults Cratos follows him. A slight pause would naturally ensue, so that Prometheus might be sure that his enemy had passed beyond the sound of his voice. These intervals enabled the former actor to take his place at some crack or opening behind the lay figure and break Prometheus' speech-lessness (vs. 88). The other actor reappears in a succession of rôles throughout the play, as Oceanus (vs. 284), Io (vs. 561), and Hermes (vs. 944); but these shifts were easily managed.

Soon after Sophocles' first appearance (468 B.C. or possibly 471 B.C.)[1] he introduced the third actor. First of all this innovation permitted a larger number of characters to be presented. In Aeschylus' two-actor plays the characters number three in the *Suppliants* in addition to the chorus and coryphaeus, four in the *Persians*, six in the *Prometheus*, and five in *Seven against Thebes*. In the three-actor plays Aeschylus' characters range from five to seven, Sophocles' from five to nine, and Euripides' from seven to eleven, except that Euripides' satyr-play, the *Cyclops*, has but three characters. Secondly, a third actor allowed greater flexibility in handling entrances and exits. An artificial pause, more or less improbably motived, to enable an actor to change his mask and costume before appearing in another rôle would now be less frequently required (see further, p. 231, below). Thirdly, it allowed three personages to appear side by side in the same scene, whereby in turn a certain aesthetic effect became possible. I refer to the varied emotions which one actor's statements or conduct sometimes produce in two other characters. An excellent illustration is afforded by the scene with the Corinthian messenger in Sophocles' *Oedipus the King*, vss. 924 ff. As the awful conviction is brought home to Jocaste that

[1] Cf. Capps, "The Introduction of Comedy into the City Dionysia," *University of Chicago Decennial Publications*, VI, 269, n. 37.

Oedipus is her son as well as her husband, she rushes from the stage to hang herself; but Oedipus, on the contrary, still lacking the fatal clue, becomes elated at the prospect of discovering his parents' identity. Similarly in the same playwright's *Electra*, vss. 660 ff, the false report of Orestes' death cheers his mother with the assurance that her murder of Agamemnon must now remain unavenged, but plunges Electra into the desperation of despair. Such situations would have been impossible in the two-actor drama. Finally, the introduction of a third actor contributed to the decay of the chorus. We have already noted in the last chapter how the importance of the chorus steadily declined, especially in comedy. But this change was quantitative as well as qualitative. In the prehistrionic period the chorus and its coryphaeus, from the nature of the case, monopolized every line. After Thespis had brought in the first actor the chorus yielded but a small place to its rival. Even in the two-actor period in our earliest extant play, the *Suppliants*, the chorus sang five hundred and sixty-five verses out of a total of a thousand and seventy-four, and in addition to this the coryphaeus spoke ninety verses. In six of Aeschylus' seven extant pieces the choral element varies from three-fifths to about one-half of the whole play. The *Prometheus*, for special reasons, is exceptional, the fraction being only one-sixth. The effect of the third actor is seen in the fact that in Sophocles the proportion varies from one-fourth to one-seventh and in Euripides from one-fourth to one-eighth.

The question naturally arises, Why were the Greek dramatists so slow in increasing the number of actors? This was due partly to a paucity of histrionic talent and partly to difficulty in mastering the dramatic technique of the dialogue.

In the dithyramb and the prehistrionic drama the poet was his own coryphaeus. Accordingly when Thespis introduced the first actor he served in that capacity himself, appointing another as coryphaeus. So did Phrynichus, Aeschylus, and the other dramatists of that period. Since there were then no retired actors and no opportunity to serve an apprenticeship, it is obvious that these early poets had to teach themselves how to act. At this stage it was not possible for anyone except a playwright to become an actor, and actors must have been correspondingly scarce. The situation improved somewhat after Aeschylus introduced the second actor, for though the poets still carried the major rôles it now became possible for men with natural histrionic ability to develop it and gain experience in minor parts. By the time of Sophocles, actors had become so plentiful, relatively speaking, that he could increase the number employed by each poet from two to three and could retire from personal participation in the public presentation of his works. His weak voice is said to have been responsible for this second innovation; but he occasionally appeared in scenes where this weakness was no great hindrance, e.g., as a harp player in *Thamyris* and as an expert ball player in *Nausicaa*. By 449 B.C. the profession was so large and its standing so well recognized that a contest of tragic actors was made an annual event in the program of the City Dionysia. This course of development reveals one reason for the long duration of the one- and two-actor stages in Greek drama.

We shall now pass to the second reason. In the prehistrionic period a series of lyric questions and answers between chorus and coryphaeus was the nearest approach to a dialogue that was possible (see p. 10, above). With the invention of the first actor this interplay of question and answer, still lyrical in form, could be carried on by the actor and the chorus (including the coryphaeus). Such a duet, which came to be known as a *commus*, continued in use, especially for dirges, as long as the chorus lasted. Side by side with this, however, there quickly developed a non-lyric interchange of spoken lines between actor and coryphaeus. But not until the second actor was added did true dialogue in the modern sense become possible. Yet the poets could not at once make full use of even these simple resources. Our analysis of Aeschylus' *Suppliants* (pp. 163 f., above) shows that in two instances Danaus stood silent and unaddressed during a conversation between the other actor and the

coryphaeus.   Moreover, priority of usage constrained the playwrights to give the actor-coryphaeus dialogue precedence over
actor-actor dialogue (cf. pp. 165 f., above).   They seemed unable
to weld the two types together with a technique which would
employ all three persons at once.   In the three-actor period the
embarrassment of riches made their helplessness the more
striking.   "A" might engage in a dialogue with "B" while
"C" remained inactive; then with "C" while "B" was silent;
and finally "B" and "C" might converse, with "A" remaining
passive.   Often the transitions are marked or the longer speeches
set off by a few more or less perfunctory verses (usually two)
spoken by the coryphaeus.   The type is not frequently worked
out as completely as I have just indicated, but the principle is
illustrated on a lesser scale in almost every play.   Compare, for
example, Euripides' *Helen*, vss. 1186–1300, and *Andromache*,
vss. 547–766.   Such an arrangement, needless to say, falls far
short of a genuine trialogue or tetralogue.   Yet we must not be
unfair in condemning this practice.   The Greek poets were
feeling their way and could not immediately attain to every
refinement.   Even in Shakespeare and the modern drama,
despite centuries of continuous experimentation and the numerous examples of superior technique, the tandem arrangement of
dialogue is still not uncommon.

A half-step in advance consisted in the silent actor interrupt-
ing the dialogue with some electrifying utterance.   For example,
in Aeschylus' *Libation-Bearers* (458 B.C.), Clytemnestra's appeal
to Orestes on the score of her motherhood stays his hand in the
very act of murdering her, and he weakly turns to his trusted
friend, Pylades, for guidance.   The latter's ringing response,

> Wilt thou abjure half Loxias' behest,
> The word of Pytho, and thy sacred troth?
> Hold all the world thy foe rather than Heaven
> [vss. 900–903, Warr's translation],

is as effective as if uttered by the god in person, and urges Orestes
on to the deadly deed.   These are the only words that Pylades
utters in the whole tragedy.   In another play belonging to the

same trilogy, the *Eumenides*, Aeschylus rose to the full possibilities of his histrionic resources—Orestes, the coryphaeus, Apollo, and Athena all participating in the conversation between vss. 746 and 753. Similarly, in Sophocles' *Oedipus at Colonus*, Antigone, Oedipus, Ismene, and the coryphaeus all speak between vss. 494 and 506, and in Euripides' *Suppliants* the herald, the coryphaeus, Adrastus, and Theseus divide four lines among them (vss. 510–13). But after all, such instances are comparatively rare and seldom extend over a very long passage.

In contradistinction to tragic practice Aristophanes in the last quarter of the fifth century employed not merely three but occasionally even four comic actors in ensemble scenes. For example, in the *Lysistrata*, vss. 78–246, Calonice, Myrrhina, Lysistrata, and Lampito engage in a running fire of conversation quite in the modern manner. Again, in the *Frogs*, vss. 1411 ff., Dionysus, Aeschylus, Euripides, and Pluto all have speaking parts, although the last two do not address one another. In the same play (vs. 555) Dionysus utters three words while three other participants in the dialogue are present. Under similar circumstances Pseudartabus interposes two verses (100 and 104) in the *Acharnians*, and Triballus parts of five verses (1615, 1628 f., and 1678 f.) in the *Birds*. In these passages the comic coryphaei have no speaking parts. Trialogues are not so rare in Old Comedy as to justify an enumeration of the instances, and they are sometimes embellished by the participation of the coryphaei. Nevertheless, the old tandem arrangement is still the more common one when three characters are present.

We thus pass from one problem to another: Why this disparity between the technique of tragedy and comedy? Must we suppose that the comic dramatists were more clever artists than their tragic confreres? By no means. Comedy was more mobile and reacted more quickly to the actual conditions of contemporaneous life; tragedy was more conventional, never could free itself entirely from the power of tradition, and could only slowly modify that tradition. The situation is clearly revealed in the field of meter. In the iambic trimeters written by Aeschylus a trisyllabic substitution (tribrach, anapaest, or dactyl) for the pure disyllabic iambus occurs only once in about twenty-five verses. In the earliest plays of Euripides such resolutions appear once in sixteen verses but gradually increase to a maximum of one in every alternate verse.[1] On the contrary, in the comedies of Aristophanes they are found in almost every line. Now we are not to suppose that Euripides required a lifetime in order to learn how to use resolutions with freedom or that he was never able to gain the facility of Aristophanes. Nor are we to suppose that Sophocles, whose iambics resemble those of Aeschylus, was never able to master this expedient. In both cases we see merely the power which convention and tradition exercised over tragedy. And the same influences made themselves felt in the comparatively archaic technique of tragic dialogue and tended to keep the tragic playwrights from making full use of their resources.

But were the resources of the tragic writers as great as those of the comedians? We have seen how the first, second, and third actors were added to Greek tragedy. Is there reason to believe that the tragedians of Athens ever followed the comedians in employing a larger number? Until recently a negative reply to this has been accepted without serious question, but in 1908 Professor Rees challenged the tradition. Three years later the old view was defended by Dr. Kaffenberger. Although neither has been able fully to establish his contentions, yet the discussion has helped to clear the air, defined the issues more sharply, and really settled certain important points. For one thing, since 1844 it has generally been taken for granted that three actors were the maximum for Old Comedy as well as for tragedy. But the passages just cited from Aristophanes would seem to be decisive against this view, and all the objections to the presentation of Greek tragedy by only three actors apply with still greater force to Old Comedy. Even Dr. Kaffenberger (*op. cit.*, pp. 9 f.) accepts this conclusion, and it is an invaluable result of Professor Rees's investigations that he has banished this phase

---

[1] Cf. Tanner, *Transactions of American Philological Association*, XLVI (1915), 185–87. For Sophocles, cf. Jebb's *Electra*, p. lvii.

of the subject from the field of controversy. Moreover, they are both agreed[1] that a fourth actor seems sometimes to be required also for New Comedy. It must be added, however, that Dr. Graf (*op. cit.*, pp. 29 ff.) dissents. But in any case the question has been restricted, so far as the fifth century is concerned, to the practice in tragedy.

It can be said at once that if we are willing to grant that the Greeks made use of certain desperate expedients it is physically possible to stage all the extant tragedies with three actors. But these expedients are so offensive to modern feeling as to be tolerable only as a last resort. It will be best to begin at a point where comparative agreement is possible, viz., with Aeschylus' earlier plays, which nearly everyone would admit were intended for two actors alone. Do they reveal any indication of this limitation?

In the analysis of Aeschylus' *Suppliants* on p. 164, the reader will remember that Danaus, having declared "I will return with helpers and defenders," took his departure at vs. 775; after an ode, the suitors' herald arrived on the scene (vs. 836) but was balked by the entrance of the Argive king (vs. 907). One would surely expect Danaus to accompany the king, but as a matter of fact he does not reappear until vs. 980. The reason for this is plain—Danaus and the herald are played by the same actor, and consequently the former can return only after the latter's departure at vs. 953. Moreover, Aeschylus sought to gloss over the blemish by having Danaus refer in advance to the possibility of his being slow in spreading the alarm (vs. 730) and by having the chorus request the king to send their father back to them (vss. 968 ff.), as if his absence had been perfectly natural. This incident teaches us four things: (1) A single actor could carry several rôles; the simplicity and sameness of ancient costumes and the ease of slipping them off and on, together with the use of masks by the actors, made this practice more feasible than it is with us. Overzealous classicists have not merely asked us to tolerate this practice but even to admire its results. Thus,

[1] Cf. Rees, *Classical Philology*, V (1910), 291 ff., and Kaffenberger, *op. cit.*, p. 10.

when one character returns to report the death of another the spectators are supposed to have been doubly moved if they could penetrate the messenger's disguise and from the identity of stature, build, and voice recognize the ghost, as it were, of the departed visibly before them (!).[1]   (2) This practice oftentimes necessitated the arbitrary withdrawal of a character from the scene of action and his enforced absence when he would naturally be present.   (3) By inventing an inner reason for this the poet strove to conceal or gloss over his yielding to external need.   (4) The intervals between the withdrawal of Danaus and the entrance of the herald (vss. 776–836) and vice versa (vss. 953–80) afford an inkling as to the length of time required for such shifts in rôles.

Further information is derived from Aeschylus' *Prometheus Bound* (see pp. 166 f., above).   (5) Supernumeraries may be employed for silent parts, e.g., that of Bia.   (6) A part may be divided between a lay figure and an actor, as in the case of Prometheus himself.   From the nature of things, this expedient would not be frequently employed;   but an analogous device (6a) is common, viz., to give the silent portions of a rôle to a mute and the speaking portions to an actor.   (7) The stubborn silence of the mutes and supernumeraries employed according to principles (5) and (6a) is sometimes extremely embarrassing and difficult to motivate.   (4a) The interval required for a "lightning" change from one character to another was much shorter than the *Suppliants* led us to suppose.   Six verses and a slight pause in the action enabled the actor impersonating Hephaestus to withdraw by the side entrance after vs. 81 and to get in position to speak from behind the wooden figure of Prometheus at vs. 88. This conclusion is confirmed by certain evidence in Plautus' translation of Greek comedies, which indicates that about thirteen lines would suffice.[2]

[1] Cf. C. F. Hermann, *De Distributione Personarum inter Histriones in Tragoediis Graecis* (1840), pp. 32–34.

[2] Cf. Prescott, "Three Puer-Scenes in Plautus and the Distribution of Rôles," *Harvard Studies*, XXI (1910), 44.   It ought to be added that some authorities deny that Prometheus was represented by a dummy, believing that this tragedy belonged to the three-actor period (see further, p. 228, below).

Still other principles are derivable from Aeschylus' *Persians*. The ghost of Darius having requested his widow to meet their son Xerxes with a change of raiment, Atossa replies (vss. 849 ff.): "I shall endeavor to meet my son . . . . and," turning to the chorus, "if he comes hither before me, do you comfort him and escort him to his palace." These words are clearly intended to prepare us for her failure to appear in the dénouement, and in fact she does not appear. But since one of the two actors is disengaged in the final scene, at first glance there seems to be no external reason for her absence. It is evident that Aeschylus valued the parts of Atossa and Xerxes so highly that he wanted them both played by the better of his two actors, the *protagonist*. If Atossa had appeared with her son, she must have been impersonated by a different actor than in the opening scenes. The poet preferred to sacrifice verisimilitude somewhat rather than to "split" Atossa's rôle in this fashion. Hence, we must conclude (8) that at any cost star parts were reserved for the leading actor, (9) that split rôles were to be avoided, and (10) that sometimes for purely technical reasons the dramatist would unnaturally keep a character off the stage entirely in certain scenes.

If we could be sure that the final scene of Aeschylus' *Seven against Thebes* is genuine, it would be possible to deduce a final principle. The main support for the charge of interpolation is that this scene in a two-actor play apparently requires three actors. From vs. 961 to vs. 1004 Antigone and Ismene engage in a lyric duet; at vs. 1005 a herald enters and converses with Antigone. From this scene, which I am inclined to accept as genuine (see p. 283, below), we must concede either that a supernumerary could occasionally bear a brief singing (or speaking) part or preferably that the herald, standing in the side entrance concealed from the spectators and already dressed for his own rôle, sang Ismene's share of the duet while a mute went through the dumb show of her part before the audience; at the conclusion of the duet he promptly appeared *in propria persona*. Though the latter alternative is offensive to present-day taste, it is not

unparalleled in the annals of the modern stage.[1]   In any case
one of these alternatives is the last principle (11) to be drawn
from the two-actor drama.

Now these eleven principles are so manifestly operative in the
other Greek tragedies as to raise an irresistible presumption that
some restriction (to three or at most to four actors) applied also
to them.   It would obviously be out of place to pass every play
in review here; I must content myself with a few typical illustrations and then consider the crucial cases.

In order to avenge his daughter, Menelaus is on the point of
murdering her rival (Andromache) and the latter's son when he
is interrupted by the arrival of Peleus, Hermione's father-in-law.
There is no reason why Menelaus should fear the old man's
blusterings; nevertheless he suddenly leaves Hermione in the
lurch and takes his departure with the words:

> Now, seeing that my leisure serveth not,
> Home will I go; for not from Sparta far
> Some certain town there is, our friend, time was,
> But now our foe: against her will I march,
> Leading mine host, and bow her 'neath my sway.
> Soon as things there be ordered to my mind,
> I will return, etc.
>
> [Euripides *Andromache*, vss. 732 ff., Way's translation]

Surely no excuse was ever less convincing than this!   No wonder
Professor Verrall's ingenuity has built up a whole reinterpretation
of the play around it.[2]   The real reason for the sudden leave-
taking is only too apparent—Orestes is presently to make his
appearance (vs. 881) and Menelaus' actor is required for his
rôle.   This exemplifies principles (1), (2), and (3).

Again, in Sophocles' *Maidens of Trachis*, Lichas, Deianira, and
a messenger are on the scene when Deianira spies Iole in a
throng of captives and questions her (vss. 307 ff.).   Iole makes
no reply whatsoever.   Lichas explains her refusal to answer by
stating that from grief and weeping she has not uttered a word

---

[1] Cf. Lewes, *Life of Goethe*[2], p. 424.

[2] Cf. *Four Plays of Euripides* (1905), pp. 1 ff.

since leaving her fatherland (vss. 322 ff.). Since the three actors are already occupied in this scene it is evident that Iole is played by a mute and cannot speak. This illustrates principles (5) and (7).

Still again, up to vs. 1245 of Euripides' *Orestes*, when he enters the palace, Pylades speaks freely. At vs. 1554 Menelaus, Orestes, Hermione, and Pylades enter the scene. The last two are now played by mutes, the third actor appearing as Apollo at vs. 1625. Orestes threatens to kill Hermione; and after vainly striving to deter him Menelaus turns to Pylades with the query (vs. 1591): "Do you, also, share in this murder, Pylades?" What is a mute to do under such circumstances? Orestes relieved the situation by saying: "His silence gives consent; my word will suffice." There can be no doubt that the playwright intended Menelaus' question to create the illusion that Pylades could have spoken had he so desired, principles (6a) and (7).

Euripides avoided an awkward silence of this sort in the *Ion* by leaving Xuthus unrepresented in the final scene, where the three actors speak in other rôles. Xuthus takes his final departure at vs. 675, intending to celebrate for his new-found son a public feast from which the host himself is most strangely absent. The poet prepares us in advance for this contingency by means of Xuthus' words to his son, as reported by a servant at vss. 1130 ff.: "If I tarry in sacrificing to the Birth-gods," a thin pretext, "place the feast before the friends assembled there," principles (1), (2), (3), and (10).

Finally, for the presentation of his *Phoenician Maids*, Euripides must have had a leading actor of great musical attainments. For such a performer the rôles of Jocaste and Antigone were especially adapted, and he seems to have played them both, principle (8). The piece opens with a soliloquy by Jocaste, who withdraws at vs. 87. Immediately a servant appears on the palace roof and tells Antigone to tarry upon the stairs until he can assure himself that there is no one near to see her and to spread scandalous reports of her indiscretion. Thus, Antigone's appearance is delayed for fifteen verses (vss. 88–102), which is sufficient to enable Jocaste's actor to shift to the new rôle, principle (4a). The protagonist continues to play both parts without difficulty, except at vss. 1264 ff. Here Jocaste summons her daughter from the palace and both are present during vss. 1270–82, the latter speaking some six verses. Obviously Antigone's lines in this brief scene must have been delivered by one of the subordinate players, though such splitting of a rôle violates Aeschylean practice, see principle (9). Perhaps the procedure in this case was condoned by the fact that Antigone's part previously and (for the most part) subsequently was entirely lyric, while her few words here are in plain iambics. The difference between the singing and the speaking voice would help to conceal the temporary substitution of another actor. It is true that by assigning Jocaste's and Antigone's rôles to different actors throughout it is possible to distribute the parts in this play among three actors without any difficulty whatever. But this would require us to ignore the peculiar technique of the opening scenes, the true inwardness of which was recognized by ancient commentators.[1]

These examples are by no means exhaustive, but it is high time that we turn to the passages which are of crucial importance to the three-actor theory. In Aeschylus' *Libation-Bearers* a servant has just informed Clytemnestra that her paramour is slain, and she cries out: "Let some one quickly give me an ax to slay a man withal" (vs. 889). We are to suppose that the slave at once makes his exit to comply with her command. She speaks two lines more and Orestes enters. They divide seven more lines between them, and Orestes' purpose is beginning to waver when he catches sight of Pylades entering and asks: "Pylades, what shall I do? Shrink from killing my mother?" Pylades' electrifying response has already been quoted (vss. 900–902; see p. 170, above). Here we have four speaking characters between vss. 886 and 900 and consequently four actors, unless the servant can be transformed into Pylades within the

[1] Cf. the scholium on vs. 93.

space of nine lines, vss. 891–99. This would be a "lightning" change indeed (4a), and it is not surprising that it has been challenged. Yet the ancient scholiast accepts it and I do not believe we are warranted in pronouncing it impossible, especially since the shift is merely from one male character to another.

Another sort of difficulty is presented by Euripides' *Andromache*. Menelaus, Andromache, and her son, Molossus, all have speaking (or singing) parts just before the entrance of Peleus at vs. 547. Since none of the earlier speakers has withdrawn and since Peleus at once begins to talk, it would seem at first glance that we had four actors indisputably before us. Not so, answer the defenders of the traditional view, for it is significant that Molossus becomes utterly dumb after Peleus enters. Therefore we are asked to believe that Molossus was played by a mute throughout, and the actor who is presently to appear as Peleus delivered from behind the scenes the words which belong to Molossus, the mute furnishing only the gestures. We have already found support for this kind of thing in a suspected scene of Aeschylus' *Seven against Thebes*, principle (11), second alternative (pp. 175 f.). But we are asked to go further and believe that this was always the practice when children seemed to sing or speak upon the Greek stage;[1] and in confirmation of this it is pointed out that whenever children have a part, as in Euripides' *Alcestis*, vss. 393 ff. and *Medea*, vss. 1271 ff., one of the actors is always off the scene and available for this purpose. The most difficult example of this problem has recently come to light in the fragments of Euripides' *Hypsipyle*, vss. 1579 ff.[2] The heroine and Amphiaraus converse from the beginning of the fragment to vs. 1589, where the latter makes his exit. Two lines of farewell (vss. 1590 f.) are addressed to him and are assigned by the papyrus to "the children of Hypsipyle." Moreover, they are of such a nature that one line must have been spoken by each of the two youths. Next, *one* of them converses with his mother until Thoas, who also has a speaking part, appears at vs. 1632.

[1] Cf. Devrient, *Das Kind auf der antiken Bühne* (1904).

[2] Cf. *Oxyrhynchus Papyri*, VI (1908), 69.

Here, then, if the children's parts are taken by actors we have four actors required in two successive scenes. The only alternative lies in supposing that mutes impersonated the boys and that Thoas' actor, already dressed for his introit at vs. 1632, spoke their lines from behind the scenes. This would include

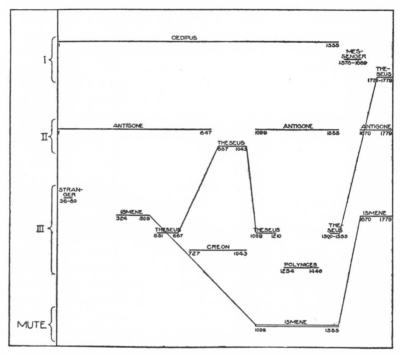

FIG. 67.—Distribution of Rôles to Actors in Sophocles' *Oedipus at Colonus*

twelve lines for one youth and one line, *in a different voice*, for the other.

But the most intractable play of all is Sophocles' *Oedipus at Colonus*. Antigone and Oedipus are on the stage continuously for the first eight hundred and forty-seven verses (the latter until vs. 1555), while the third actor appears successively as a stranger, Ismene, Theseus, and Creon (Fig. 67). So far there is no difficulty; but at this point Creon hopes to bring Oedipus to time by announcing that his guards have already seized Ismene (off-scene) and by having them now drag Antigone away. Creon threatens to carry off Oedipus as well, but at vs. 887 Theseus reappears and prevents further outrage. Note, however, that if only three actors were available Theseus must now be impersonated by Antigone's actor, whereas previously he was represented by the actor who is now playing Creon's part. Such splitting of a rôle is directly contrary to Aeschylean practice, principle (9), and has not in this instance the justification which Euripides had for splitting Antigone's part in the *Phoenician Maids* (p. 178, above). For Theseus' second actor participates in the dialogue more extensively than did hers and his lines are prose throughout, while hers were entirely prose for one actor and (almost) entirely lyric for the other. But there are still other obstacles ahead. At vs. 1043 Creon and Theseus withdraw; after a choral ode Antigone, Theseus, and Ismene rejoin Oedipus (vs. 1099). Inasmuch as Ismene now has no speaking part she is evidently played by a mute, principle (6a). Presumably the other two are represented by the same actors as at the beginning, although this second transfer in Theseus' rôle doubles the chances of the audience noticing the shift. The only alternative, however, is to split also Antigone's rôle at this point. Theseus retires at vs. 1210 and reappears at vs. 1500, his actor having impersonated Polynices in the interval (vss. 1254–1446). At vs. 1555 all the characters exeunt. In the final act a messenger is on the stage from vs. 1578 to vs. 1669. Since Antigone and Ismene enter immediately thereafter (vs. 1670), it is necessary to suppose that they are played by the same actors as at the beginning and that Oedipus has become the messenger. At vs. 1751 Theseus makes his final entrance, represented this time by Oedipus' actor, so that this important rôle is played in turn by each of the three actors! This means splitting Theseus' rôle twice. It is also possible to split his rôle and Ismene's (or Antigone's) once each, or to split his rôle once and to have the final actor in this part sing from behind the scenes the few words which fall to Ismene just before Theseus' last entrance, principle (11). On the other hand, though a fourth actor would obviate all these difficulties we should then have no explanation for the complicated system of entrances and exits and for the strange silence of Ismene during vss. 1099–1555, especially during vss. 1457–99 (see p. 187, below).

I do not consider it warrantable to draw a categorical conclusion from the data considered in the last fifteen paragraphs. But in my opinion the technique of almost every tragedy is explicable only on the assumption that the regular actors were restricted to three; and, as I stated at the beginning, it is physically possible to stage every play with that number. In the case of a few pieces, however, this limitation imposes practices which so outrage the modern aesthetic sense that we instinctively long for some manner of escape. According to late and unreliable evidence an extra performer was called a *parachoregema*. This name would indicate that he was an extra expense to the man who financed each poet's plays (the choregus, see pp. 186 and 270f., below), and consequently that his employment would be determined by the wealth or liberality of the latter. But whether it was in fact possible for the tragic playwrights occasionally to have the services of such an extra, and, if so, under what conditions and how, are questions which in the present state of our knowledge can receive only hypothetical answers. It must be recognized, however, that the paucity of actors in the early days resulted, as we have just seen, in conventions of staging which perhaps were afterward accepted as part of the tradition, however unnecessary they may in the meanwhile have become. The technique of composition also makes it clear in my opinion that extra performers, if such were in fact engaged, were not on a par with the other three nor employed freely throughout the whole play but merely recited or sang a very few lines at those crises in the dramatic economy which were occasioned by the limitation in the number of regular actors.

We have now discovered why the dialogue technique of tragedy was more restricted than that of comedy, but there still remains a further question. Why was the number of actors in tragedy usually or always restricted to three, while four actors were not uncommon in comedy? So long as the poets did their own acting, there was no occasion for the state to interfere in the selection of actors. And this situation would naturally continue for some time after the plays were presented largely or wholly by actors alone—the poets would still have the matter in their charge. In fact there is no reason to suppose that the state interposed its authority before the establishment of the contest for tragic actors at the City Dionysia in 449 B.C. This supposition affords the best explanation for certain ancient notices. For example, Aeschylus is said to have used Cleander as his first actor and afterward to have associated Mynniscus with him, and Sophocles to have employed Tlepolemus continuously. Whatever truth or error may lie back of these statements they imply that in the first half of the fifth century the choice of actors rested solely with the poets. The same implication is inherent in the fact that the second and third actors were introduced by Aeschylus and Sophocles respectively. The poets must have made these additions upon their own initiative. For the state could not have shown partiality by providing Sophocles, for example, with more actors than were furnished the other dramatists in the same contest; and if they were all alike given an increased number, there would be no reason for crediting any one of them with the innovation. The state must have assumed supervision of the histrionic features of the dramatic contests at the same time that it established a prize for actors, viz., in 449 B.C. And since the tragedies of this period were presented by three actors, this number became crystallized, and so was never thereafter, so far as the state was concerned, exceeded in tragedy. Tragedies were added to the Lenaean program and a prize for tragic actors established for that festival simultaneously, about 433 B.C. Naturally the conventional number of tragic actors would be transferred from the older contest to the newer. In comedy, however, the development and tradition were entirely different (see pp. 52 f., above). Primitive comedies in Attica were performed by a double chorus of choreutae, who constituted an undifferentiated crowd and assumed no individual rôles, but sang (or spoke) singly, antiphonally, or in unison. Shortly before 450 B.C. regular actors were introduced in contradistinction to the choreutae; and Cratinus, imitating contemporaneous tragedy, set their number at three. Yet the choreutae did not for a long time entirely give up their old license and self-assertiveness. Consequently, it is not surprising that the number of performers did not remain at the tragic norm. The fact that a contest of comic actors was not established at the Lenaea until about 442 B.C. (at the City Dionysia not until about 325 B.C.) allowed a slight interval for this reaction to assert itself before usage became legalized. Such, then, are the reasons for the number of actors being less restricted in comedy than in tragedy.

For about a century, beginning with 449 B.C., the state annually engaged three tragic protagonists to be assigned by lot to the three poets who were about to compete with plays. Each protagonist seems to have hired his own subordinate actors (deuteragonist and tritagonist) and with their assistance presented all the plays (at the City Dionysia three tragedies and one satyric drama) which his poet had composed for the occasion. The victorious actor in each year's contest was automatically entitled to appear the following year. The other two protagonists were perhaps selected by means of a preliminary contest, such as is mentioned for comic actors on the last day of the Anthesteria. These regulations applied, *mutatis mutandis*, also to the contest of comic actors and to the tragic and comic contests at the Lenaea. Thus at the Lenaea of 418 B.C. Callippides acted in the two tragedies of Callistratus, and Lysicrates in the other dramatist's two plays. And it should be noted that, whereas Callippides won the prize for acting, Callistratus was defeated in the competition of tragedies. This must have been a point of considerable difficulty, for an actor's chances must have been greatly hampered by his being required to present a poor series of plays; and a poet, likewise, must have suffered by reason of an inferior presentation of his dramas. But sometime in the fourth century, when the playwrights were no longer required to write satyr-plays (see p. 199, below), a more equitable system was introduced. Each of the protagonists in turn now acted one of the three tragedies of each poet, the histrionic talent at the disposal of each dramatist being thus made exactly the same. For example, at the City Dionysia of 341 B.C. (Fig. 76) Astydamas was the victorious playwright; his *Achilles* was played by Thettalus, his *Athamas* by Neoptolemus, and his *Antigone* by Athenodorus. The same actors likewise presented the three tragedies of Evaretus and those of the third dramatist. On this occasion Neoptolemus won; a year later, under similar conditions, he was defeated by Thettalus.

We have seen how slow was the rise of actors into a profession distinct from the poets. At a later time, however, they were strongly organized into guilds under the name of "Dionysiac artists" (οἱ ἀμφὶ τὸν Διόνυσον τεχνῖται). Their strongest "union" (κοινόν or σύνοδος) was centered at Athens and it was also the earliest (fourth century B.C.). Others were situated at Thebes, Argos, Teos, Ptolemais, Cyprus, and in all parts of the Greek-speaking world. Now already in the fifth century traveling troupes had presented at the country festivals plays which had won popular acclaim in Athens. For economic reasons it was to the advantage both of the players who had to divide their emoluments and of the communities which hired them to make these traveling companies as small as possible and consequently to restrict their repertoire to plays capable of being performed by a minimum of actors. With the organization of guilds the presentation of dramas "in the provinces" or even at important festivals would be taken over by them; and the same economic causes as before would operate to restrict the number of players in a company. There is reason to believe that a normal troupe in the time of the *technitae* consisted of three actors.[1] Inscriptions for the Soteric festival at Delphi for the years 272–269 B.C. inclusive contain the names of ten companies of tragic actors and twelve of comic actors. These performers belonged to the Athenian guild and in every case there are three names to a

[1] Cf. Rees, *American Journal of Philology*, XXXI (1910), 43 ff.

company. There is no reason to doubt that this number was customary also in the wandering troupes of the pre-technitae period. Some maintain that already in the fifth century a fourth actor was called a parachoregema, as being an extra burden upon the choregus (cf. p. 182, above). But Professor Rees has made it seem very probable that the term took its rise in the time of the technitae. For in later usage *choregein* ($\chi o \rho \eta \gamma \epsilon \hat{\imath} \nu$) in most cases no longer meant "to defray the expense of the chorus," "to act as choregus," but simply "to furnish" without any reference to the choregic system at all. Parachoregema, therefore, would signify "that which is furnished in supplement," "an extra." In other words, if the officials of a city contracted with the union for one or more troupes for a dramatic festival they would be provided with three-actor companies; but if they desired to witness some four-actor play or to avoid the infelicities arising from the splitting or ill-assorted doubling of rôles (see pp. 191 f., below) they might *at extra expense* secure a parachoregema in the form of a fourth actor and so gratify their wishes. According to either interpretation, therefore, the term may refer, *inter alia*, to a fourth actor, but there is a wide difference as to the theory of the circumstances and situation which produced this meaning.

Since our extant plays belong exclusively to the fifth and fourth centuries, the size of the troupes furnished by the guilds could have exerted no influence upon them. But it is quite possible that the dramatists of later times deliberately adapted their technique to the needs of subsequent presentation by such companies. For example, the number of characters who can have a speaking part in a dialogue naturally cannot exceed the number of actors at the poet's disposal. Whatever may have been the situation previously, in the technitae period this would be three. Therefore if the technitae did not give rise to, they at least fixed the so-called aesthetic law that if a fourth character is present at a conversation between three others he must keep silent. This rule is expressed by Horace[1] in the words: "Let no fourth character strive to speak," and it is often mentioned by

[1] Cf. Horace *Ars Poetica*, vs. 192; see also p. 53, n. 1, above.

writers of the Alexandrian and Roman periods. The scholiasts belong to this time and their comments frequently reveal an attempt to foist the aesthetic law upon the fifth-century dramas. The difficulty which the fifth-century writers encountered in mastering even the three-part dialogue (see p. 170) lends to such an attempt a misleading facility. In tragedy the normal restriction of actors to three makes the task especially easy, but even here the law is only superficially observed. For the coryphaeus often participates so freely in a conversation between actors (see pp. 164f. and 169f., above) that only by courtesy can it be called a three-part dialogue. In Seneca's Roman tragedies, on the contrary, the coryphaeus never speaks if more than one actor is present.[1] Now Professor Rees would trace the aesthetic law back to fifth-century times, but Dr. Kaffenberger (*op. cit.,* pp. 22f.) rightly demurs. He points out that in Sophocles' *Oedipus at Colonus*, vss. 1099–1555, Oedipus, Antigone, and Ismene are continuously present but that Ismene says never a word. What is the cause of this silence? During vss. 1099–1210 and vss. 1500–1555 Theseus is also present and during vss. 1249–1446 Polynices is present. In these scenes, therefore, it is possible to explain Ismene's silence on the basis of the aesthetic law. But during vss. 1447–99 Oedipus and his two daughters are left alone, and Ismene still remains silent. Consequently the aesthetic explanation breaks down at this point and we must stand by our earlier conclusion (see pp. 181 f., above) that throughout these scenes Ismene is impersonated by a mute. Moreover, since Oedipus forbids his daughters sharing his final moments with him, why does the poet not let him take leave of them on the stage instead of resorting to a messenger's narrative (cf. vss. 1611 ff.)? The answer is obvious. In such a situation Ismene simply *must* have spoken and this a mute could not have done for her. Moreover, there is no aesthetic reason why the law should not be as binding in comedy as in tragedy. Nevertheless, fifth-century comedies indisputably violated it and possibly fourth-century comedies did also (see pp. 171–73, above). Therefore, if

---

[1] Cf. Leo, *Rheinisches Museum für Philologie*, LII (1897), 513.

tragedy was more scrupulous it must have been because its actors were less numerous. But in truth it was not until the period of the technitae and their three-actor troupes that a hard-and-fast rule was established. Notwithstanding, the grammarians as a result of their closet study of Attic drama seized upon the observance of the law in fifth-century tragedy and usually in New Comedy, which was greatly influenced by Euripides, as a justification for tracing the practice back to an earlier origin. Except in one scene Seneca always observed the law.[1] But when Plautus and Terence attempted to transplant New Comedy to Italian soil, they encountered a difficulty. It was the use of masks which enabled the Greek playwrights to shift their actors from one rôle to another with lightning speed. But masks are said not to have been employed on the Roman stage until the next century. Therefore, even if the Greek comedies had been translated without modification it would have been quite impossible to present them at Rome with only three or four (maskless) actors. Accordingly, Plautus and Terence seem to have employed five or six performers and occasionally even more, and then proceeded to make further use of them so as to gratify the Roman desire for spectacular effects. By combining Greek plays into one Latin version (by "contaminating" them, to use the technical term) and by altering them freely they produced many scenes in which four or five persons participate in the same dialogue.

The fact that women's parts in Elizabethan drama were played by boys has been used to explain the fondness of Elizabethan heroines for masquerading in masculine attire. Now the Greek theater, likewise, knew no actresses—all parts, regardless of sex, were presented by men. Can any effect of this practice be traced in the extant plays? First, Greek drama also was not unacquainted with the spectacle of masculine performers impersonating women disguised as men or vice versa; cf. the rôle of Mnesilochus in Aristophanes' *Women at the Thesmophoria*, and the chorus and several characters in the same

[1] Cf. Seneca's *Agamemnon*, vss. 981 ff.

author's *Women in Council*. But in the Greek theater this occurrence was too rare to be significant. Secondly, it has frequently been observed that the heroines of Greek tragedy are as a rule lacking in feminine tenderness and diffidence and are prone to such masculine traits as boldness, initiative, and self-reliance. On the other hand the women who have speaking parts in comedy are usually either impaired in reputation or disagreeable in character—courtesans, ravished maidens, shrews, scolds, jealous wives, intriguing mothers-in-law, etc.[1] Now these facts are doubtless the resultant of many factors. For example, tragedy has little direct use for the modest violet type of woman, and the sharp demarcation between dramatic genres (see p. 201, below) tended to prevent their indirect employment in scenes meant merely to relieve the tragic intensity of the main plot. Likewise, social conditions must have had a great deal to do with the exclusion of women of unblemished reputation and attractive years from the comic stage (see pp. 277–79, below). Nevertheless when all is said I consider it quite possible that the representation of women by men actors was partially responsible for such a choice and for the delineation of female rôles. At least male performers must have found such types of women much easier to impersonate. Finally, if children were represented only in pantomime and their words spoken by a grown actor from behind the scenes (see pp. 179 f., above) we can understand why girls never have a speaking part and one reason why the words put in boys' mouths are often too old for them. A competent critic has declared: "Euripides' children do not sing what is appropriate to children in the circumstances supposed but what the poet felt for the children and for the situations. In particular the song of the boy over the dead body of his mother in the *Alcestis* is one of his grossest errors in delineation."[2] This situation, also, is capable of several explanations, but who will deny that the practice of having children's parts declaimed by adults belongs among them?

[1] Cf. Lounsbury, *Shakespeare as a Dramatic Artist*, pp. 111 f.

[2] Cf. U. von Wilamowitz-Möllendorff, *Herakles*[2], I, 119, note, and Euripides' *Alcestis*, vss. 393 ff.

In France the court compelled actors to furnish amusement and the church damned them for complying. In Rome the actors were slaves or freedmen and belonged to the dregs of society. Only in Greece did no stigma rest upon the histrionic profession. As we have seen (pp. 131f., above) the actors were active participants in a religious service and during the festival performances their persons were quasi-sacrosanct. As such, they were entitled to and received the highest respect, and their occupation was considered an honorable one. Consequently, they were often the confidants and associates of royalty and wielded no mean influence in the politics of their native lands. In particular as they traveled from court to court they often acted as intermediaries in diplomatic negotiations. Thus Aeschines, an ex-actor, was almost as influential in the Athenian faction which favored the Macedonians as was Demosthenes in that which opposed them. And though the latter in his speeches indulged in frequent sneers at Aeschines' theatrical career, this was not on account of his profession per se but because Demosthenes claimed he had been a failure at it. Aeschines and Aristodemus, another actor, twice went as ambassadors from Athens to Philip, king of Macedonia, with whom the latter was *persona gratissima*. Thettalus was an especial favorite of Alexander the Great, who sent him as an emissary to arrange his marriage with a Carian satrap's daughter. When Thettalus was defeated by Athenodorus at Tyre in 332 B.C. Alexander said that he would rather have lost a part of his kingdom than to have seen Thettalus defeated. These men were contemporaries of Aristotle, who declared in his *Rhetoric* that in his day actors counted for more in the dramatic contests than the poets.[1] The huge fees that they received are often mentioned. In view of all this it is not surprising that they arrogated to themselves many liberties. Aristotle states that Theodorus always insisted upon being the first actor to appear in a play, doubtless on a principle analagous to that which Mr. William Archer[2] mentions: "Where it is

[1] Cf. Aristotle's *Rhetoric* 1403*b*33, quoted as the motto of this chapter.
[2] Cf. *Play-making*, p. 129.

desired to give to one character a special prominence and pre-dominance, it ought, if possible, to be the first figure on which the eye of the audience falls. . . . . The solitary entrance of Richard III throws his figure into a relief which could by no other means have been attained." This anecdote may mean merely that Theodorus assumed the rôle of the first character, however insignificant, in order to appear first upon the scene. But some have thought that he actually had the plays modified so that the character which he was to enact might appear first. Even upon the first hypothesis, however, slight alterations might sometimes have been necessary. For example, if he wished to impersonate Antigone in such a play as Euripides' *Phoenician Maids* and if no passage were provided like vss. 88–102 to enable the actor to shift from Jocaste, who opens the tragedy, to Anti-gone (see pp. 177 f., above), then perhaps the simplest solution would have been to interpolate a few such lines for this purpose. But however this may have been in Theodorus' case there can be little doubt that the actors did sometimes take such liberties with their dramatic vehicles. To correct this abuse Lycurgus, who was finance minister of Athens in the last third of the fourth century B.C. and "completed" the theater (see p. 69, above), is said to have had state copies of old plays provided from which the actors were not allowed to deviate; and Lycon was fined ten talents, which Alexander paid, for having interpolated one line in a comedy.

Naturally most actors were peculiarly adapted to certain types of characters. Thus Nicostratus was most successful as a messenger, Theodorus in female rôles, etc. The interesting significance of the parts borne by Apollogenes, an actor of the third century, has only recently been recognized. At Argos he impersonated Heracles and Alexander, at Delphi, Heracles and Antaeus, at Dodona, Achilles, etc., in addition to winning a victory in boxing at Alexandria. Evidently this actor was a pugilist for whom rôles and plays were carefully chosen which would display his physique and strength to the best advantage. Now these special predilections and accomplishments of the actors, as well as their physical qualities, must often have run afoul of the constant doubling and the occasional splitting of rôles as required by the restricted number of players. Professor Rees makes good use of such points in arguing against the three-actor limitation in fifth-century tragedy.[1] But in such matters custom is all-important; we cannot be sure to what extent the Greeks were offended by infelicities of this nature. In my opinion such considerations are not strong enough to break down the arguments drawn from dramatic technique (see pp. 173–82, above).

I ought not to conclude this chapter without a few words concerning the manner in which act divisions arose from the alternation of choral odes and histrionic passages in ancient drama. The earliest tragedies, such as Aeschylus' *Suppliants* and *Persians*, began with the entrance song of the chorus, which is called the *parodus*. In later plays it was customary for one or more actors to appear before the choral parodus in a so-called *prologue*. The first instance of this which is known to us occurred in Phrynichus' *Phoenician Women* (476 B.C.). After the parodus came an alternation of histrionic scenes (*episodes*) and choral odes (*stasima*), concluding with a histrionic *exodus*. These are nontechnical definitions and do not cover every variation from type, but they will suffice for present purposes. Thus Aeschylus' *Prometheus Bound* falls into the following divisions: prologue, vss. 1–127; parodus, vss. 128–92; first episode, vss. 193–396; first stasimon, vss. 397–435; second episode, vss. 436–525; second stasimon, vss. 526–60; third episode, vss. 561–886; third stasimon, vss. 887–906; exodus, vss. 907–1093. Though the number of stasima (and of episodes) was more usually three, as in this case, there was originally no hard-and-fast rule on the subject. In several plays there were four stasima and four episodes, and in Sophocles' *Antigone* five of each. Therefore in a normal tragedy like the *Prometheus* the number of histrionic divisions would be five—prologue, three episodes, and exodus. In the early plays which had no prologue the histrionic

[1] Cf. *The So-called Rule of Three Actors in the Classical Greek Drama*, pp. 45–60.

divisions fell to four—three episodes and an exodus.   In several
of the later plays, on the other hand, they rose to six, and in the
Antigone to seven.   As the lack of connection between chorus
and plot increased and the size and importance of choral odes
diminished (see pp. 126 f., 136–49, and 168, above) there was the
more excuse for ignoring the choral elements and for concen-
trating attention upon the histrionic divisions.   The development of comedy led to similar results.   The composition of an
Old Comedy has already been discussed (see pp. 40 f., above).
So long as the agon and the parabasis persisted, the structural
differences between tragedy and comedy were unmistakable;
but with the disappearance of these features early in the fourth
century (see pp. 42 f., above) the assimilation of the two genres
rapidly proceeded.   Moreover, as the activity of the comic
chorus was confined to *entr'actes* and as their entertainment
became so foreign to the plot as no longer to be written in the
manuscripts but merely to be indicated by XOPOY (see pp. 147 f.),
this tendency to ignore the choral element in favor of the histrionic became pronounced.   Now the number of histrionic
divisions in Old Comedy and in New Comedy was limited to
five even less frequently than in tragedy.   And in either literary
genre there was no more reason for such a restriction, whether on
historical or technical grounds, than there would be in modern
drama.   In every period such a detail depends, or ought to be
left to depend, entirely upon the requirements of the story
chosen for dramatic presentation.   Nevertheless, since the histrionic divisions in tragedy were more usually five and since
comedy fell more and more under the domination of tragedy,
the rigid principle was at last set up for both tragedy and comedy
that each play should contain five acts, no more, no less; cf.
Horace's pronunciamento: "Let a play neither fall short of nor
extend beyond a fifth act."

It should be observed, however, that our English word "act"
conveys a misleading impression in this connection.   The Greek
word was simply "part" ($\mu\epsilon\rho os$) and denoted merely a division
of the play as determined by choral *divertissement*, whether

written or interpolated. These "parts," therefore, depended upon the more or less accidental and haphazard activity of the chorus and often two or three of them would be required to make up an act in the modern sense. In other words the modern notion of an act as an integral part of the story, marking a definite stage in the unfolding of the plot, was for the most part yet to be developed, especially in comedy.

The leveling effect of the five-act rule is seen in the modern editions of Plautus and Terence. It is certain that neither four nor any other fixed number of pauses was employed at the premier performances of these dramatists' works. In some cases they seem to have been given continuous representation with neither choral intermezzi nor pauses at the points where the Greek originals had had *entr'actes*. From this, however, we must not infer that Plautus and Terence did not know where the acts or the "parts" began and closed. If for no other reason, the recurrence of ΧΟΡΟΤ in at least most of the Greek comedies which they were translating and adapting would not have permitted them to be ignorant on this point, for in my opinion, so far as pauses were inserted in the Roman performances, they coincided with the corresponding points of division in the Greek plays. But by this I do not mean that the Latin divisions were always as numerous as the Greek; in my judgment, owing to contamination and other modifying influences they were uniformly fewer. Moreover, when these comedies were first published for the use of a reading public, it seems that the manuscripts contained no indication of act divisions. Within a century of Terence's death, however, partisans of the five-act dogma were already attempting to force their Procrustean theory upon his works. A later effort of this sort is preserved to us in the commentary of Donatus (fourth century A.D.) and passed into the printed editions, with some modifications, about 1496 A.D. Likewise, the Renaissance scholars, obsessed by the tradition of what had come to be considered an inviolable law, proceeded to divide each of Plautus' twenty plays into five acts; cf. Pius' edition of 1500 A.D. The divisions in both poets rest upon no adequate authority and are easily shown to be incorrect. Yet, unfortunately, it is now impossible to re-establish the acts as known to their Latin authors. If we revert to the Greek terminology, however, somewhat more definite results may be obtained, though, even so, agreement is not possible in every case. Technical criteria now at our disposal would indicate that the original "parts" ($\mu\acute{\epsilon}\rho\eta$) in these comedies ranged from a minimum of two or three to a maximum of seven or eight.

But Aristophanes was at the same time a dramatist contending for a prize, and had no wish to alienate the greater part of his audience.—T. G. TUCKER.

CHAPTER IV

THE INFLUENCE OF FESTIVAL ARRANGEMENTS[1]

We have already seen that the performance of plays at Athens was confined to two festivals of Dionysus, and the time when the various dramatic genres began to be presented at each has been stated (see pp. 119 f., above). Since the Lenaea came at the end of January (Gamelion), when navigation was not yet considered entirely safe, few strangers were present; and in consequence this festival became more private and intimate, more like a family gathering of the Athenians by themselves. On the contrary the City Dionysia took place toward the end of March (Elaphebolion), when the allies were accustomed to send their tribute to Athens and the city was crowded with visitors from all parts of the Greek world. As a result this occasion was more cosmopolitan than the other, and every effort was expended to make it as splendid as possible. All this explains an episode in the life of Aristophanes. At the City Dionysia of the year 426 B.C. was produced his *Babylonians*, in which he represented the Athenian state as a mill where the allies suffered from the tyrannous exactions of Cleon, its manager. Cleon accordingly lodged with the senate an information (εἰσαγγελία) charging lèse majesté, aggravated by being committed in the presence of strangers (παρόντων τῶν ξένων). Therefore, in his next play, the *Acharnians*, produced at the Lenaea of 425 B.C., Aristophanes prefaced some frank expressions of opinion with the following statement: "And what I shall say will be dreadful but just, for Cleon will not be able *now* to malign

[1] In addition to the works mentioned on pp. xvii and xx f., above, cf. A. T. Murray, *On Parody and Paratragoedia in Aristophanes* (1891); Mazon, "Sur le Proagôn," *Revue de Philologie*, XXVII (1903), 263 ff.; Rees, "The Significance of the Parodoi in the Greek Theater," *American Journal of Philology*, XXXII (1911), 377 ff.; Graeber, *De Poetarum Atticorum Arte Scaenica* (1911); Robert, *Die Masken der neueren attischen Komödie* (1911); and the bibliography listed on p. 318, below.

me for defaming the state to alien ears.   For we are alone; this
is the Lenaea, and the aliens are not yet here, nor the tribute from
the federated states, nor our allies; but we are alone *now*."[1]
Similarly, Demosthenes tried to make Midias' assault upon him
at the City Dionysia of 350 B.C. seem more heinous by pointing
out that it was committed "in the presence of many, *both strangers
and citizens*."[2]

Since we have no exact information as to when the City
Dionysia began or ended, we are in doubt as to its duration.[3]
But it is probable that it lasted for six days, certainly five.   The
first day was occupied with the procession, as already described
(see pp. 121 f., above).   The second day, and possibly the third,
was devoted to dithyrambs, the literary type from which tragedy
had sprung.   There were five choruses of boys and five of men,
each of the ten tribes annually standing sponsor for one chorus.
We happen to know that the contest of men was added to this
festival in 508 B.C.   Inasmuch as each chorus consisted of fifty
amateur performers, it will be seen that no inconsiderable portion of the free population received every year a musical training
which could not but enhance their appreciation of the choral and
lyrical parts of the dramas and likewise improve the quality of the
material from which the dramatic choruses were chosen.

The last three days of the festival seem to have been given
over to the dramatic performances, but just what the arrangements were is not known.   In Aristophanes' *Birds*, vss. 786 ff.,
the chorus, praising the use of wings, remarks that "if one of you
spectators were so provided and became wearied with the tragic
choruses, he might fly away home and dine and then fly back
again to us."   From this passage it has been plausibly concluded
that the comedies came later in the day than the tragedies.   It
would seem as if the three tragic playwrights must have produced

[1] Cf. *Acharnians*, vss. 501 ff., Starkie's edition, excursus V, and Croiset,
Aristophanes and the Political Parties at Athens, pp. 42 ff. (Loeb's translation).

[2] Cf. Demosthenes' *Against Midias*, § 74.

[3] It probably began upon the tenth day of Elaphebolion (cf. Adams, *Transactions of American Philological Association*, XLI [1910], 60 ff.) and closed on the
fifteenth.

their plays on as many successive mornings, the comedies following later each day in similar rotation.

It is well known that at the City Dionysia each of three tragic poets brought out four plays in a series, three tragedies and one satyric drama (see pp. 23 f., above). Such a group was termed a *didascalia* ("teaching"). It was Aeschylus' frequent practice to have all four plays treat different aspects of the same general theme, the levity of the concluding piece counterbalancing somewhat the seriousness of the three tragedies. In that case the set of four was called a tetralogy; but if the satyric drama dealt with a different topic than the tragedies, the latter were said to form a trilogy. No tetralogy or didascalia is extant and only one trilogy, the *Agamemnon*, *Libation-Bearers*, and *Eumenides*, which Aeschylus brought out in 458 B.C. The satyric drama in this series is not preserved but was entitled *Proteus*. It may have dealt with the shipwreck of Menelaus, Agamemnon's brother, on his return from Troy. After Aeschylus the four pieces in a didascalia were usually unrelated in subject.

According to canonical doctrine satyric drama was the intermediate stage in the development of tragedy from the dithyramb and was retained in the festival program as a survival. Within recent years, as this hypothesis has been subjected to searching criticism, its supports have slowly crumbled away. My own opinion is that tragedy and the satyr-play are independent offshoots of the dithyramb (see pp. 1–35, above). In either case, since the dramatic performances were part of a Bacchic festival and since the Bacchic element had long since been discarded by tragedy (see p. 123, above), it is no doubt true that the satyric drama was in the program partly in order to keep up the religious associations, as revealing its connection with Dionysus more plainly than did mature tragedy. Nevertheless the same tendencies which had broken down the exclusively Dionysiac themes in tragedy were at work here also and would not be denied. We have already seen (see pp. 126 f., above) how the writers of satyr-plays arbitrarily superimposed Silenus and a chorus of satyrs upon some non-Dionysiac subject. Both in

Euripides' *Cyclops* and in Sophocles' *Trackers*, the sole exc.nt representatives of the genre, the Bacchic element is restricted to these followers of his, and Dionysus himself figures only as he is apostrophized or mentioned by them.   In 438 B.C. Euripides introduced a further innovation by bringing out the *Alcestis* as the last play in his didascalia.   Neither Silenus nor the chorus of satyrs appears in this piece, the theme being entirely non-Dionysiac; but the drunkenness of Heracles and the brutal frankness in the quarrel between Admetus and his father suggest the spirit of the old satyric drama, while the happy ending and the humor remind us of a comedy.   These incongruities and the exceptionable circumstances under which the play was produced have occasioned the controversy, which began in antiquity and still continues, as to how the *Alcestis* is to be classified as a literary type.   Is it a tragedy, comedy, satyr-play, tragi-comedy, melodrama, *Schauspiel*, *Tendenz-Schrift*, or what?[1]   How far Euripides' innovation in substituting such a play for the usual satyric drama may have met with the approval and emulation of his fellow-playwrights we have no means of knowing; but an extant inscription of a century later shows that the satyr-play had then been degraded still further (Fig. 76).   At the City Dionysia of 341, 340, and 339 B.C. the poets were no longer compelled each to conclude his group of pieces in the old way, but a single satyric drama was performed, before the tragedies began at all, as ample recognition of the Dionysiac element which had once been all-pervasive in the festivals.

During the latter part of its history five comic poets competed each year at the City Dionysia, and each presented but a single play; there is some reason for believing that the number was five also at the beginning, but possibly there were then only three competitors.   At any rate there were certainly not more than three for a while during the Peloponnesian War (431–404 B.C.).[2] When the comedies were restricted to three they were naturally

---

[1] Cf. the Introduction to Hayley's edition, pp. xxiii ff.

[2] Cf. Capps, in *Classical Philology*, I (1906), 219, note on l. 5, and Wilhelm, *Urkunden dramatischer Aufführungen in Athen*, pp. 195 ff.

performed one on each of the last three days, after that day's tragedies and satyr-play, as we have just seen.   But what the arrangement was when the larger number was presented is not so obvious.   Was a second comedy crowded into the program on two of the days ?   Or were comedies produced also on the second and third days of the festival, after the dithyrambic choruses ?   The latter alternative would be my choice, and this would explain why in the inscriptional records the comedies preceded the tragedies, though in the chronological sequence of the last three days they followed them.   When Aristophanes brought out his *Women in Council* he was so unfortunate in the drawing of lots as to be forced to perform his play first in the series of comedies.   Therefore he had his chorus say (vss. 1158 ff.):

> Let it nothing tell against me, that my play must first begin;
> See that, through the afterpieces, back to me your memory strays;
> Keep your oaths, and well and truly judge between the rival plays.
> Be not like the wanton women, never mindful of the past,
> Always for the new admirer, always fondest of the last.
>
> [Rogers' translation]

This close juxtaposition of tragedy and comedy at the same festival must have strengthened a practice which in any case would have been inevitable, viz., that the comic poets should parody lines, scenes, or even whole plots of their tragic confrères. In a community as small as Athens it was impossible that advance knowledge of a tragic plot or even the exact wording of striking lines should not sometimes reach the ears of a comic playwright and be turned to skilful account by him.   Even when the secret had been guarded until the very moment of presentation, it must have been feasible for a comedian whose play was to be produced on a subsequent day of the festival to incorporate a few lines or a short scene in his comedy overnight.   But this is mere theorizing, for I remember no passage where such "scoops" are mentioned. The parodying of tragedies brought out at previous festivals, however, was exceedingly common.   The extant plays preserve some instances of this, and the scholiasts tell us of many others.

Parodies of no less than thirty-three of Euripides' tragedies are preserved in the remains of Aristophanes' comedies. But the situation is too well known to merit further amplification here, cf. Murray, *op. cit., passim.*

On the other hand, though tragedy, comedy, and satyric dramas were juxtaposed at the festivals, they were not intermingled. The lines of demarcation were kept distinct. With very rare exceptions, like the *Alcestis,* the audience always knew what kind of a play it was about to hear, and (what was even more important) the poet always knew what kind of a play he was supposed to write. Of course, this is not the same as saying that all Greek tragedies were alike or that all Greek comedies seemed to be poured from the same mold. Within the type there was room for the greatest diversity, but the types did not overlap or borrow much from one another. This practice was a natural outgrowth of the Greek love for schematizing which displayed itself in the formulation and observance of rigid laws in every branch of art and especially in literature; in the field of drama this tendency was strengthened by the festival arrangements. Contrast with this the modern confusion of all the arts and all the literary genres which, in the sphere of drama, results in plays harder to classify than Polonius' "tragical-comical-historical-pastorals." This is one of the things that Voltaire had in mind when he declared that Shakespeare wrote like "a drunken savage."

The simplicity of the Greek effect is aptly characterized by Mr. Clayton Hamilton:[1] "Although the ancient drama frequently violated the three unities of action, time, and place, it always preserved a fourth unity, which we may call unity of mood." Possibly regard for this fourth unity caused Euripides to employ the *deus ex machina* at the conclusion of his *Iphigenia among the Taurians.* It is well known that this is the play that lends least support to the frequent charge that Euripides used the *deus* to cut the inextricable tangle of his plots. Here the final, insurmountable difficulty is of the poet's own choosing.

[1] Cf. *The Theory of the Theater,* p. 118.

Orestes and his party have at last got their vessel free of the shore, and all the playwright needed to do was to allow them to sail on in safety and thus bring his play to a close.   But arbitrarily he causes a contrary wind and sea to drive their ship back to land, making divine intervention indispensable.   Of course this device enabled him to overleap the unity of time and bring events far in the future within the limits of his dramatic day, and frequently that was all that Euripides had in mind in having recourse to this artifice (see p. 295, below).   But in the present instance I think he had an additional motive, one which has a place in this discussion.   The gist of the matter is well expressed by Mr. Prickard:[1]   "If the fugitives had simply escaped, snapping their fingers at Thoas, the ending would have been essentially comic: perhaps, after the grave and pathetic scenes which have gone before, we should rather call it burlesque.   But the appearance of the *deus ex machina*, a device not itself to be praised, enables the piece to be finished after all with dignity and elevation of feeling."

In connection with the foregoing arises another point: when the line between tragedy and comedy was drawn so sharply, we should hardly expect to find the writer of tragedies and the writer of comedies united in one and the same person.   As a matter of fact not a single case is known in all Greek drama.   "The sock and buskin were not worn by the same poet";[2] the Greek theater knew no Shakespeare.   This very versatility of the Elizabethan poet helps to explain why his tragedies contain much that is humorous and his comedies much that is painful, a characteristic which has been so offensive to his French critics.   Very similar is the situation among the actors.   At the City Dionysia, beginning with 449 B.C., a prize was awarded to the best actor in the tragedies brought out each year, and about 325 B.C. a contest was established for comic actors.   At the Lenaea, prizes were offered for comic and for tragic actors from about 442 B.C. and about 433 B.C., respectively.   These arrangements would tend

---

[1] Cf. his *Aristotle on the Art of Poetry*, pp. 48 f.

[2] Cf. Dryden, *Dramatic Essays* (Everyman's Library edition), p. 20.

still further to keep each actor within his specialty.   No performer in both tragic and comic rôles is indubitably known until
Praxiteles, who performed at Delphi in 106 B.C. as a comedian
and nine years later as a tragedian.   Two other instances
occurred a little later.   In the second century B.C. Thymoteles
seems to have been both a tragic poet and a comic actor.   These
examples exhaust the list in pre-Christian times.

In the preceding discussion some changes in the festival
program have already been mentioned, for the program was not,
like Athena, fully grown at birth.   For example, the requirement
that each tragic poet should present three tragedies and a satyric
drama in a group did not go back to the introduction of tragedy
by Thespis in 534 B.C. and cannot be established for any poet
before Aeschylus.   It is likely that this regulation, together with
the main outlines of the program as known at a later period,
dates from about 501 B.C., when the festival seems to have been
reorganized (see p. 319, below).   This is the period with which
the official records began, when also the κῶμοι, that is, the volunteer performances from which formal comedy was derived,
were first added to the festival.   In addition to the changes that
have already been noticed we may now mention the following:
It was not customary for plays to be performed more than once at
Athens.   It is true that the more successful plays in the city might
be repeated at the Rural Dionysia, which were held in the various demes (townships) during the month Posideon (December),
and that some of these provincial festivals, notably that at the
Piraeus, were almost as splendid as those at Athens itself; yet
the fact remains that at Athens the repetition of a play was an
exceptional thing.   Thus, when Aeschylus died in 456 B.C., honor
was shown him by the provision that his plays might be brought
out in rivalry with the new productions of living tragedians, and
they are said to have won the prize in this way several times.[1]
This explains what Aeschylus is represented as saying in Aristophanes' *Frogs* (vss. 866 ff.), where he protests against contending with Euripides "here in Hades" on the ground that they will

[1] Cf. Philostratus, *Apollonius of Tyana*, p. 245.

not be on equal terms, "for his poetry," he says, "died with him [and came down to Hades], so that he will be able to recite it, but mine did not die with me." There is here not only the obvious meaning that Aeschylus thought his poems had achieved an immortality which Euripides' never could, but also an allusion to the special privileges bestowed upon them. Again, the Athenians conceived such an admiration for the parabasis of Aristophanes' *Frogs*, doubtless on account of the sensible and patriotic advice therein given the citizens to compose their differences, that the play was given a second time by request. As a result of such precedents, in 386 B.C. the repetition of one old tragedy was given a regular place in the program, as a separate feature, however, no longer in rivalry with new works; and in 339 B.C. this arrangement was extended also to old comedies. It must further be remembered that the program was susceptible of considerable modification from year to year. When a single satyr-play was brought out as a substitute for one in each poet's group (see p. 199, above), naturally each playwright presented three tragedies and nothing more, and this actually happened in 341 B.C. But in the following year each of the three poets produced but two tragedies. The program was therefore flexible enough to meet special needs or emergencies.

It must be understood that the discussion of the festival program up to this point applies as a whole to the City Dionysia alone and only in part to the Lenaea. For example, at the Lenaea there were no dithyrambic contests, and there is no evidence for the presentation of old plays or even of satyric dramas. Our most tangible information is an inscription for the years 419 and 418 B.C. (see p. 184, above). On these occasions there were two poets and each brought out two tragedies.

Possibly the first thing, apart from physical conditions, which would strike the modern theatergoer's attention after entering an ancient Greek theater would be the fact that he was provided with no playbill. For this lack he received compensation in three ways: The first was the *proagon* (προαγών; πρό "before"+ἀγών "contest"), i.e., the ceremony before the contest.

This was held in the nearby Odeum on the eighth day of the month Elaphebolion (end of March), which was probably the second day before the City Dionysia proper began. In this function the poets, the actors (without their masks and stage costumes), the choregi (see pp. 270 f., below), and the choruses participated. As the herald made announcement each poet and choregus with their actors and chorus presented themselves for public inspection. It was therefore possible for anyone interested, simply by being present on this occasion, to learn what poets were competing, the names of their actors and plays, the order of their appearance, and similar details. Moreover, the mere titles of the plays by themselves would often convey considerable information to the more cultured members of the audience. Thus, names like Aeschylus' *Seven against Thebes*, Sophocles' *Oedipus at Colonus*, and Euripides' *Iphigenia at Aulis* or *Iphigenia among the Taurians* indicate the locale and general theme of the play on their face, and to the more cultivated spectators titles such as Sophocles' *Oedipus the King* or Euripides' *Alcestis* would be equally significant. On the other hand, such names as Euripides' *Suppliants* or *Phoenician Maids* would be either mystifying or misleading, especially if the hearer was well enough versed in Greek drama to remember that Aeschylus and Phrynichus, respectively, had applied these titles to plays which actually dealt with entirely different incidents.

The proagon furnished the name and scene for one of Aristophanes' (or Philonides') comedies, but unfortunately we have no inkling as to how the theme was treated. In 406 B.C. the news of Euripides' death came from Macedonia just before this ceremony. Sophocles appeared in garments indicative of mourning and had his chorus leave off their accustomed crowns. The spectators are said to have burst into tears. In Plato's *Symposium* (194B) Socrates is represented as referring to the proagon at the Lenaean festival of the year 416 B.C. as follows: "I should be forgetful, O Agathon, of the courage and spirit which you showed when your compositions were about to be exhibited, when you mounted the platform with your actors and faced so large an audience altogether undismayed, if I thought you would on the present occasion [a celebration in honor of his first victory] be disturbed by a small company of friends."

The second compensation for the absence of a playbill was provided within the plays themselves. First, with reference to the imaginary scene of action. The mythological stories which uniformly supplied the tragic playwrights with their themes were always definitely localized, and the tragic poets seemed to feel the necessity of indicating the place of action. This was commonly done by having an actor refer to "this land of so-and-so," or even address it or some conspicuous object. At the beginning of Sophocles' *Electra* the aged servant says to Orestes, "This is ancient Argos for which you longed" (vs. 4); in the *Bacchanals*, Dionysus in a typical Euripidean prologue states, "I come to this land of the Thebans" (vs. 1); Apollo begins Euripides' *Alcestis* with the words, "O house of Admetus!" (vs. 1); and Eteocles in Aeschylus' *Seven against Thebes* addresses the spectators, "O citizens of Cadmus" (vs. 1). When the scene is changed within a play each locality is clearly identified. Thus at the beginning of Aeschylus' *Eumenides*, Delphi is indicated as the scene in the usual way; a little later Apollo bids Orestes "go to the city of Pallas" (vs. 79), and still later, when the shift is supposed to have taken place, Orestes enters and says, "O Queen Athena, I come at the bidding of Loxias" (vs. 235). Euripides was most punctilious about this matter: he usually identified his scene within the first five lines and always within the first fifty. Aeschylus and Sophocles were not always so particular: in the *Antigone*, Thebes is not mentioned until vs. 101; and in the *Persians*, though it early becomes apparent that the action is laid in Persia, Susa is not actually shown to be the place of action before vs. 761. On the other hand, Euripides sometimes plays a little joke upon his audience; for example, the *Andromache* begins, "O pride of Asia, city of Thebe, whence I came to Priam's princely halls as Hector's bride," as if the scene were laid in Asia Minor; but in vs. 16 we learn that the scene is really placed in Phthia!

In comedy the situation was somewhat different.   Except in mythological parodies the stories are independent of tradition and newly invented, and usually are very slightly attached to any definite locality.   As a result the plays of Old Comedy are generally thought of, somewhat vaguely, as taking place in Athens, though this fact is seldom expressly stated, and we rarely have any indication as to precisely where in the city the scenic background is supposed to stand.   Occasionally we hear of the Pnyx (*Acharnians*, vs. 20) or Chloe's temple (*Lysistrata*, vs. 385). But there is not a word in the *Clouds* or in the *Women at the Thesmophoria* to show where in Athens Socrates' thinking-shop or Agathon's house is situated.   A shift of scene is not uncommon.   At the beginning of the *Frogs*, Dionysus visits his brother Heracles.   Since no other location is specified, this scene is probably laid in Athens.[1]   At vs. 182 the orchestra represents the subterranean lake, and at vs. 436 the chorus informs Dionysus that he has reached Pluto's door (see pp. 88–90, above).

By the time of New Comedy, unless we are definitely informed to the contrary, the scene is so uniformly laid in Athens that there was no necessity of saying so.   It is true that Athens is mentioned in Plautus' *The Churl*, vss. 1 ff.: "Plautus asks for a tiny part of your handsome walls where without the help of builders he may convey Athens," but it is evident that these words were added by the Roman poet to the original and so are no exception to the Greek practice.   That the action did customarily take place in Athens is expressly stated in Plautus' *Menaechmi*, vss. 8 ff.: "And this is the practice of comic poets: they declare that every thing has been done at Athens, so that their play may seem more Greek to you."   So thoroughly was this principle ingrained in the playwrights' consciousness that they were in danger of a lapse when they evaded it.   Thus Calydon is the imaginary scene of Plautus' *The Carthaginian* (cf. vs. 94); nevertheless at vs. 372 one character says to another, "If you will but have patience, my master will give you your freedom and make you an Attic citizen," as if they were in Athens!   When the poet,

[1] Cf. note on vs. 38 in Tucker's edition.

as in this instance, deviated from the usual scene of action, he had one of the actors, generally the prologus, warn the audience by saying, "This town is Ephesus" (Plautus' *The Braggart Captain*, vs. 88); "Diphilus wished this city to be named Cyrene" (Plautus' *The Fisherman's Rope*, vs. 32), etc.   It is only natural that this same period should witness the rise of the convention that the side entrance (parodus) at the spectators' right led to the harbor or the market place and that at their left into the country, since the scene was regularly placed in Athens and since these were the actual topographical relationships in the Athenian theater (see p. 233, below).   So firmly was this convention established that in Plautus' *Amphitruo*, Thebes, an inland town, is represented as having a harbor like Florence, Milan, Rome, etc., in Shakespeare, or as Bohemia has a seacoast in *The Winter's Tale*.

But the plays not only informed the audience where the scene was laid, but also made known the identity of the dramatic characters.   It is obvious that the first character to appear would have to state his own name with more or less directness and then introduce the next character.   The latter he might do (*a*) by announcing bluntly "Here comes so-and-so," (*b*) by addressing the newcomer by name, (*c*) by himself inquiring his name and so eliciting his identity, or (*d*) by loudly summoning him out of the house or from a distance.   All four of these means are actually resorted to.   Now the earliest Greek plays have no prologue, but begin with the entrance song of the chorus (the parodus, see p. 192, above).   Accordingly, in Aeschylus' *Persians* the very first words are intended to reveal the personnel of the chorus:

> We are the Persian watchmen old,
> The guardians true of the palace of gold.
> Left to defend the Asian land,
> When the army marched to Hellas' strand.
>
> [Blackie's translation]

At the conclusion of their ode, as Atossa enters they address her as follows:

> Mistress of the low-zoned women, queen of Persia's daughters, hail!
> Aged mother of King Xerxes, wife of great Darius, hail!
>
> [Blackie's translation],

thus removing all possibility of doubt as to the identity of the new arrival. In this connection it ought to be said that introducing an actor did not necessarily involve a proper name; often it was enough to indicate the station, occupation, or relationship of the new character. This rule applies not only to the humbler folk, such as messengers, herdsmen, nurses, heralds, etc.—in fact Sophocles usually ignored the entrance of servants, since their costume showed their position clearly enough—but it sometimes applies also to those of the highest rank, as in this instance to Atossa.

Aeschylus' earlier play, the *Suppliants*, resembles the *Persians* in having no prologue, and so at vs. 12 of the parodus the choreutae disclose their identity by declaring that Danaus is their father. Moreover, since Danaus enters the orchestra simultaneously with the chorus, this statement serves to introduce him also, though he has no chance to speak until vs. 176. When he does speak, however, he makes assurance doubly sure by addressing the chorus as his "children." Still again, in the fourth-century *Rhesus*, which also has no prologue, the chorus marches in and summons Hector by name from his quarters (vs. 10).

Thus from the fact that the early plays had no prologues, there grew up the practice of having the chorus (or coryphaeus) introduce not merely the first actor but every new character, as he appeared. For example, when the king of Argos makes his entrance in the *Suppliants* he engages in conversation with the Danaids, ignoring their father, and in reply to their question declares his name and station (vss. 247 ff.). Originally this technique was doubtless due in part also to the exigencies of the one-actor period (see p. 165, above), and it continued to be the regular practice, even after prologues were *en règle*, in all the plays of Aeschylus and in the earlier ones of Sophocles and Euripides. In comedy this method of procedure was less common, partly because this was no longer the usual convention in contemporaneous tragedy and partly because comedy closely approximates the manners of everyday life, which do not indorse this kind of introduction. When employed in comedy it was often intended to give a tone of tragic parody. For instance, in Aristophanes' *Acharnians*, vss. 1069 f., the approach of a messenger is announced by the chorus as follows: "Lo, here speeds one 'with bristled crest' as though to proclaim some message dire," the tragic tone of which in the original is unmistakable.[1]

Phrynichus' *Phoenician Women* was the first play which we know to have had a prologue (476 B.C.). Aeschylus' *Seven against Thebes* has the earliest extant prologue (467 B.C.). Of course, this change in the economy of the play involved a change also in dramatic technique. Now the entrance of actors preceded that of the chorus. If one actor came alone he had to introduce himself, as Eteocles does in the *Seven:* "If we succeed, the credit belongs to heaven; but if we fail, Eteocles alone will loudly be assailed throughout the town." If two actors enter together at the beginning of the play they may by alternately addressing each other by name make their identity clear to the audience, as Cratus and Hephaestus do in Aeschylus' *Prometheus Bound*. Moreover, before his exit Cratus calls Prometheus, whom he has helped to nail to the rocky background, by name (vs. 85). We have seen that when the chorus opened a play they introduced the actors who followed them. It would be natural that when the relative position of actors and chorus was interchanged the technique of introduction should also be reversed; in other words, that one of the actors in the prologue should now introduce the on-coming chorus as the latter had previously introduced the actors. This actually occurs in this play: when the choreutae appear, the bound Prometheus addresses them as "children of Tethys and Oceanus," vss. 136–40. The same artifice recurs in Aeschylus' *Libation-Bearers*, vss. 10–16 (see below). But it is self-evident that this manner of introducing the chorus would seldom be satisfactory. In truth, as the chorus gradually but unmistakably lost its importance, its individuality faded away, and the need of formally introducing or identifying it almost disappeared.

[1] Cf. note on these lines in Starkie's edition, and Murray, *op. cit.*, p. 30.

The chorus soon lost the exclusive privilege of introducing actors by *addressing* them. We have seen that Cratus and Hephaestus exercise this function for one another, and the former does the same for Prometheus. But the poets continued much longer to use the chorus in *announcing* the approach of a new character. Dr. Graeber (*op. cit.*, p. 26) claims that Euripides was the first to employ an actor for this purpose. In his *Alcestis* (vss. 24 ff.), Apollo says:

> Lo, yonder Death;—I see him nigh at hand,
> Priest of the dead, who comes to hale her down
> To Hades' halls, etc. [Way's translation]

But just twenty years before, in Aeschylus' *Libation-Bearers* (vss. 10–17), Orestes announced the approach of the chorus and Electra as follows:

> What see I now? What company of women
> Is this that comes in mourning garb attired?
> . . . .
> Or am I right in guessing that they bring
> Libations to my father, soothing gifts
> To those beneath? It cannot but be so.
> I think Electra, mine own sister, comes,
> By wailing grief conspicuous. [Plumptre's translation]

Possibly Graeber did not consider the last instance formulaic enough to count. But however this may be, at last the actors largely took over the function of announcing new characters, as they previously had that of addressing them.

In comedy proper names, and consequently introductions, are less important. The names of tragedy were largely traditional and conveyed a meaning to all educated persons in the audience as soon as they heard them (see pp. 127 f., above); but in comedy a character might almost as well have no name at all as one which had no associations for the spectators. Accordingly, Aristophanes and Plautus left many of their characters nameless. Of course when well-known citizens of Athens, such as Socrates, Euripides, or Lamachus, were ridiculed, they were definitely named at their first appearance. When a significant comic name

was employed it was not mentioned until the audience was in a
position to appreciate the point of the joke, sometimes not until
well along in the play.   Thus in Aristophanes' *Birds* the names
of Pisthetaerus (Plausible) and Euelpides (Hopeful) are first
mentioned at vss. 644 f.

I conclude this section with three examples of clever introductions. In Euripides' *Bacchanals* (vss. 170 ff.) the blind
Tiresias cries:

> Gate-warder, ho! call Cadmus forth the halls
> . . . . Say to him that Tiresias
> Seeks him—he knoweth for what cause I come,

and Cadmus, coming out, replies:

> Dear friend, within mine house I heard thy voice,
> And knew it, the wise utterance of the wise.
>
> [Way's translation]

The announcement of a new character's coming was usually a
pretty artificial device, but it is plausibly employed a little
farther on (vss. 210 ff.) in this same play, when Cadmus says:

> Since thou, Tiresias, seest not this light,
> I will for thee be spokesman of thy words.
> Lo to these halls comes Pentheus hastily.
>
> [Way's translation]

Again, at the beginning of Sophocles' *Oedipus at Colonus*, Oedipus
inquires: "To what place have we come, Antigone? Who will
receive the wandering Oedipus?"   In a blind man these questions are especially natural, and the use of the proper names
identifies the actors' rôles.   Soon a stranger approaches, and
to him Oedipus repeats his first question (vs. 38).   His replies
reveal the location and significance of the scenic setting.   The
directness of the play's first line finds a parallel in Shakespeare's
Twelfth Night, Act I, scene 2:

> VIOLA.   What country, friends, is this?
> CAPTAIN.   This is Illyria, lady.

The third compensation for the lack of a playbill was afforded
by the use of masks (see pp. 221 ff., below).   In Old Comedy
contemporaneous personages were often introduced, and we are

FIG. 68.—Mask of a Slave in New Comedy.

See p. 213, n. 1

FIG. 69.—Terra Cotta Mask in Berlin Representing a Courtesan in New Comedy.

See p. 213, n. 1

told that their masks were true enough to life for their identity to be recognizable before the actors had uttered a word.   According to a late anecdote, at the presentation of Aristophanes' *Clouds*, Socrates rose from his place and remained standing during the whole performance so that strangers in attendance might recognize the original of his double on the stage.   In the *Knights* (vss. 230 ff.), Aristophanes explains the absence of a portrait-mask for Cleon on the ground that the mask-makers were too apprehensive of that demagogue's vengeance to reproduce his features.   But the playbill value of masks was seen more fully in the case of more or less conventionalized characters, especially in New Comedy (Figs. 68 f.).[1]   Pollux, a writer of the second century A.D., describes twenty-eight such masks for tragedy and forty-four for New Comedy.   The hair, of varying amount, color, coiffure, and quality, seems to have been the chief criterion, but dress, complexion, facial features, etc., were also taken into account.   The make-up of every stock character was fixed with some definiteness and must have been well known to all intelligent spectators.   Thus the first glimpse of approaching actors enabled an ancient audience to identify the red-headed barbarian slave, the pale lovelorn youth, the boastful soldier, the voracious parasite, the scolding wife, the flatterer, the "French" cook, the maiden betrayed or in distress, the stern father, the designing courtesan, etc., much more easily than a playbill of the modern type would have done.

If our modern playgoer in ancient Athens were an American and so accustomed to staid conduct in a theatrical audience, he would be surprised at the turmoil of an Athenian performance. A Frenchman, familiar with the riots which greeted Victor Hugo's *Hernani* or Bernstein's *Après Moi*, would be better prepared for the situation.   But in any case he would soon discover that a prize was to be awarded both in tragedy and in comedy, and that each poet had his friends, partisans, and claque. The comic poets at least made no attempt to conceal the fact that there was a prize and that they were "out" for it.   In

[1] Figs. 68 f. are taken from Robert, *op. cit.*, Figs. 55 and 77, respectively.

almost every play Aristophanes' choruses advance reasons, sometimes serious, sometimes fantastic, for favoring their poet and giving him the victory. A few examples will suffice. In the *Women in Council* (vss. 1154 ff.) the chorus says:

> But first, a slight suggestion to the judges.
> Let the wise and philosophic choose me for my wisdom's sake,
> Those who joy in mirth and laughter choose me for the jests I make;
> Then with hardly an exception every vote I'm bound to win. . . . .
> Keep your oaths, and well and truly judge between the rival plays.
> > [Rogers' translation]

Birds, vss. 1101 f.:

> Now we wish to tell the judges, in a friendly sort of way,
> All the blessings we shall give them, if we gain the prize today.
> > [Rogers' translation]

Aristophanes was bald-headed, and therefore the chorus humorously appeals for the votes of all those similarly afflicted; cf. *Peace*, vss. 765 ff.:

> It is right then for all, young and old, great and small,
> > Henceforth of my side and my party to be,
> And each bald-headed man should do all that he can
> > That the prize be awarded to me.   [Rogers' translation]

The *Birds* (vss. 1763 ff.) concludes with a sort of "Lo, the conquering hero comes," an adaptation of Archilochus:

> Raise the joyous Paean-cry,
> Raise the song of Victory.
> Io Paean, alalalae,
> Mightiest of the Powers, to thee!   [Rogers' translation],

where Rogers comments: "These triumphal cries not only celebrate the triumph of Pisthetaerus [in the play], but also prognosticate the victory of Aristophanes in the dramatic competition." Similarly, at the end of the *Women in Council* (vss. 1179 ff.):

> Then up with your feet and away to go.
> > Off, off to the supper we'll run.
> With a whoop for the prize, hurrah, hurrah,
> With a whoop for the prize, hurrah, hurrah,
> > Whoop, whoop, for the victory won!
> > [Rogers' translation],

where the same editor and translator again comments as follows:
"These Bacchic cries (*Evoi, Evae*) do not merely celebrate the
success of Praxagora's revolution, they also prognosticate the
poet's own success over his theatrical rivals in the Bacchic
contest." In tragedy we naturally could not expect anything
so frank and undisguised as the first three passages just cited,
but for the last two an adequate parallel is found in the tag
which Euripides employed at the conclusion of his *Iphigenia
among the Taurians, Orestes*, and *Phoenician Maids:*

> Hail, reverèd Victory:
> Rest upon my life; and me
> Crown, and crown eternally.   [Way's translation],

which the ancient scholiast and modern editors rightly interpret
as a prayer for victory in the contest.

But if this were the extent of the influence which the fact of
there being a contest exercised upon Greek drama, the matter
might quickly be dismissed. Actually, however, the system involved deeper consequences. It is unnecessary here to rehearse
the cumbersome process by which the judges were appointed and
rendered their decision upon dramatic events (see p. 272, below).
While designed to prevent bribery or intimidation, it had two
other effects as well. One was that, since we have no reason to
believe that the choice of judges was restricted in any way or
that they were not selected from the entire free population, the
judges would therefore represent the average intelligence and
taste, and a poet who cared for victory had to accommodate
himself to this situation and could not make his appeal merely to
the superior attainments of the favored, intellectual class.
Secondly, like most officials at Athens, the judges were liable to
be called to account for their conduct. In fact on the second
day after the conclusion of the City Dionysia a special popular
assembly was held in the theater for the express purpose of airing
complaints concerning the management of the festival; and if
the judges were thought to have been recreant to their duties or
guilty of favoritism, action could be taken against them at that
time while the popular anger was still hot and by the votes of

the very persons whose wishes had been balked. The total effect of these arrangements was to render the judges extremely sensitive to the public's expression of opinion, which was manifested by whistling, catcalls, applause, knocking the heels against the seats, etc. Especially in the dithyrambic contests, where tribal rivalry entered in, feeling sometimes ran very high and personal encounters were not infrequent. To quell such riotous disorders it became necessary to appoint certain officials to maintain order, like sergeants-at-arms. In view of these conditions, it is not surprising that Plato[1] complains that the choice of victor had practically been intrusted to a general show of hands and that the necessity of pleasing the popular taste had corrupted the very poets themselves. Let us consider just how this tendency manifested itself.

First of all, then, in the *Knights*, Aristophanes appeals to the audience to impress the judges by a hearty burst of applause; cf. vss. 544 ff.:

> So seeing our Poet began
> In a mood so discreet, nor with vulgar conceit rushed headlong
>   before you at first,
> *Loud surges of praise to his honour upraise; salute him, all hands,*
>   *with a burst*
>   *Of hearty triumphant Lenaean applause,*
> That the bard may depart, all radiant and bright
> To the top of his forehead with joy and delight,
>   *Having gained, by your favour, his cause.*
>
>   [Rogers' translation]

But some of Aristophanes' contemporaries stooped far lower than this. In the *Wasps* he warns the audience not to expect "two slaves scattering nuts among the spectators out of a basket" (vss. 58 f.), animadverting upon a scene in a recent play by Eupolis. Again, in the *Plutus* (vss. 789 ff.) one of the characters refuses an invitation to have titbits distributed and adds: "It is beneath the dignity of a poet to scatter figs and delicacies to the spectators, and on these terms to force their laughter." In the *Peace* (vss. 962 ff.) he ridiculed such practices by providing every spectator with at least one grain of barley! A more

[1] Cf. *Laws* 659A–C.

drastic parody was perpetrated by Hegemon, who brought a cloakful of stones into the orchestra to be thrown at the spectators! It is only fair to state that Aristophanes did not lower himself by using such unprofessional appeals, but the point which I am urging is confirmed by the practice of his rivals and by the fact that he sometimes explains his own defeats by his unwillingness to resort to their methods.

From the nature of the case, tragedy could exhibit no appeals so undisguised as the above. To judge from Plato's language, just cited, in some of the tragedies of his day we might have found closer parallels to these artifices of the comic playwrights. Nevertheless, fifth-century tragedy does reveal how the tragic poets tickled the palates of their auditors. They did this in two ways: first, they appealed to national pride by rewriting the mythology in such a way as to assign to Athenian worthies a part which non-Attic tradition did not recognize; and secondly, they aroused the chauvinistic spirit by the sentiments, whether eulogistic of Athens or derogatory to her enemies, which they placed in their characters' mouths. These points might be illustrated at great length; it will suffice to mention a few examples.

According to Attic tradition, Medea sojourned for a while at Athens. Euripides took advantage of this fact in order to introduce the Aegeus episode into his *Medea* and thus bring the Attic king into connection also with an earlier part of the Colchian's career. His character in this play is presented in agreeable contrast to that of both Medea and Jason, and his chivalry in offering Athens to Medea as an asylum from her enemies would bring a thrill of pride to every Attic heart. Furthermore, his presence served to motivate the famous choral ode (vss. 824 ff.) beginning:

> O happy the race in the ages olden
>   Of Erechtheus, the seed of the blest Gods' line,
> In a land unravaged, peace-enfolden,
>   Aye quaffing of Wisdom's glorious wine, etc.[1]

[Way's translation]

---

[1] See pp. xvii f. above, and cf. Bartsch, *Entwickelung des Charakters der Medea in der Tragödie des Euripides* (Breslau, 1852), p. 24. For the Boeotian version of the incident in Euripides' *Suppliants*, cf. Pausanias i. 39. 2.

Athens as a place of refuge for suppliants was a favorite note: the conduct of Demophon in Euripides' *Children of Heracles* and that of Theseus in Euripides' *Suppliants* and Sophocles' *Oedipus at Colonus* must have given great pleasure to an Athenian audience.

Still more striking are the sentiments of the dramatic characters.   When Euripides' *Children of Heracles* was produced, the Spartans were accustomed to invade and ravage Attica every year.   To the ancestors of these pillagers Iolaus says in the play (vss. 309 ff.):

> Boys, we have put our friends unto the test:—
> If home-return shall ever dawn for you,
> And your sires' halls and honours ye inherit,
> Saviours and friends account them evermore,
> And never against their land lift hostile spear,
> Remembering this, but hold them of all states
> Most dear. [Way's translation]

Think what indignation at such ingratitude must have welled up in every spectator's heart!   Later on in the same play (vss. 1026 ff.) the Argive king, Eurystheus, whom Athens has just defeated in battle, is made to say:

> But I bestow
> On Athens, who hath spared, who shamed to slay me,
> An ancient oracle of Loxias,
> Which in far days shall bless her more than seems, etc.
> [Way's translation]

Again, in Euripides' *Alcestis* (vs. 452) the chorus of Pheraean elders drags in an allusion to "wealthy, splendid Athens," using the adjective λιπαραί.   Aristophanes said (*Acharnians*, vs. 640) that the Athenians could refuse nothing to anyone who applied this epithet to their city.   In Euripides' *Trojan Women* the choreutae are represented as wondering to what part of Greece the allotment of the spoils will send them, and express the wish that they "might come to the renowned, heaven-blest land of Theseus" (vss. 208 f.).   There was absolutely no reason why Trojans should entertain such a partiality toward Athens, and this undramatic sentiment is frankly directed to the *amor patriae*

of the playwright's compatriots.   In the same poet's *Andromache*
the title-character is made to burst out into the following invective against Sparta (vss. 445 ff.):

> O ye in all folk's eyes most loathed of men,
> Dwellers in Sparta, senates of treachery,
> Princes of lies, weavers of webs of guile,
> Thoughts crooked, wholesome never, devious all,—
> A crime is your supremacy in Greece! etc.[1]
>
> [Way's translation]

Thus, in effect the mythological heroes were dragged upon the
stage before the Athenian populace and forced to affirm: "Your
friends shall be my friends, and your enemies my enemies."

It would be easy greatly to extend this list, but I shall close
with two instances in which it is particularly obvious that
dramatic illusion has been sacrificed.   In Euripides' *Suppliants*
the Theban herald inquires, "Who is despot of this land?"
which gives Theseus an opportunity to say (vss. 403 ff.):

> First, stranger, with false note thy speech began,
> Seeking a despot here.   Our state is ruled
> Not of one only man: Athens is free.
> Her people in the order of their course
> Rule year by year, bestowing on the rich
> Advantage none; the poor hath equal right.
>
> [Way's translation]

Equally effective with any jingoes in the audience would be the
scene in the *Persians*.   Here Aeschylus "pays a pleasant com-
pliment to Athenian vanity" by means of the following dialogue
(vss. 231 ff.):

ATOSSA.   Where, O friends, is famous Athens on the broad face of the
earth?

CHORUS.   Far in the west: beside the setting of the lord of light the sun.

ATOSSA.   This same Athens, my son Xerxes longed with much desire to
take.

CHORUS.   Wisely: for all Greece submissive, when this city falls,
will fall.

[1] There is a tradition that this play was not produced in Athens, and some
maintain that it was first played at Argos.   In that case, in addition to appealing
to the convictions of the pro-Athenian, anti-Spartan party in Argos, there must
also have been the political motive of gaining converts for that party.

ATOSSA.   Are they many? do they number men enough to meet my son?

CHORUS.   What they number was sufficient once to work the Medes much harm.

ATOSSA.   Other strength than numbers have they? wealth enough within themselves?

CHORUS.   They can boast a fount of silver, native treasure to the land.

ATOSSA.   Are they bowmen good? sure-feathered do their pointed arrows fly?

CHORUS.   Not so. Stable spears they carry, massy armature of shields.

ATOSSA.   Who is shepherd of this people? lord (ἐπιδεσπόζει) of the Athenian host?

CHORUS.   Slaves are they to no man living, subject to no earthly name.

ATOSSA.   How can such repel the onset of a strong united host?

CHORUS.   *How* Darius knew in Hellas, when he lost vast armies there.

[Blackie's translation]

From a dramatic standpoint these questions are out of place, since Atossa's ignorance is improbable and is shown to be feigned by vss. 348 and 474 f. The first question is especially artificial. Nevertheless, point by point Atossa has drawn out all the distinctive points of pride in her son's enemies: their commanding influence, their numbers, their resources, their national weapon, their freedom, and their previous exploits. Aeschylus valued dramatic verisimilitude less highly than the fervent response that each of these couplets would evoke in every Athenian breast.

So we see that the tragic playwrights, more subtly than their comic confrères but fully as effectively, knew how to commend themselves to the good graces of the populace by incidents and sentiments no less palatable than the nuts and figs of comedy. If such conduct seem to some to be beneath the dignity of transcendent geniuses like Aeschylus and Euripides, a corrective may be found in the words of Schlegel:[1] "The dramatic poet is, more than any other, obliged to court external form and loud applause. But of course it is only in appearance that he thus lowers himself to his hearers; while, in reality, he is elevating them to himself."

[1] Cf. *Lectures on Dramatic Art and Literature,* translated by Black and Morrison, p. 38.

For to set up the Grecian method amongst us with success, it is absolutely necessary to restore, not only their religion and their polity, but to transport us to the same climate in which Sophocles and Euripides writ; or else, by reason of those different circumstances, several things which were graceful and decent with them must seem ridiculous and absurd to us, as several things which would have appeared highly extravagant to them must look proper and becoming with us.—JOHN DENNIS.

CHAPTER V

THE INFLUENCE OF PHYSICAL CONDITIONS[1]

Whether the use of masks in Greek drama originated in the mere desire for a disguise or in some ritualistic observance has not been definitely established. At any rate their employment was peculiarly well adapted to the genius of the ancient theater. First of all they enabled a small number of actors to carry a much larger number of parts (see p. 173, above). Secondly, the mouth-piece is claimed by some to have magnified the sound of the actor's voice, and thus helped to counteract the outstanding fact in the physical arrangement of ancient theaters, viz., their huge size (see p. 121, above). But in particular I wish to stress their bearing upon another feature of the classic drama—the hugeness of ancient theaters, together with the lack of opera glasses, made impossible an effect which modern audiences highly appreciate. I refer to the delicate play of expression on the mobile faces of the performers. In antiquity such refinements could scarcely have been seen outside of the orchestra. A partial substitute was occasionally found in a change of mask

[1] In addition to the works mentioned on pp. xvii and xxf., above, and the bibliography listed on pp. 57–59, above, cf. Hense, *Die Modificirung der Maske in der griechischen Tragödie* (1905); Dignan, *The Idle Actor in Aeschylus* (1905); Flickinger, "Scaenica," *Transactions of the American Philological Association*, XL (1909), 109 ff.; Robert, *Die Masken der neueren attischen Komödie* (1911); Rees, "The Significance of the Parodoi in the Greek Theater," *American Journal of Philology*, XXXII (1911), 377 ff., and "The Function of the Πρόθυρον in the Production of Greek Plays," *Classical Philology*, X (1915), 117 ff.; Harms, *De Introitu Personarum in Euripidis et Novae Comoediae Fabulis* (1914); Mooney, *The House-Door on the Ancient Stage* (1914); and Rambo, "The Wing-Entrances in Roman Comedy," *Classical Philology*, X (1915), 411 ff.

during the performance. This became possible if a character was off-stage at the time when his physical or mental state was supposed to be modified by some misfortune or accident.   Thus when some one's eyes are dashed out behind the scenes, as in Sophocles' *Oedipus the King*, Euripides' *Hecabe* and *Cyclops*, etc., the mask with which he appears after this event would naturally be different from that previously worn.   Similarly in Euripides' *Hippolytus* that hero, young and handsome, proudly leaves the stage at vs. 1102.   At vs. 1342 he is borne back in a dying condition, battered and torn by his runaway team.   It is plausible to suppose that this change is reflected by a modification of his mask and costume.   Still another type is seen in Euripides' *Phoenician Maids*.   A seer has demanded that Creon's son be slain to redeem the fatherland, but at vs. 990 Creon departs with the assurance that Menoeceus will seek safety in flight.   When he reappears at vs. 1308 his brow is said to be clouded by the news that his son had changed his mind and immolated himself for his country's good.

At best such a change of masks was but a clumsy and inadequate evasion of the difficulty; yet even this was out of the question whenever the catastrophe befell the character while on the scene.   In these cases the dramatists sometimes try to explain the immobility of the actor's mask.   An unusually successful instance occurs in Sophocles' *Electra*.   Electra had believed her brother dead, and now she unexpectedly holds him in her arms, alive and well.   But not a spark of joy can scintillate across her wooden features either then or later.   Her subsequent passivity is motivated by Orestes' request that she continue her lamentations and not allow their mother to read her secret in her radiant face (vss. 1296 ff.).   Electra replies that 'old hatred of her mother is too ingrained to allow her countenance to be seen wreathed in smiles, but that her tears will be tears of joy,' which has the merit of explaining also the present unresponsiveness of her features.   Sometimes the actor's face is hidden at times when strong emotions might be expected to play thereon.   For example, in Euripides' *Orestes*, Electra and the chorus stand in the orchestra and look toward the palace within which Helen is being slain and from which her dying cries issue. Inasmuch as their backs are turned to the audience, the spectators are free to suppose that their faces are working with excitement and horror. This fiction will be destroyed as soon as the performers wheel around toward the front again. Accordingly Electra is made to say:

> Belovèd dames, into the jaws of death
> Hermione cometh! Let our outcry cease:
> For into the net's meshes, lo, she falls.
> Fair quarry this shall be, so she be trapped.
> Back to your stations step with quiet look,
> With hue that gives no token of deeds done:
> And I will wear a trouble-clouded eye,
> As who of deeds accomplished knoweth nought.
>
> [Vss. 1313 ff.; Way's translation]

Electra's "trouble-clouded eye" does not refer to sorrow at Helen's death but at her brother's evil plight, and has characterized her mask from the beginning of the play.

Being largely balked in this matter, the Greeks characteristically turned the limitation to good account. The maskmakers did not attempt to fashion a detailed portrait—that would have suffered from the same difficulty as the naked human physiognomy; like our newspaper cartoonists, they reduced each character to the fewest possible traits, which were suggested in bold strokes and were easily recognizable by even the most remote spectator. Under close inspection representations of ancient masks seem grotesque and even absurd (Figs. 4, 8, 17–21, 66, and 68 f.), but it must be remembered that distance would to a great extent obliterate this impression. Moreover, such masks were admirably adapted to, and at the same time reinforced, the Greek tendency to depict types rather than individuals (see pp. 213 and 266 f.). On the modern stage masks are practically unknown. We must not allow that fact to prejudice us against their possible effectiveness. So respectable an authority as Mr. Gordon Craig declares "the expression of the human face as used by the theaters of the last few centuries" to be "spasmodic and ridiculous," that "the mask is the only right medium of portraying the expressions of the soul as shown through the expressions of the face," and that they "will be used in place of the human face in the near future"; and Mr. Cornford testifies to the baffling, tantalizing effect of a similar device at the Elizabethan Stage Society's representation of Marlowe's *Doctor Faustus*.[1]

The size of ancient theaters exercised an influence also in another direction. In the absence of arches and domes or modern steel girders it was impossible to roof over such a structure without a multitude of supports to obstruct the view and hearing. Accordingly, the proceedings were exposed to every caprice of the weather. For example, in the time of Demetrius Poliorcetes an unseasonable cold spell and frost broke up the procession. On the other hand the lack of an adequate and easily controlled artificial illuminant such as gas or electricity would have prevented the satisfactory lighting of a roofed theater, could they have built one. Therefore, like the Elizabethans, their dramas were presented in the daytime, and the constant harmony between lighting effects and dramatic situation, which to us is a commonplace, was entirely beyond their powers. But since it was also beyond their ken, it doubtless did not bother them especially, and like much else was safely left to the well-trained imaginations of the spectators. Thus dramatic characters frequently address the heavenly constellations in broad daylight, and ostensibly the entire action of the *Rhesus* and much of that in Euripides' *Cyclops* fall within the hours of night. Nevertheless, we know that the playwrights were sometimes self-conscious concerning this discrepancy. In Aristophanes' *Frogs* most of the action is supposed to be laid in Hades, and ancient opinion was unanimous in considering that a place of gloom. Since the poet could not count upon the sun going behind a cloud to suit his convenience, he undertook to put the audience on their guard against the incongruity.

[1] Cf. Craig, *On the Art of the Theatre* (1911), pp. 13 and 54 ff., and Cornford, *Thucydides Mythistoricus* (1907), p. 142, n. 2.

Toward the beginning of the play, when Dionysus is seeking directions for his journey to the lower world and the scene is still upon earth, Heracles tells him: "Next a breathing sound of flutes will compass you about and you will see a light most fair, *even as here*" (vss. 154 f.). Furthermore, shortly after the action is transferred to the realm of Pluto, the matter is once more called to the spectators' attention by the chorus of initiates singing (vss. 454 f.): "We alone have a sun and gracious light."

So far as I have observed, the tragedians never stooped to apologize for this absurdity, but they were willing, whenever possible, to accommodate themselves to actual conditions. The dramatic exercises are said to have begun at sunrise. Consequently, it is not surprising that the action of tragedies like Aeschylus' *Agamemnon* and Euripides' *Iphigenia at Aulis*, which stood first in the series presented on the same day, should open before daybreak. I must add, however, that such scenes occur also in comedies and in tragedies which did not stand first in their series, both of which must have been presented in the full light of day. These instances of incongruity are to be explained by stating that the arrangements and physical conditions which caused the Greek playwrights usually to crowd the action of their dramas within a period of twenty-four hours (see p. 250, below) would also lead them to make the dramatic day as long as possible by beginning the action of their plays at early morning.

Lessing and others have unfavorably contrasted Voltaire's employment of ghosts with Shakespeare's practice. The comparison rests principally upon two points: that the ghost of Hamlet's father complied with "recognized ghostly conditions" by appearing in the stillness of night and speaking to but one, unaccompanied person, while the ghost of Ninus in *Sémiramis* outraged accepted beliefs by stalking out of his tomb in broad daylight and making his appearance before a large assembly. Now it is interesting to observe that Greek practice is liable to these same criticisms. Thus in Aeschylus' *Persians* (vss. 681 ff.) the ghost of Darius appears in the full light of day and before his queen and no less than twelve councilors.   In Euripides' *Hecabe* (vss. 1 ff.) the difficulties are somewhat obviated by placing the appearance of Polydorus' ghost in the prologue, before any other actor or the chorus has come in; and perhaps Hecabe's words in vss. 68 f., "O mirk of the night," etc., are intended to suggest that the preceding scene took place in darkness.   In any case, whatever make-believe the dramatists might choose to practice, the considerations just mentioned, together with the almost constant presence of the chorus, normally compelled apparitions appearing in Greek drama to violate two provisions in the standard code of ghostly etiquette.

It is well known that in the earliest extant Greek plays, viz., the *Suppliants, Persians*, and *Prometheus Bound* of Aeschylus, the scene is laid in the open countryside with not a house in sight and with no scenic accessories except an altar, tomb, or rock, respectively.   But that this circumstance was explicable by the character of the Athenian theater did not become evident until Dr. Dörpfeld's excavations on that site in 1886, 1889, and 1895 (see pp. 65 ff., above, and Figs. 32 and 32a).   From 499 B.C. until about 465 B.C. the theater at Athens consisted of an orchestral circle nearly ninety feet in diameter and somewhat south of the present orchestra, and an auditorium arranged partly about it on the Acropolis slope.   Immediately behind the orchestra there was no scene-building or back scene, but a six-foot declivity.   Only within the orchestra itself, at the center or to one side, might there be erected for temporary use some such theatrical "property" as an altar or tomb.   Consequently it was inevitable that playwrights of the early fifth century in choosing an imaginary scene for their plays should react to these physical conditions and localize the dramatic action in more or less deserted spots.   Even as late as Aeschylus' *Seven against Thebes* (467 B.C.), although the scene no longer is laid in the countryside but on the Theban Acropolis, yet this is still a place without inhabitants or houses.   It should be noted that at this period the exclusive mode of ingress and egress was by the side entrances, the parodi; under normal conditions, any movement into the orchestra or out of it, at the rear, was entirely precluded by the declivity. That such a primitive theater would suffice for the needs of that or even a later period is proved by the remains of the structure at Thoricus (Figs. 70 f.),[1] which was never brought to a higher state of development (see p. 103, above), and by the fact that even at a later period dramatists sometimes voluntarily reverted

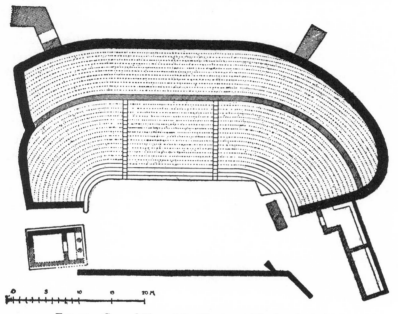

Fig. 70.—Ground Plan of the Theater at Thoricus in Attica

See p. 227, n. 1

to this unpretentious stage setting. For example, in Sophocles' *Oedipus at Colonus* the background represented the untrodden grove of the Eumenides, so that practically all the entrances and exits were restricted to the parodi. An exceptional rear exit is afforded by Aeschylus' *Prometheus Bound*, and an exceptional rear entrance by the next play in the trilogy, the *Prometheus*

[1] Fig. 70 is taken from Dörpfeld-Reisch, *Das griechische Theater*, Fig. 43; Fig. 71 is from a photograph taken by Professor L. L. Forman and furnished by Dr. A. S. Cooley.

Unbound. We have already seen (see pp. 166 f. and 174, above) how in the former play the hero, being represented by a dummy, cannot speak until Hephaestus leaves the scene by a side entrance and makes his way behind the rock upon which Prometheus is bound. In the absence of a scene-building, the six-foot declivity must have been utilized to conceal the second half of this movement. Now the *Prometheus Bound* ends as the Titan and his crag sink into the depths; at the beginning of the *Prometheus Unbound* this crag has emerged from the abyss. What was the reason for this maneuver? Obviously to enable an actor to be substituted for the lay figure of Prometheus. So long as the hero was fixed in his place, an actor concealed behind him experienced little difficulty in speaking his lines for him; but as the time drew near for his release a living impersonator was required. How was this substitution managed? I conceive that a wooden frame-work, rudely suggesting a rock, was propped up at the outer extremity of the orchestra. At the moment of the catastrophe the supports were removed and the structure allowed to collapse into the declivity. After an interval sufficient for the exchange had elapsed, the rocky background was once more raised into its place and braced.

About 465 B.C. an advance step in theatrical conditions was taken when a scene-building was erected on and just behind the orchestra, where the declivity had previously been (see pp. 66 and 339 ff.). This first scene-building must have been very simple, probably of only one story, with parascenia but no proscenium (Fig. 74), and capable of being readily rebuilt so as to be accommodated to the needs of different plays. The extant dramas show that from the first the new background was pierced by at least one door and that the number was soon raised to three, though they were not all used in every production. The different doorways were conventionally thought of as leading into as many separate houses or buildings. Thus, whereas the actors had hitherto been able to enter and depart only through the two parodi, from one to three additional means of entrance were now provided. Moreover, the mere fact of having a background was

FIG. 71

AUDITORIUM AND ORCHESTRA OF THE THEATER AT THORICUS

See p. 227, n. 1

no small advantage. For example, it enabled Aeschylus to introduce a distinct improvement in dramatic technique. Heretofore scenes of violence must either have been boldly enacted before the spectators' eyes or reported by a messenger. Since the sacrosanctity of the actor while engaged in a performance and the Greeks' aesthetic sense interfered with the first alternative (see pp. 127–32, above), doubtless the second had usually been resorted to. Now Aeschylus is said to have invented the very effective device of having a character killed behind the scenes during the play. In view of the physical conditions it will be understood that the failure of Aeschylus' predecessors to avail themselves of this expedient was due to no lack of inventive genius on their part but simply to the entire absence in their time of a back scene to use for the purpose. It is not known just how long it took Aeschylus to discover this possibility in the new arrangements; but it was certainly not later than the *Agamemnon* (458 B.C.), in which the king's agonized death cries from behind the scenes (vss. 1343 and 1345) still have power to affect even modern audiences. Further modifications of this artifice have already been mentioned on p. 128.

One of the most troublesome problems that confront a playwright is inventing plausible motives to explain the entrances and exits of his characters. The fundamental nature of this problem appears from the words of a modern dramatist, Mr. Alfred Sutro: "Before I start writing the dialogue of a play, I make sure that I shall have an absolutely free hand over the entrances and exits: in other words, that there is ample and legitimate reason for each character appearing in any particular scene, and ample motive for his leaving it." Now in the interior scene, and especially in the box set, moderns have a marvelously flexible instrument for shifting personages on and off the scene; yet few can avoid abusing this resource and can repeat Mr. Bernard Shaw's boast: "My people get on and off the stage without requiring four doors to a room which in real life would have only one."[1] To the ancient writer the difficulty was still

[1] Cf. *Three Plays for Puritans*, p. xxxvi.

greater. Prior to 465 B.C., when some uninhabited spot was perforce chosen as the scene of action and the two parodi were the sole means of ingress, it was fairly easy to motivate a person's *first* entrance and withdrawal; but a reappearance proved a more difficult matter, and each additional character complicated the problem still further. Consequently, the ancient playwrights not infrequently frankly abandoned all search for a solution and considered that to leave a character standing in idleness during a whole scene or choral ode was less awkward and improbable than any motive which they could provide for his exit and re-entrance. Thus in Aeschylus' *Suppliants*, Danaus enters the orchestra with the chorus consisting of his daughters and remains at the altar, without a single word to say, during their parodus of a hundred and seventy-five lines. After a short scene the king of Argos appears, and then for over two hundred lines (vss. 234–479) Danaus is again ignored (see pp. 163 f., above). In this play the town of Argos is thought of as lying some distance away from the scene of action. Only an important errand would take Danaus there, and evidently the poet experienced difficulty in inventing as many errands as dramatic propriety required. Similarly at vss. 181 ff. of Aeschylus' *Seven against Thebes*, Eteocles rebukes the chorus for their fears and lamentations; yet apparently he has been standing there during their whole parodus (vss. 78–180) without a single word of protest! But it was not characteristic of the Greek genius tamely to submit to hindrances, and accordingly we are not surprised that Aeschylus actually secured a striking dramatic effect by leaving characters like Niobe and Achilles for considerable intervals speechless and immovable on the scene. When finally uttered, their startling cries of anguish were greatly enhanced by their previous long-continued silence. It may not be amiss to note that Molière obtained similar suspense by means quite opposite. In *Tartuffe*, contrary to all the accepted rules, the principal character does not appear upon the scene until after the beginning of the third act. But the conversation and disputes of the other dramatic personages have so inflamed our curiosity concerning him that we can scarcely wait to catch a glimpse of him, and his entrance finally is thrice as effective as if it had come earlier in the play.

The erection of a scene-building about 465 B.C. somewhat relieved the difficulty of the playwrights' problem. First of all the places of entrance were increased 50 per cent or more. Secondly, the new entrances were nearer the orchestra than were the parodi and enabled an actor to come in or depart more quickly. Thirdly, the presence of buildings almost required the scene to be laid in a town or city and correspondingly multiplied the possible motives for visiting it. And finally, since the doorways often represented the homes of certain of the dramatic characters, no elaborate motivation was needed to explain their passing in and out at frequent intervals. When his work was done, the useless actor could be temporarily eliminated with neatness and dispatch. These considerations and the introduction of the third actor at about the same time (see p. 167, above) soon doubled the amount of coming and going in the plays (cf. Mooney, *op. cit.*, p. 54). The influence of the former factor appears in Euripides' *Suppliants*, the action of which takes place before a temple. It so happens, however, that the temple doors in this case are not used for entrances and exits. Consequently of all Euripides' tragedies this one has the least passing to and fro. On the other hand the influence of the second factor is seen in the fact that this piece and Sophocles' *Oedipus at Colonus* (see p. 227, above), both making practically no use of their back scene but both employing three actors, are higher in "action" than the corresponding plays of Aeschylus, which belong to the two-actor period.

Nevertheless, when all is said, the erection of a scene-building still left the ancient dramatists far behind the moderns in the easy and plausible motivation of their characters' movements, and no further advance (from this point of view) was subsequently made in the theatrical arrangements. All the dramatic personages still had to come to the same (usually a public) place; they could not dodge in at one door and out at another at their creator's caprice, but whether entering or leaving had to walk a considerable distance in plain view of the spectators. Consequently the silent actor is found after 465 B.C. as well as before. Thus in Euripides' *Suppliants* one or more characters are being neglected at almost every point. But in my opinion this phenomenon is no longer due primarily to the inadequacy of the theatrical arrangements but to other considerations. For example, the limited number of actors often resulted in prolonged or awkward silence on the part of a character who was being impersonated by a mute (see pp. 174–82, above). Again, in the *Alcestis*, after Heracles has brought the queen back from her grave, she utters never a word. Euripides himself explains this on the ground that she may not speak until her consecration to the gods of the lower world be undone and the third day come (vss. 1144 ff.). This is a clever pretext but not the real reason. Nor do I think, as some do, that in this instance the limitation of actors is responsible, since only two actors speak in this scene and the play belongs to the three-actor period. Alcestis' silence springs rather from the impossibility of placing in her mouth a message worthy of her experiences, one which "telling what it is to die had surely added praise to praise." Still again the silence frequently arises from inability to master the technique of the trialogue (see pp. 169 f.) or from the nature of the plot. In any trial scene it is almost inevitable that both the judge and the accused should remain inactive for considerable intervals. Thus in Aeschylus' *Eumenides* the silence of Athena (vss. 585–673 and 711–33) and of Orestes (vss. 244–63, 307–435, 490–585, and 614–743) is scarcely more noteworthy than that of the Duke and Antonio in Act IV of *The Merchant of Venice*. When his case was about to be decided, Orestes terminated a silence of one hundred and thirty lines by the thrilling ejaculation, "O Phoebus Apollo, what shall the judgment be!" (vs. 744)—another example of the dexterity with which the Greek poets could transmute base metal into pure gold.

It need not be said that the same difficulty of plausible motivation puzzled the comic as well as the tragic writers of antiquity, and they extricated themselves with no less ingenuity

in their own way. For the further unfolding of the plot in
Plautus' *Pseudolus* it became necessary that that crafty slave
should explain to his accomplices certain developments which
had already been represented on the scene. Actually to repeat
the facts would have been tedious to the spectators, while to
motive an exit for all the parties concerned until the information
could be imparted and then to motive their re-entrance might
have proved difficult and certainly would have caused an awkward pause in the action. The poet therefore chose the bolder
course of dropping for the moment all dramatic illusion and at
the same time of slyly poking fun at the conventions of his art:
"This play is being performed for the sake of these spectators.
They have been here, and are aware of developments. I'll tell
you about them afterwards"(!) (vss. 720 f.).

We have already referred to the fact that topographical
conditions in Athens gave rise to a convention regarding the
significance of the parodi (see p. 208, above). As the spectator
sat on the south slope of the Acropolis at Athens, with the
orchestra and scene-buildings before him, the harbor of the
Piraeus and the market place lay toward his right and the open
country on his left (Fig. 29). And since the theater was roofless
and the performances given in daylight, these relationships were
visible and must at all times have been present to the consciousness of the audience. The matter was, therefore, one of more
consequence than in the modern theater, where many spectators,
being unable to see points of orientation outside, would be
puzzled to indicate the points of the compass. In the Athenian
theater, on the contrary, if the scene were laid locally no poet
or stage manager could have allowed a character from the Piraeus
to enter by the left (east) parodus without committing a patent
absurdity. In such a case there was, at the beginning, no
convention; the plays simply reacted to actual local conditions.
But the fifth-century plays were rarely laid in Athens, and in
them comparatively little is said of harbor, market place, or
countryside, whether at Athens or elsewhere. Apart from a rigid
convention, there would be no point in staging Aeschylus'

Suppliants, the scene of which is laid just outside the city of Argos, or Aristophanes' *Birds*, whose scene is supposed to be in the clouds, in such a way as to conform to Athenian topography. In fact, incidental allusions in the fifth-century plays, the comparative infrequency in them of references to harbor, country, and market place, and minor infelicities arising from any attempt to foist this convention upon them, would all seem to indicate that these plays had been written without much regard for local geography. But with increasing frequency Athens became the imaginary scene of comedies, and the relationships which had become a fixed rule for them were transferred to tragedy also, and soon to other theaters whose setting bore little or no resemblance to that of the theater of Dionysus Eleuthereus. Certainly by the time of New Comedy the convention was firmly established, and except for characters leaving or entering the houses in the background almost every exit or entrance was oriented for the audience with reference to country, harbor, or market place. When Greek comedy was transplanted to Italian soil the convention was taken over, too, and reappears, possibly with some modification, in the plays of Plautus and Terence.

Regardless of the convention, however, and the period of its origin there is one blemish which careful stage managers nowadays seek to avoid. When a door closes upon a departing character, it should not be immediately opened again to admit another character, whom the first character must have brushed against in the hall. A slight pause is somehow provided to enable the two characters to avoid meeting and to give the sense of space beyond the room on the stage. Now in Euripides' *Alcestis* a violation of this common-sense principle of stage craft seems to occur. At vs. 747 Admetus and the chorus have departed bearing the body of Alcestis to its last resting place. In the ensuing scene Heracles at last learns the identity of the deceased and at vs. 860 rushes out to wrestle with the king of the dead beside the grave. *In the very next verse* Admetus returns. According to the Hellenistic convention Heracles must have departed and Admetus have re-entered through the parodus at the audience's left.   But which parodus was employed does not in this case greatly matter.   The point is that since Heracles was bound for the spot from which Admetus was returning, they must have used *the same parodus*.   Nevertheless, later developments show that they did not meet; indeed, certain telling features of the dénouement would have been spoiled if they had. Yet how could they avoid doing so?   The play furnishes no reply.   So far as I can see the only way in which the difficulty can be obviated is by supposing that vss. 747–860 take place before a slightly different part of the palace from the rest of the play.   Scholars, however, do not commonly accept a change of scene in this piece (see pp. 250 f., below).

The space between the two parodi and leading past the scene-building was usually thought of as representing a street or road-way (see p. 86, above).   In the Hellenistic theater at Athens a stone proscenium ran across the front of the scene-building from one parascenium to the other (see p. 70, above) (Fig. 38), and it is likely that a wooden proscenium occupied the same space from about 430 B.C.   It is true that the stone foundation of the parascenia, which served as a framework for the proscenium, cannot be dated much earlier than 415–421 B.C. (see p. 67 and n. 1, above).   But there is now reason to believe that parascenia entirely of wood were erected long before permanent foundations were provided for them, perhaps as early as 465 B.C. (see pp. 342 f.), and the proscenium colonnade seems to have been employed at least as early as Euripides' *Hippolytus* (428 B.C.) and Aristophanes' *Clouds* (423 B.C.).   Confirmation for this conclusion may be found in the fact that the crane ($\mu\eta\chi\alpha\nu\dot{\eta}$) was introduced at about this same time (see p. 289, below).   When the scene was laid before a private house or a palace, the colonnade was in place as signifying its prothyron ($\pi\rho\dot{o}\theta\upsilon\rho\sigma\nu$) or "porch."   When the background was thought of as a temple the proscenium was its *pronaos* ($\pi\rho\dot{o}\nu\alpha\sigma$) or "portico."   Moreover, when a less conventional setting was required, painted panels ($\pi\dot{\iota}\nu\alpha\kappa\epsilon\varsigma$) could be inserted in the intercolumniations in order to suggest the desired locality, and in some theaters the proscenium columns were shaped so as to hold such panels more firmly in place (Fig. 72).[1] Thus the action in Sophocles' *Oedipus at Colonus* takes place before a grove, and that in Plautus' *The Fisherman's Rope*, along a beach. The interruption of natural scenery by columns at regular intervals would be disturbing to us; that it did not seem so to the Greeks was due not only to their ignorance of modern scenery but also to the sketchy shorthand which they practiced in other fields of art. On ancient vases, for example, a whole forest is frequently represented by a single tree. A

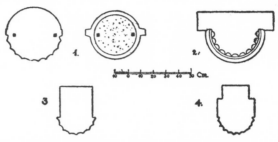

Fig. 72.—Horizontal Sections of Proscenium Columns at Megalopolis and Eretria (1), Epidaurus (2), Delos (3), and Oropus (4).

See p. 236, n. 1

similar convention obtains in the drama of modern Persia, where "the desert is represented by a handful of sand on the platform, the river Tigris by a leather basin full of water."[2] Sophocles is said to have invented scene painting during the lifetime of Aeschylus (see p. 66, above), but this must be interpreted as meaning that he had the panels applied directly to the front of the scene-building, the proscenium being not yet introduced. It has also been suggested, on the basis of certain vase paintings (Fig. 73),[3] that an actual porch (prothyron) was sometimes built

[1] Fig. 72 is taken from Puchstein, *Die griechische Bühne*, Fig. 3.

[2] Cf. Ridgeway, *Dramas and Dramatic Dances of Non-European Races*, p. 83.

[3] Fig. 73 is taken from Baumeister, *Denkmäler*, Fig. 980. Within the prothyron are the king of Corinth and his daughter, Jason's second wife. The latter is being assisted by her brother. In front lies an opened box which contained the poisoned gifts. From the other side the queen comes rushing. In the foreground is Medea slaying one of her children, while a youth tries to rescue the other. In

extending from the center of the proscenium or taking the place
of a proscenium and extending from the center of the scene-
building's front wall.   But perhaps these paintings are only
conventionalized representations of the proscenium colonnade

Fig. 73.—A Fourth-Century Vase in Munich Representing the Vengeance
of Medea.

See p. 236, n. 3

itself.   In any case it is important to observe that no background
corresponding to the scene-building is indicated on the vases.

Now it will be noted that these theatrical arrangements
made no provision for an interior scene.   The dramatic action
was necessarily laid in the open air, usually before a palace,

the center is Oistros, the demon of madness, mounted upon a dragon chariot.
Further on Jason is hastening to aid his boys, and on the extreme right is the ghost
of Aeetes, Medea's father.   The design is apparently not based upon Euripides'
Medea.   Cf. Earle's edition, pp. 60 f.

private house, or temple. Though occasional plays, like **Mr.** Louis Parker's *Pomander Walk,* show that the thing can still be managed, in general modern dramatists would be paralyzed by such a requirement. Nor is it correct to state that the classical poets "seldom had occasion to show an interior scene." The truth is precisely the opposite: having no way in which to show an interior they were constrained to rest content with alfresco scenes. Yet the situation was not so desperate as it would seem. Corneille pointed out that Greek kings could meet and speak in public without a breach of etiquette.[1] At the French court, and consequently on the French stage, such conduct would have been intolerable. In the second place the mildness of a southern climate justified some practices which might appear strange to more northern peoples. Many things which we would consider must be kept strictly within doors would sometimes take place in the street. Semi-privacy was afforded by porches and porticoes, that is, theatrically speaking, by the colonnade of the proscenium. Our nearest parallel would be sun parlors or screened porches and even these fall short. Doubtless this difference in weather conditions has something to do with the fact that modern playwrights of the classic school, who, though freed from the material restrictions of the ancients, have yet slavishly imitated them in so much else, have not followed them in this partiality for outdoor scenes. Allowance must also be made for the fact that in comedy the characters uniformly belonged to the lower strata of society. Accordingly we need feel little surprise that in Aristophanes' *Clouds* (vss. 1 ff.) Strepsiades and his son are disclosed sleeping before their home in the open air, though we have no reason to believe that they are either actual or prospective victims of tuberculosis. In Euripides' *Orestes* (vss. 1 ff.) the matricide, wasted by illness, lies on his couch before the palace in Argos under his sister's care. In Plautus' *The Churl* (vss. 448 ff.), Phronesium reclines on a bed before the house, pretending that she has given birth to a child. In Plautus' *The Haunted House* (vss. 248 ff.), Phile-

[1] Cf. *Discours des trois unités,* I, 119 (Regnier's edition; 1862).

matium asks her maid for a mirror, jewel box, etc., and a scene
of prinking ensues in the open air.   Scenes of outdoor feasting
and carousing are too numerous to deserve individual mention.
I cannot accept the contention that the action of such scenes
takes place in an "imaginary interior."   They are frankly out
of doors; in this connection such expressions as "outside the
house," "before the doors," etc., are frequent.   These scenes
were enacted in the colonnade of the proscenium and are correctly
copied from ancient life.   Of course I concede that in real life
they would take place indoors as often as out, or even more often;
but they were common enough as open-air scenes to justify the
playwrights in constantly transcribing them in this fashion.

But the significance of the considerations mentioned in the
last paragraph must not be overestimated.   The difficulty
arising from physical conditions in the theater was cumulative.
In other words the placing of any particular scene in the open
air was generally justifiable by ancient habits of living and not
difficult to motivate; but to place *every* scene in *every* play out
of doors and under these conditions to invent a plausible motive
for every entrance taxed the dramatists' powers to the utmost
and sometimes exceeded them.[1]   No wonder, then, that occasionally they abandoned all attempts to explain their characters'
movements and coolly allowed them to leave their dwellings and
to speak, without apology or excuse, of the most confidential
matters in a public place.   Many instances of this license,
however, seem to have been conditioned by definite rules.   For
example, if a character leaves his house while engaged in conversation with another, no reason is given for their entrance,
i.e., for their not having concluded the conversation where it was
begun.   Examples of this technique do not occur until about
400 B.C. (see p. 310, below, and the instances there cited).
Secondly, no entrance motive is provided when a character is to
take part in a dialogue with another who is already on the scene
and whose own entrance has been motived.   Thus in Euripides'
Alcestis, Heracles enters at vs. 476 in order to seek hospitality

[1] Cf. Legrand, *The New Greek Comedy*, pp. 356 f., Loeb's translation.

at Admetus' palace; at vs. 506 the chorus announces the king's emergence, which is entirely unmotived. Six other examples of this technique occur in Greek tragedy.

Nevertheless, in general the ancient playwrights displayed an amazing fertility of invention in explaining why their characters came out of doors and spoke in so public a place of matters which might more naturally have been reserved for greater privacy. Thus in Euripides' *Alcestis*, Apollo explains his leaving Admetus' palace on the ground of the pollution which a corpse would bring upon all within the house (vss. 22 f.) and Alcestis herself, though in a dying condition, fares forth to look for the last time upon the sun in heaven (vs. 206). Oedipus is so concerned in the afflictions of his subjects that he cannot endure the thought of making inquiries through a servant but comes forth to learn the situation in person (Sophocles' *Oedipus the King*, vss. 6 f.); Carion is driven out of doors by the smoke of sacrifice upon the domestic altar (Aristophanes' *Plutus*, vss. 821 f.); Polyphemus leaves his cave intending to visit his brothers for a carousal (cf. Euripides' *Cyclops*, vss. 445 f. and 507 ff.). In Euripides' *Andromache*, Hermione's nurse, worn out in the attempt to save her mistress from self-destruction, hurries out and appeals to the chorus for assistance; a moment later Hermione herself escapes from the restraining clutches of her attendants and rushes upon the stage (vss. 816 ff.). Agathon cannot compose his odes in the winter time unless he bask in the sunlight (Aristophanes' *Women at the Thesmophoria*, vss. 67 f.). In Plautus' *The Haunted House* (vss. 1 ff.) one slave is driven out of doors by another as the result of a quarrel. The lovelorn Phaedra teases for light and air (Euripides' *Hippolytus*, vss. 178ff.). Medea's nurse apologizes for soliloquizing before the house with the excuse that the sorrows within have stifled her and caused her to seek relief by proclaiming them to earth and sky (cf. Euripides' *Medea*, vss. 56 ff. and pp. 307 f., below). And Antigone informs her sister that she has summoned her out of doors in order to speak with her alone (Sophocles' *Antigone*, vss. 18 f.), as if that were the most natural place in the world for a tête-à-tête. In connection with this last instance it must be remembered that the interior of ancient houses was arranged differently than ours and was more favorable for eavesdropping (cf. Terence's *Phormio*, vss. 862–69).

The difficulty inherent in the exclusive use of exterior scenes appears very strikingly in Euripides' *Cyclops*. Here the action would naturally take place in Polyphemus' cave, as it does in Homer's *Odyssey;* but, theatrical conditions making that impossible, the scene is laid before the cave's mouth. Contrary to verisimilitude, therefore, the poet is obliged to allow Odysseus to pass in and out without let or hindrance. Why, then, does he make no attempt to escape? Euripides anticipated this query and explained Odysseus' remaining by regard for his companions' safety (vss. 479 ff.). But why was it not equally feasible for his comrades to leave the cave and for all to be saved together? The poet can think of no better motive than that Odysseus' pride and sense of honor caused him to desire to take vengeance on Polyphemus for having murdered some of his followers (vss. 694 f.).

Being unable actually to represent an interior scene the Greek playwrights gladly availed themselves of several substitutes. The most common of these was the messenger's speech (see p. 164, above), by which occurrences that had taken place indoors were related to the chorus or to actors before the house. Another substitute was found in the cries of characters murdered behind the scenes (see pp. 128 and 229, above). A third method consisted in throwing open the doors in the background and revealing a scene of murder done within (see p. 128, above). We are told further that sometimes, when the doors were flung open, a platform, with a tableau mounted upon it, was pushed forward for a few moments (see the discussion of the *eccyclema* on pp. 284–89, below). A fourth evasion of the restriction occurs in Euripides' *Hippolytus*, vss. 565 ff. Phaedra from her couch in the proscenium colonnade hears the voices of her confidential slave and Hippolytus engaged in conversation within doors. She invites the chorus in the orchestra near by to join her in listening at the door—a proposal which for obvious dramatic reasons the choreutae cannot accept; but her own cries and exclamations of despair as she listens stir the audience much more profoundly than the conversation itself could have done. Thus the main portion of the dialogue between Hippolytus and the slave is supposed to take place indoors. It is concluded before the house, the two interlocutors entering the stage at vs. 600.

Still again, the dramatists of New Comedy were fond of representing a character in the act of passing through a doorway and shouting back parting injunctions to those within—an artifice which is sufficiently transparent and is justly ridiculed in Terence's *Andrian Girl*. A nurse has been summoned in a confinement case and issues her final instructions while leaving the house. Simo, who thinks no child has been born and that it is all a trick to deceive him, turns fiercely upon the scheming slave at his side: "Who that knows you would not believe this to be the product of your brain? She did not tell what must be done for the mother in her presence; but after taking her departure she screams from the street to the attendants within. O Davus, do you scorn me so? Pray do I seem so suitable a victim for you to beguile with such transparent stratagems? You ought to work out the details of your plots more exactly, so that I might at least *seem* to be feared in case I learned the truth" (vss. 489 ff.). Be it noted, however, that such a stickler for realism as Ibsen occasionally made use of this same device (cf. *Pillars of Society*, Acts II and III). A close parallel occurs in Aristophanes' *Acharnians*, vss. 1003 ff.

As a final illustration of the artificiality of the exterior scene I may refer to the manner in which characters are brusquely called out of their homes to meet the demands of the dramatic situation. Thus in Euripides' *Iphigenia at Aulis* a messenger enters and unceremoniously shouts to his queen within doors:

> Daughter of Tyndareus, Clytemnestra, come
> Forth from the tent, that thou mayst hear my tale.
>   [Vss. 1532 f.; Way's translation],

and in Euripides' *Children of Heracles*, Iolaus calls:

> Alcmene, mother of a hero-son,
> Come forth, give ear to these most welcome words.
>   [Vss. 642 f.; Way's translation]

To judge by such a dramatic expedient, the front walls of ancient houses must have been pretty thin![1]   It is interesting to contrast the uproar which is required in Shakespeare's *Othello* (Act I, scene 1) before Brabantio can be brought to his window.   Perhaps the most amusing instance of this convention occurs in Plautus' *Braggart Captain*.   In that play a slave had to be deluded into believing that two women of identical appearance lived in adjoining houses.   Accordingly he is first sent into one house and then into the other, while directions are shouted to the one woman in question to move back and forth by means of a secret passage so as always to meet him (vss. 523 ff.). This of course presupposes that the walls will be thin enough for the woman to hear through but too thick for the slave to do so!

The publicity thus inevitably attending conversations of the most private nature was rendered still more incongruous by the constant presence of the chorus; but this topic has already been treated on pages 154–57, above.

Whether the fifth-century theater was provided with a drop curtain has often been discussed.   I am inclined to think there is no conclusive evidence for the constant and regular use of one. The considerations upon which the argument mainly rests are a priori.   That is to say, in several Greek plays the actors must arrange themselves and be in position before the action begins. This is the situation in Euripides' *Orestes* and Aristophanes' *Clouds* (see p. 238, above).   Did Orestes take to his sick bed in full view of the assembled audience?   But he is said (cf. vs. 39) already to have been there for five days!   And though the action of the *Clouds* begins just before dawn, Strepsiades and his son are supposed to have lain before the house all night.   In such matters we must not permit our own prepossessions to mislead us.   In mediaeval drama though a character was in view of the audience he could be thought of as, in effect, behind the scenes until his part began.   Similarly in oriental theaters today performers are treated as if they could put on the mask of

[1] For another interpretation cf. Mooney, *op. cit.*, p. 19 and n. 13.

invisibility. The only standing concession which I can make to modern feeling consists in granting that the proscenium columns partially screened the actors from the audience while they were taking their places. In my opinion the nearest approach to the use of a curtain occurs in Sophocles' *Ajax* and is quite exceptional. That hero committed suicide on the stage, and his body was found in a woodland glen (νάπος, vs. 892) near the seashore. I suppose that the door in the front of one of the parascenia[1] (Fig. 74) was left open to represent the entrance to the glen, and that around and behind it were set panels painted to suggest the woodland coast and the glen (see pp. 235 f., above). Into this opening Ajax collapsed as he fell upon his sword. At vs. 915, Tecmessa "conceals him wholly with this enfolding robe." Possibly this means that the cloth was fastened about the corpse and across the doorway, thus enabling a mute or a lay figure to be substituted for the corpse and releasing this actor to appear as Teucer in the remainder of the play (see p. 174, above). Whatever the means employed, it is certain that a substitution was effected.

It has often been maintained that the abrupt endings of so many modern plays is due to the fact that we possess a drop curtain which can be brought down upon the action with a bang, and that the quieter endings of, for example, Elizabethan plays arise from their being written for curtainless theaters. I do not entirely disapprove of this suggestion, but wish to point out that the difference originates, at least in part, also in a difference in taste at different times and among different peoples. It is true that the Greeks probably had no drop curtain and that their dramas usually end upon a note of calm. But the same kind of close is normal in other fields of their literature, where the presence or absence of a curtain did not enter into consideration.

---

[1] The *Ajax* is one of the earliest among Sophocles' extant plays, but its exact date is not known. I have assumed that it preceded the introduction of a proscenium about 430 B.C. (see p. 235, above). If it was written after that innovation, the statement in the text would have to be altered accordingly, but the general method of procedure remains the same in either case.

For example, there is a distinct tendency for modern orators to close speeches with a peroration which is intended to sweep auditors off their feet.   Not so in Greek oratory.   "Wherever pity, terror, anger, or any passionate feeling is uttered or invited, this tumult is resolved in a final calm; and where such tumult has place in the peroration, it subsides before the last sentences of all."[1]   The same situation obtains likewise in the case of the Greek epic as in Homer's *Iliad* and *Odyssey*.

[1] Cf. Jebb, *The Attic Orators*, Vol. I, p. ciii.

The unities, sir, are a completeness—
a kind of a universal dovetailedness with
regard to place and time—a sort of a
general oneness, if I may be allowed to
use so strong an expression. I take those
to be the dramatic unities, so far as I
have been enabled to bestow attention
upon them, and I have read much upon
the subject, and thought much.—
CHARLES DICKENS.

CHAPTER VI

THE INFLUENCE OF PHYSICAL CONDITIONS (*CONTINUED*): THE UNITIES[1]

The dramatic unities, three principles governing the structure of drama and supposedly derived from Aristotle's *Poetics*, are a subject of perennial interest. They are known as the unities of time, place, and action, respectively, and require that "the action of a play should be represented as occurring in one place, within one day, and with nothing irrelevant to the plot." The essential facts concerning them were recognized at least as long ago as the publication of Lessing's *Hamburgische Dramaturgie* (1767). But so deep-rooted is the popular impression that the Greeks formulated these rules arbitrarily and observed them slavishly that no attempt to state the true situation can be superfluous. The current doctrine is based on the fact that the classic dramatists in France and Italy blindly obeyed the rules as a heritage of the past, without regard to the demands of the theater at their own disposal; and, consequently, the inference has been easily and naturally drawn that the ancient practice was equally irrational.

[1] In addition to the works mentioned on pp. xvii and xxf. and the bibliography listed on pp. 57–59, above, cf. Campbell, *Classical Review*, IV (1890), 303 ff.; Verrall in his edition of Euripides' *Ion* (1890), pp. xlviii ff.; Krause, *Quaestiones Aristophaneae Scaenicae* (1903); Kent, "The Time Element in the Greek Drama," *Transactions of the American Philological Association*, XXXVII (1906), 39 ff.; Felsch, *Quibus Artificiis Adhibitis Poetae Tragici Graeci Unitates Illas et Temporis et Loci Observaverint* (1907); Polczyk, *De Unitatibus et Loci et Temporis in Nova Comoedia Observatis* (1909); Marek, *De Temporis et Loci Unitatibus a Seneca Tragico Observatis* (1909); Wolf, *Die Bezeichnung von Ort und Zeit in der attischen Tragödie* (1911); Butcher, *Aristotle's Theory of Poetry and Fine Art*[4] (1911), pp. 274 ff.; Brasse, *Quatenus in Fabulis Plautinis et Loci et Temporis Unitatibus Species Veritatis Neglegatur* (1914); and Manning, *A Study of Archaism in Euripides* (1916).

But in the Greek theater, where there was no drop curtain, no scenery to shift, and a chorus almost continuously present, a change of scene was difficult to indicate visually.   Nevertheless Aristotle nowhere mentions the unity of place, and the Greek dramatists not infrequently violate it.   The most familiar instances occur in Aeschylus' *Eumenides* and Sophocles' *Ajax*. The former play opens at the temple of Apollo in Delphi, whither the avenging Furies have pursued Orestes after his mother's murder.   During a momentary lapse from their watchfulness Orestes makes his escape, but the Furies soon awaken and take up the trail once more.   The scene is thus left entirely vacant (vs. 234) and is supposed to change to Athens, where all parties presently appear for the famous trial before the Council of the Areopagus.   The beginning of the latter play takes place before Ajax' tent, and Sophocles wished to introduce the very unusual motive of having a scene of violence enacted before the audience. As the presence of the chorus was an insuperable obstacle to such a deed, Ajax was allowed to leave the scene and, suspicion being soon aroused, the chorus was sent in search of him (vs. 814). Thus, the scene is again entirely deserted by both actors and chorus, and Ajax returns, not to his tent, but to some lonely spot near the seashore (see pp. 129 and 244, above).   This was by far the most natural and logical method of leading up to a change of scene, was infinitely superior to Shakespeare's practice in *King Henry V*, where Chorus is introduced in the prologue of each act to acquaint the spectators with the scene of the succeeding action, but was so difficult to motivate that only some half a dozen examples are known to us in the whole Greek drama.   On the other hand, such a technical device was usually not well adapted to represent considerable shifts of scene, since it would seem unnatural for so large a body of persons as the chorus always to accompany the dramatic characters to widely separated localities. To this general restriction, however, the *Eumenides* furnishes a brilliant exception, because it was the especial duty of the Furies to track the guilty Orestes wherever he might flee.   In Old Comedy, ever fantastic and intentionally impossible, greater freedom was naturally allowed than in tragedy, so that in Aristophanes' *Frogs* no less than five different scenes are successively required (see pp. 88–90, above).

At the same time the need of such scene-shifting was largely obviated by the arbitrary placing of almost all scenes before a building, by the exclusion of interior scenes, and by the various devices substituted therefor (see pp. 237–42, above).   In particular the use of the messenger's speech enabled dramatists to bring indirectly before their audiences events which had taken place, not merely in the scene-house interior, but at far distant spots. Very commonly the unity of place was observed by conventionally bringing together as close neighbors structures or localities which would actually be separated by considerable intervals. Thus the murderers of Agamemnon would not wish his grave to stare them in the face and to remind their subjects of their crime; nevertheless in Aeschylus' *Libation-Bearers* palace and tomb stand side by side.   Likewise in Euripides' *Helen*, King Theoclymenus has buried his father in front of his palace.   Now these arrangements are not to be interpreted in the light of the prehistoric custom of placing the dead within the house or before its threshold.   It is purely a theatrical convention, and Euripides shows what he thought of it by deeming it necessary to put an excuse on the Egyptian king's lips:

> Hail, my sire's tomb!—for at my palace-gate,
> Proteus, I buried thee, *to greet thee so;*
> Still as I enter and pass forth mine halls,
> Thee, father, I thy son Theoclymenus hail.
>
> [Vss. 1165 ff.; Way's translation]

Many similar instances of incongruous juxtaposition in Greek drama can be cited, and those who remember the use of the continuous set in mediaeval theaters will feel no surprise.

Slightly different but no less efficacious is the method of procedure in the *Persians*.   For dramatic effect Aeschylus wished to introduce the ghost of Darius.   But according to ancient notions on the subject ghosts do not normally wander far from their tombs, and the real grave of Darius was at

Persepolis. Furthermore, under the conditions supposed the Persian elders, the royal messenger, and Xerxes himself would not naturally resort thither. Consequently, without the slightest compunction, Aeschylus transferred the dead monarch's tomb to Susa!

Sometimes the unity of place was observed by causing a character to come to a spot to which he would not naturally resort. The scene of Euripides' *Phoenician Maids*, for instance, is laid in Thebes, and the poet wished to show a meeting of the Theban king and his brother. Since the latter is considered a traitor and the enemy of his country, is in banishment and at the head of an invading army, such a meeting in real life would almost inevitably be held between the hostile lines. Yet Polynices is forced to intrust his head to the lion's jaws and enter the city. He expresses his own misgivings in vss. 261 ff., concluding:

> Yet do I trust my mother—and mistrust,—
> Who drew me to come hither under truce.
>
> [Vss. 272 f.; Way's translation]

At vss. 357 ff. he alludes to the matter once more.

Similarly, a character is oftentimes forced to remain upon the scene of action when he would not naturally do so. Thus, in Plautus' *Menaechmi*, owing to a failure to distinguish Menaechmus I from his brother, his father-in-law and a physician consider him insane and make arrangements, in his hearing, for his apprehension. Notwithstanding, when they both leave the stage at vs. 956 he makes no attempt to escape—an act which would transfer the next two scenes elsewhere—but unconcernedly awaits developments.

Finally I may mention one especially amusing artifice. In Euripides' *Iphigenia among the Taurians*, Orestes has left the scene and is now supposed to be some distance away. Notwithstanding, Athena addresses him and apologetically adds: "For, though absent, you can hear my voice, since I am a goddess" (vs. 1447). The same situation recurs, without apology, at vs. 1462 and in Euripides' *Helen*, vss. 1662 ff.

Likewise, the unity of time arose, not from the whim of ancient writers, but from the same theatrical arrangements which resulted in the unity of place, viz., the absence of a drop curtain and the continuous presence of the chorus. Under these conditions an intermission for the imaginary lapse of time could be secured only by the withdrawal of the chorus, and without such intermissions the constant and long-continued presence of the same persons in the same place without food or slumber was in danger of becoming an absurdity. Now we have seen how difficult it was to invent motives for the successive reappearances of actors; to motivate the movements of a body of twelve (fifteen) tragic or twenty-four comic choreutae was naturally still more difficult (see pp. 229–33 and 150–52, above). Consequently the chorus is rarely removed from the stage during the action. Two instances have already been mentioned (p. 247, above). In the *Ajax* advantage is taken of the withdrawal to change the scene slightly; naturally a slight interval of time is also supposed to elapse, but in this instance this is negligible and without significance. In the *Eumenides* the case is different. Here the scene is not shifted a few rods merely but from Delphi clear to Athens. As the crow flies this was a distance of about eighty miles and, in view of the physical conditions and ancient methods of travel, would require two or three days to traverse. Accordingly a considerable lacuna in the dramatic time of the play must be assumed. What is still more remarkable is that, except for the empty stage, the spectators are given nothing to help "digest the abuse of distance." At vs. 80 Apollo dispatches Orestes to the city of Pallas, at vs. 179 he begins to drive the chorus of Furies from his shrine, at vs. 234 he leaves the stage and the scene is empty. Up to this point we are still at Delphi. In the very next verse (235) Orestes rushes into the theater and exclaims, "O queen Athena, I come at the bidding of Loxias." He has reached Athens! In Euripides' *Alcestis* the chorus forms part of the queen's funeral cortège and is absent during vss. 747–860. Although it is not usually so regarded I am inclined to think that there is a slight change of scene here (see p. 235, above); there is also a slight condensation of time, but neither constitutes a serious violation of these unities.   This is one of the rare cases where the withdrawal of the chorus resulted naturally from the normal development of the plot.   For if the choreutae had been present when Heracles announced his intention of rescuing Alcestis from death (vss. 840 ff.) the poet must have invented a reason for their not reporting this news to Admetus or have spoiled certain features of the finale.   It was much simpler to avoid the difficulty by allowing the chorus to do the natural thing.   In the following instances apparently no change of scene or undue compression of time is involved.   In Euripides' *Helen* (vs. 385) the chorus accompany their mistress inside the palace to consult the seeress Theonoe and re-enter at vs. 515. The only advantage that seems to accrue from this maneuver is to prolong Menelaus' uncertainty as to the identity of his newly recovered wife.   In Aristophanes' *Women in Council* (vs. 311) the women of the chorus, disguised as men, leave for the assembly in order to vote the management of the state into their own hands, returning at vs. 478.   Unless the playwright wished to have the assembly scene enacted before the audience he had to withdraw the chorus.   As it is their doings are reported by a messenger (Chremes) in vss. 376 ff.   In the pseudo-Euripidean *Rhesus* the chorus is absent during vss. 565–674, being sent in front of the camp to receive Dolon (cf. vss. 522 ff.).   The presence of Trojan guards would have prevented the intervening scene between the Greek marauders, Odysseus and Diomedes. It will be noted how few are the instances of the withdrawal of the chorus in the extant plays and that the observance of the unities figures in just half of them.   In New Comedy the chorus appeared only between acts (see p. 145) and it would have been feasible to assume a lacuna several times in each play.   That this was not done was probably due to the fact that the other practice had become stereotyped and that concentration of action resulted in greater unity of plot.   Sometimes the stage is left empty *before the entrance of the chorus* by the retirement of all the actors on the scene either between the prologue and the

parodus or between monologues (or dialogues) in the prologue.
Euripides' *Alcestis* (vs. 77) furnishes an example of the former
and his *Iphigenia among the Taurians* (vs. 66) of the latter. So
far as I have observed such pauses are not made use of to
accelerate the time unduly.

Since it was not often possible to suspend the audience's
sense of time by removing the chorus, the poets had recourse
to the next best expedient, the choral odes. Inasmuch as several
of these occurred in every play, this artifice was far more available than the other. In many respects the chorus moved upon a
different plane from the actors, and we are now dealing with one
of these differences. As Professor Butcher expressed it: "The
interval covered by a choral ode is one whose value is just what
the poet chooses to make it. While the time occupied by the
dialogue has a relation more or less exact to real time, the choral
lyrics suspend the outward action of the play and carry us still
farther away from the world of reality. What happens in the
interval cannot be measured by any ordinary reckoning; it is
much or little as the needs of the piece demand. A change of
place directly obtrudes itself on the senses, but time is only what
it appears to the mind. The imagination travels easily over
many hours; and in the Greek drama the time that elapses during
the songs of the chorus is entirely idealized" (*op. cit.*, p. 293).
Thus the choral songs were roughly equivalent to the modern
intermission, and after them the action is often farther advanced
than the actual time required for chanting them would warrant.
For example, during a single stasimon of Aeschylus' *Suppliants*
(vss. 524–99) the Argive king must leave the scene, summon his
subjects to public assembly, state the object of the meeting, and
allow discussion before the final vote—all in time for Danaus to
report the people's decision at the beginning of the following
episode! An analogy to ancient practice occurs in Shakespeare's
The Winter's Tale, where Time as Chorus announces the passage
of sixteen years between Acts III and IV.

But at the same time that the chorus conferred this liberty
it restricted it. The presence of such a body of performers at

all the scenes of a play could seldom be entirely natural. Yet that the same persons should be found standing about, in the same place, at various intervals during the day is conceivable, though it does not often happen. But that they should be found there at every moment chosen for representation during weeks or months or years is inconceivable and ridiculous. Only by shortening the supposed action of the piece and the supposed lacunae in the plot could the convention be tolerated at all. However, Professor Verrall was lacking in historical imagination when he maintained that "the point at which the discrepancy between the facts presented and the natural facts began to be flagrant and intolerable was when the audience were told to pass in imagination *from day to day*. Night is the great natural interrupter of actions and changer of situations" (*op. cit.*, p. l). To the spoiled theatergoer of today this would seem to be true. But the ancient drama knew no lighting effects (see p. 224, above). On the stage day and night looked the same to them. Scenes at midday, in the darkness of night, in the gloom of Hades, were alike enacted in the glare of the sun. Ostensibly the entire action of the anonymous *Rhesus* and much of that in Euripides' *Cyclops* fell within the hours of night, and characters frequently addressed the heavenly constellations in (actual) daylight. So far were the playwrights from avoiding the discrepancy involved in passing from one day to another that in Terence's translation of Menander's *Self-Tormentor*, when a night is supposed to elapse between Acts II and III, attention is deliberately called to it by Chremes' words, "It is beginning to grow light here now" (vs. 410). In my opinion this play extends over about as much time as the conditions which obtained in ancient drama would normally allow; and it should be noted that it does not exceed the twenty-four hours permitted by the unity of time.

In the third place, perhaps it is unnecessary to point out that acceleration of time is possible in all drama quite apart from an empty stage or choral songs. Instances can be cited even from dramatists who owned no allegiance to the unities—note, for example, the striking of the half-hour every twenty or twenty-five

lines at the close of Marlowe's *Doctor Faustus*.   In Aristophanes'
Plutus the blind god is escorted from the stage for a night's
treatment in the temple of Asclepius (vs. 626), the chorus remaining in its place but apparently not singing.[1]   At the very next
verse one of the escort returns to announce that Plutus has
recovered his sight and to relate the events of the night!   But
here again, despite the transition from one day to another, the
action does not exceed twenty-four hours.   In the same writer's
Acharnians, Amphitheus goes from Athens to Sparta and returns
again during the dialogue contained between vss. 133 and 174.
There is no hint, however, that his reappearance is premature or
that his trip would occupy more than the apparent space
allotted it.

But neither the ordinary acceleration of time in drama nor
the use of stasima nor yet the stage left empty by the retirement
of chorus and actors tells the whole story of Greek practice.
Nowadays the playbill clearly informs us how much time has
elapsed between acts, and the piece is constructed accordingly.
If a character in the third act has occasion to refer to something
which occurred in the first act ten years or so ago he must not
speak of it as if it happened yesterday.   Not so in ancient drama.
The Greek audiences had no playbills, and even the introductions
to Greek plays prepared by Alexandrian scholars contained no
such information as this.   I fancy that the Greek dramatist
never laid his finger upon a given line and said: "Here we must
assume a lapse of several days, or months, or years."   The
events of a drama, regardless of actualities, were conventionally
treated as occupying no more than twenty-four hours.   A like
convention was customary in the Greek epic: when once a
Homeric character was given a definite age or form he maintained each unchanged throughout.[2]   For example, Telemachus
is introduced in the first book of the *Odyssey* as a young man just
reaching his majority, ready and anxious to assume the duties of

[1] XOPOΥ is printed at this point in most editions but occurs in no manuscript
(see p. 145, above); it has been inserted by the editors.

[2] Cf. Scott, *Classical Philology*, VIII (1913), 453 ff.

manhood; but nine years before, when he could not have been more than twelve years of age, he is spoken of as just as old and as already a man among men (cf. Book xi, vss. 185 f. and 449). Again, in the third book of the *Iliad*, Helen is pictured in the prime of youth and beauty; ten years later and thirty years after her elopement with Paris she is likened to the same goddess as is the Maiden Nausicaa (cf. *Odyssey* iv. 121 f. and vi. 102 ff.). In Greek drama time relations are similarly ignored. At the opening of Aeschylus' *Agamemnon* the watchman sights the signal fire which announces the capture of Troy, and within a few hundred lines Agamemnon has finished the sack, traversed the Aegean, and appeared before his palace! No hint is given, however, that there is anything unusual about all this; not a word[1] indicates that the action is disconnected at any point.

This is the most flagrant instance, and I conceive that it is to be interpreted as follows: The performance of Greek drama in the fifth century was continuous in the sense that with negligible exceptions (see pp. 250 f., above) actors or chorus or both were constantly before the audience. Notice that this is not the same as saying that the *time* of the plays was continuous. When critically examined it is found to have been interrupted by numerous gaps, as we have already seen and shall see again. But the continuity of performance gave a *semblance* of continuity also to the action. Therefore when a modern playwright like Pinero restricts his action to one day and represents the lapse of several hours by the fall of the curtain between acts, he does not thereby observe the unity of time in the Greek sense. The dramatic events were tacitly treated by the poets as if they occupied no more than a day and were so accepted by the public. By "tacitly" I mean that if such crowding involved a physical or moral impossibility the dramatists never stooped to apologize or explain but placed their events in juxtaposition just the same. In Plautus' *Captives*, Philocrates travels from Aetolia (the scene of action) to Elis and back again between vss. 460 and 768. In

---

[1] Πάλαι in vs. 587 is entirely subjective; cf. Conrad, *The Technique of Continuous Action in Roman Comedy* (1915), pp. 22 ff.

real life such a trip would have required several days, but in the play it consumes less than one! Do we positively know this? Beyond the shadow of a doubt. A parasite is introduced at intervals during the play scheming to be invited to a meal. He is first seen at vs. 69 and does not get a satisfactory invitation until vs. 897. A more detailed statement would show conclusively that the same day's meal is under discussion throughout. Moreover, this is no mere *lapsus calami*, such as a few phrases which are found in an opposite sense,[1] but is unmistakable in its import and is closely interwoven with the plot. If anyone feels amazed at so deliberate a contradiction he may console himself with a study of the use of "double time" in Shakespeare. It would be possible, but is quite unnecessary, to cite other plays in which restriction of time to a single day is indicated with sufficient exactness. Of course the Greek dramatists did not consistently introduce references to the precise date or to the time of day. In general they were wise enough to act upon the principle which Corneille[2] expressed as follows: "Above all I would leave the length of the action to the imagination of the hearers, and never determine the time, if the subject does not require it. . . . . What need is there to mark at the opening of the play that the sun is rising, that it is noon at the third act, and sunset at the end of the last?"

It is somewhat remarkable that Professor Verrall, who fully recognized the dependence of this unity upon local conditions and published eminently sensible observations on the subject, nevertheless felt constrained to challenge the obvious interpretation of two plays in which a glaring violation of the unity of time occurs. In the *Agamemnon* he supposed the watchman and the populace (including the chorus) to be misinformed as to the meaning of the beacon and that it really served to Clytemnestra, Aegisthus, and their supporters as a warning of Agamemnon's

---

[1] For example, the slips which occur in Aristophanes' *Lysistrata* (vss. 725 and 881).

[2] Cf. *Discours des trois unités*, I, 113 f. (Regnier's edition), quoted by Butcher, *op. cit.*, pp. 294 f.

being close at hand! His elucidation of Euripides' *Andromache* was still more ingenious and complicated.[1] But to bolster up such interpretations Mr. Verrall ought to have explained away all similar instances as well—to explain, for example, how in Euripides' *Suppliants* an Attic army can march from Eleusis to the vicinity of Thebes and fight a battle there, and how tidings of the victory can be brought back to Eleusis, all between vss. 598 and 634, which, as Dryden[2] expressed it, "is not for every mile a verse." Nevertheless not the slightest attention is paid to such patent impossibilities, and in every case the whole action is unmistakably supposed to fall within a day.

In view of the foregoing it is not surprising that Aristotle does mention the unity of time, though only incidentally. His exact language is: "Tragedy and epic differ, again, in their length: for tragedy endeavors, so far as possible, to keep within a single circuit of the sun (περίοδος ἡλίου), or but slightly to exceed this limit; whereas the epic action has no limits of time."[3] "Endeavors" (πειρᾶται) was mistranslated as *doit* by some French writers. Aristotle rather commends the unity of time as a rough generalization which works out well in practice than enjoins it as an invariable rule. Actually the restriction was further reduced, in most cases, to the hours of daylight, and Dacier even maintained that περίοδος ἡλίου means no more than twelve hours. But Aristophanes' *Plutus* and Terence's *Self-Tormentor* (see pp. 253 f., above) furnish clear examples of dramatic action beginning in the late afternoon of one day and not concluding until the next day.

It remains to consider some of the expedients which the poets found useful in solving the difficulties (both of time and place) caused by local conditions. In the first place the practice of writing a series of three plays on the same general subject (see p. 198, above) often enabled the playwright to distribute his

---

[1] Cf. the introduction to his edition of the *Agamemnon*, and *Four Plays of Euripides*, pp. 1–42.

[2] Cf. *Dramatic Essays* (Everyman's Library edition), p. 18.

[3] Cf. *Poetics* 1449b12–14.

incidents in different places and time-spheres without loss of verisimilitude, for a whole trilogy was about as long as the average modern play, and each tragedy would thus correspond to a single act and, since the chorus was withdrawn at the close of each play in the trilogy and its place taken by another entirely different, changes of time and place between plays were absolutely without restriction.   Thus Scythia of Aeschylus' *Prometheus Bound* becomes Caucasus in the second piece in the trilogy, the *Prometheus Unbound;* in the former was shown the binding of the Titan and in the latter his release, and he is said to have been bound for 30,000 years.   All but two days of this time elapses between plays!   In Aeschylus' Orestean trilogy the scene of the *Agamemnon* and *Libation-Bearers* is laid in Argos; that of the *Eumenides* in Delphi and Athens.   Several years are supposed to pass by in the two interims.

But even Aeschylus did not always employ the trilogic form, and Sophocles and Euripides rarely did.   When, therefore, the three or four plays in each series were severally devoted to utterly unrelated material, it sometimes became necessary to bring almost as many events within the scope of one play as would otherwise be dealt with in a whole trilogy.   Inasmuch as a large fraction of these events could not possibly be conceived of as taking place in the same locality or within the same day, it was imperative either to exclude them or to include them in some indirect fashion.   Now two striking peculiarities of Euripidean technique were admirably adapted to help solve these difficulties. His prologues regularly take the form of a monologue, which, with scant regard for dramatic illusion, rehearses the story of the myth up to the point where the play begins.   Again, Euripides' dramas frequently terminate with the epiphany of a deity.   This device was the accustomed recourse of unskilful playwrights, when their plots had become complicated beyond the possibility of disentanglement by natural means, in order that a god's fiat might resolve all difficulties.   It has often been charged that this was also Euripides' motive, but most unjustly (see pp. 293 ff., below).   He rather "wished, by the help of a divine foreknowledge, to put before the spectators such future events or unknown circumstances as should settle their minds, satisfy all curiosity, and connect the subject of the piece with subsequent events or even with the times of living men."[1] Thus in Euripides' *Andromache* the complications of the plot are entirely solved before Thetis' appearance at vs. 1231, and she merely gives directions for Neoptolemus' burial and prophesies the future of Peleus, Andromache, and Molossus, and of the latter's posterity. When these two pieces of technique were combined in the same play, the prologue, the body of the tragedy, and the epilogue sometimes corresponded roughly to the successive dramas of a whole trilogy. This appears most clearly in the case of Euripides' *Electra* and Aeschylus' Orestean trilogy. The opening monologue of the former (vss. 1–53) passes in rapid review the Greek expedition against Troy, the murder of Agamemnon, and the present fate of his children. With the exception of the last item, which is brought out in the second play of the *Oresteia*, these are the matters contained in the prologue, which naturally is comparatively short, and in the action of Aeschylus' *Agamemnon*. The body of the *Electra* corresponds to the second tragedy in the trilogy, the *Libation-Bearers*. At the *Electra's* conclusion (vs. 1238) Castor as *deus ex machina* forecasts among other things the acquittal of Orestes at Athens, which is the theme of Aeschylus' *Eumenides*. Whatever other explanations, therefore, may be advanced for Euripides' prologues and epilogues (see pp. 294 f. and 299 f., below) this consideration must also be allowed a certain weight, viz., that they permitted him to bring events of the most diverse nature within the scope of his piece without violating the unities of time and place.

A fourth device looking to the same ends consisted in setting conversations at times and places which would naturally be different. Even such a master of dramatic technique as Sophocles represented Orestes as communicating to his fellow-conspirators the result of his inquiry at Delphi only after they

---

[1] Cf. England's edition of Euripides' *Iphigenia at Aulis*, p. xxvii.

had reached Argos (*Electra*, vss. 32 ff.), and as waiting to formulate a definite plan of action until they were in the most unfavorable place in all the world for such a purpose—before Clytemnestra's palace (vss. 15 ff.).   The latter incongruity does not occur in Euripides' version of the same story because the scene of his *Electra* is laid, not in the city of Argos, but before Electra's hut in the country.   The device under consideration was conveniently supplemented by the convention that if two or more characters enter the stage together no conversation is thought of as passing between them until they have come within the hearing of the audience (see p. 310, below).   It will be seen that the passage just cited from Sophocles' *Electra* conforms to this rule.   Another instance occurs in Euripides' *Madness of Heracles*, vss. 822 ff.   Iris appears above Heracles' palace with Madness, whom she orders to incite the hero to the murder of his children.   Madness protests but is overborne and forced to perform her bidding.   Though Iris and Madness must have come a considerable distance together, all discourse between them is apparently postponed until they reach their destination. Furthermore, these instructions would naturally have been given to Madness elsewhere and somewhat earlier.   In that case the audience must have lost an effective scene.   The device discussed in this paragraph enabled the poet to circumvent the unities and place the scene before his audience; and the convention which I have mentioned preserved it for them in its entirety.

We have seen that the unities of time and place are largely due to the striving for illusion in a theater comparatively bare of scenery and of facilities for scene-shifting.   Conversely, their observance in the modern theater with its ample scenic provision would naturally militate against the scenic extravagance and actualism of which the present-day theatocracy is so enamored. Thus it would seem that the much-abused unities are not without a meaning and truly artistic tendency even today, for some of the most significant influences in contemporaneous staging are directed against excesses along these lines.   Even a modern producer, Henry W. Savage, included the following in his advice to a young playwright: "Do not distribute your scenes so widely that you have one on an island, another at Herald Square, and a third at Chicago. Make the action of your play take place all in one day, if possible"[1]—in other words the unity of time expressly and an approximation to the unity of place. Ibsen surely retained no theatrical conventions merely because they were old; yet he usually observed the unities. A recent critic has written: "Though the unities of time and place were long ago exploded as binding principles—indeed, they never had any authority in English drama—yet it is true that a broken-backed action, whether in time or space, ought, so far as possible, to be avoided. An action with a gap of twenty years in it may be all very well in melodrama and romance, but scarcely in higher and more serious types of drama."[2]

The unity of action is the only one that is universal, since it alone springs from the inmost nature of the drama. Yet even here local conditions make themselves felt. The modern playwright, free (if he pleases and has a producer complaisant enough) to change the scene ten times within a single act and with superior facilities for motivating entrances and exits, delights in shifting different sets of characters back and forth and thus secures an alternation of light and shade, an intermingling of comedy and tragedy quite beyond the ancient dramatist's reach. The preceding discussion has shown the immobility of the ancient theater in these respects and, consequently, one reason why the Greeks ruthlessly excluded everything that was not strictly germane to their action (see also p. 201, above).

This unity, it is needless to say, plays an important part in Aristotle's *Poetics*. He recognized that "plot is the first essential and soul of tragedy and that character comes second."[3] The most lengthy statement runs as follows: "Let us now discuss the proper construction of the plot, as that is both the first and

[1] Cf. *The Bookman*, XXX (1909), 37.

[2] Cf. Archer, *Play-making*, pp. 123 f.　　　[3] Cf. *Poetics* 1450a38 f.

the most important thing in tragedy.   We have laid it down that tragedy is an imitation of an action that is complete and whole, having a certain magnitude, for there is also a whole that is wanting in magnitude.   Now a whole is that which has a beginning, a middle, and an end.   A beginning is that which is not itself necessarily after anything else and after which something else naturally is or comes to be; an end, on the contrary, is that which itself naturally follows some other thing either as its necessary or usual consequent, and has nothing else after it; and a middle is that which is both itself after one thing and has some other thing after it.   Accordingly, well-constructed plots must neither begin nor end at haphazard points, but must conform to the types just mentioned."[1]   These principles were excellently restated by Lowell:

> In a play we not only expect a succession of scenes, but that each scene should lead, by a logic more or less stringent, if not to the next, at any rate to something that is to follow, and that all should contribute their fraction of impulse towards the inevitable catastrophe.   That is to say, the structure should be organic, with a necessary and harmonious connection and relation of parts, and not merely mechanical with an arbitrary or haphazard joining of one part to another.   It is in the former sense alone that any production can be called a work of art.[2]

Though it is now admitted on all sides that the unity of action is the *sine qua non* of dramatic composition, many fail to realize the meaning and extent of its limitation.   Aristotle indicated a mistaken notion current in his day, and likewise in ours, in the following words: "The unity of a plot does not consist, as some suppose, in its having one man as its subject. An infinite multitude of things befall that one man, some of which it is impossible to reduce to unity, and so, too, there are many actions of one man which cannot be made to form one action.   Hence, the error, as it appears, of all the poets who have composed a *Heracleid*, a *Theseid*, or similar poems.   They suppose that, because Heracles was one man, the story also of Heracles must be one story."[3]   Freytag discussed the matter

[1] Cf. *Poetics* 1450b22–35.

[2] Cf. *The Old English Dramatists*, III.   [3] Cf. *Poetics* 1451a15–22.

with keen discrimination and exemplified it by showing how Shakespeare remodeled the more or less chaotic story of Romeo and Juliet's love into a unified plot whose incidents follow one another almost as inexorably as Fate. The passage is unfortunately too long for quotation here, but is highly instructive.[1]

The same reasoning reveals the shortcoming in Professor Lounsbury's contention: "What, indeed, is the objection to this mixture of the serious and the comic in the same play? By it is certainly represented, as it is not in pure comedy or pure tragedy, the life we actually live and the mingled elements that compose it. . . . . As there was no question that sadness and mirth were constantly intermixed in real life, it was impossible to maintain that the illegitimacy of this form of dramatic composition was due to its improbability."[2] The word "pure" gives away the whole case. Aristotle would have to grant that Shakespeare's plays are admirable, even sublime; but he could hardly admit that they were "pure" tragedies or "pure" comedies, however legitimate in other respects. They fall short in the quality which Mr. Albert H. Brown placed in the forefront of his definition: "A great drama is a *clearly focused* picture of human conditions."

Aristotle also pointed out that epic poetry has an advantage in that it can present many events simultaneously transacted, while the drama is restricted to but one.[3] A curious violation of this self-evident principle occurred in a recent American play. Toward the end of Act II in Eugene Walter's *Paid in Full*, Emma Brooks is disclosed making an appointment with Captain Williams over the telephone. In the next act we are transferred to Captain Williams' quarters, and the dramatic clock has in the meanwhile been turned back some fifteen minutes, for presently the telephone bell rings and the same appointment is made over again. In other words, Act III partially overlaps Act II in time, but the scene is different. It can scarcely be

---

[1] Cf. *Technique of the Drama*, MacEwan's translation[2], pp. 30 ff.

[2] Cf. *Shakespeare as a Dramatic Artist* (1902), pp. 150 f.

[3] Cf. *Poetics* 1459b22–28.

denied that the dramatic situation has been enhanced by this device, but this gain has been secured at the sacrifice of verisimilitude and dramatic illusion. Such "cut-backs" may be all very well in moving picures, but they hardly have a place in spoken drama.

Thus, the Greek masters were so far from evolving unities out of their inner consciousness or from observing them invariably that they constantly violated the unities of time and place in both letter and spirit. Their practice throughout simply reacted to theatrical conditions as they found them. It has remained for their successors, whose theater has for the most part been quite dissimilar, to observe the unities with a literalness and exactness such as never characterized the great dramatists of Greece. That both ancients and moderns have produced masterpieces under these restrictions is, of course, beyond dispute. In fact, some of our most impressive plays of recent date such as Kennedy's *Servant in the House*, have conformed to them. That many modern plays would have been improved by observing them is doubtless also true. Even so uncompromising an admirer of Shakespeare as Professor Lounsbury[1] wrote:

Let it not be imagined, however, that any attempt is made here to deny the merit of modern plays which observe the unities, or to maintain that a powerful drama cannot be produced upon the lines they prescribe. Such a contention would be only repeating on the side of the opponents of this doctrine the erroneous assumptions which its advocates put forth. He who ventures to take a position so extreme can hardly escape a feeling of serious discomfort if called upon, in consequence, to decry the productions of Corneille, Racine, and Molière, to say nothing of some of the most brilliant pieces which have adorned the English stage. Nor, furthermore, need it be denied that there are conditions in which the observance of the unities may be a positive advantage. Especially will this be the case when the characters are few and all the incidents of the plot are directed to the accomplishment of a single result. The concentration of the action is likely to contribute, in such pieces, to the effect of the representation. He who sets out to imitate the simplicity of the Greek drama will usually find himself disposed to adopt, as far as possible, its form. Within its limitations great work can be accomplished by the drama which regards the unities, and, to some extent, it will be great work because of its limitations.

[1] Cf. *op. cit.*, p. 92.

But that the unities should be arbitrarily imposed upon every drama without exception is absurd, since the theatrical conditions that called them forth are no longer the same. That Aeschylus and Sophocles, if present with us in the flesh, would avail themselves of the greater flexibility and adaptability of the modern theater I cannot doubt. At any rate that restless spirit, Euripides, would certainly have gloried in its freedom.

As a cumulative result of the conditions already described the action of a Greek drama was restricted to the culmination alone, corresponding to the fifth act of most modern plays. Though we have seen that the Greek poets arbitrarily juxtaposed, as if within the confines of a sun's circuit, events which were actually separated by considerable intervals, yet even the widest license would hardly permit a whole series of transactions, of sufficient dignity and importance to be chosen for tragic representation, to be compressed within a single day and limited to a single spot. As Dryden[1] expressed it, the ancient playwrights "set the audience, as it were, at the post where the race is to be concluded; and, saving them the tedious expectation of seeing the poet set out and ride the beginning of the course, they suffer you not to behold him, till he is in sight of the goal, and just upon you." Thus in Aeschylus' *Suppliants* we see nothing of the unwelcome suit of Aegyptus' sons and of the events which led the daughters of Danaus to take refuge in flight. All this lies in the past and is brought before us indirectly. The action begins when the Danaids have reached another land and are on the point of being overtaken by their cousins. Similarly, in Euripides' *Alcestis* we learn by hearsay the long story of Apollo's servitude at the court of Admetus, of his providing a way of escape from death for the king, and of the latter's disheartening search for a substitute. Only the final stage in the action, the day of the queen's self-immolation and rescue, is chosen for actual representation. The same situation recurs in almost every piece. Of course in trilogies it was possible to select three different time-spheres and three different localities for the

---

[1] Cf. *Dramatic Essays* (Everyman's Library edition), pp. 12 f.

dramatic action. But here again only the crests of three crises in the story were put before the spectators' eyes; all the rest was narrated. So invariable a method of attack would seem monotonous to us today, but its successful employment by Ibsen and many another in modern times proves that there is nothing blameworthy in the practice per se.

Finally, since the dramatic action was confined to a single day (however elastic) at the culmination of the story, it was rarely possible for the dramatis personae to experience any particular change or development of character during the course of the play. This fixity of type was not only a natural result of theatrical conditions in ancient times and of the use of masks but was also in thorough accord with Homeric conventions (see pp. 254f., above). Moreover, it harmonized completely with the Greek fondness for schematization. Horace's words in his *Ars Poetica* are entirely Hellenic in spirit: "Either follow tradition, or invent that which shall be self-consistent. In the former case, let Achilles be impatient, irascible, ruthless, keen . . . . ; let Medea be untamed and unconquerable, Ino tearful, Ixion treacherous, Io ever roving, and Orestes in sorry plight. In the latter case, keep the character to the end of the play as it was at the beginning and let it be consistent" (vss. 119 ff.). All this implies more than we would think desirable today. Not only was a positive development into a character seemingly inharmonious with that seen at first rarely possible, but the singleness of purpose in ancient plays, which has been called the unity of mood (see p. 201, above), crowded out incidents which might have revealed other phases, no matter how consistent, of a dramatic personage's character. The taste of some critics objected to even the slight modifications in rôle which ancient conditions did permit. For example, to modern readers the manner in which Medea, in Euripides' tragedy of that name, wavers between love for her children and the desire to punish her recreant husband by murdering them is esteemed one of the finest touches in ancient drama. But the Greek argument which is prefixed to this play reports that "they blame Euripides because he did not maintain

Medea's rôle but allowed her to burst into tears as she plotted against Jason and his second wife." Again, so excellent a critic as Aristotle cites the title rôle in Euripides' *Iphigenia at Aulis* as an example of inconsistency,[1] inasmuch as the Iphigenia who pleads for her life at vss. 1211 ff. in no wise resembles her later self, who willingly approaches the altar. To modern feeling, since the change is psychologically possible and is plausibly motived by the sudden realization that her death can serve her country, it seems entirely unobjectionable. But these two passages and the usual practice of the Greek stage reveal a discrepancy between the ancient and the modern points of view. The simplicity of character-drawing which resulted from Greek methods is strikingly described, in a different connection, by Mr. Cornford:

Agamemnon, for instance, is simply Hybris typified in a legendary person. He is a hero flown with "insolence" (the pride and elation of victory), and that is all that can be said of him. He is not, like a character in Ibsen, a complete human being with a complex personality, a center from which relations radiate to innumerable points of contact in a universe of indifferent fact. He has not a continuous history: nothing has ever happened to him except the conquest of Troy and the sacrifice of Iphigenia; nothing ever could happen to him except Pride's fall and the stroke of the axe. As we see him he is not a man, but a single state of mind, which has never been preceded by other states of mind (except one, at the sacrifice in Aulis), but is isolated, without context, margin, or atmosphere. Every word he says, in so far as he speaks for himself and not for the poet, comes straight out of that state of mind and expresses some phase of it. He has a definite relation to Cassandra, a definite relation to Clytemnestra; but no relation to anything else. If he can be said to have a *character* at all it consists solely of certain defects which make him liable to Insolence; if he has any *circumstances*, they are only those which prompt him to his besetting passion.[2]

[1] Cf. *Poetics* 1454a31 ff.

[2] Cf. *Thucydides Mythistoricus* (1907), p. 146.

There seems no human thought so primitive as to have lost its bearing on our own thought, nor so ancient as to have broken its connection with our own life.—E. B. TYLOR.

CHAPTER VII

THE INFLUENCE OF NATIONAL CUSTOMS AND IDEAS[1]

It is unnecessary to state that the differences between ancient life in Greece and modern life in America and Western Europe are endless. To attempt to enumerate them all would require a separate volume. In the present chapter I shall undertake to touch upon some of the features which more intimately affected Greek drama.

First of all a modern can scarcely avoid a feeling of surprise that plays were almost always brought out in competition; but no instinct was more thoroughly imbedded in the Greek consciousness than this. From the time of the first celebration of the Olympian games in 776 B.C. or before, a contest of some kind formed, to their minds, the most natural setting for the display of athletic, musical, and literary skill. Associated with this fact was another, viz., that the prizes awarded upon these occasions were usually more honorific than intrinsically valuable. The victors in the Olympian games received a garland of wild olive and a palm branch. It is true that the delighted fellow-citizens of the victors usually supplemented the award by something more substantial, but the fact remains that these trivial objects were the sole official reward for many arduous months of preparation and training. In like manner we are informed by the most ancient tradition that the original prize in tragic

[1] In addition to the works mentioned on pp. xvii and xx f., above, cf. Petersen, *Preisrichter der grossen Dionysien* (1878); Hayley, "Social and Domestic Position of Women in Aristophanes," *Harvard Studies*, I (1890), 159 ff.; Lounsbury, *Shakespeare as a Dramatic Artist* (1902); Goodwin's edition of Demosthenes' *Against Midias*, Appendix IV (1906); Capps, "Epigraphical Problems in the History of Attic Comedy," *American Journal of Philology*, XXVIII (1907), 179 ff.; Legrand, *Daos; Tableau de la comédie grecque pendant la periode dite nouvelle* (1910), translated by Loeb in 1917 under the title *The New Greek Comedy;* Sheppard, *Greek Tragedy* (1911); and Ruppel, *Konzeption und Ausarbeitung der aristophanischen Komödien* (1913).

contests was a goat (see p. 13 f. above); and what is more, it is
said to have been customary for the victorious poet to offer up
his prize in immediate sacrifice to the god of the festival. After
the reorganization of the City Dionysia about 501 B.C., however,
it seems likely that pecuniary awards were established for the
tragic victors. Though we are in ignorance as to their amount,
some notion can be formed from the fact that prizes of ten, eight,
and six minae,[1] respectively, were granted dithyrambic victors
at the Piraeus festival toward the close of the fourth century B.C.
Three prizes seem to have been available in tragedy at the City
Dionysia also, so that every contestant was sure of some
compensation. In other words, to be chosen to compete at all
was sufficient honor to entitle even the poorest of the three to a
suitable reward. Only the winner of the first prize, however,
was technically regarded as "victor." In comedy, according to
tradition, the original prize was a jar of wine, which likewise
gave place to financial awards after comedy came under state
control at the City Dionysia of 486 B.C. These arrangements
were extended to the Lenaea, when first comedy and then
tragedy were introduced there (see p. 119, above), and to contests
between actors, as these were established at the two festivals
(see p. 202, above). The successful playwrights, actors, and
"choregi" (see below) seem to have been crowned with garlands
of ivy by the presiding archon—the archon eponymus at the
City Dionysia and the king archon at the Lenaea.

In several particulars the government under which the
Athenians lived was indirect in its provisions. For example,
though valuable mines belonged to the state, they were not
worked by government officials but were leased to private
parties. Accordingly, although the dramatic festivals were
under the direct control of the state, the financial management
was relegated to lessees, who agreed to keep the theater in repair
and to pay a stipulated sum into the public treasury in return for

---

[1] A mina was equivalent to one hundred drachmae and was worth about $18,
though allowance must be made for the greater purchase value of money in those
days.

the privilege of collecting an admission fee. During the fourth century B.C. the lessees of the Piraeus theater paid thirty-three minae annually. This system explains why the authorities, when they wished to enable even the poorest citizens to attend the dramatic exhibitions, did not simply throw open the doors to all or issue passes. Instead, toward the end of the fifth century it was provided that any citizen might receive two obols from the "theoric" fund in order to pay his own way into the day's performances (see p. 120, above).

Another instance of the indirect exercise of governmental functions is seen in the practice of various kinds of "public service" (λειτουργία). Thus when the Board of Generals had provided the hull of a warship ("trireme") they did not proceed also to rig it and to hire a commander. Instead some rich citizen was required to contribute toward its rigging and upkeep and to command it for one year. This obligation was laid upon the wealthier citizens in rotation; and if anyone considered that he was being called upon too frequently or that someone of greater substance was escaping his just responsibilities, he could challenge him to an exchange of property (ἀντίδοσις). According to law the man so challenged was restricted to the two options of either assuming the burden or trading estates. This system of liturgies applied to the maintenance not only of the naval service but also of dramatic and dithyrambic contests, the torch race, etc. It was provided that no one need act as trierarch more frequently than once in three years, bear any liturgy two successive years, or two liturgies in the same year. But it was the glory of Athenian citizenship that they served oftener and spent their means more generously than the law demanded. The bearers of the theatrical liturgies were called *choregi* (χορηγοί), and there was no surer method of displaying one's wealth and of currying favor with the populace than by voluntary and lavish assumption of the choregia. The evidence is not sufficient to establish just how the charges were distributed. The state seems to have paid the actors, and the choregus to have been responsible for assembling and hiring a body of choreutae, engaging a trainer to drill them, purchasing or renting costumes for the chorus, employing mute characters, providing showy extras of various kinds, etc. As regards the flute-player a distinction was perhaps drawn between the dithyrambic and dramatic contests, the state employing him in the former and the choregus in the latter. The question of an additional actor has already been discussed (see pp. 172–82, above). A speaker in one of Lysias' orations[1] claims to have spent, within a period of seven years, thirty minae for a tragic choregia, sixteen minae for one in comedy, fifty minae for a dithyrambic chorus of men, fifteen minae for a chorus of boys, three hundred and sixty minae for six trierarchies, twelve minae as gymnasiarch, etc. Since this man's ambition led him to do more than his share, these outlays are probably somewhat larger than they need to have been; in fact, he declares that the law would not have required of him one-fourth as much. But in addition to indicating how much some were willing to spend, the figures are valuable also as showing the comparative expense of the different events. Needless to state, a poet's chance of victory was considerably affected by the wealth and disposition of his choregus. An ambitious and lavish man like Nicias, who is declared by Plutarch[2] never to have been worsted in any of his numerous choregias, could manifestly do much to retrieve a poor play. But woe betide the playwright whose success was largely in the keeping of a sponsor who would spend no more than law and public opinion could wring from him. In 405 and 404 B.C., while Athens was experiencing a financial stringency just before the close of the Peloponnesian War, the number of choregi at the City Dionysia was temporarily doubled, so that two synchoregi might divide between them the burden which normally fell to one man. Finally about 308 B.C. the dearth of rich men caused the abandonment of the choregic system and the annual appointment of an *agonothete* (ἀγωνοθέτης) or "master of contests," whose own resources were supplemented by a state subsidy and who assumed

---

[1] Cf. Lysias xxi, §§ 1–5.

[2] Cf. his *Life of Nicias*, III.

entire control and financial responsibility for all the dithyrambic and dramatic contests at the festival.

One of the most characteristic features of the Athenian
democracy was the large rôle assigned to the lot in the selection
of officials. For example, in Aristotle's day the nine archons
were chosen by lot from five hundred men, who had themselves
been previously chosen by lot, fifty from each of the ten tribes.
Whatever may have been the other objects of this system, at
least one was the prevention of bribery and manipulation; and
without a doubt this was the motive which led to the use of the
lot in theatrical matters. Thus the judges in the contests seem,
though the scheme is largely conjectural and depends upon
insufficient notices, to have been selected and to have rendered
decisions somewhat as follows: Some days before the festival a
certain number of names was taken from each tribe and deposited
in ten sealed urns on the Acropolis. Just before the contest
began, these vessels were brought into the theater and the presiding archon drew one name from each tribal urn. The men so
chosen came forward and swore to judge truly. When the
performances were over, each judge wrote down his verdict and
the ten ballots were placed in a single urn. The archon now
drew out half of these, which were alone used in arriving at the
ultimate decision! So cumbersome a system can be justified
only by its results; and it must be allowed that, so far as we can
now determine, no poet suffered any great injustice from its
operation. The playwrights usually won whom later critics
were unanimous in considering the greatest. Each of the tragic
triad wrote about one hundred plays: Aeschylus, whose career
fell before the admission of tragedy to the Lenaea, gained
thirteen victories at the City Dionysia; Sophocles, eighteen City
and at least two Lenaean victories; and Euripides, fifteen (or
possibly only five) victories at both festivals (see p. 325, below).
It must be remembered that several plays would be simultaneously crowned at each victory in tragedy (see p. 198, above). The
most astounding reversal occurred when Philocles, Aeschylus'
mediocre nephew, defeated Sophocles' didascalic group in which

was included his *Oedipus the King*, perhaps the greatest tragedy of ancient times! However, this apparent lapse of judgment is possibly to be explained by the factor mentioned in the last paragraph, a parsimonious choregus.

The lot was employed also in another connection. Immediately after the beginning of each civil year in Hecatombaeon (July), the archon eponymus and the king archon attended to the appointment of tragic choregi for the City Dionysia and the Lenaean festival, respectively. During the fifth century they chose the comic choregi as well, but Aristotle informs us that in his day their selection was managed by the tribes.[1] After this detail had been arranged the archons proceeded to "grant a chorus" to a suitable number of playwrights. For this purpose doubtless an untried poet was required to submit a more or less finished copy of what he wished to produce; from seasoned writers probably the presentation of a scenario or even less was deemed sufficient. At any rate Dr. Ruppel has shown that in Aristophanes' comedies the plot was sometimes essentially modified by or even integrally depended upon events which took place but a few weeks before the festival. It is evident that the archons exercised considerable discretion in selecting the playwrights; at least we are told that no less a personage than Sophocles was once refused a chorus when one was granted to an obscure Gnesippus.[2] When poets and choregi had finally been chosen, the troublesome task of matching them still confronted the officials. Naturally the important consequences which we have seen to grow out of the assignment of a generous or niggardly choregus to a poet served only to enhance the difficulty of the situation. And in the light of what has just been said concerning the Athenian fondness for the lot, it is not surprising that the problem was met by its use. After the actors passed from private to public management, about 449 B.C. (see p. 183, above), the lot was employed also to distribute the protagonists among the dramatists. In the fourth century the

[1] Cf. Aristotle, *Constitution of Athens*, c. 56.

[2] Cf. Kock, *Comicorum Atticorum Fragmenta*, I, 16, fr. 15 (Cratinus).

more equitable system became possible of permitting each protagonist to appear in a single one of each tragedian's three plays (see p. 185, above).

One of the most prominent traits of the Greek, and especially of the Athenian, character was litigiousness. Inasmuch as from the time of Pericles citizens of Attica received a slight stipend for serving upon juries, which ranged from 201 to 2,500 in membership and sometimes reached an aggregate of 6,000, there was scarcely an Athenian but was personally acquainted with courtroom procedure and not a few practically supported themselves in this way. Moreover, this situation was intensified by the fact that the fifth century witnessed the rise of formal oratory at Athens and its exploitation by numerous rhetorical and sophistic teachers. It is hardly possible that all these influences should have allowed contemporaneous drama to escape unscathed. Their first effect is seen in the actual introduction of a courtroom scene, as in Aeschylus' *Eumenides*, in which Orestes is put on trial before the Council of the Areopagus for having murdered his mother. Athena is the presiding judge, Apollo the attorney for the defense, and the chorus of Furies conducts the prosecution. Aristophanes satirized the Athenian weakness in his *Wasps*, the chorus of which appeared in the guise of those quarrelsome insects; and that inveterate juryman, Philocleon, was provided with a domestic court wherein one dog was duly arraigned by another for having pilfered a round of Sicilian cheese! Again, certain scenes in other plays, though not ostensibly placed in the courtroom, are practically treated as if they were. For example, in Euripides' *Trojan Women*, Menelaus meets his truant wife for the first time since her elopement. Will he pardon or slay her? Helen herself naturally hopes to be forgiven and restored to her husband's favor; but the Trojan women, who hold her responsible for their country's downfall, wish condign punishment to be meted out to her. Consequently the play degenerates into a quasi-trial in which Menelaus presides as judge, Hecabe, ex-queen of Troy, represents the prosecution, and Helen pleads her own cause. In the third

place, when a court scene was out of the question a debate of
some kind was often dragged in.   Of course "struggle" is of the
essence of drama and a formal "agon" was by derivation almost
indispensable in Old Comedy (see pp. 42–44), but I am now referring to something different.   Perhaps the most glaring instance
is found in Euripides' *Madness of Heracles* (vss. 158 ff.).   Lycus
has resolved upon Amphitryon's speedy death, yet they both
stop to argue whether it be better to fight with the spear or the
bow!   Finally, since in the law courts the addresses of the
contending parties were equalized by means of the "water-
clock" (the *clepsydra*), it is not surprising that the speeches of
sharply contrasted characters in tragedy are occasionally made
of exactly the same length.   The best example occurs in Euripides' *Hecabe*, where Polymestor's speech of fifty-one lines is
exactly balanced by that of the Trojan queen (cf. vss. 1132–82
and 1187–1237).   In Aeschylus' *Seven against Thebes* there are
seven pairs of contrasted speeches, two of which are exactly equal
(cf. vss. 422–36 = 437–51, and 568–96 = 597–625, and two others
are nearly so; cf. vss. 375–96 ≠ 397–416 and 631–52 ≠ 653–76).
If we had before us the *ipsissima verba* of the tragic writers it is
likely that these and some other minor inequalities would be
resolved.   Thus in Euripides' *Medea*, Jason speaks fifty-four
lines in reply to the heroine's fifty-five (cf. vss. 465–519 ≠ 522–75);
but there is some reason for believing that vs. 468 is interpolated.
Again, in Sophocles' *Antigone* the speeches of Creon and Haemon
would precisely correspond (cf. vss. 639–80 and 683–723), if we
suppose a verse to have dropped out after vs. 690.   In conclusion
it ought to be stated that such balancing was quite congenial to
the fondness for symmetry which characterized the Greek genius
in every field of endeavor.

Perhaps the one idea which was most fixed in the popular
consciousness of ancient Greece was that of Nemesis, the goddess
who punished the overweening presumption arising from long-
continued prosperity and success.   Herodotus' history exemplifies the notion both in its main theme, the crushing defeat
which brought Persia's long series of victories to a close, and in

numerous digressions, such as the story of Polycrates and his ring. Accordingly, when Phrynichus in his *Phoenician Women* and afterward Aeschylus in his *Persians* undertook to celebrate the Persian rout they were careful to avoid a display of the pride which had ruined the invading host, by laying the scene in the Orient and exhibiting the mourning of Persia, not the triumph of Greece (see p. 124, above). Again, in the seven pairs of contrasted speeches just mentioned as occurring in Aeschylus' *Seven against Thebes*, a messenger states in turn the name of the Argive champion who is to assail each of the seven gates of Thebes, describing his actions, words, the device upon his shield, etc., and the king in a similar manner matches each enemy with a warrior of his own. It is not without significance that to a Greek mind "the boasts and blazons of the champions convict them of presumption, and doom them beforehand to failure. The answers of Eteocles are always right, take advantage of the enemy's insolence, and secure divine favour by studied moderation."[1] Still again, in the same playwright's *Agamemnon* appears an incident which to the uninitiated modern reader seems forced and unworthy of the prominence and space assigned to it. Clytemnestra has been untrue to her lord during his long absence at Troy and is now prepared by her paramour's help to murder him. Agamemnon himself, thanks to the recent smiles of fortune, is in the sort of position which would easily expose him to the vengeance of Nemesis. In the play (vss. 905–57) Clytemnestra skilfully takes advantage of this situation in order to array the powerful goddess upon her side. She urges Agamemnon not to set his conquering foot upon the common earth but to pass from his chariot into the palace over a purple tapestry. The king shrinks from an act which would be more becoming to a god than a mortal, but finally yields to his wife's insistence. The result is that to a Greek audience he would seem to invite and almost to deserve the doom which his unfaithful spouse quickly brings upon him. These instances from the many available suffice to indicate Greek feeling on the subject.

[1] Cf. Sheppard, *op. cit.*, p. 58.

The poets of New Comedy leaned heavily upon the "long arm of coincidence." The young women who are the recipients of the gilded youths' favors are frequently found in the outcome to be free-born, the children of respectable parents, and acceptable wives. In several instances the victim of violence at some nocturnal festival has unwittingly become the spouse of her ravisher. The situation is aggravated by the unity of time. Men who have been absent from their homes for months or years must some day return to their households, pregnant women must at last be delivered of their offspring, long-standing debts must finally fall due, and the escapades of spoiled sons must at some time be brought to light and receive the attention of "hardhearted" parents. Coming singly, such occurrences occasion no surprise. But when several of that sort are crowded into a period of twenty-four hours or less in play after play, to our minds the coincidence becomes well-nigh intolerable. It seems likely, however, that the ancients regarded such concatenations of events with more kindly eyes, for the reason that Chance or Fortune (Τύχη) was commonly accepted as exercising supreme authority over the lives and fortunes of men. This conception also helps to explain the curious immunity from punishment which was usually enjoyed by the scheming slaves in comedy. Of course to a race whose national characteristics were embodied in the wily Odysseus, cleverness, however unscrupulous, always seemed to elevate its practitioners above the rules of ordinary morality. But more. Just as "in the days of the *Odyssey* a man merely required to be skilful at deceiving his fellows to become a favorite of Athena's, so in the days of New Comedy this quality gave him a claim to the favor of the queen of the world —omnipotent Tyche."[1]

It is not always realized how almost oriental was the seclusion in which respectable women were kept at Athens during the period of its greatness in drama. Respectable women of good family were not permitted to leave their homes except for special reasons, nor to converse with men other than near relatives or

[1] Cf. Legrand, *op. cit.*, pp. 312–15 and 455 f.

slaves.   When it is remembered that the physical arrangements
of the Greek theaters did not readily admit of interior scenes
(see pp. 237 ff., above) it will be understood how difficult it was
for an ancient playwright to bring women of the better class
upon his stage.   This applies particularly to comedy as being a
more accurate mirror of contemporaneous manners; in tragedy,
as will presently appear, it was counteracted by another factor.
At weddings, funerals, and religious festivals women, especially
married women, were allowed greater liberty than at other times.
Thus, in Aristophanes' *Women at the Thesmophoria* the coming
of the *festa* affords them an opportunity of carrying on the business of the play.   In the same writer's *Women in Council* they
act in secret and disguised as men until their coup d'état has
succeeded and the government has been voted into their hands.
The situation in Aristophanes' *Lysistrata* is quite as abnormal,
being nothing more or less than a "sex strike!"   In more conventional plays the speaking characters, apart from divinities,
are practically restricted to women of the demimonde, foreign
residents (*metics*), female slaves, those other virtuous but vulgar
creatures whom poverty has compelled to seek a livelihood in
various business pursuits of the humbler sort, and finally women
advanced in years, shrewish in disposition, and unattractive in
person.   The first and last types are especially common in New
Comedy, while Plautus' *Persian* is said to be unique in its
presentation of a chaste and free-born maiden in an active rôle.[1]
Even the girl who has excited the young man's affections and
whose counterpart in modern drama would be a conspicuous
figure is seldom seen and is not always heard.   The most that
she seems normally capable of doing is to ejaculate a cry of agony
from behind the scenes at the moment of childbirth.   This is
the more surprising since the fact of her Attic citizenship is
rarely established and sometimes is not even suspected until the
very close of the play.   The poet's consciousness of what he
intends to make of her—a free-born citizen and a legal wife—
apparently constrains him to protect her from an unconvention-

[1] Cf. Prescott in *Classical Philology*, XI (1916), 132.

ality of conduct which, though suitable to her present condition, would afterward be looked back upon with regret by herself, her husband and newly recovered relatives, and even by the spectators themselves. Truth to tell, the girls from whom an Athenian was required to take his bride were scarcely fitted to be his intellectual companions or to grace a dialogue in drama, while the best of the courtesans could qualify in either capacity. According to American notions the marriage of convenience arranged by the parents is hardly warranted to produce domestic felicity. But the hero of Greek comedy often selected a mistress for graces of mind and person and afterward, when her legitimate birth was discovered, gladly made her his wife. At least such matches ought to have resulted happily. Yet surprisingly little is ever said of married bliss and affection arising from any sort of union. While this social situation prevented the ancient dramatist from introducing certain scenes which are the stock in trade of the modern playwright, in one respect it was of service to him. Since practically no attention was paid to the girl's wishes in such matters and almost none to the youth's, the speed with which engagements could be made and unmade or consummated in wedlock aided materially in observing the unity of time. The plots and concentrated action of many plays in the New Comedy (cf. for example Terence's *Andrian Girl*) would be quite impossible if women in such a case were not passive and helpless instruments in the hands of others. Professor Lounsbury (*op. cit.*, pp. 120 ff.) has convincingly shown what a stumbling-block the unity of time proved to the classical dramatists of Western Europe who tried to conform to the unities but lived in a society to which such rapidity in courtship was repugnant.

In Greek tragedy the representation of women is strikingly different from that in comedy. Whereas in this respect the latter reacted to the usage of contemporaneous society, tragedy reverted to the practice of Homer. In the *Iliad* women like Helen and Andromache, suitably attended, not only traverse the Trojan streets but appear on the walls and among the men without losing caste or being regarded as immodest; and though Helen's elopement with his brother was the source of all Troy's present woes, Hector addresses her with far more consideration than he shows the wayward Paris.   In the fourth book of the *Odyssey* she assists Menelaus at their Spartan home in entertaining the strangers from Ithaca and Pylus, and freely participates in the conversation without embarrassment and as an equal. How faithful a picture these poems present of the social situation in Homer's own day is largely beside the question, since it is evident that they portray the events of a bygone age, viz., the close of that "Aegean" or "Minoan" civilization which has been unearthed by Schliemann on the Greek mainland and more recently by Evans and others in Crete.

It is certain that women must have lived on a footing of greater equality with the men than in any other ancient civilization, and we see in the frescoes of Knossos conclusive indications of an open and easy association of men and women, corresponding to our idea of "Society," at the Minoan Court unparalleled till our own day.[1]

The extant remains clearly demonstrate that Homer's delineation was at the least derived from a genuine tradition.   In view of the fact that with three or four exceptions (see pp. 123 f., above) the themes of tragedy were always selected from Homeric or other mythological sources, it was natural that the Greek tragedians should take over from him a social system which so conveniently liberated them from the restrictions of contemporaneous customs.   It is unnecessary to cite passages to prove that they actually did this; the women of almost every tragedy move about with a freedom and conduct themselves with an independence such as no respectable woman among the playwright's contemporaries could have asserted.

Nor is it peculiar that so artificial a pose is not consistently maintained.   Occasionally, an unconscious sense of outraged propriety causes the dramatist to put words into a woman's mouth which stand in glaring contrast with the rest of the scene.

[1] Cf. Hall, *The Ancient History of the Near East*[2] (1913), p. 48.

In Euripides' *Andromache*, Hermione's confidential slave brings their dialogue to a close by saying to her mistress:

> Nay, pass within; make not thyself a show
> Before this house, lest thou shouldst get thee shame,
> Before this palace seen of men, my child.
> > [Vss. 877 ff.; Way's translation]

In real life these words would furnish an excellent motive for withdrawing; how artificial they are in tragedy appears from the fact that, though a strange-looking man is now seen approaching, Hermione remains upon the scene! In the same author's *Electra* (vss. 341 ff.) that heroine's peasant-husband finds her conversing with her brother and Pylades (though she recognizes neither) and exclaims:

> How now?   What strangers these about my doors?
> > . . . . Beseemeth not
> That with young men a wife should stand in talk.
> > [Way's translation]

The man's lowly birth and usually deferential attitude toward his wife make these words seem especially incongruous, and Electra promptly apologizes for them. Sometimes these anachronisms are intentional and fulfill a deliberate purpose. In Euripides' *Phoenician Maids* (vss. 88 ff.), Antigone and a servant are about to appear on the flat roof of the palace in order to catch a glimpse of the invading army; but for technical reasons (see pp. 177 f., above) it is necessary that Antigone's entrance be slightly delayed. Accordingly, the slave comes into view first and is made to afford an excuse for her tardy appearance which would have been legitimate for a fifth-century princess but which to a Homeric woman or one at the period of the dramatic time of the play would have seemed to spring from false modesty.

> Fair flower of thy sire's house, Antigone,
> Albeit thy mother suffered thee to leave
> Thy maiden-bower at thine entreaty, and mount
> The palace-roof to view the Argive host,
> Yet stay, that I may scan the highway first,
> Lest on the path some citizen appear,
> And scandal light—for me, the thrall, 'twere naught,—
> On thee, the princess.   [Way's translation.]

Again, when they are ready to withdraw, the approach of the chorus reinforces the same motive (see p. 93, n. 1, above):

> Daughter, pass in . . . .
> Lo, to the royal halls a woman-throng
> Comes, ...
> And scandal-loving still is womankind, etc.
>
> [Vss. 193 ff.; Way's translation]

As intimated at the beginning it would be possible to extend this chapter indefinitely. One more point must suffice. The belief was widespread among the Greeks that if a man's body failed of burial his shade was forced to wander for a season on this side of the river Styx and was thus cut off from association with the great majority of departed spirits; the obligation of attending to the funeral rites rested upon the nearest kin of the deceased. It was inevitable that a doctrine so intimately connected with the life of the people should frequently appear in their literature. Thus the *Iliad* does not close with the deaths of Patroclus and Hector, but two whole books are devoted to an account of their funerals. Likewise in the *Odyssey*, however unsympathetic has been his delineation of the suitors' conduct, nevertheless Homer does not pass by the final disposition of their bodies in silence (cf. xxiv. 417). In tragedy, which often involves the death of the hero, naturally this matter is frequently mentioned. In Sophocles' *Antigone* it provides the mainspring of the action. Because Polynices fell in arms against his native country, Creon forbade his burial, but before the call of a duty so sacred Antigone deemed not her life precious and performed the formal rites for her brother's body in defiance of the king's command. According to modern feeling, when the hero falls upon his sword at vs. 865 of Sophocles' *Ajax*, the dénouement must have arrived and the ending be close at hand; as a matter of fact, the play continues for over five hundred verses. To the Greeks no less important than the fact of his death was the treatment which was to be accorded his corpse, and the honors which Ajax received in Attica as a "hero" in the technical, religious sense of that term made this a matter of far more moment than would have been true even in the case of an ordinary man. Aeschylus' *Seven against Thebes* concludes with a dirge between Antigone and Ismene over the bodies of their two brothers, and an altercation between a public herald and Antigone in which she declares her intention of defying the state edict by burying Polynices. The genuineness of these scenes has been assailed on technical grounds but in my opinion unwarrantably (see p. 175, above). They have been charged also with carrying the play (and the trilogy) past the natural stopping-point and to an inconclusive close. But despite any considerations which can be urged in its support, this objection ignores the Greek feeling concerning the paramount importance of interment and cannot be allowed. Even modern audiences have sometimes felt a certain sympathy with this point of view "The typical Elizabethan tragedy does not deal with the mistakes of a night, but with the long—often life-long—struggles of its hero. Such a play must have an appropriate ending. After the audience has sympathized with a Hamlet or a Brutus through many a scene, it is not satisfied with a sudden death and a drop of a curtain with a thud. It asks to see the body solemnly and reverently borne off the stage as if to its last resting place. And this was the respect which the honored dead received on the Elizabethan stage."[1]

[1] Cf. Albright, *The Shakesperian Stage* (1909), pp. 148 f.

I find them one and all to be merely
examples of a new artificiality—the artificiality of naturalism.—GORDON CRAIG.

CHAPTER VIII

THE INFLUENCE OF THEATRICAL MACHINERY
AND DRAMATIC CONVENTIONS[1]

We have already noted that the Greek theater had no facilities
for the direct representation of interior scenes (see pp. 237–42,
above). Of the many subterfuges there mentioned as available
for or utilized by the ancient playwrights it is now in place to
elaborate upon one. I refer to the *eccyclema*, one of the strangest
and most conventional pieces of machinery that any theater
has ever seen.

If it were desired to disclose to the audience the corpse of
someone who has just been done to death behind the scenes,
perhaps with the murderers still gloating over their crime, or to
set any similar interior view before the faithful eyes of the spectators, the simplest device was to fling open the appropriate door
of the scene-building and thus to display the desired objects or
persons close behind the opening. Whatever may be said for
such a method under other conditions, in the Greek theater it
ran afoul of certain practical considerations. For example, the
wings of the auditorium extended around so far (Fig. 22) that
spectators seated there could have obtained no satisfactory view
through the opened doors of the scene-building. Nevertheless,

[1] In addition to the works mentioned on pp. xvii and xx f., above, cf. Thirlwall,
"On the Irony of Sophocles," *Philological Museum*, II (1833), 483 ff.; Neckel,
Das Ekkyklema (1890); Trautwein, *De Prologorum Plautinorum Indole atque
Natura* (1890); Dörpfeld-Reisch, *Das griechische Theater* (1896), pp. 234 ff.; Bethe,
Prolegomena zur Geschichte des Theaters im Alterthum (1896), pp. 100 ff.; Exon,
"A New Theory of the Eccyclema," *Hermathena*, XI (1901), 132 ff.; Leo, *Der
Monolog im Drama, ein Beitrag zur griechisch-römischen Poetik* (1908); Polczyk,
De Unitatibus et Loci et Temporis in Nova Comoedia Observatis (1909); Flickinger,
"Dramatic Irony in Terence," *Classical Weekly*, III (1910), 202 ff.; Arnold, *The
Soliloquies of Shakespeare* (1911); Fensterbusch, *Die Bühne des Aristophanes*
(1912), pp. 51 ff.; Harms, *De Introitu Personarum in Euripidis et Novae Comoediae
Fabulis* (1914); and Rees, "The Function of the Πρόθυρον in the Production of
Greek Plays," *Classical Philology*, X (1915), 134 ff.

during the last quarter-century not a few scholars have maintained that this was the sole means which the Greek playwrights employed for such a purpose. But the ancient commentators often speak of a contrivance which was used to bring a supposedly interior scene out of the opened doors and more fully into the view of the audience. This device is sometimes described as "turning" or "revolving" (στρέφειν)[1] and sometimes as being "rolled out" (ἐκ, "out"+κυκλεῖν, to "wheel"). And though eccyclema (ἐκκύκλημα) was used as the generic term I am persuaded that there were in fact two types of machine corresponding to different conditions in the Athenian theater.

When the first scene-building was erected, about 465 B.C., it must have been simple and unpretentious, having parascenia but no proscenium. Probably it consisted also of but a single story, though in Fig. 74[2] I have given it a low clerestory with small windows for the admission of light into the scene-building. The roof would thus have been better suited for the occasional appearance of actors upon the housetop, as in Aeschylus' *Agamemnon* (458 B.C.). In addition to the usual doors in the parascenia and scene-building (*A*, *C*, and *E* in Fig. 74), I believe that a butterfly valve, to the base of which a semicircular platform was attached, was used to close one or more other openings. In Fig. 74 one of these is shown closed and not in use at *B* and another open and in action at *D*. The size of the semicircular platform would be limited only by the depth of the scene-building and the space between the front doors, and there would be ample room for several persons upon the eccyclema at a time. Therefore when a deed of violence had been committed indoors it was possible, by revolving one of the valves after a tableau had been posed upon its platform, to place a quasi-interior scene

[1] Cf. scholia to Aeschylus' *Eumenides*, vs. 64, Aristophanes' *Acharnians*, vs. 408 and *Clouds*, vs. 184, and Clemens Alexandrinus, p. 11 (Potter).

[2] Fig. 74 is specially drawn, but owes several features to Figs. 93 f. in Dörpfeld-Reisch, *Das griechische Theater*. Since Exon's discussion and drawing of the eccyclema presuppose a theater with a stage, it has been necessary to modify his conception so as to bring it into conformity with the Dörpfeld theory. See p. 358.

before the spectators. This is Mr. Exon's theory of the eccyclema, and it admirably fits the conditions in the Athenian
theater at an early date.

Thus, Aeschylus' *Eumenides*, which belongs to this period
(458 B.C.), opens with a monologue of the Pythian priestess
(see p. 305, below). At vs. 33 she enters the temple, but immediately returns, so shaken by the sight within that she cannot

FIG. 74.—The Athenian Theater of About 460 B.C. Showing the Earlier Type
of Eccyclema.

See pp. 285, n. 2, and 358.

walk, but crawls. She has seen a blood-stained man (Orestes)
at the omphalus and before him a sleeping band of hideous Furies
(vss. 34–63). At vs. 64 we must suppose that the eccyclema
revolves with Apollo, Hermes, and Orestes mounted upon it.
The first named bids the matricide to leave Delphi and speed to
Athens and Hermes to guard him on his journey. Whereupon
the two step from the platform and flee through one of the parodi,
and the eccyclema, with Apollo still upon it, is revolved back
into its original position (vs. 93). Here we may note a curious

incongruity; the platform of the eccyclema is actually out of doors; nominally it is indoors. If the latter fact were kept steadfastly in mind, a character could not step directly from the eccyclema into the orchestra (as Orestes does here) but could only pass out through one of the doors after the eccyclema had been closed again. It is of a piece with this that the characters are not only spoken of as being indoors but sometimes as being out of doors. At vs. 94 the ghost of Clytemnestra appears in the orchestra (or perhaps is merely heard from within the scene-building) calling upon the Furies to waken and pursue their escaping prey. Beginning at vs. 117 their cries and ejaculations are heard at intervals, and at vs. 143 they burst into the orchestra for their entrance song (the parodus). At its conclusion (vs. 178) Apollo comes out and drives them from his precinct.

Sometimes the opening and shutting of the back scene is distinctly referred to. Thus in Sophocles' *Ajax*,[1] vs. 344, the coryphaeus cries to the attendants: "Open there; perhaps even by looking upon me he may acquire a more sober mood"; and as Tecmessa replies "Lo! I open," the door of the hero's tent is opened and Ajax is seen amid the slaughtered cattle, the victims of his misdirected vengeance. After playing a prominent lyrical and speaking part in the scene which follows, Ajax orders the door to be closed with all speed and disappears from view (vs. 593).

But the eccyclema was also described as a low, trundle platform,[2] large enough to accommodate several persons and narrow enough to be pushed through the doors of the scene-building, and this type would be more suitable for the conditions which obtained in the Athenian theater from about 430 B.C. (see pp. 235 and 292).[3] At this period the scene-building was slightly moved and raised to a second story; it was embellished with a wooden proscenium; a crane came into use, etc. Under these conditions the earlier type of eccyclema could no longer be so large nor so

[1] See p. 244, n. 1, above.

[2] Cf. scholia to Aristophanes' *Acharnians*, vs. 408 and *Women at the Thesmophoria*, vs. 284; Pollux iv. 128, and Eustathius, p. 976, 15. [3] See pp. 339 ff.

easily seen, being hampered in both particulars by the proscenium. On the other hand the new type could be made as
long as the scene-building was deep and could be pushed forward
as far as might be necessary.¹ Thus in Aristophanes' *Acharnians*
(425 B.C.), Dicaeopolis appears before the house of Euripides,
who is lounging within doors. In response to the former's
knock and summons "to be wheeled out" Euripides says "I will
be wheeled out," and is pushed upon the stage (ἐκκυκλήθητι
. . . . ἐκκυκλήσομαι, vs. 408). The conversation which ensues
between Dicaeopolis outdoors and Euripides supposedly indoors
does not conclude until vs. 479, when the latter exclaims: "The
fellow is insolent; shut the doors." Perhaps in this instance,
for parodic effect, a trundle couch itself is shoved through the
door instead of a stationary couch upon a trundle platform.²
Very similar is the scene in Aristophanes' *Women at the Thesmophoria* (about 411 B.C.), where Agathon is wheeled out before
Euripides and Mnesilochus. Here again the verbs ἐκκυκλούμενος
in vs. 96 and εἰσκυκλησάτω at the conclusion of the scene in
vs. 265 do not permit me to doubt that the eccyclema, or a comic
substitute, was employed. It is probably no accident that
Euripides figures in both of these scenes. He is "hoist with his
own petar" as having invented, or been a frequent user of, this
mechanism.

The passage of tragedy in which most authorities concede
the employment of the eccyclema is Euripides' *The Madness
of Heracles* (vss. 1029–1402). Chronologically this play falls
somewhere between the *Acharnians* and the *Women at the
Thesmophoria*. In his madness Heracles has slain his wife and
three children within the palace and at last has fallen into a dazed
torpor; whereupon his friends have bound him to a broken

---

¹ The *exostra* (ἐξ, "out"+ὠθεῖν, to "push") seems to have performed about
the same function as the eccyclema; cf. Pollux iv. 129; perhaps it was only the more
specific name for this later type.

² On the basis of ἀναβάδην in vs. 399, for which the scholiasts preserve two
interpretations, some writers would have us believe that Euripides was shown in
the second story. Tracks for the wheels of an eccyclema have been reported on
the logium level of the theater at Eretria (see p. 107, above).

column.   As the chorus chant "Alas! Behold the doors of the
stately palace fall asunder" (vss. 1029 f.), the hero bound to
a pillar amid the slain is pushed forward on the eccyclema.
At vs. 1089 he recovers consciousness and begins to speak; at
vs. 1123 Amphitryon loosens him; and at vs. 1163 Theseus
enters and finally (vs. 1402) persuades him to descend into the
orchestra.

Still another theatrical contrivance was called the μηχανή
("machine"), which about 430 B.C. came to be used to bring
divinities before the ancient audiences.   This was a crane and
pulley arrangement, mounted in one of the side wings (parascenia), whereby persons or objects could be brought from
behind the second story (the episcenium) and held suspended
in the air or let down upon the roof of the scene-building or into
the orchestra, or could be lifted in an opposite direction.   This
development is of interest also from the structural standpoint as
indicating that whatever the situation may have been earlier,
at least from this time on the scene-building was provided with
an episcenium (see pp. 67 f., above).

Before considering the use of the *machina* further, it will be
worth while to trace briefly how gods played their parts in the
Greek theater.   Prior to the erection of a scene-building, about
465 B.C., the scene was perforce laid in the open countryside (see
p. 226, above) and the playwrights had no option but to place
divinities and mortals in immediate juxtaposition, after the
Homeric fashion, in the orchestra.   For the same reason, however
these characters might be thought of as traveling before they
entered the theater, they rested under the prosaic necessity, as
soon as they were seen by the spectators, of moving upon the
solid earth.   Thus in Aeschylus' *Prometheus Bound*, Oceanus
enters at vs. 284 with the words:

> From my distant caves cerulean
> This fleet-pinioned bird hath borne me;
> Needed neither bit nor bridle,
> Thought instinctive reined the creature.
>
> [Blackie's translation]

As a preliminary to his departure at vs. 397, he says:

> I go, and quickly.   My four-footed bird
> Brushes the broad path of the limpid air
> With forward wing: right gladly will he bend
> The wearied knee on his familiar stall.
>
> [Blackie's translation]

It will be noted that there is nothing here which requires or implies flight through the air within sight of the audience. Evidently Oceanus rides upon a fantastic creature which is rolled along by hidden power or which walks on disguised human legs. A similar interpretation must be set upon the lines which refer to the chorus' mode of entrance in the same play.   At vs. 124 Prometheus cries out:

> Hark again!   I hear the whirring
> As of wingéd birds approaching;
> With the light strokes of their pinions
> Ether pipes ill-boding whispers!—
> Alas! Alas! that I should fear
> Each breath that nears me.

To which the Oceanides, as they come into view, reply:

> Fear nothing; for a friendly band approaches;
> Fleet rivalry of wings
> Oared us to this far height.   [Blackie's translation]

They remain upon their winged car until the Titan invites them, at vs. 272, to step upon the earth.   They accept in the following language:

> Not to sluggish ears, Prometheus,
> Hast thou spoken thy desire;
> From our breeze-borne seat descending,
> With light foot we greet the ground.
> Leaving ether chaste, smooth pathway
> Of the gently winnowing wing,
> On this craggy rock I stand.   [Blackie's translation]

Here again there is no need of supposing that the choral car does not rest solidly upon the ground. Its aërial motion is entirely off-scene.

Even at a later period, when more sophisticated devices were available, the gods still continued on occasion to use strictly terrestrial means of locomotion and to stand in the orchestra on a level with purely human characters. For example, in Sophocles' *Ajax*, Athena appears before the tent of that hero and converses first with Odysseus and then with Ajax. In Euripides' posthumous *Bacchanals*, Dionysus is seen *in propria persona* before the house of Pentheus and afterward (in disguise) enters and departs from its portals. Still again, in the pseudo-Euripidean *Rhesus*, which is usually regarded as a fourth-century production, Athena comes before Hector's tent to advise and encourage Odysseus and then to deceive Paris (cf. especially vss. 627 f.). On the contrary, the words of the chorus in vss. 885 f. of this play show that the Muse appears above their heads. Thus it is an error to think that the more primitive methods of presenting divinities were entirely superseded by later ones; the different methods existed side by side and might even be used in the same play.

After the erection of a scene-building, about 465 B.C., it became possible to employ the roof as a higher stage for certain scenes. At the beginning of Aeschylus' *Agamemnon* the guard is found posted upon the palace roof, on watch for the last in the series of beacon lights from Troy. In Euripides' *Phoenician Maids*, Antigone and an old servant appear on top of the royal palace in order to view the hostile army (cf. vss. 88 ff.). In these and other instances the roof of the scene-building (or at a later period the top of the proscenium) was pressed into service. Moreover, although this spot was of course not the exclusive place of speaking, yet, since it was never used for dancing but only for speaking, it came to be called the logium (λογεῖον) or "speaking-place" *par excellence* (see p. 59, above). This arrangement was especially useful when a scene was to be thought

of as taking place in heaven.   So in Aeschylus' lost play entitled
The Weighing of Souls, Zeus was represented as placing the fates
of Achilles and Memnon into the scales, while Thetis and Eos
prayed for their sons.   The same meaning is assigned the logium
also in Aristophanes' *Peace*, in which Trygaeus on the back of
his beetle mounts from earth to heaven, i.e., from the orchestra
to the top of the proscenium.   The dramatists were not slow
to perceive that no other part of the theater was so well adapted
for the awe-compelling theophanies with which the Greeks were
so fond of terminating their tragedies.   There is no doubt that
this method of introducing divinities was employed in several
of our extant plays, but the absence of stage directions makes it
difficult to differentiate the instances sharply.

Finally about 430 B.C. the machine ($\mu\eta\chi\alpha\nu\dot{\eta}$) came into use.
Possibly this is employed in Euripides' *Medea* (431 B.C.) in order
to carry away that heroine and the bodies of her children in the
chariot of the sun-god, but the situation is doubtful.   It is almost
certainly a mistake, however, to attribute the machine, as some
do, to the time of Aeschylus.   Whether Euripides was its
inventor or not, he was extraordinarily fond of using it.   Indeed
it has been remarked that "in almost every play of Euripides
something flies through the air."   At any rate the earliest sure
instance of the machine occurs in Euripides' lost *Bellerophon*,
which was brought out some time before 425 B.C.   By its means the
hero in this play was enabled to mount from earth to heaven, i.e.,
from the orchestra to the top of the proscenium, upon the winged
steed, Pegasus.   This scene is parodied in Aristophanes' *Peace*
(421 B.C.), in which Trygaeus makes a similar flight on the back
of a beetle.   Somewhat later the same device enabled Perseus
in Euripides' lost *Andromeda* to fly to the rocks upon which that
heroine had been bound.   In Aristophanes' *Clouds* (423 B.C.)
it was employed to suspend Socrates in a basket, whence he could
look down upon the troubles of mortals and survey the heavenly
bodies.   Especially important is the situation in Euripides'
Orestes (408 B.C.).   Orestes and Pylades have fled to the palace
roof, dragging Hermione with them.   Menelaus is outside the

bolted door below. Suddenly Apollo appears (vs. 1625) with Helen at his side. The divinity begins to speak as follows:

> Menelaus, peace to thine infuriate mood:
> I, Phoebus, Leto's son, here call on thee.
> Peace thou, Orestes, too, whose sword doth guard
> Yon maid, that thou mayst hear the words I bear.
> Helen, whose death thou hast essayed, to sting
> The heart of Menelaus, yet hast missed,
> Is here,—whom *wrapped in folds of air ye see* (ἐν αἰθέρος πτυχαῖς),—
> From death delivered, and not slain of thee, etc.
>
> [Way's translation]

The italicized words show that Apollo and Helen stand above all the other actors in the drama, who are themselves standing on two different levels; and it is evident that the machine was utilized for this purpose.

The last example is typical of a large class of instances in which a divinity appears as a splendid climax to the events of the play. It is plain that in all or practically all of these the god is raised above the other performers, as would be only appropriate for an effective close; but whether the deity merely came forward upon the logium or was brought into view by means of a machine is not always an easy matter to determine. By a natural extension of meaning, however, such an apparition at the close of a play came to be called a "god from the machine" (θεὸς ἀπὸ μηχανῆς; *deus ex machina*) regardless of the method used for his appearance. By a further extension of meaning μηχανή was used to designate any mechanical artifice, such as the "long arm of coincidence," for example. Thus Aristotle criticized the μηχανή in Euripides' *Medea*, but from another passage it becomes clear that he was referring, not to the use of an actual machine at the dénouement, but only to the improbability involved in the appearance of King Aegeus in the course of the play.[1]

There are several ancient notices which refer to the use that inexpert playwrights made of the deus ex machina in order to extricate their characters when the plot had become complicated

[1] Cf. *Poetics* 1454b1 and 1461b21.

beyond the possibility of disentanglement by purely natural means. It would seem that in the hands of second-rate poets the deus was frequently so employed. In particular it has often been charged that Euripides was guilty of this practice, but in my opinion without due warrant. It is true that he concluded fully half of his eighteen extant plays in this manner, besides several other instances in the plays now lost; but with only one exception his principal motive was never to relieve himself of the embarrassment into which the confusion of his plot had involved him. The truth of this statement appears most clearly in the *Iphigenia among the Taurians* (see pp. 201 f., above). At vs. 1392 all the immediate requirements of the drama have been met: Orestes, Iphigenia, and Pylades have made good their escape, bearing the image of Artemis. The poet could have stopped here without requiring the aid of a divinity. Instead he preferred to plunge himself into such a plight as only a deity could rescue him from, for in the succeeding verses a messenger reports that contrary wind and wave are driving the refugees back to land. King Thoas just has time to issue quick commands when Athena appears (vs. 1435) and bids him cease his efforts. Surely the playwright's difficulties here are self-imposed and must be regarded as having furnished the excuse rather than the reason for the use of the deus ex machina. What other objects might he have had in mind? It has already been suggested (p. 202, above) that this device enabled him to bring the melodramatic course of the action to a more dignified and truly tragic close. Also he thus found it possible to rescue the chorus, who had been promised a safe return to Greece but had been left behind. But the fact that the chorus in the same poet's *Helen* is irremediably left in the lurch after the same fashion (see pp. 160 f., above) implies that this was a lesser consideration. Again, toward the close of Euripides' *Suppliants*, Adrastus has vowed the eternal gratitude of Argos to Athens for having secured the return of her slain. But the appearance of Athena at vs. 1183 makes her a witness to this, and her demand that Adrastus' promise be ratified by an oath converts it into a sacred obligation.

But after all these are only occasional motives, while a more important result is obtained again and again. In the *Iphigenia*, Euripides took advantage of Athena's presence to have her foretell the heroine's later career and final decease in Attica. It is unnecessary to point out that the presence of a divinity was highly serviceable and appropriate for such a purpose. We have already seen (p. 259, above) that exactly the same situation obtains in the *Andromache*. In this way the poet was enabled to burst through the restricting influences which caused the normal observance of the unities of time and place and to include other days and other places within the purview of his play. Frequently there is included in this an aetiological explanation of rites which were observed in the dramatist's own day. Thus in Euripides' *Hippolytus* (vss. 1423 ff.), Artemis promises that the maidens of Troezen will perform certain ceremonies in honor of the hero's sufferings, and in the *Iphigenia among the Taurians* (vss. 1446 ff.), Athena enjoins upon Orestes to establish the temple and worship of Artemis Tauropolos at Brauron in Attica.

It would take too long to examine here every instance of the deus ex machina in Euripides. For that I must refer the reader to Professor Decharme's interesting discussion.[1] Suffice it to state that in every case the element of prediction is brought into play. This appears even in the *Orestes*, the only piece in which the theophany is frankly and undisguisedly employed to provide Euripides with a dénouement. Orestes and Electra stand condemned to death for having murdered their mother. Being disappointed in the hope of receiving succor from their uncle, Menelaus, they determine to punish him for his recreancy by slaying Helen and to hold his daughter Hermione as a hostage in order to force him to secure the recall of the decree against them. Helen has now supposedly been slain, Menelaus stands angry and baffled before the bolted doors, Orestes with his sword at Hermione's throat taunts him from the palace roof. If any regard is to be paid to verisimilitude or human psychology, no

[1] Cf. *Euripides and the Spirit of His Dramas*, pp. 263 ff., Loeb's translation (1906).

reconciliation between these conflicting elements is possible; but at this moment Apollo appears, and his fiat (see p. 293) resolves every feud.   The god goes beyond this, however, and in typical fashion predicts (or ordains) the later career of each character.

It is but fair to Euripides to state that even Sophocles, that master of dramatic writing, found the deus ex machina as indispensable in his *Philoctetes* as did the former in his *Orestes*. Philoctetes had come into possession of the bow of Heracles, and having been abandoned on the island of Lemnos by the leaders of the Greek expedition against Troy he cherished an implacable hatred against his former associates.   But now the Greeks have received an oracle to the effect that the person and weapons of Philoctetes are necessary for the capture of Ilium.   In Sophocles' play the task of meeting these conditions has been laid upon the wily Odysseus and the noble Neoptolemus.   By a trick they succeed in gaining possession of the bow and by another trick are in a fair way of enticing the inexorable hero on board a ship bound for Troy, when the generous son of Achilles refuses to proceed further with so infamous a scheme and finally returns his weapons to Philoctetes.   This development was inevitable if the character of Neoptolemus is to be maintained consistently; but it leaves the characters in a hopeless deadlock.   At this juncture (vs. 1408) the deified Heracles appears to reveal the purposes of Zeus, and Philoctetes abandons his resentment. Here again the element of prophecy is associated with the deus ex machina, Heracles foretelling the healing of Philoctetes' wound and his future career of glory at Troy and elsewhere.

Much nonsense has been indulged in by modern authorities in ridiculing this contrivance of the Greek theater.   This has sprung partly from a misapprehension of the real situation and partly from a failure to realize that devices fully as forced and artificial have been employed by the supreme masters of dramatic art in modern times.   Of course I do not mean that an actual μηχανή has often been brought to view in modern theaters or that divinities have frequently trod the stage.   Nevertheless a close equivalent of the deus ex machina, in the broader sense, has not rarely been resorted to.   For example, at the close of Shakespeare's *Cymbeline* the king declares, *as the result of an oracle:*

> *Although the victor*, we submit to Caesar
> And to the Roman empire, promising
> To pay our wonted tribute.

Again, in *As You Like It* everything has been satisfactorily settled except one point: the spectators would hardly rest content to think of the characters as spending the remainder of their lives in the Forest of Arden.   This detail is adjusted by means of a messenger, who reports that the usurping duke had addressed a mighty power with which to capture his brother and put him to the sword:

> And to the skirts of this wild wood he came;
> Where *meeting with an old religious man,*
> After some question with him, was converted
> Both from his enterprise and from the world;
> His crown bequeathing to his banish'd brother,
> And all their lands restored to them again
> That were with him exiled.

Finally, not to extend this list unduly, in Molière's *Tartuffe* by the time that Orgon has at length unmasked the hypocrite he had played into his hand to such an extent, by deeding him his property and by intrusting him with incriminating papers, that it is impossible to conceive how he can be extricated.   But at this crisis an officer of police in the name of the French king (almost a divine figure in those days) rescues him from his troubles:

Monsieur, dismiss all anxious fears.   We live beneath a prince the foe of fraud,—a prince whose eyes can penetrate all hearts; whose mind the art of no impostor can deceive. . . . . This one was powerless to mislead him; those wily schemes he instantly detected, discerning with his keen sagacity the inmost folds of that most treacherous heart.   Coming to denounce you, the wretch betrayed himself; and by the stroke of some high justice the prince discovered him, by his own words, to be a great impostor, ... In a word, the monarch . . . . ordered me to follow him here and see to what lengths his impudence would go, and then to do justice on him for your sake. Yes, I am ordered to take from his person the papers which he boasts of holding, and place them in your hands. The king, of his sovereign power, annuls the deed you made him of your property; and he forgives you for the secret to which your friendship for an exile led you. [Wormeley's translation.]

Who, with such examples of artificial and mechanical dénouements before him, will cast the first stone at the deus ex machina of the Greeks ?[1]

In a technical sense "prologue" came to denote the histrionic passage before the entrance song of the chorus (the parodus) (see p. 192, above). Such prologues are not found in Aeschylus' *Suppliants* and *Persians*, which begin with the choral parodus. The earliest prologue of which we have knowledge occurred in Phrynichus' lost play, the *Phoenician Women* (476 B.C.), in which a eunuch opens the action by spreading places in the orchestra for the counselors of the Persian empire and at the same time announcing the defeat of Xerxes in Greece. On the other hand, according to a late authority, prologues were the invention of Thespis.[2] In my opinion this contradiction is to be explained as a confusion between the technical and non-technical uses of the term. There is every reason for believing that prologues in the technical sense just mentioned did not go back to the time of Thespis. But the fully developed prologue was naturally employed as a vehicle for the exposition, and the task of acquainting his audience with data preliminary to the action and necessary for comprehending the plot of course confronted Thespis no less than later playwrights. Now it is evident that he could accomplish this in any one of three ways: (1) He could utilize the choral parodus for this purpose, as Aeschylus partially did in his *Agamemnon*. Though this play has a prologue, the parodus is

---

[1] According to late authorities Greek theaters were provided with revolving prisms (*periacti*) with a different view painted on each of their three sides. These could be turned to indicate a change of scene. There is no evidence, however, that this contrivance was employed during the classical period of Greek drama, although Dörpfeld thought that a place was provided for it in the earlier parascenia at Epidaurus (cf. *Das griechische Theater*, p. 126). The *geranos* ("crane") and the *krade* ("branch") were probably only other names for the μηχανή.

[2] Cf. Themistius *Oration* xxvi, 316 D.

employed to rehearse the story of Iphigenia's sacrifice and other pertinent events. Somewhat similar is the parodus of Aeschylus' *Persians*, which in the absence of a regular prologue opens the play. Accordingly, the ancient argument to this play remarks: "A chorus of elders 'speaks the prologue'" (προλογίζει), using the word in a popular sense. (2) The drama might begin with a dialogue or duet between the chorus and an actor, somewhat in the manner of the pseudo-Euripidean *Rhesus*. It is perhaps unlikely that this technique was employed as early as Thespis. (3) The exposition might be intrusted to the character who speaks first after the choral parodus. Since the drama was then in the one-actor stage, such a "prologue" would necessarily be monologic. Some justification for this nomenclature may be found in the ancient argument to Sophocles' *Oedipus at Colonus*, where it is stated that Oedipus προλογίζει. Since Antigone and a stranger take part in this prologue as well as Oedipus, the verb must here mean that Oedipus "makes the first speech." Now whatever may be true about Thespis having employed (1) or (2), he certainly must have employed the third type of exposition, and a "prologue" of this non-technical sort he can truthfully be said to have invented.

It is a peculiarity of Euripides that he oftentimes combined startling innovations with a reversion to archaic, or at least much earlier, technique. Therefore, it is not surprising that he preferred prologues which smack somewhat of this primitive type. Of course this statement is not to be taken so literally as to imply that he placed his prologues after the parodus. It means that instead of retailing the essential antecedents of the action piecemeal in the manner of Sophocles and Ibsen, he regularly set the whole body of data before the spectators at once in an opening soliloquy. This is normally succeeded by a dialogue with which the dramatic action really begins. In other words there is a prologue within a prologue: the histrionic passage before the choral parodus (the prologue in the technical sense) opens with a sharply differentiated monologue (a prologue in the old, non-technical sense). In my opinion the latter must be regarded as consciously harking back to Thespian practice. An excellent example of this technique is afforded by the *Alcestis*. Here Apollo apostrophizes the palace of Admetus, thus revealing the location of the scene (see p. 206). He then proceeds to relate in detail how he had been forced to serve in the house of a mortal, how considerately Admetus had treated him, how in gratitude he had tricked the Fates into permitting Admetus to present a voluntary substitute when premature death threatened him, how Queen Alcestis is the only one found willing to die for the king, that this is the day appointed for her vicarious act, etc. It is noticeable that scant regard is here paid to dramatic illusion: Apollo tells what the spectators need to know and because they need to know it. He explains his leaving the palace on the ground of the pollution which the death of Alcestis would bring upon all indoors at the time (vs. 22). But no excuse is provided for his long soliloquy. We have seen that the apostrophe to the palace served another purpose; and in any case, since (unlike the elements) houses were never regarded by the Greeks as either divine or even animate, it would be no adequate motivation for the monologue. The prologue concludes and the action proper is set in motion by a quarrel between Apollo and Death, who is now seen approaching.

This prologue is one of Euripides' best. They are often interminable and marred by long genealogies and other jejune matter. Some of them are not undeserving of the strictures which critics, both ancient and modern, have heaped upon them. Yet they served many useful purposes, too, and there is no warrant for utterly condemning the type as a whole. We have already seen (p. 258, above) that such a device enabled a dramatist to circumvent the conditions which caused the conventional observance of the unities of time and place and to bring earlier events more explicitly within the scope of his play. The fact that Euripides more often chose different themes for the plays in each group instead of writing trilogies or tetralogies made brevity of exposition a desideratum. Again, a desire for novelty and the fact that Aeschylus and Sophocles had anticipated him in so many of his subjects caused him to depart widely from the traditional accounts. Unless some warning of this were given, it would sometimes be almost impossible for the ordinary spectator to comprehend the action, and no other place was so appropriate for such an explanation as the prologue. For example, in the *Helen*, Euripides abandoned the account given by Homer and most others in favor of the version invented by Stesichorus. The audience had to comprehend not only that Helen had been the chaste and loyal wife of Menelaus throughout but also that there were two Helens—one the true Helen who spent the years of the Trojan War in Egypt, and the other a cloud-image Helen who eloped with Paris and was recovered by Menelaus at the capture of the city. Surely a very clear statement was required to render such a revamping of the legend clear to everyone. Even the genealogical table was not without its utility in this prologue, for the Egyptian king Theoclymenus and his sister would mean nothing to most spectators until their lineage was traced to the familiar names of Proteus and Nereus.

Quite apart from these considerations, however, there is still something to be said for the Euripidean type of prologue. Knowing that the spectators had no playbill, whatever the dramatist wished to tell them concerning the antecedents of the dramatic action he had to tell them in the play itself. And though the plots of most tragedies were based upon oft-told myths, yet we have the authority of Aristotle[1] for the statement that even the best-known tales were known to but a few. Furthermore, the Greek practice of attacking the series of dramatic incidents, not at the beginning or in the middle, but only at the end, of excluding everything but the culmination or fifth act (see pp. 265 f., above), prevented the earlier events from actually being represented upon the stage. There was, therefore, a considerable body of facts which the poet had either to relate frankly and succinctly in a mass at the beginning or to attempt to weave into the play and disclose gradually as they were needed. Euripides preferred the former method, which he

[1] Cf. *Poetics* 1451b26.

employed in all of his extant plays except possibly the *Iphigenia at Aulis*. It was borrowed by Sophocles in his *Maidens of Trachis*, was extensively imitated by Aristophanes despite his caustic criticisms, and was exceedingly popular among the writers of New Comedy. Even in modern times, notwithstanding all that has been said against it both by ancients and moderns, there have always been playwrights to whom this manner of approach has made the stronger appeal. The principle involved is well stated by a contemporaneous student of dramatic technique:[1] "It may not unreasonably be contended, I think, that, when an exposition cannot be thoroughly dramatized—that is, wrung out, in the stress of the action, from the characters primarily concerned—it may best be dismissed, rapidly and even conventionally, by any not too improbable device."

Frequently the opening soliloquy of the prologue was spoken by a divinity, and in Euripides' *Hecabe* it is spoken by a ghost! Their prophetic powers enabled such personages to predict the course of the action. Thus in Euripides' *Hippolytus* (vss. 42 ff.), Aphrodite declares that Phaedra's love for her stepson will be made known to his father, whose curses will bring Hippolytus to destruction, and that Phaedra herself will die, though with name untarnished; and these things actually come to pass in the play. Indeed, an outstanding difference between ancient and modern tragedy, doubtless arising from the fact that the former dealt with traditional material whose outlines were fairly well known to at least some and could be modified only within certain limits, consists in this, that the Greek tragedians usually made little or no attempt to keep their audiences in the dark as to the outcome. It is true that there are occasional exceptions. For example, in Euripides' *Ion*, Hermes explains in the prologue that Apollo is Ion's father by a secret union, but expressly states that the Delphian deity will bring the youth into his just deserts without letting his own misdeed become known. Consequently when Ion's very life seems to depend upon his parentage transpiring, the hearts of the spectators are harried with fear for his

[1] Cf. Archer, *Play-making*, p. 119.

safety until Athena appears in her brother's stead as deus ex machina and unexpectedly reveals his secret after all.   Euripides' *Orestes* provides another instance of an attempt to baffle the spectators.   The contrast of a few such cases, however, serves only to call attention to the more usual procedure.   Here again the Greek practice has not lacked defenders.   Lessing wrote:[1] "I am far removed from believing with the majority of those who have written on the dramatic art that the dénouement should be hid from the spectator.   I rather think it would not exceed my powers to rouse the very strongest interest in the spectator even if I resolved to make a work where the dénouement was revealed in the first scene.   Everything must be clear for the spectator, he is the confidant of each person, he knows everything that occurs, everything that has occurred, and there are hundreds of instances when we cannot do better than to tell him straight out what is going to occur."   A somewhat different point of view is presented by Professor Murray:[2]   "But why does the prologue let out the secret of what is coming?   Why does it spoil the excitement beforehand?   Because, we must answer, there is no secret, and the poet does not aim at that sort of excitement. A certain amount of plot-interest there certainly is: we are never told exactly what will happen but only what sort of thing; or we are told what will happen but not how it will happen.   But the enjoyment which the poet aims at is not the enjoyment of reading a detective story for the first time; it is that of reading *Hamlet* or *Paradise Lost* for the second or fifth or tenth."

But the prologue was not always spoken by a divinity; oftentimes a mortal appeared in this capacity.   Sometimes this mortal took no further part in the dramatic action, and sometimes he did.   In the latter case he occasionally displayed as prologist a greater knowledge of the situation and of what was going to happen than he afterward seemed to possess as an acting character.   This difficulty occurs in Plautus' *Braggart Captain*. At vss. 145 ff. (in the prologue) Palaestrio boasts how he will

[1] Cf. *Hamburgische Dramaturgie*, Zimmern's translation, p. 377.

[2] Cf. *Euripides and His Age*, p. 206.

cause his fellow-slave "not to see what he has seen" and even explains the trick which will be used for this purpose. But in the scene following the prologue, when he must make good his braggadocio, he seems as perplexed and confounded as would one who had not foreseen this emergency.

In later times the soliloquy of the prologist was sometimes deferred until after an introductory scene or two. Such "internal" prologues occur in the *Casket* and the *Braggart Captain* of Plautus. The meager beginnings of this system can be traced in Aristophanes and Euripides, but there is no evidence for its full development prior to the time of Alexis, a poet of Middle Comedy. His nephew, Menander, who belonged to the New Comedy, employed it in his *Hero* and *Girl with Shorn Locks.* In Plautus' *Amphitruo*, Mercury speaks an opening prologue (vss. 1–152), then engages in a dialogue with Sosia (vss. 153–462), after which he continues the prologue for some thirty additional verses!

The six comedies of Terence all begin with "dissociated" prologues. These give the name and Greek authorship of the Latin play and bespeak the friendly consideration of the audience. They devote no attention, however, to the dramatic situation in the comedy or to future complications therein, but are employed for polemical purposes against the poet's detractors. It used to be supposed that this was an absolutely new departure on Terence's part, but it is now found to be only the last in a series of developments which began in Greek comedy.[1]

Of course monologues were not the invention of the playwrights, being found as early as Homer. Yet true soliloquies, as seen in Shakespeare, are a late development in Greek drama. The epic hero, when alone, may appeal to some divinity or the elements, or he may address his own soul; he never simply thinks his thoughts out loud. So long as the tragedies began with a parodus the choreutae would nearly always be present; and a character who was otherwise alone could address his remarks to them. Consequently no monologues occur in either the *Suppli-*

[1] Cf. Reitzenstein, *Hermes*, XXXV (1900), 622 ff.

ants or the *Persians* of Aeschylus. But with the introduction of a prologue the way was opened up. It would be interesting to know how the words of the eunuch at the beginning of Phrynichus' *Phoenician Women* were motivated, but no evidence is available. In the extant plays of Aeschylus only three soliloquies are found—in the *Prometheus Bound* (vss. 88 ff.), *Agamemnon* (vss. 1 ff.), and *Eumenides* (vss. 1 ff.). The first is addressed to the elements (ether, breezes, rivers, ocean, earth, and sun) and the other two begin with prayer. There are also some other speeches which are delivered in the presence of the chorus or of another character but with little or no reference thereto. If completely detached, however, they are addressed to divinities as before. It must be added that though monologues in Aeschylus and other tragedians may be thus motivated at the beginning, they frequently trail off into expressions which are not strictly appropriate. It is noticeable, then, that of the two types of motivation found in Homer only the first occurs in Aeschylus. In Sophocles the situation is practically the same.

But already in the oldest of Euripides' extant tragedies, the *Alcestis*, a development may be detected. Apollo's monologue at the beginning of this play has just been discussed. It is apparent that when a divinity utters a soliloquy he would rarely address his words to some absent deity or to the elements, as mortal personages did in Aeschylus and Sophocles. This factor helps to account for the fact that dramatic illusion suffers here. For all practical purposes Apollo might just as well have frankly addressed himself to the spectators, as the comic poets sometimes allowed their characters to do. Such prologizing deities are careful to explain the reason for their presence in the place where we find them; but they are absolved from the necessity of accounting for their soliloquizing. Their speeches sometimes degenerate into business-like notices which are almost brusque in their abruptness. For example, Posidon begins Euripides' *Trojan Women:*

> I come, Posidon I, from briny depths
> Of the Aegean Sea, where Nereids dance, etc.
> [Way's translation]

This new freedom, which thus came first to divine prologists, was soon extended also to mortals. Thus the heroine in Euripides' *Andromache* exclaims (vss. 1 ff.):

> O town of Thebes, beauty of Asian land,
> Whence, decked with gold of costly bride-array,
> To Priam's royal hearth long since I came, ...
> Here on the marshes 'twixt Pharsalia's town
> And Phthia's plains I dwell.   [Way's translation]

The artificiality of Euripides' opening soliloquies strikingly appears in his *Orestes*. Referring to Clytemnestra's murder of her husband, Electra says (vss. 26 f.):

> Wherefore she slew,—a shame for maid to speak!—
> I leave untold, for whoso will to guess.   [Way's translation]

These words, together with certain other phrases, show clearly that the speaker is conscious of an audience.

It will be worth our while to note and comment also upon the other monologues in the *Alcestis* and the first one in the *Medea*, these being the oldest of Euripides' extant tragedies. At vss. 243 ff. the dying Alcestis, in the presence of her husband and the chorus and interrupted by the former at regular intervals, bids a final farewell to sun, earth, palace, etc. This belongs to the type found in Homer and Aeschylus and is paralleled by Sophocles' *Antigone* (vss. 806 ff.) and *Ajax* (vss. 372 ff.). At vs. 746 of the *Alcestis* occurs one of the few instances of a chorus retiring during the course of a Greek play. Advantage is at once taken of this circumstance. A reason for the servant's leaving the palace at this point can readily be imagined but none is expressly mentioned. Nor is the bluntness of his monologue softened by any motivation. At vs. 773 Heracles appears and a dialogue ensues between them. At vs. 837 the servant withdraws; Heracles tarries and bursts forth as follows (incidentally obviating in this way the necessity of their departures in opposite directions exactly synchronizing):

> O much-enduring heart and hand of mine, etc.

It will be observed that such an introduction for the following soliloquy is a reversion to the second Homeric type, which now

makes its first appearance in tragedy. At vs. 861 Admetus
re-enters with the chorus and apostrophizes his bereaved palace.
His speech at vs. 934 begins with the words "my friends,"
referring to the chorus, and closes in the same way at vs. 961.
Except for these artificial sutures his words constitute in effect a
soliloquy. This play is especially valuable for our present
purpose as indicating what a hindrance the chorus was to the
unhampered use of monologues outside of the prologue, and how
quickly and freely they were called into requisition during its
withdrawal. The same deduction may be drawn also from
comedy. In the Old Comedy of Aristophanes, the chorus still
being active and vigorous, soliloquies were employed hardly
more freely than in Aeschylus or Sophocles. But by the time
of New Comedy, when the chorus had so far lost its functions
as to appear only for *entr'actes* and when Euripides' innovations had had time to work their full effect, monologues occur
with great frequency and are usually unmotived. In fact,
Professor Leo endeavored to use them in the plays of Plautus
and Terence, which are taken from originals of the Greek
New Comedy, as a criterion to determine the position of act
divisions.

From the *Medea* I wish to cite only the opening monologue,
which is spoken by the Colchian's nurse:

> Would God that Argo's hull had never flown
> Through those blue Clashing Rocks to Colchis-land,
> . . . . My mistress then,
> Medea, ne'er had sailed to Iolcos' towers
> With love for Jason thrilled through all her soul.
>
> [Way's translation]

An admirable quality here is the passionate emotion which does
not always dominate Greek soliloquies. A little later (vs. 49) a
man slave enters and inquires:

> O ancient chattel of my mistress' home,
> Why at the gates thus lonely standest thou,
> Thyself unto thyself discoursing ills?
> How wills Medea to be left of thee?   [Way's translation]

She replies:

> . . . . For I have sunk to such a depth of grief,
> That yearning took me hitherward to come
> And tell to earth and heaven my lady's plight.
>
> [Way's translation]

It is noteworthy, however, that despite this statement her opening monologue had not in fact been addressed to earth or sky. Since Ibsen the soliloquy has been tabooed on the modern stage. Yet inasmuch as people do at times talk aloud, when alone, it would seem that the present-day reaction had gone too far and that monologues, under proper psychological conditions, might sometimes be allowed. Furthermore it must be supposed that among impulsive southern races, like the Greeks and Romans, soliloquizing would be more common than with us, and in consequence it would naturally claim a larger part in their drama. Nevertheless, we have seen that, until Euripides, the playwrights restricted its use to such instances as could be motivated with some degree of naturalness. Of these motives it must be allowed that the least satisfactory was that founded on an appeal to the elements. Of course most commentators have refused to recognize this as a mere expository convention and have expatiated upon the innate feeling for and sympathy with nature among the Greeks. But as for myself I fear that this explanation has been pressed unduly. Euripides, I am sure, felt self-conscious in utilizing a device so threadbare and patent. My conviction is based on the retroactive way in which he employed the motive here in the *Medea,* on the fact that he often preferred to introduce monologues without any motive than to resort to one so bald and artificial as this, and especially on the guilty phrase which he slips into the heroine's soliloquy in his *Iphigenia among the Taurians* (vss. 42 f.):

> What visions strange the night hath brought to me
> I'll tell to ether, *if doing so brings help.*

Though it is unsafe to set too much value upon the jibes of the comic poets, yet it is not without interest to observe their attitude in this matter. Philemon placed a close parody of this *Medea* passage in the mouth of a boastful cook:[1]

> For yearning took me hitherward to come
> And tell to earth and heaven—my cuisinerie!

And Plautus in his *Merchant* (vss. 3 ff.) preserved a more explicit passage from the same poet of New Comedy:

> I do not do as I've seen others do
> In comedies, who through the power of love
> Tell night, day, sun, or moon their miseries.

The foregoing statement of Euripidean usage is far from exhaustive. Yet it is necessary to hasten on. Quite apart from the effects which may be secured from monologues in choral drama, there are no less than three additional uses to which they can easily be put in chorusless plays. In terms of classical drama, therefore, they will appear most frequently in Greek New Comedy and in Plautus and Terence.

In the first place when two characters meet on the stage and talk it is necessary for them either to appear simultaneously at the two entrances (and it is self-evident that this method cannot be employed very often without seeming ridiculous) or for one of them to enter first and fill up a slight interval before the other's arrival by soliloquizing. Such an entrance monologue occurs at the beginning of Aristophanes' *Lysistrata*, where the bearer of the title-rôle complains:

> Now were they summoned to some shrine of Bacchus,
> Pan, Colias, or Genetyllis, there had been
> No room to stir, so thick the crowd of timbrels.
> And now!—there's not one woman to be seen.
> Stay, here comes one, my neighbor Calonice.
> Good morning, friend.   [Rogers' translation]

Perhaps I may be pardoned for digressing here a moment in order to discuss what happens when two characters make a simultaneous introit through the same entrance. In most cases it is natural to suppose that they have been together for some little while and that some talk has already been carried on

[1] Cf. Kock, *Fragmenta Comicorum Atticorum*, II, 500, fr. 79.

between them.   On the contrary in the fifth-century plays the conversation regularly does not begin until after they have entered the stage.   Two instances of this have already been noted on pages 259 f., above, Orestes coming all the way from Phocis to Argos before he acquaints his associates with the Delphian oracle or formulates a plan of action with them, and Iris accompanying Madness from Olympus but reserving her instructions until Thebes has been reached.   Of course it is easy to see why this convention was employed, but a little thinking enabled the playwrights to secure the same results without violating verisimilitude quite so patently.   Only twice in fifth-century drama do characters enter with words which indicate that they have already been engaged in conversation.   In Aristophanes' *Frogs* (405 B.C.) (vs. 830), Euripides says to Dionysus, as they emerge with Pluto from the latter's palace: "I would not yield the throne of tragedy to Aeschylus; do not urge me to."   Again in Euripides' posthumous *Iphigenia at Aulis* (vss. 303 ff.), Agamemnon's slave enters in expostulation: "Menelaus, outrageous is your boldness. . . . . You ought not to have unsealed the tablet which I bore."   The former of these quotations clearly implies words off scene, and the latter implies action and presumably words as well.   But in New Comedy and the Latin comedies this technique has, not unnaturally, pre-empted the field.   Two instances must suffice.   In Terence's version of Menander's *Andrian Girl* (vss. 820 f.), Chremes enters complaining: "My friendship for you, Simo, has already been put sufficiently to the test; I have run enough risk.   Now make an end of coaxing me."   Again, in Terence's *Brothers* (vs. 517), Ctesipho and Syrus enter together, the former saying: "You say my father has gone to the country?"   It is characteristic of this technique that the very first words make plain the fact that the stage conversation is a continuation of one already begun off stage and likewise disclose the topic under discussion.   It will be remembered that simultaneous entrances of this sort, when made from the abode of one of the characters involved, are generally left unmotivated (see p. 239, above).

After this digression we may return to the second use which New Comedy made of monologues, viz., as exit speeches. Since there was no drop curtain in the Greek theater, all characters had to go off as well as come on; no tableau effects to terminate a scene were possible. Moreover, in order to avoid the simultaneous exit of all the persons in a scene, it often seemed best to detain one of them beyond the rest and allow him to fill a brief interval with a soliloquy. As already mentioned this technique occurs so frequently in Plautus and Terence that an attempt has been made to utilize it as a criterion for a division of the Roman comedies into acts. Such an exit soliloquy has already been noted in Euripides' *Alcestis*, vss. 837 ff. (p. 306, above).

In the third place, unless a new character is to enter the stage at the very instant that an old one leaves it, the actor who engages in successive dialogue with each of them must cause a slight pause by soliloquizing. Such a soliloquy is technically known as a "link." One is found in the monologue which Strepsiades utters between the withdrawal of his son and the entrance of Socrates' pupil (Aristophanes' *Clouds*, vss. 126 ff.). Links are often extremely short, sometimes being no more than a cough or hem; they are frequently employed to cover the condensation of time, especially when they occur between the exit and re-entrance of the same character. Furthermore, they occur in playwrights who reject other forms of soliloquy, no less than five instances appearing in Ibsen's *Pillars of Society* alone.

So long as the chorus retained its vigor, dramatists found it easier, except in the prologue or during occasional withdrawals of the chorus in the course of the action, to fill gaps by remarks addressed to the coryphaeus than by entrance soliloquies, exit soliloquies, or links. Yet they do occur in choral drama, and I have cited one instance illustrative of each type from fifth-century plays. In comedies of subsequent date, in which the chorus was greatly curtailed or nonexistent, they may be found by the score.

It still remains to speak of another kind of soliloquy, viz., the aside or, more accurately speaking, the apart, by which the grim ghastliness of modern tragedy has often been enhanced. The vastness of Greek theaters and the almost constant presence of from twelve to twenty-four choreutae rendered this artifice an awkward one for ancient playwrights. Nevertheless, asides are occasionally found in Greek drama. In Euripides' *Hippolytus* (vss. 1060 ff.), that hero, unable to clear himself of false accusations except by violating his oath of secrecy, exclaims to himself:

> O Gods, why can I not unlock my lips,
> Who am destroyed by you whom I revere?
> No!—whom I need persuade, I should not so,
> And all for nought should break the oaths I swore.
>
> [Way's translation],

entirely unheard by his father and the chorus close at hand. Half-asides occur in Euripides' *Hecabe* (vss. 736–51), where the Trojan queen utters no less than four aparts, an aggregate of ten verses, in an effort to decide whether to appeal to Agamemnon for aid. His interruptions indicate that he is aware that she is speaking but does not catch the drift of her words. It should be noted, however, that these passages do not contain the ironic values which have usually inhered in the use of aparts upon the modern stage. The obstacles hampering the employment of asides in fifth-century times appear most plainly from scenes like Euripides' *Ion* (vss. 1520 ff.), where two actors wish to speak to one another privately. Their confidences must be uttered loud enough to be heard by the seventeen thousand spectators, but the nearby chorus catches not a word. With the virtual disappearance of the chorus in New Comedy the apart, not unnaturally, came into more frequent use and was employed more as it has been in modern times.

For the absence of ironic aparts, however, Greek tragedy was richly compensated by the frequent occurrence of dramatic irony. Irony of course is a mode of speech by means of which is conveyed a meaning contrary to the literal sense of the words, and may be divided into two classes—"verbal" and "practical" (to use Bishop Thirlwall's term) or "dramatic." In the former the dissimulation is manifest to all concerned, else the sarcasm, passing unrecognized, would fail of its effect and recoil upon the speaker, while in the latter (which alone interests us here) concealment of the hinted truth is essential. It may be the speaker himself who fails to perceive the inner meaning of his own words (and then we call it "objective" irony), or he may employ "subjective" irony, i.e., consciously use his superior knowledge, to gloat over his victim or inveigle him to doom by an ambiguous utterance. In either case, however, the *double entente* is usually known to the audience, a considerable part of whose pleasure consists in viewing with prophetic insight the abortive efforts of the dramatic characters to escape the impending catastrophe.

An excellent instance of conscious irony occurs in Middleton and Rowley's *Changeling*, Act III, scene 2. There De Flores is guiding Alonzo about the castle where he intends to murder him, and significantly says:

> All this is nothing; you shall see anon
> A place you little dream on.

The unconscious irony, however, is likely to be more tragic in its tone. So when Iago first conceives his groundless suspicions of his wife and Othello he vows that he will be

> evened with him, wife for wife. [*Othello*, Act II, scene 2],

and these words are fulfilled in a sense far different than he intended, by the death of both wives. For this sort of irony Sophocles was especially renowned, and his *Oedipus the King* abounds in instances. One must suffice. Oedipus has slain his own father, the reigning king, though these facts are unknown to him. Being now directed by an oracle to investigate his predecessor's death, he declares, with more meaning than he realized: "I will fight this battle for him as for mine own sire" (vss. 264).

It is possible to draw still one more distinction. Dramatic irony consists, not only in the contrast between the outer, apparent meaning and the real, inner meaning of an ambiguous phrase, but also in the contrast between the real and the supposed situation.   Thus a man whose ruin is impending often mistakes the position of his affairs so utterly as to indulge in entirely unjustified expressions, feelings, gestures, or acts of rejoicing and triumph.   The difference between these two varieties of dramatic irony may be seen in Sophocles' *Maidens of Trachis*. In the first place we have the contradiction between the real meaning of the oracle that Heracles' "release from toils will be accomplished" and Heracles' own mistaken interpretation thereof (vss. 167 f. and 1170 ff.); and in the second place there is the "irony of situation" in that Deianira sends him a gift which she hopes will woo back his love but which actually results in his death.   Euripides' *Bacchanals* offers other examples in the boastful and confident attitude of Pentheus, whom the spectators know to be doomed to a frightful end, and in the mock humility of Dionysus, whose intended vengeance they foresee.   Again, in Sophocles' *Oedipus the King* (vss. 1014 ff.) there is a striking contrast between the intended and the actual effect when the Corinthian messenger informs Oedipus that Polybus was not his father.   This irony of situation often consists in the clash or shock of conflicting intrigues, as may be seen in Shakespeare's *Measure for Measure*.

But dramatic irony was not confined to tragedy, as a brief analysis of one of Terence's plays will disclose.   In comedy, however, the effect was naturally somewhat different, being more humorous than tragic.   In the *Andrian Girl,* Simo intrigues to test his son's obedience, pretending that he has arranged an immediate marriage for him with Chremes' daughter.   Accordingly there is irony of situation in the consternation which this false announcement causes (vss. 236 ff. and 301 ff.).   Pamphilus' slave (Davus), however, soon sees through the trick and persuades him to turn back the intrigue (and, consequently, the irony) upon his father by apparent compliance (vss. 420 ff.). But Simo at once proceeds to get Chremes' consent in fact, so that the dramatic situation is again reversed, as the too clever slave discovers to his surprise when he facetiously inquires why the wedding is being delayed (vss. 581 ff.). Especially galling are Simo's words (said without a full comprehension of how true they are): "Now I beseech you, Davus, since you alone have brought about this marriage . . . . exert yourself further that my son be brought into line" (vss. 595 f.). There is also irony in the conduct of Charinus, who is a suitor for Chremes' daughter and is naturally (though needlessly) disturbed at the thought of Pamphilus' marrying her (vss. 301 ff., 625 ff., and 957 ff.). Of course there is always irony involved when a man leads himself astray or allows another so to lead him; but as these are the standard themes of comedy, one need not cite every such instance.

The best instance in this play, however, can be appreciated only on second reading or as the memory of the spectator recalls its real significance. Simo wishes his son to marry Chremes' daughter, but Pamphilus' affections are already pledged elsewhere. Now unknown to all the parties concerned this sweetheart is also Chremes' daughter. There is, therefore, more meaning than he intends or perceives in Pamphilus' despairing question: "Can I in no way avoid relationship with Chremes?" (vs. 247).

This is similar to Admetus' words in Euripides' *Alcestis* (vs. 1102) when Heracles insists that he receive into his home a veiled woman (really Admetus' own wife restored to life): "Would you had never won her in a wrestling bout!" But in the present instance the identity of Pamphilus' mistress does not transpire until later, so that, as I have stated, the irony is not at first apparent. There is here a point of difference between tragedy and comedy in antiquity: the themes of tragedy were almost invariably drawn from mythology and the outlines of the story would therefore be known to practically everyone of consequence in the audience; furthermore, the not infrequent practice of foretelling the dénouement in the prologue would put even the ignorant in a position to recognize subtleties in the language of the characters. That the ancient playwrights themselves appreciated this difference appears from the words of the comic poet, Antiphanes, already quoted on page 127, above. As a result, in ancient tragedy the irony of a situation or ambiguous phrase would be recognized at once without any preparation for it whatsoever, while in ancient comedy and in modern plays, whether tragic or comic, these effects usually have to be led up to. Two other considerations ought also to be mentioned, however. First, audiences exercise a sort of clairvoyance in looking beneath the bare words and divining the course of events, so that (paradoxical as it sounds) the surprises of the stage usually are long foreseen by the spectators and only the expected events happen. Secondly, the dénouement here in question, the discovery that Pamphilus' sweetheart is the daughter of free parents and, in particular, of someone among the dramatis personae, was so hackneyed in New Comedy, occurring in no less than five of Terence's six plays, that any frequent theatergoer would have been on the lookout for it and might easily have recognized any subtle effects dependent thereon.

In conclusion, we have to consider the dramatic purpose of tragic irony and its effect upon the audience. Bishop Thirlwall (*op. cit.*, p. 489) pointed out:

There is always a slight cast of irony in the grave, calm, respectful attention impartially bestowed by an intelligent judge on two contending parties, who are pleading their causes before him with all the earnestness of deep conviction, and of excited feeling. What makes the contrast interesting is, that the right and the truth lie on neither side exclusively: that there is no fraudulent purpose, no gross imbecility of intellect, on either: but both have plausible claims and specious reasons to allege, though each is too much blinded by prejudice or passion to do justice to the views of his adversary. For here the irony lies not in the demeanor of the judge, but is deeply seated in the case itself, which seems to favor both of the litigants, but really eludes them both.

This analogy is especially true when the irony arises from clashing intrigues, and the audience, admitted to the author's confidence and sitting at his side, as it were, joins with him in awarding praise here and condemnation there. Again the playwright is the omnipotent creator and ruler of the little world that moves upon the stage. And the spectator, beholding the dramatic characters' fruitless toil and plotting, baseless exultation, and needless despondency seems to be admitted behind the scenes of this world's tragedy and to view the spectacle through the great dramatist's eyes, learning that man must be content with little, humble ever, distrustful of fortune, and fearful of the powers above. Thus the slighter themes and less important reverses of comedy bring a purification (κάθαρσις) in their train no less truly than the more somber catastrophes of tragedy.[1]

[1] Aristotle's theory of the purificatory effects of tragedy has not fallen within the scope of my text, but I cannot forbear citing Fairchild, "Aristotle's Doctrine of Katharsis and the Positive or Constructive Activity Involved," *Classical Journal*, XII (1916), 44 ff.   Stuart, "The Function and the Dramatic Value of the Recognition Scene in Greek Tragedy," *American Journal of Philology*, XXXIX (1918), 268 ff., maintains that Aristotle's terms ἔλεος and φόβος, which are usually translated "pity and fear," must be interpreted as including also such emotions as "sympathy" and "suspense."

Footprints on the sands of time.—
H. W. LONGFELLOW.

CHAPTER IX

THEATRICAL RECORDS[1]

The technical word used of bringing out a play was διδάσκειν ("to teach"), and the technical name for the director of the performance was *didascalus* (διδάσκαλος) or "teacher." We have already noted (p. 198, above) that *didascalia* (διδασκαλία; "teaching") was the name for a group of plays brought out by a tragic playwright at one time, and the same word was applied to a record of the theatrical contests. At the beginning the didascalus and the author were identical, for the reason that the primitive poets taught the choreutae what they were to sing, that the poets in the one-actor period carried the histrionic parts themselves and still taught the choreutae their rôles, and that even when they had ceased to act in their plays they yet continued to train those who did.

The Athenian archons seem to have kept records of the contests at the Dionysiac festivals, the archon eponymus for the City Dionysia and the king archon for the Lenaea. These records, of course, were not compiled in the interests of literary research such as flourished in Alexandrian times but merely for the private convenience of the officials and for documentary purposes. Apparently they consisted of a bald series of entries,

[1] Cf. Capps, "Dramatic Synchoregia at Athens," *American Journal of Philology*, XVII (1896) 319 ff.; "Catalogues of Victors at the Dionysia and Lenaea," *ibid.*, XX (1899), 388 ff.; "The Dating of Some Didascalic Inscriptions," *American Journal of Archaeology*, IV (1900), 74 ff.; "The Introduction of Comedy into the City Dionysia," *Decennial Publications of the University of Chicago*, VI (1904), 259 ff.; and "Epigraphical Problems in the History of Attic Comedy," *American Journal of Philology*, XXVIII (1907), 179 ff.; Wilhelm, *Urkunden dramatischer Aufführungen in Athen* (1906), and "Eine Inschrift aus Athen," *Anzeiger d. Akademie d. Wissenschaften in Wien, phil.-hist. Klasse*, XLIII (1906), 77 ff.; Clark, "A Study of the Chronology of Menander's Life," *Classical Philology*, I (1906), 313 ff.; *Oxyrhynchus Papyri*, IV (1904), 69 ff., and X (1914), 81 ff.; O'Connor, *Chapters in the History of Actors and Acting in Ancient Greece* (1908); Jachmann, *De Aristotelis Didascaliis* (1909); and Flickinger, "Certain Numerals in the Greek Dramatic Hypotheses," *Classical Philology*, V (1910), 1 ff.

chronicling the choregi, tribes, poet-didascali, actors, plays, and victors in the various dithyrambic and dramatic events. In the fourth century B.C. these archives were published by Aristotle in a work entitled *Didascaliae*. His service probably was mainly that of unearthing the material and arranging it in chronological sequence and of making it available to a wider public, for Dr. Jachmann has made it seem clear that he did not edit the archons' record to any great extent. In consequence Aristotle's book contained too much and was overloaded with unimportant details. Its main value consisted in being a court of last resort and a source from which smaller and less unwieldy lists might be compiled.

Some of these indirect products of Aristotle's industry were entered upon stone and are still preserved in fragments. The first of these is for convenience referred to as the Fasti ("calendar" or "register") and contained the annual victors in each event at the City Dionysia from about 502/1 B.C. when volunteer comuses were first given a place in the festival program. This inscription was cut upon the face of a wall built of four rows of superimposed blocks and almost six feet in height. The text was arranged in vertical columns. There were originally sixteen of these and most of them contained one hundred and forty-one lines. The presence of a heading over the first five columns, however, reduced the lines upon them to one hundred and forty. For the most part the lines in adjoining columns were placed exactly opposite one another, but toward the bottom of col. 13 the writing was crowded so that this column perhaps contained no less than one hundred and fifty-three lines. As the entries for 346–342 B.C. fell in this space, most authorities accept Dr. Wilhelm's conclusion that the body of the inscription was cut at that period and received additional entries, year by year, for subsequent festivals until about 319 B.C.[1] Whoever was

---

[1] Reisch, however, in his review of Wilhelm in *Zeitschrift f. östr. Gymnasien*, LVIII (1907), 297 f. maintained that the original cutting went to the bottom of col. 14. This would postpone the preparation of the inscription until about 330 B.C. and would make it a feature of the completion of the theater by Lycurgus at about that time. He suggests that the Fasti stood in the left parodus of the theater.

responsible for the original inscription must have excerpted the appropriate items from Aristotle's *Didascaliae* and, for the brief period intervening between the publication of Aristotle's book and 346–342 B.C., from the original archives.

— πρῶτ]ον κῶμοι ἦσαν τῶ[ι Διονύσωι —

[Ξ]ενοκλείδης ἐχορήγε	Πανδιονί[ς ἀνδρῶν]	[ὁ δεῖνα ἐχορήγει]
[Μ]άγνης ἐδίδασκεν	Κλεαίνετ[ος Κυδαθη: ἐχορήγει]	[ὁ δεῖνα ἐδίδασκε]
τραγωιδῶν	κωμωιδῶ[ν]	[ὑποκριτὴς ὁ δεῖνα]
Περικλῆς Χολαρ: ἐχορή	Θαρ[— — ἐχορήγει]	['Επὶ Τιμαρχίδου 447/6]
5 Αἰσχύλος ἐ[δ]ίδασκε	[ὁ δεῖνα ἐδίδασκε]	[—ὶς παίδων]
['Επὶ Χάρητος 472/1]	[τραγωιδῶν]	[ὁ δεῖνα ἐχορήγει]
[— παίδων]	[. . . . .]: ἐχορή	'Ε[ρεχθηὶς ἀνδρῶν]
[ὁ δεῖνα ἐχορήγει]	[. . . . . . .] ἐδίδασκεν	Βίω[ν ἐχορήγει]
[— ἀνδρῶν]	['Επὶ Φιλο]κλέους 459/8	κω[μωιδῶν]
10 [ὁ δεῖνα ἐχ]ο[ρήγει]	[Οἰ]νηὶς παίδων	'Ανδ[— ἐχορήγει]
[κωμωιδῶν]	Δημόδοκος ἐχορήγε	Καλ[λίας ἐδίδασκεν]
[ὁ δεῖνα ἐχ]ορήγει	'Ιπποθωντὶς ἀνδρῶν	τρα[γωιδῶν]
[. . . . . ἐδίδ]ασκεν	Εὐκτήμων 'Ελευ: ἐχορή	Θαλ[— ἐχορήγει]
[τραγωιδῶν]	κωμωιδῶν	Κα[ρκίνος ἐδίδασκε]
15 [ὁ δεῖνα ἐχ]ορήγει	Εὐρυκλείδης ἐχορήγει	ὑπ[οκριτὴς ὁ δεῖνα]
Πολυφράσμω]ν ἐδίδασ	Εὐφρόνιος ἐδίδασκε	'Επ[ὶ Καλλιμάχου 446/5]
['Επὶ Πραξιέργο]υ 471/0	τραγωιδῶν	[κτλ.]
[. . . . . ντὶς πα]ίδων	Ξενοκλῆς 'Αφιδνα: ἐχορή	
[. . . . . . . ἐχο]ρήγει	Αἰσχύλος ἐδίδασκεν	
20 [. . . . . . . ἀνδρ]ῶν	'Επὶ "Αβρωνος 458/7	
[. . . . . ἐχ]ορήγ	'Ερεχθηὶς παίδων	
[κωμωιδῶν]	Χαρίας 'Αγρυλῆ: ἐχορή	
[. . . . . ἐχορήγε]ι	Λεωντὶς ἀνδρῶν	
[κτλ.	Δεινόστρατος ἐχορ[ήγει]	
	κωμωιδῶν	
	[. . . . . . ἐχ]ορήγ[ει	

FIG. 75.—Wilhelm's Transcription and Restoration of Two Fragments of the Athenian Fasti.

See p. 320, n. 1

The character of the Fasti will appear most clearly from Fig. 75,[1] a transcript and restoration of two fragments on which were originally cut the tops of cols. 3–5. The Greek letters within brackets are restorations where the stone is broken away or illegible. Inasmuch as the entries follow a fixed order from

[1] Fig. 75 is taken from Wilhelm, *Urkunden dramatischer Aufführungen in Athen*, p. 18, and represents fragments *a* and *f* of *Corpus Inscriptionum Graecarum*, II, 971.

year to year and occupy a definite number of lines, except as
slight changes were occasionally introduced into the program, it
is often easy to restore everything but proper names. Of the
heading of the inscription, which extended over the first five
columns, only the center is preserved. When complete it
probably read somewhat as follows: οἵδε νενικήκασιν . . . . ἀφ'
οὗ πρῶτ]ον κῶμοι ἦσαν τῶ[ι Διονύσωι 'Ελευθερεῖ ("The following
gained the victory . . . . since first there were comuses in
honor of Dionysus Eleuthereus"). Let us examine more closely
the record of the year which begins at line nine in the second
column of Fig. 75 (col. 4 in the complete inscription). The
entries for each year begin with ἐπί ("in the time of"), followed
by the name of the Athenian archon eponymus in the genitive
case. The archon for this year was Philocles, whose term ran
from July, 459 B.C., to July, 458 B.C. Since the festivals came
in the spring the record under consideration is for the City
Dionysia of 458 B.C. The inscription is so formulaic and condensed that it has necessarily been expanded somewhat in the
following translation:

> In the archonship of Philocles.
> The tribe Oeneis was victorious with
>   a dithyrambic chorus of boys;
> Demodocus was choregus.
> The tribe Hippothontis was victorious
>   with a dithyrambic chorus of men;
> Euctemon of Eleusis was choregus.
> In the contest of comedians:
> Euryclides was choregus,
> Euphronius was didascalus.
> In the contest of tragedians:
> Xenocles of Aphidnae was choregus,
> Aeschylus was didascalus.

This was the year in which Aeschylus competed in Athens for
the last time and was victorious with his Orestean trilogy.

About 278 B.C. two other inscriptions were compiled from
Aristotle's publication of theatrical records. I refer to the
stone Didascaliae and to the Victors'-Lists. The former gave

the full program of the dramatic, but not the dithyrambic, events for each year and fell into four divisions, dealing respec-

tively with tragedy and with comedy at each of the two festivals. Fig. 76a[1] gives a transcript of two fragments which reproduce the programs of tragedy at the City Dionysia in 341 and 340 B.C. They may be freely translated, as shown on p. 323.

There are several matters here which are worthy of comment. It will be noted that by 341 B.C. the tragic poets no longer closed each group of plays with a satyric drama, but one satyr-play was performed instead as a preface to the tragic contest. It followed that the playwrights, the number of whose dramas now corresponded to that of the star performers, were no longer handicapped by being allotted the exclusive services of a single star and his troupe but were placed upon terms of perfect equality by having all the stars in turn at their command, each for a different tragedy. This explains why in 340 B.C., when we must

[’Επὶ Σωσιγένους σατυρι] 342/1
[— —]
[παλαι]ᾶι Νε[οπτόλεμος]
[’Ιφιγε]νείαι Εὐρ[ιπ]ίδο[υ]
[ποη]: ’Αστυδάμας
[’Αχι]λλεῖ ὑπε: Θετταλός
5 ’Αθάμαντι ὑπε: Νεοπτόλ[εμος]
[’Αν]τιγόνηι ὑπε: ’Αθηνόδω[ρος]
[Εὐ]άρετος δ[εὐ:] Τεύκρωι
[ὑπ]ε: ’Αθηνόδωρος
[’Αχι]λλεῖ ὑ[πε]: Θετταλός
10 [. . . ε]ι ὑπ[ε: Ν]εοπτόλεμος
[’Αφαρεὺς] τρί: Πελιάσιν
[ὑπε: Νεοπτ]όλεμος
-κι ’Ορέστηι [ὑπε: ’Αθηνόδωρος]
Αὔγηι ὑπε: Θεττα[λός]
15 ὑπο: Νεοπτόλεμος ἐνίκ[α]
5 ’Επὶ Νικομάχου σατυρι   341/0
Τιμοκλῆς Λυκούργωι
παλαιᾶι: Νεοπτόλεμ[ος]
-αι ’Ορέστηι Εὐριπιδο
20 ποη: ’Αστυδάμας
Παρθενοπαίωι ὑπε: Θετ[ταλός]
[Λυκά]ονι ὑπε: Νεοπτόλε[μος]
[. . . ο]κλῆς δεύ: Φρίξωι
-ι [ὑπε:] Θετταλός
25 [Οἰδί]ποδι ὑπε: Νεοπτολ[εμος]
[Εὐάρ]ετος τρί
[’Αλκ]μέ[ων]ι: ὑπε: Θεττα[λός]
[. . . λ]ηι: ὑπε: Νεοπτό[λε]
[ὑπο: Θ[εττάλος ἐνίκα
30 [’Επὶ Θεο]φράστου σα[τυρι 340/39
[. . . . .] Φορκίσ[ι]
[παλαιᾶι· Νικ?]όστρ[ατος]
[. . . . . . . Εὐ]ριπί[δου]
[. . . . .]ο [. . .

[1] Fig. 76a is taken from Wilhelm, op. cit., p. 40, and represents Corpus Inscriptionum Graecarum, II, 973.

FIG. 76a.—Wilhelm's Transcription and Restoration of Two Fragments of the Stone Didascaliae at Athens.

See p. 322, n. 1

suppose that three players of the first rank with their supporting companies were for some reason not available, the

In the archonship of Sosigenes (342/1 B.C.). Satyr-play:
—— was poet with his ——.
Old tragedy: Neoptolemus
acted in Euripides' *Iphigenia*.
Poets: Astydamas was first
with the *Achilles* acted by Thettalus
with the *Athamas* acted by Neoptolemus
with the *Antigone* acted by Athenodorus;
Evaretus was second with the *Teucer*
acted by Athenodorus
with the *Achilles* acted by Thettalus
with the —— acted by Neoptolemus;
Aphareus was third with the *Daughters of Pelias*
acted by Neoptolemus
with the *Orestes* acted by Athenodorus
with the *Auge* acted by Thettalus;
the actor Neoptolemus was victor.
In the archonship of Nicomachus (341/0 B.C.). Satyr-play:
Timocles was poet with his *Lycurgus*.
Old tragedy: Neoptolemus
acted in Euripides' *Orestes*.
Poets: Astydamas was first
with the *Parthenopaeus* acted by Thettalus
with the *Lycaon* acted by Neoptolemus;
——cles was second with the *Phrixus*
acted by Thettalus
with the *Oedipus* acted by Neoptolemus;
Evaretus was third
with the *Alcmeon* acted by Thettalus
with the —— acted by Neoptolemus;
the actor Thettalus was victor.

FIG. 76b.—Translation of Inscription in Fig. 76a

number of tragedies presented by each playwright was likewise reduced to two and the histrionic talent was thus kept evenly distributed. The fact that the tragic writers no longer devoted whole trilogies to different aspects of the same theme made it easy to reduce the number of tragedies in any year in order to conform to an emergency in the histrionic conditions.

Furthermore, old tragedies were not now permitted to compete with new ones, as was said to have been the practice in the case of Aeschylus' plays after his decease (see p. 203, above); but beginning at the City Dionysia of 386 B.C., as we learn from the Fasti, an old tragedy was performed, outside of the contest, every year. It is interesting to observe that in both these years and again in 339 B.C. (see next to the last line in Fig. 76a) plays of Euripides were chosen for this purpose, and this is in accord with the steady growth of that poet's popularity as compared with Aeschylus and Sophocles. As already stated, the Didascaliae were inscribed in 278 B.C., but the record was kept up to date by contemporaneous entries for over a century subsequently.

The Victors'-Lists were prepared at the same time as the stone Didascaliae and were likewise derived from Aristotle,[1] but they were very different in character. They recorded the aggregate of victories won by poets and actors in tragedy and comedy at each of the two festivals—eight lists in all. I shall content myself with citing one fragment from the list of tragic poets who were victorious at the City Dionysia (cf. Fig. 77 a and b).[2] The names were arranged in the chronological order of their first victory at the festival in question, in this case the City Dionysia; and after each name was entered the total number of victories gained at that festival. We are especially interested in two names in this list, Aeschylus and Sophocles. Of course the former's name did not originally head the list; it stood in the eleventh line. The numeral is broken away from behind his name, but we know from other sources that he won thirteen (ΔΙΙΙ) victories. He died before the establishment of the tragic contest at the Lenaea, so that his competition was

---

[1] Körte, "Aristoteles' NIKAI ΔΙΟΝΥΣΙΑΚΑΙ," *Classical Philology*, I (1906), 391 ff., maintained that the Victors'-Lists were transferred to stone straight from another book of Aristotle's entitled Νῖκαι Διονυσιακαὶ 'Αστικαὶ καὶ Ληναϊκαὶ ("Victories at the City Dionysia and the Lenaea"). Our knowledge of the nature of this work is confined to what can be inferred from its title and is too vague to justify dogmatic conclusions.

[2] Figs. 77a and b are taken from Wilhelm, *op. cit.*, 101, and represent *Corpus Inscriptionum Graecarum*, II, 977a and ab respectively.

FIG. 77a.—A Fragment of the Athenian Victors'-List

See p. 324, n. 2

<table>
<tr><td></td><td>[. . . . . .]ασ[—]</td><td></td></tr>
<tr><td></td><td>[Καρκί]νος ΔI</td><td></td></tr>
<tr><td>10 __</td><td>['Αστ]υδάμας ΓII [—?]</td><td></td></tr>
<tr><td>[Αἰ]σχύ[λος —]</td><td>[Θεο]δέκτας ΓII</td><td></td></tr>
<tr><td>[Εὐ]έτης I</td><td>['Αφα]ρεύς II</td><td></td></tr>
<tr><td>[Πο]λυφράσμ[ων —]</td><td>[. . . . ω]ν II</td><td>AI</td></tr>
<tr><td>[Νόθ]ιππος I</td><td>. . . . . .</td><td>Φρ-</td></tr>
<tr><td>15 [Σοφ]οκλῆς ΔΓIII</td><td>. . . . . II</td><td>'Ομ-</td></tr>
<tr><td>[. . . .] τος II[—?]</td><td></td><td>ΔΙ</td></tr>
<tr><td>['Αριστί]μ, [—]</td><td></td><td>Ξ-</td></tr>
</table>

FIG. 77b.—Wilhelm's Transcription and Restoration of Two Fragments of the Athenian Victors'-List.

See p. 324, n. 2

restricted to the City Dionysia. But Suidas reports that according to some Aeschylus had gained twenty-eight victories.
Perhaps the larger number is not to be rejected as worthless
but is to be regarded as including the victories which Aeschylus'
plays are said to have won after his decease in competition, at
both festivals, with the works of living tragedians. To Sophocles
the inscription assigns eighteen (ΔΓΙΙΙ) victories at the City
Dionysia, and that is the number which most authorities give.
But Suidas, who regularly records the aggregate of victories at
both festivals, credits him with twenty-four victories. Sophocles
must, therefore, have been victorious six times at the Lenaea.
Euripides' name does not appear upon any extant portion of the
Victors'-List. He is usually stated to have won five victories,
but some notices report fifteen. Possibly we are to understand
that he won ten Lenaean victories. His comparative lack of
success while living thus stands in striking contrast to his
popularity subsequently.

Dr. Reisch has propounded an ingenious and plausible theory
with reference to the housing of the Didascaliae and the Victors'-
Lists (cf. *op. cit.*, pp. 302 ff.). He believes that these catalogues
were prepared for the master of contests (the agonothete, see
p. 271, above) for the year 278 B.C., who also erected a special
structure in the precinct of Dionysus Eleuthereus to receive
them. The dedicatory inscription is extant, but unfortunately
the name of the agonothete is broken away. He supposes this
building to have been hexagonal, with three sides of solid wall
and the other three left open. This arrangement was designed
to afford a maximum of light for reading the inscriptions on the
interior of the building. On the left wall, as one passed through
the main entrance, were cut the tragic Didascaliae of the City
Dionysia. On the architrave above was the Victors'-List for
the tragic poets at this festival, and on the architrave over the
adjoining (open) side to the right was the Victors'-List for the
tragic actors. On the next wall to the right were the comic
Didascaliae of the City Dionysia, and on the architrave above
that side and the adjoining (open) one were the Victors'-Lists of

the comic poets and actors who had won victories at this festival. On the third wall stood both the comic and also the tragic Didascaliae of the Lenaea. On the architrave above this wall were the Victors'-Lists of the comic poets and actors at the Lenaea, and on the architrave above the sixth (open) side were those of the tragic poets and actors at the same festival. Dr. Reisch's reconstruction may be incorrect in some minor details, but must certainly be accepted in principle.

One matter in connection with all these inscriptions has been a subject of keen controversy among scholars, and the end is not yet. The problem is too complicated to be discussed upon its merits here, but the general situation may be outlined. When a poet did not serve as his own didascalus but brought out his play through someone else, did the name of the didascalus or that of the poet appear in the records? On a few points general agreement is possible. For example, when a poet had applied for a chorus in his own name but died before the festival and someone else had to assume his didascalic duties, care seems to have been taken at all periods to indicate the original didascalus. Again, in cases of deliberate deception, as when a man without dramatic powers secured the consent of a playwright to bring out the latter's work as his own and applied for a chorus as if for his own play, naturally the name of the pseudo-author would be the only one to appear in the records. The crucial case remains, viz., when a dramatist wished to be relieved of the burden of stage management and arranged for a didascalus to ask for a chorus and assume responsibility for the performance. The matter becomes important with reference to Aristophanes and the correct restoration of the Victors'-Lists for comic poets at the City Dionysia and the Lenaea.

When Aristophanes had written his first play, the *Banqueters*, youth, inexperience, diffidence, or some other motive for desiring to avoid the responsibility of staging his play caused him to intrust it to Callistratus for production at the Lenaea of 427 B.C. The same process was repeated at the City Dionysia of 426 B.C. and the Lenaea of 425 B.C., when Callistratus brought out Aristophanes' *Babylonians* and *Acharnians*, respectively. The former piece was apparently unsuccessful, but the latter was awarded the first prize. At the Lenaea of 424 B.C. Aristophanes was equally successful with the *Knights*, which, however, he produced *in his own name*. In vss. 512 ff. of this play the chorus declares that many Athenians approached the poet and expressed their surprise that he had not long before asked for a chorus in his own name. This passage implies that the real authorship of Aristophanes' earlier pieces was known to a large section of the public, and makes it clear that he had produced no earlier plays in his own name. Therefore if he had won a City victory during this period the comedy with which he won it must have been brought out in the name of another. The earliest City Dionysia, then, at which he could have produced a play in his own name was in 424 B.C., two months later than the *Knights*. Now in the Victors'-List for comic poets at the City Dionysia (Fig. 78),[1] the letters 'Aρι appear in line seven of the second column. Is the name of Aristophanes or that of Aristomenes to be restored here?

We know that Eupolis, whose name stands next below in the list, won a victory at the City Dionysia of 421 B.C. and that Hermippus and Cratinus were successful at the City festival in 422 and 423 B.C., respectively. This leaves the City Dionysia of 424 B.C. for some unknown victor, who may have been Aristophanes producing a play in his own name. But, on the other hand, these victories of Hermippus and Cratinus were certainly not their first, and it is possible that the victory of Eupolis in 421 B.C. was also not his first. If any of these men was in fact the City victor in 424 B.C., Aristophanes' name could be read at this point on the stone only by supposing that he had won a City victory at some date prior to the *Knights* and consequently with a play which had been brought out by another. If this hypothesis is correct, it would automatically be established that at this

---

[1] Fig. 78 is taken from Wilhelm, *op. cit.*, p. 107 and represents *Corpus Inscriptionum Graecarum*, II, 977*i* and *k*, together with two previously unpublished fragments.

period victories were credited to the actual poet rather than to his didascalus. The argument here is by no means conclusive, however, and most authorities follow Dr. Wilhelm in restoring the name of Aristomenes, another poet who belonged to the same general period.

The same problem recurs in connection with the comic Victors'-List for the Lenaea (Fig. 79).[1] Here Aristophanes' name

[Ἀστικαὶ ποιητῶν]	[Τηλεκλεί]δης |||	Νικοφῶ[ν —]
[κωμικῶν]	[. . . . .]s		Θεόπομπ[ος —]
[Χιωνίδης —]	—	Κη]φισό[δοτος —]
—	—	. . .]ι[ππος ? —]
5 —		Φερ[εκράτης —]	—
[. . . . .]s		Ἑρμ[ιππος —]	—
—	Ἀρι[στομένης —]	—
[Μάγνη]s Δ|	Εὔ[πολις —]	—
[. . . . . o]s		Κα[λλίστρατος —]	—
10 [Ἀλκιμέ]νη[s]		Φρύ[νιχος —]	—
[. . . . .]s		Ἀμ[ειψίας —]	—
[Εὐφρόν]ιος		Πλά[των —]	—
[Ἐκφαν]τίδης ||||	Φιλ[ωνίδης —]	—
[Κρατῖ]νος ⌐|	Λύκ[ις —]	—
15 [Διοπ]είθης ||	Λεύ[κων —]	—
[Κρά]της |||		
[Καλλία]s ||		

FIG. 78.—Wilhelm's Transcription and Restoration of Four Fragments of the Athenian Victors'-List.

See p. 327, n. 1

is certainly to be restored somewhere in the lacuna below the name of Eupolis in the first column. But whether his name stood in a position corresponding to his own victory in 424 B.C. or in one corresponding to his victory through the agency of Callistratus in the previous year, or whether (to state it differently) the name of Callistratus must be restored ahead of Aristophanes' own name because of his victory in 425 B.C., are

[1] Fig. 79 is taken from Wilhelm, *op. cit.*, p. 123, and represents *Corpus Inscriptionum Graecarum*, II, 977d, e, f, g, and h.

questions which are still incapable of categorical answers. Lack of space will prevent a further argument of the matter, and I must close with a summary of Dr. Jachmann's conclusions. His discussion is not only the latest but takes certain factors into account which had previously been ignored. He points out that the archons' records, Aristotle's *Didascaliae*, and the different types of inscriptions must be sharply differentiated and that the first named are the ultimate source of all the others.

[Ληναικ]α[ὶ ποη]τῶν	Πο[. . . . .] Ι	Φιλέ[ππος Γ ?]ΙΙ	—	
[κωμικ]ῶν	Με[ταγένη]s ΙΙ	Χόρη[γος —]	Διο[νύσι]ος Ι	
[Ξ]ενόφιλος Ι	Θέο[πομπ]ος ΙΙ	'Αναξα[νδρί]δης ΙΙΙ	Κλέ[αρχ]ος [Ι.]	
[Τ]ηλεκλείδης Γ	Πολ[ύζηλο]s ΙΙΙΙ	Φιλέτα[ιρο]s ΙΙ	'Αθηνοκλῆs[	
5 'Αριστομένης ΙΙ	Νικοφ[ῶν —]	Εὔβουλος ΓΙ	Πυρ[ήν?] Ι	5
Κρατῖνος ΙΙΙ	'Απο[λλοφάνη]s Ι	Εφιππος Ι[.?]	'Αλκήνωρ Ι	
Φερεκράτης ΙΙ	'Αμ[ειψίας —]	['Α]ντιφάν[ης] ΓΙΙΙ	Τιμοκλῆς Ι	
Ἕρμιππος ΙΙΙΙ	Ν[ικοχάρης —]	[Μ]νησίμ[αχος] Ι	Προκλείδης Ι	
Φρύνιχος ΙΙ	Ξενο[φ]ῶν Ι	Ναυ[σικράτ]ης ΙΙΙ	Μ[έν]ανδρος Ι[—	
10 Μυρτίλος Ι	Φιλύλλιος Ι	Εὐφάνη[s —]	Φ[ι]λήμων ΙΙΙ	10
[Εὔ]πολις ΙΙΙ	Φιλόνικος Ι	Ἄλεξις ΙΙ [—]	'Απολλόδωρο[s—]	
—	[. . . . . . .]s Ι	['Αρ]ιστ[οφῶν —]	Δίφιλος ΙΙΙ	
—	[Κηφισόδοτος Ι	—	Φιλιππίδης ΙΙ[—	
—	—	—	Νικόστρατος [—	
15 —	—	—	Καλλιάδης Ι	15
—	—	—	'Αμεινίας Ι	
—	—	['Ασκληπιό?δω]ρος Ι	Ι Ι Ι	

FIG. 79.—Wilhelm's Transcription and Restoration of Five Fragments of the Athenian Victors'-List.

See p. 328, n. 1

The archons, of course, kept their records with no thought of later literary investigations but mainly with a view to having a definite list of men whom they were to hold responsible for different events upon their programs. Naturally, then, they had no interest in current or subsequent charges of plagiarism, pretended authorship, etc. Jachmann maintains that prior to about 380 B.C. the archons entered the name of the didascalus alone, but after that date they recorded the names of both didascalus and poet when these differed. He supposes the change to have been due to a law, which was made necessary by the increasing practice of intrusting plays to men who were

not their authors and to the consequent differentiation of function between poets and didascali. According to Jachmann the
same situation probably obtained also in Aristotle's *Didascaliae;*
but in the Victors'-Lists and the inscriptional Didascaliae only the
didascali were listed before 380 B.C. and after that date only
the poets. In the Fasti, on the contrary, only the didascali, as
the use of the verb ἐδίδασκε would indicate, appeared at any time.

Besides some other inscriptions of lesser importance than
those already discussed, Aristotle's *Didascaliae* was the source,
directly or indirectly, also of several treatises, collections of
classified data, catalogues, etc., dealing with various phases of
Greek theatrical history and compiled by such men as Dicaear-
chus, Callimachus, and Aristophanes of Byzantium. I shall
close with an account of one of these. I refer to the system of
numbering which was applied to ancient plays. Thus, according
to the ancient hypothesis (argument) to Sophocles' *Antigone*
that drama "was counted the thirty-second" (λέλεκται δὲ τὸ
δρᾶμα τοῦτο τριακοστὸν δεύτερον), and the first hypothesis to
Aristophanes' *Birds* declares that that comedy "is the thirty-
fifth" (ἔστι δὲ λέ). Before going farther it will be best to state
that the latter numeral is inexplicable under any theory, but
that Dindorf's substitution of ιέ for λέ ("fifteen" for "thirty-
five") is a satisfactory and convincing emendation. With the
publication of the Vatican hypothesis to Euripides' *Alcestis* in
1834 a third numeral came to light: τὸ δρᾶμα ἐποιήθη ιζ̅ ("the
drama was made seventeenth"). By far the most significant
numeral, however, was published in the *Oxyrhynchus Papyri*
in 1904. Here at the top of the last column of a hypothesis to
Cratinus' lost *Dionysalexandros* stood the following heading,
doubtless repeated from the beginning of the hypothesis, which
is now lost:

Διονυσ[αλεξανδρος]	"The Dionysalexandros
η̄	Eighth
κρατ[εινου]	Of Cratinus"

Finally, one of the fragmentary hypotheses to two of Menander's
plays published in the *Oxyrhynchus Papyri* of 1914 begins as

follows: "The *Imbrians*, commencing 'For how long a time, Demeas, my good man, I . . . . you.' This he wrote in the archonship of Nicocles, being his 7[.]th play (ταύτην [ἔγρα]ψεν ἐπὶ Νικοκλέο[υς . .]την καὶ ἑβδομηκοστ[ήν]), and he gave it for production at the Dionysia; but on account of the tyrant Lachares the festival was not celebrated. Subsequently it was acted by the Athenian Callippus." This numeral is partly illegible, but was in the seventies, probably seventy-first, seventy-third, seventy-sixth, or seventy-ninth, possibly seventy-fourth or seventy-fifth.

The interpretation of these numerals has suffered from the fact that they did not become known simultaneously and from the further fact that for the most part explanations have been advanced by editors who contented themselves with proposing the most plausible interpretation of the particular numeral before them without taking the others into consideration. Of the many suggestions offered I shall here confine my discussion to two, the chronological and the alphabetical. The former interpretation is the oldest and receives confirmation from the fact that Terence's comedies are not only arranged chronologically in our manuscripts but are provided with numerals on that basis in the didascalic notices which are prefixed to these Latin plays. These numbers, of course, would trace back the system only to the Romans and to about the time of Varro in the first century B.C. But inasmuch as Aeschines' speeches are arranged on the same principle, there can be no doubt that the Alexandrian Greeks were familiar with it. The chronological interpretation, however, has been open to three objections: (1) It is impossible for Aristophanes' *Birds* to have been thirty-fifth in a chronological arrangement of his plays. This obstacle may be evaded by accepting Dindorf's emendation. (2) The *Antigone* and *Alcestis* numerals are somewhat smaller than we might expect, since they seem to assign too few plays to the earlier years of Sophocles' and Euripides' activity as playwrights. This is not a serious objection but must be taken into account. (3) The *Alcestis* took the place of a satyric drama and therefore stood fourth in its group. Consequently its numeral ought to be divisible by four, and the number seventeen does not satisfy this requirement and does not seem consistent with the tetralogic system employed at the City Dionysia during this period.

These difficulties are not insuperable, but first I wish to refer to another interpretation, which has enjoyed great popularity. There is no doubt that the Greeks were acquainted, and at an early date, with the alphabetical arrangement of titles. The Oxyrhynchus arguments to Menander's plays, for example, seem to have been arranged in accordance with this principle. The objection that there would be no point in recording numerals derived from an alphabetical system for the reason that it would be as easy to turn to a given play by means of its initial letters as by means of its number is invalid because in alphabetical lists the Greeks ignored all letters except the first. For example, fifteen of Euripides' extant titles begin with alpha, and there was no a priori method of knowing which of the fifteen places available the *Alcestis* would occupy (Fig. 80).[1] It becomes necessary, then, to examine the alphabetical explanation without prejudice, and fortunately it is now possible to reach an incontrovertible conclusion. The numerals have never lent themselves cordially to this interpretation, but the final *coup de grâce* was delivered by the recent discovery of the numeral for Menander's *Imbrians*. Menander is said to have written from one hundred and five to one hundred and nine pieces, but only eighty-six titles are now known. Fifty-one of these, however, have initial letters which come after iota in the Greek alphabet. Now the smallest restoration which is possible for the Menander numeral is seventy-one, and seventy-one plus fifty-one make one hundred and twenty-two, or thirteen more than the largest number recorded by any authority as the aggregate of Menander's works. Therefore the alphabetical explanation must be rejected.

[1] Fig. 80 is taken from a photograph by Giraudon (Paris) and furnished by Professor D. M. Robinson. Note that the first play in the list on the background is the ΑΛΚΗΣΤΙΣ.

ΑΛΚΗΣΤΙΣ
ΑΡΧΕΛΑΟΣ
ΑΙΓΕΥΣ
ΑΙΟΛΟΣ
ΑΛΟΠΗ
ΑΝΤΙΓΟΝΗ
ΑΝΚΥΑΙΩΝ
ΑΝΔΡΟΜΕΔΑ
ΑΛΕΞΑΝΔΡΟΣ
ΑΥΓΗ
ΑΝΔΡΟΜΑΧΗ
ΑΝΤΙΓΟΝΗ
ΑΥΤΟΛΥΚΟΣ
ΒΑΚΧΑΙ
ΒΕΛΛΕΡΟΦΟΝΤΗΣ
ΒΟΥΣΙΡΙΣ
ΔΙΚΤΥΣ
ΔΑΝΑΗ
ΕΙΦΙΓΕΝΕΙΑ
ΕΛΕΝΗ
ΕΙΝΩ
ΕΚΑΒΗ
ΕΡΕΧΘΕΥΣ
ΕΥΡΥΣΘΕΥ
ΕΠΕΟΣ

ΚΡΗΤΕΣ
ΚΡΗΣΣΑ
ΚΡΕΣΦΟΝΤΥΣ
ΚΥΚΛΩΨ
ΛΙΚΥΗΝΙΟΣ
ΜΕΛΑΝΙΠΠΟΣ
ΜΗΔΕΙΑ
ΜΕΛΕΑΓΡΟΣ
ΟΙΝΕΥΣ
ΟΙΔΙΠΟΥΣ
ΟΡΕΣΤΗΣ

FIG. 80

THE VILLA ALBANI STATUE OF EURIPIDES IN THE LOUVRE WITH
THE BEGINNING OF AN ALPHABETICAL LIST OF HIS PLAYS

See p. 332, n. 1

We may now return to the chronological interpretation, and first let us note the light which the *Dionysalexandros* numeral throws upon the situation. It is significant that this number is not incorporated within the hypothesis but stood at the top of the last column and had doubtless appeared also at the beginning of the hypothesis (now lost). In my opinion this was the original form of such a notice and shows why in the fuller form of statement found elsewhere a different verb is employed in each case—λέλεκται, ἔστι, ἐποιήθη, and ἔγραψεν. When Aristophanes of Byzantium, or whoever was responsible for the change, transferred these items from the heading and made them integral parts of the hypothesis, finding no verb in the original version before him and resting under the necessity of now using one, he did not deem it essential to paraphrase the information always in the same way but, as was natural, employed now one expression and now another. If it be true that the original function of the numerals was as we find it in the Cratinus hypothesis, only one explanation is possible— it was a device for the convenience of some library, probably that at Alexandria. If so, every play in the collection would bear a number and these numbers would run consecutively for each author. In other words, if any play were not pre-served in the library, that fact would not be indicated by an unoccupied number being left as a gap in the enumeration. Of course it is conceivable that the basis of arrangement was purely arbitrary and even varied with each author, and in fact there has been a distinct tendency among recent authorities to accept some such pessimistic conclusion. But it is more prob-able, until the contrary be proved, that some rational system (alphabetical, chronological, etc.) was employed and employed consistently.

Now there can be little room left for doubt as to what system was actually chosen, when it is observed that the foregoing statement of the numerals' purpose and use obviates two of the three objections to the chronological interpretation. Euripides produced his first play in 455 B.C. and died in 406 B.C. He is said to have written ninety-two plays, or an average of one and four-fifths per annum. If the *Alcestis* were actually his seventeenth piece he must have written less than one play a year between 455 B.C. and 438 B.C., when the *Alcestis* was produced, and two and one-third plays a year thereafter. It is true that Euripides' career opened slowly and that many of his later works are characterized by hasty and careless execution. But this disparity is too great, even apart from the objection that *ex hypothesi* the *Alcestis* numeral ought to be a multiple of four. If we suppose, however, that only the plays that were preserved received a number, the situation at once clears. We are informed that seventy-eight of Euripides' works (four of them spurious) were preserved. This is confirmed by the fact that seventy-two of his titles are now known, for the number of titles now extant generally approximates closely the number of an author's plays which were known by the ancients. If, then, the *Alcestis* was seventeenth among the seventy-eight works which were passing under the name of Euripides in antiquity and if it retained the same relative position as in the complete list, it must have been about the twentieth play which he brought out. This number, being divisible by four, would be suitable for the last play of a tetralogy and would have the merit of reducing slightly the disproportion between the earlier and the later activity of the poet. Moreover, since the earlier plays of a dramatist are more likely to have been lost than the later ones, it is possible to suppose that the *Alcestis* may have been twenty-fourth or even twenty-eighth in a complete list (chronological) of his writings. The point is that the purpose of the numerals as deducible from the *Dionysalexandros* instance is capable of obviating all objections to the chronological interpretation of the *Alcestis* numeral.

Similarly, Sophocles is said to have written one hundred and twenty-three plays, and his career extended from about 468 B.C. to 406 B.C., yielding an average of about two plays per annum. Inasmuch as the *Antigone* was probably performed in 441 B.C. and bears the numeral thirty-two, an unmodified chronological interpretation would give an average of one and one-seventh plays a year for Sophocles' earlier period and of two and three-sevenths for his later period. But we now have fragments of somewhat more than one hundred Sophoclean plays; and if the *Antigone* was thirty-second among these and retained the same relative position as at first, it would have been about the thirty-seventh play which Sophocles wrote. Of course this is a mere estimate, but again this solution has the merit of assigning a slightly larger number of plays to the earlier years of the poet and of reducing, to that extent, the only objection to the chronological interpretation of this numeral.

Aristophanes' first comedy was produced in 427 B.C., and his last one not much later than 388 B.C. To him were attributed forty-four plays, four of which were considered spurious. Apparently all of his works were known to the ancients. The *Birds* was produced at the City Dionysia of 414 B.C. in the fourteenth year of his activity as a playwright. There is, therefore, no a priori reason for refusing to believe that it was Aristophanes' fifteenth play. Nor does any obstacle arise from the chronology of the plays, so far as they can be dated. On the other hand the traditional numeral, thirty-five, is inexplicable under any logical system of enumeration, while Dindorf's emendation is paleographically simple. Therefore we must accept the substitution and the chronological interpretation.

Cratinus' career began about 452 B.C. and closed in 423 B.C. or soon thereafter. Most scholars suppose his *Dionysalexandros* to have been brought out in 430 or 429 B.C., though I was myself at first inclined to favor an earlier date. He is said to have written twenty-one plays. Twenty-six titles, however, were accepted for him by Meineke and Kock in their editions of the Greek comic fragments. Probably a few of these titles must be rejected as spurious or transferred to the younger Cratinus, but it is also possible that Cratinus was much more productive than is commonly supposed and that twenty-one was the number of his preserved works in Alexandrian times, not of all that he had composed. As the custom of publishing comedies seems to have started only at about the beginning of Cratinus' career (see p. 55, above), it would not be surprising if many of his plays, especially of his earlier plays, were lost.   At any rate in a chronological arrangement of twenty-one comedies, whether they were the whole or only the preserved part of Cratinus' work, the *Dionysalexandros* could be the eighth.   These conclusions are acceptable to Professor R. H. Tanner, who will shortly publish a dissertation dealing with the chronology of Cratinus' plays and whose results on the point now under discussion he has kindly permitted me to summarize here.   He follows Croiset in assigning the *Dionysalexandros* to the Lenaea of 430 B.C.; six plays he definitely dates before the *Dionysalexandros*, and a seventh somewhat less positively.   In the thirteen remaining he has found nothing to indicate a date prior to 430 B.C.   Some of them certainly belong to the period subsequent to 430 B.C. It will be seen that these conclusions are in thorough accord with my interpretation of the numeral.

The chronology of Menander's life is not free from uncertainties, but these do not seriously affect the present discussion. His first play was performed perhaps as early as 324 B.C., and his decease probably took place in 292/1 B.C.   During these thirty-three or thirty-four years he composed some one hundred and nine pieces or slightly over three per annum.   Now Nicocles was archon in 302/1 B.C.   If, then, the hypothesis is correct in assigning the *Imbrians* to the archonship of this man, the number seventy-one (the smallest restoration which is possible) or seventy-nine (the largest possible) would almost perfectly fit the requirements of the case.   Eighty-six Menandrian titles are now known, and it is not likely that many of his plays were lost in Alexandrian times.

We may, therefore, summarize the preceding discussion as follows: If we follow Dindorf in reading $\iota\acute{\epsilon}$ for $\lambda\acute{\epsilon}$ in the hypothesis to Aristophanes' *Birds*, the numerals are capable of a uniform interpretation; they were a library device and were assigned to the plays represented in some collection, most probably that at Alexandria, according to the dates of their premières. It is needless to state that in establishing the chronological sequence of the plays in their possession the library authorities would depend upon Aristotle's *Didascaliae* or other handbooks derived therefrom.

CORRIGENDA ET ADDENDA

P. xii, ll. 1 f. The plays of Chaeremon and the other ἀναγνωστικοί mentioned in Aristotle's *Rhetoric*, 1413*b*12, were "capable of being read" with enjoyment in addition to being performed, rather than "closet dramas" in the modern sense. Cf. Haigh, *The Tragic Drama of the Greeks*, pp. 426–29.

P. xvii, ll. 10 ff. To the works cited should now be added Goodell's *Athenian Tragedy* (1920), and Norwood's *Greek Tragedy* (1920).

Pp. xx f. To the works cited should now be added Bieber's *Die Denkmäler zum Theaterwesen im Altertum* (1920), a profusely illustrated corpus of scenic data which at last antiquates Wieseler's *Theatergebäude und Denkmäler des Bühnenwesens bei den Griechern und Römern* (1851). For Frickenhaus, *Die altgriechische Bühne* (1917), see Allen's review in *Classical Philology*, XVII (1922), pp. 166 ff.

P. xxviii, bottom. Considerations of space have necessitated that the following new illustrations be listed here:

Fig. 24*a*.—Cross-Section of the Proscenium (*Bühnenfassade*) of the Graeco-Roman Theater at Ephesus, *p.* 61.

Fig. 82*a*.—Relationships between Aeschylean and Lycurgus Theaters according to Allen's Revised Theory, *p.* 349.

Fig. 85.—Part of Gladiatorial Scene Painted upon Wall Surrounding the Orchestra of the Graeco-Roman Theater at Corinth, *facing p.* 354.

Fig. 86.—Ramp Leading to Rear Entrance of the Theater at Thoricus, *facing p.* 357.

Fig. 87.—Charon's Stairs in the Theater at Eretria, *facing p.* 357.

Fig. 88.—Columns from the Proscenium of the Theater at Oropus, *facing p.* 357.

P. 4, l. 33: In addition to literary evidence cited elsewhere in this volume, cf. Athenaeus, p. 630C: "And all satyric poetry, also, in ancient times consisted of choruses, as did tragedy of that day. Therefore they did not even have actors."[1] Stahl, "Arion und Thespis," *Rheinisches Museum für Philologie*, LXIX (1914), 590, n. 2, pointed out that Suidas (*s.v.* Simonides) mentioned τραγῳδίαι among the works of that poet and failed to list his dithyrambs, although his dithyrambs were famous and he is not known to have composed tragedies (in the usual sense). He therefore concluded (p. 590) that τραγῳδία was applied to two different kinds of performances (*a*) lyric tragedies, which both earlier and later were usually called dithyrambs, and (*b*) dramatic tragedies.

---

[1] Συνέστηκε δὲ καὶ σατυρικὴ πᾶσα ποίησις τὸ παλαιὸν ἐκ χορῶν, ὡς καὶ ἡ τότε τραγῳδία· διόπερ οὐδὲ ὑποκριτὰς εἶχον.

P. 5, l. 18. Cf. Norwood, *op. cit.*, pp. 42 f.: "As to the value of Aristotle's evidence we must distinguish carefully between the facts which he reports and his comment thereon. The latter we should study with the respect due to his vast merits; but he is not infallible. When, for instance, ... he blames Euripides because 'Iphigenia the suppliant in no way resembles her later self,'[1] we shall regard him less as helping us than as dating himself. But as to the objective facts which he records he must be looked on as for us infallible. He lived in or close to the periods of which he writes; he commanded a vast array of documents now lost to us; he was strongly desirous of ascertaining the facts; his temperament and method were keenly scientific; his industry prodigious. We may, and should, discuss his opinions; his facts we cannot dispute."

P. 9, ll. 33 f. and n. 4. Cf. schol. Pindar *Olymp.* xiii. 26b (Drachmann): "The most serious (σπουδαιότατον) of Dionysus' dithyrambs appeared first in Corinth."

P. 16, l. 22. That the first actor was an "answerer" to the dominating chorus of the period is not only probable on theoretical grounds but is attested by such a dithyramb as Bacchylides' *Theseus*, see p. 10, above; at any rate it is now all but universally accepted. But that ἀποκρίνεσθαι was the first verb used to express the actor's function is perhaps not so certain. It is usually so stated on the basis of a few indirect phrases such as Pollux iv. 123: ἔλεος δ' ἦν ἀρχαία τράπεζα ἐφ' ἦν πρὸ Θέσπιδος εἷς τις ἀναβὰς τοῖς χορευταῖς ἀπεκρίνατο (translated on p. 18, above), but more especially because of Photius *s.v.* ὑποκρίνεσθαι· τὸ ἀποκρίνεσθαι οἱ παλαιοί. καὶ ὁ ὑποκριτὴς ἐντεῦθεν, ὁ ἀποκρινόμενες τῷ χορῷ. But Allen[2] has pointed out that already in Homer ὑποκρίνεσθαι (not ἀποκρίνεσθαι) was used in the sense of "answer" (as well as "interpret"), and that Photius' definition is wrongly punctuated not only in citations but in the editions of Photius and should read as follows: ὑποκρίνεσθαι· τὸ ἀποκρίνεσθαι· οἱ παλαιοί· καὶ ὁ ὑποκριτὴς ἐντεῦθεν, ὁ ἀποκρινόμενος τῷ χορῷ. The traditional punctuation made it appear that ἀποκρίνεσθαι was the archaic verb signifying "to act" (in addition, of course, to other meanings), while according to the new punctuation ὑποκρίνεσθαι originally meant "to answer." The latter punctuation is not only in accordance with the formula usually followed by Photius but is also supported by Homeric usage.

Accordingly, it is no longer necessary to ask when and why ἀποκρίνεσθαι became ὑποκρίνεσθαι to denote the actor's function, but rather when and why ὑποκρίνεσθαι became so technical in this sense that it was almost necessary or at least convenient to use a new term (ἀποκρίνεσθαι) in the nontechnical sense of "to answer."

[1] See p. 267, above.

[2] Cf. *Classical Philology*, XVIII (1923), 284 f., in a review of the second edition of the present work.

The old explanations, however, may be applied almost as well to the new interpretation as to the traditional one. Thus, Bywater,[1] who rejected the equation ὑποκριτής = "answerer," wrote: "The actor is called a ὑποκριτής . . . . because he was the poet's spokesman, who interpreted his text to the public. . . . . The term must have acquired this sense at the time when, by a division of labour, the poet left the acting to others, instead of being himself the performer of his pieces, as he originally was. . . . . The position of the ὑποκριτής in fact was analogous to that of the ῥαψῳδός; they were both of them intermediaries, who interpreted the words of a poet to the public. It is to be noted that in describing the rhapsodist in the *Ion* Plato in one place terms him a ἑρμηνεύς and in another a ὑποκριτής, apparently without any difference of meaning." Another explanation is afforded by Albrecht Dieterich:[2] ". . . . wer den Gott spielte, musste des Gottes grosse Maske aufsetzen, und das ist der Ursprung der sog. 'tragischen' Maske. Dieser erste Schauspieler, der vor den Chor trat, ist der ὑποκριτής, er ὑποκρίνεται unter der Maske, unter dem Gotte, wie der ὑποφήτης unter dem Gotte spricht." Kranz,[3] on the other hand, stresses the fact that the earliest actor occupied a distinctly subordinate (ὑπό) position as a mere "answerer" to the chorus, which was then the indisputable protagonist in the action.

P. 17, n. For new interpretations of Aeschylus' statement concerning Homer, cf. Scott, *The Unity of Homer* (1921), pp. 27 f., and Radin, "Homer and Aeschylus," *Classical Journal*, XVII (1922), 332 ff.

P. 20, ll. 20 ff. Thespis' choruses could not have consisted exclusively of satyrs, else he would have been celebrated as the inventor of satyric drama; cf. Stahl, *Rheinisches Museum für Philologie*, XLIX (1914), 592, n. 4. He suggests that the Thespian chorus may have been "mixed" as in comedy (see p. 42, above), i.e., only in part consisting of satyrs.

P. 24, ll. 6 f. Stahl's contention (*op. cit.*, p. 593) that satyric drama never existed independently of tragedy is very improbable.

P. 25, n. 1. Tillyard, *The Hope Vases* (1923), pp. 79–81, has now observed that on one of the Deepdene craters (Fig. 1 in Cook, *Zeus*, I, Plate XXXIX) there is an inscription, καλὸς ηφαρστος, an obvious error for καλὸς Ἥφαιστος. He plausibly suggests that the scene was based upon a satyric drama entitled *Hephaestus* and written by Achaeus of Eretria, whose dramatic career began about 447 B.C. On stylistic and technical grounds the vase has been assigned to *ca.* 450 B.C.

P. 26, ll. 6–15. Miss Bieber, *Die Denkmäler zum Theaterwesen im Altertum* (1920), p. 92, maintains that a mere actor must not sit, as the figure whom I have named Hesione does, upon a god's seat. She therefore inter-

---

[1] Cf. his edition of Aristotle's *Poetics*, note on 1449a15.

[2] Cf. *Kleine Schriften*, p. 422.

[3] Cf. *Neue Jahrbücher für das class. Altertum*, XLIII (1919), 155 f.

prets this personage as a Muse holding the mask of Hesione. Who, then, wore this mask? Are we to understand that this arrangement is to suggest that Hesione's rôle was carried as a double by one of the other three actors? See p. 173, above.

P. 30 f. In view of Tillyard's ascription of the scene upon the Deepdene crater to Achaeus (see above) I am no longer inclined to admit that the Pandora vase (Fig. 9, above) has anything to do with satyric drama. I would now accept one of the interpretations proposed by Reisch (see p. 30, n. 2, above) and would minimize the whole "penultimate stage" in the evolution of the satyric chorus.

P. 32, n. 1. On the gable relief of the old poros temple in the precinct of Dionysus Eleuthereus (see p. 63, above) the figures, whether satyrs or silenoi, have equine tails and *phalloi* like the silenoi on the François vase; cf. Frickenhaus, "Zum Ursprung von Satyrspiel und Tragödie," *Jahrbuch d. arch. Instituts*, XXXII (1917), Abb. 1. Frickenhaus (*op. cit.*, p. 3) believed "die Satyrn aber sind in Athen auch nicht länger heimisch als das Fest," i.e., the City Dionysia, established in 534 B.C.

P. 39, ll. 2 ff. The earliest extant reference to Middle Comedy is contained in the title of the work by Antiochus of Alexandria, περὶ τῶν ἐν μέσῃ κωμῳδίᾳ κωμῳδουμένων ποιητῶν, which has recently been assigned to the first century B.C. Cf. Rademacher, "Zur Frage der μέση Komödie," *Anzeiger der Akademie d. Wissenschaften in Wien, philos.-hist. Klasse*, LVIII (1922), 55.

P. 43, ll. 33 ff. "Drama means something more than persons in costume reciting a ritual," D. C. Stuart, "The Origin of Greek Tragedy in the Light of Dramatic Technique," *Transactions American Philological Association*, XLVII (1916), 203.

P. 56, ll. 5 ff. Aeschylus' visits to Sicily have been used to explain also the unusual features in the *Prometheus Bound* and to defend its genuineness and integrity; cf. Alfred Körte, "Das Prometheus-problem," *Neue Jahrbücher für d. klass. Altertum*, XLV (1920), 213.

P. 58, n., ll. 5–8. Dr. Dörpfeld was my guest at Pompeii February 20–24, 1924, and "confessed that he had at last been forced to relinquish all hope of ever revising *Das griechische Theater*, but he stated that he planned before long to prepare a book on the Athenian theater alone, with new plans and interpretations. I am informed that, with a view to the execution of this purpose, he has had further excavations made in the Athenian theater early in the current year (1925) with new and valuable results and that he has engaged a competent architect, Professor Orlandos, to prepare new drawings"; cf. Flickinger, "Some Problems in Scenic Antiquities," *Philological Quarterly* (State University of Iowa), V (1926), 112. The appearance of this volume will be awaited with eagerness. See p. 360, below.

P. 60, n. 1. For an example of this primary meaning of θέατρον, cf.

Xenophon *Hellenica* vii. 4. 31, and Flickinger, *Plutarch as a Source of Information on the Greek Theater* (1904), pp. 23 f. For a slightly different view, cf. Dyer, "The Olympian Theatron and the Battle of Olympia," *Journal of Hellenic Studies*, XXVIII (1908), 250–68, especially pp. 251, n. 2, and 267. Another early meaning of θέατρον is "audience" or "spectators" (οἱ θεαταί); cf. Herodotus vi, 21 : ἐς δάκρυα ἔπεσε τὸ θέητρον. In Pliny iv. 7. 2 *auditorium* is used in a similar way.

P. 62, l. 13. Cf. *Travels in Greece*, pp. 61 ff., published in 1776 but referring to a journey taken in 1765.

P. 63, n. 3. Cf. Timaeus *Lexicon Platonicum:* ὄρχηστρα . . . . καὶ τόπος ἐπιφανὴς εἰς πανήγυριν, ἔνθα ʽΑρμοδίου καὶ ʼΑριστογείτονος εἰκόνες, and Frazer's commentary on Pausanias, Vol. II, pp. 92 f. and 220.

P. 63, n. 4. In my judgment the alternative theory has now been rendered impossible by later developments. Professor Bethe, "Der Spielplatz des Aischylos," *Hermes*, LIX (1924), 108–17, maintains that the shift in the site of the theater (see pp. 65 and 68, above) took place *ca.* 499 B.C. But he ignores the period of the earliest performances in the old market place, still talks of a 24 m. orchestra-terrace, is apparently ignorant of the inscribed stone seat found by Bulle and Lehmann-Hartleben (see p. 350, below, *addendum* to p. 68, ll. 21 f.), partially misreads the evidence to be drawn from Aeschylus' plays, and in general is revealed as out of touch with the present situation.

P. 65, l. 10, "about eighty-eight feet in diameter." In my first edition the diameter of the orchestra-terrace was given as seventy-eight feet (24 m.). This statement was derived from Dörpfeld himself, cf. *Das griechische Theater*, pp. 26 f. In *Philologische Wochenschrift*, XLI (1921), 1213, however, he pointed out that in the drawings of his earlier publication this circle was given a diameter of 26 m. (!), and he is now willing to accept a diameter of 27 m. This discrepancy between Dörpfeld's text and his drawings is most surprising and had escaped the attention of all subsequent writers on the subject. But a compass will quickly establish the fact that a circle of 26 m. or 27 m. is required to include the stones B and C and the cutting at A in Figure 32, above. In the following discussion a diameter of eighty-eight feet (27 m.) is accepted as correct (see, however, p. 348 and n. 2, below).

Pp. 66 ff. Our knowledge of the Athenian theater has been substantially increased by Allen, "The Greek Theater of the Fifth Century before Christ," *University of California Studies in Classical Philology*, Vol. VII (1919). Like the rest of us, Professor Allen accepted 24 m. as the diameter of the early orchestra-terrace; but fortunately his conclusions were largely based upon Dörpfeld's drawings and so he was dealing with a 26 m. circle without knowing it. Nevertheless it is necessary to recast his statements somewhat in view of the situation disclosed in the preceding paragraph.

If then 27 m. be accepted as correct for the diameter of the early orchestra-terrace, it is identical in size with a hypothetical orchestral-terrace
of the Lycurgus theater as determined by the front line of the lowest row
of seats in the auditorium of this period (Fig. 81).[1] Now if this orchestra-
terrace, together with the orchestra and scene-buildings of the Lycurgus
theater, be thought of as pushed a few feet south and east back to the
original site of the theater and until it coincides with the orchestra-terrace
of Aeschylus (Fig. 82,)[2] some interesting relationships are brought to light.[3]
In the first place, the inner corners of the parascenia touch the inner edge
of the terrace's retaining wall, and the wall connecting the parascenia at the
rear forms a tangent to the terrace wall. Secondly, if a line be drawn
between the parascenia in their new position at the same distance back of
their front line as the Hellenistic proscenium stood back of the Hellenistic
parascenia (viz., about four feet, this probably being the position also of
the wooden proscenium in the Lycurgus theater, see pp. 69 f., above), this
line would be "an exact chord of the outermost circumference of the old
terrace-wall." Also, the fragments K K' in Figure 82 are contemporaneous
with fragments B and C of the early orchestra-terrace (Fig. 32) and probably
belonged to the retaining wall of the parodus in the first half of the fifth
century. If a line determined by these fragments be continued to the east,
it will intersect the retaining wall of the orchestra-terrace at about the same
point as does the chord. It is to be observed, also, how closely the position
of this chord as deduced from the position of the proscenium in the Hellenistic theater approximates that of the south side of a square inscribed
in the orchestra-terrace, see Figures 43 and 82. Finally, the Lycurgus
orchestra, 19.61 m. in diameter and separated from the north boundary of
the Aeschylean orchestra-terrace by the same distance (2.5 m.) as from the
hypothetical orchestra-terrace of the Lycurgus theater (see E F and G H in
Fig. 81), almost has as its tangent the line connecting the front walls of the
parascenia.

These discoveries at once confirm the common assumption that the
"fourth century structure probably reproduced in stone the main outlines
of the earlier theater in which the later tragedies of Sophocles and Euripides
and all the plays of Aristophanes were performed" (see p. 70, above), and
also make clear that this theater was itself a reproduction, on a slightly
different site, of the still earlier scenic arrangements. It thus becomes evident that the shift in the position of the theater took place about 430 B.C.

[1] Fig. 81 is specially drawn but is partially based upon Noack (see Fig. 32a,
above) and Allen, *op. cit.*, Fig. 17.

[2] Fig. 82 is specially drawn from an outline kindly furnished by Professor
Allen to illustrate his position (in 1922).

[3] These are somewhat confused in Dörpfeld's review of Allen, *Philologische
Wochenschrift*, XLI (1921), 1212 ff.

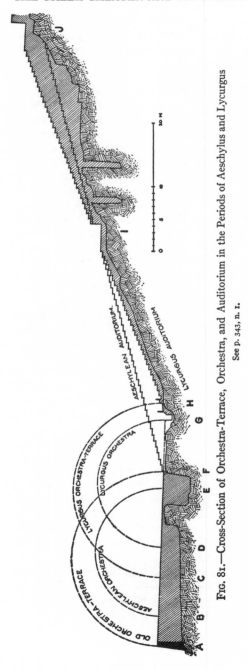

FIG. 81.—Cross-Section of Orchestra-Terrace, Orchestra, and Auditorium in the Periods of Aeschylus and Lycurgus

See p. 343, n. 1.

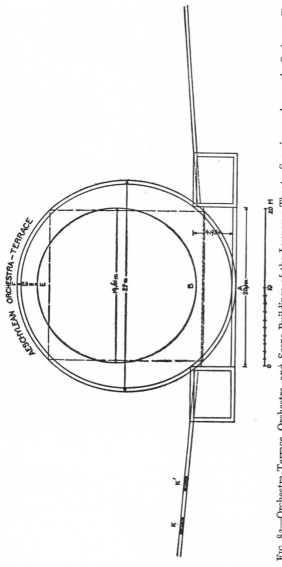

FIG. 82—Orchestra-Terrace, Orchestra, and Scene-Buildings of the Lycurgus Theater Superimposed upon the Orchestra-Terrace of Aeschylus; Constituting also a Plan of the Supposed Theater of about 460 B.C.

See p. 343, n. 2.

and not about 465 B.C., a point which in my first edition I considered still to be a matter of doubt.

Further inferences are more uncertain. Allen believes the earliest portion of the scene-building, the "Aeschylean σκηνή," to have been a small stoa-like structure erected wholly on the orchestra-terrace along the chord above mentioned. He thinks that this was built primarily as a background, and hints that it may have been used in the time of Aeschylus' *Seven against Thebes* or *Persians*, or even of the *Suppliants*, certainly several years before 458 B.C. At an early date, perhaps as early as the *Eumenides*, this σκηνή was extended beyond the circle of the terrace and two parascenia were added at its ends so as to afford a more effective and more ornamental screen for actors passing behind the scenes from one parodus to the other and also to increase the dressing-room facilities. These parascenia and portions of the enlarged σκηνή stood outside of the orchestra-terrace (Fig. 82). Finally, he believes that not later than about 430 B.C., when the position of the theater was shifted for two reasons mentioned on page 68, above, a real scene-building (two stories) was built behind the rear wall of the old σκηνή (in its new position), which was thus automatically converted into a proscenium. Thus, the proscenium of the fully developed theater was not a later addition or an afterthought but a transformation of the original unit of the structure.

I find myself unable, however, to accept this series of developments as correct at all points. I find plausibility in Noack's contention[1] that originally there was only one entrance to the orchestra-terrace; this was a ramp leading up to the terrace from the west and was delimited on the south by an ancient retaining wall, of which two fragments are located at $K K'$ in Figure 82. Therefore, it is probable that, when scenic accessories such as an altar or tomb were required in a certain play, they were located on the terrace with reference to the line of this wall. Before long, I believe, a quasi-permanent structure was erected for this purpose just outside the terrace where one of the parascenia afterward stood. When the requirements of a play demanded a second structure, the obvious position was that afterward occupied by the other parascenium on the opposite side of the terrace. The earliest of the preserved plays which demands two doorways is Aeschylus' *Libation-Bearers*, where the women's quarters and the men's quarters are expressly referred to (vss. 712 and 878), and the doors leading into them were undoubtedly visible to the audience; but of course this innovation must have been introduced several years before the date of that play (458 B.C.). It must quickly have occurred to someone that there

[1] Cf. Σκηνὴ Τραγικὴ, *Eine Studie über die scenischen Anlagen auf der Orchestra des Aischylos und der anderen Tragiker* (1915), p. 5. Noack's reconstruction of the scene-buildings, however, is invalidated by Allen's discovery.

would be an advantage in concealing the movements of actors and "stage-hands" behind the scenes by connecting these two buildings with a low wall erected along a chord of the terrace.   It is probable that this development had already taken place in the time of Aeschylus' *Seven against Thebes* (467 B.C.); at least, such a *mise en scène* would suitably suggest two redoubts and the parapet of the Theban acropolis where the action of this play is laid.   When matters had reached this stage, further developments came thick and fast, for the structures were all more or less temporary and there is an ancient tradition that in the early days the theater setting was reconstructed annually.[1]   When a third doorway was desired, perhaps thought of as leading into a more pretentious building, what more natural than to enlarge the connecting wall between the parascenia (to use the later term for them) into a long, oblong chamber with a central door in its front wall and its rear wall forming a tangent to the terrace at *A* (Figs. 81 f.; also Fig. 74). About 430 B.C., when the expanding needs of Athenian drama called for larger scenic accommodations, the orchestra and its structures were moved about thirty-five feet north and west so that a more ample scene-building could be erected behind the tangent at *C* on the new (hypothetical) orchestra-terrace, and this was one of the compelling reasons for the shift in location.   Simultaneously, as I believe, a wooden colonnade was built in front of the parascenia and the intermediate portion of the new scene-building along a line corresponding to the old chord, thus providing a proscenium.   Perhaps it was at this time, also, that two additional doors were placed in the front wall of the scene-building, and those in the parascenia closed.   At least this is the situation in the Lycurgus theater (Fig. 32), which probably follows its predecessor in this respect.   Unfortunately it is quite impossible to date all these developments with exactness or even to trace their precise sequence.   Allen, it will be remembered, favors a proscenium-like σκηνή as early as 450 B.C.   On the other hand, no permanent proscenium was erected before Hellenistic times (see p. 70, above).

The last six paragraphs I have found it necessary to retain almost word for word from the second edition.   In the meanwhile Professor Allen has restated his theory in two papers in *University of California Publications in Classical Philology:* "The Orchestra-Terrace of the Aeschylean Theater," VII (1922), 121–28 (reviewed by Dörpfeld in *Philologische Wochenschrift,* XLIII [1923], 441–43) and "Problems of the Proscenium," VII (1923), 197–207.   In the latter (pp. 205 f.) he expresses a willingness to accept the series of developments which I sketched four years ago as repeated above in the last paragraph.   Now that I am free from administrative duties, I hope to be able in the near future to return to this matter and to elaborate, improve, and substantiate with arguments the position which I then put

[1] Cf. Kaibel, *Comicorum Graecorum Fragmenta,* I, 22 (Tzetzes).

forward.[1] A discussion of the general situation, however, I have already included in my paper entitled "Some Problems in Scenic Antiquities," *Philological Quarterly* (State University of Iowa), V (1926), 97–113.

Professor Allen has revamped his theory substantially as outlined on pp. 342 ff., above. He has now relinquished the attempt to measure the diameter of the Aeschylean orchestra-terrace and *assumes* that it was 26.84m.,[2] the same as that of the great circle of the Lycurgus theater if inscribed just inside the row of thrones according to the calculation in *Das griechische Theater*, Figure 26. The resulting relationships are partially shown in Figure 82a,[3] where the heavy lines indicate the actual position of the scene-building and parascenia in the Lycurgus theater and the lighter, dotted lines indicate the orchestra-terrace and the supposed position of the orchestra, "parascenia," and connecting walls in the Aeschylean theater. In this drawing there are two things that surprise me: (*a*) for some reason which I cannot divine Allen has failed to include the great circle of the Lycurgus theater corresponding in size and function to the orchestra-terrace of the Aeschylean theater, and (*b*) he has again failed to inscribe a square in the larger circles according to the formula of Vitruvius for the *theatrum Graecorum* (see pp. 76–78, above). In Figure 82 I added this square to the drawing furnished by Professor Allen, and the closeness with which its south side escaped coinciding with the chord that marks the position of the later proscenium seems to me to explain a curious circumstance: in spite of the error about the diameter of the Aeschylean orchestra-terrace, Dörpfeld seemed well disposed toward Allen's second paper and inclined to accept his theory in principle; but Allen's third paper found him apathetic and ready to throw every difficulty in its path.[4]

In truth, the drawings at Allen's disposal were merely those in Dr. Dörpfeld's book and were not drawn upon a scale large enough to serve as a

---

[1] I am now inclined to question the statement (p. 347, ll. 20 ff., above) that a wooden proscenium was introduced "simultaneously" with the shifting of the theater to a slightly different position. The chord between the "parascenia" may well have been occupied by a row of columns or pillars, resembling the later proscenium, already during the closing years of Aeschylus' career.

[2] A plot of the two fragments (see p. 65, above), made for me by a competent architect in Athens, indicated a diameter of 25.26 m. For the value of this figure, the possibility that the two fragments do not belong to the same circle, and kindred matters, cf. *Philological Quarterly*, V (1926), 105–13, especially 108 and 112.

[3] Fig. 82a is reproduced from *California Publications*, VII (1923), 204, Fig. 3.

[4] Contrast Dörpfeld's reviews in *Philologische Wochenschrift*, XLI (1921), 1211–16 and XLIII (1923), 441–43, and cf. *Philological Quarterly*, V (1926), 109 ff. for my analysis. He has not yet reviewed Allen's fourth article, though published in July, 1923.

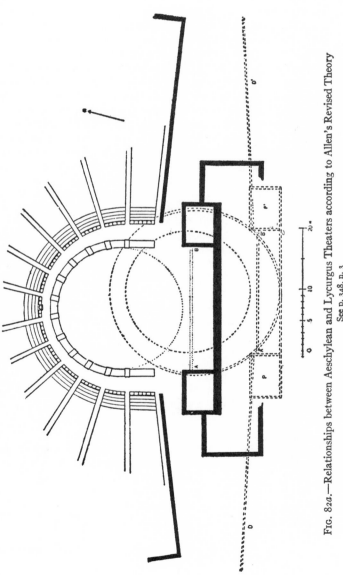

Fig. 82a.—Relationships between Aeschylean and Lycurgus Theaters according to Allen's Revised Theory

See p. 348, n. 3

basis for the exact correspondences which Professor Allen at first proposed. In my opinion he has erred again in assuming that the Aeschylean orchestra-terrace was of exactly the same diameter as the great circle of the Lycurgus theater and that the retaining wall of this orchestra-terrace was of the same width as obtained in the Epidaurus theater.[1] Nevertheless he has strengthened his theory by making it less precise in certain particulars, and in general I think he is right. The kernel of his argument is that dramatic performances in the Aeschylean theater were not centered in the whole orchestra-terrace but only in a smaller circle corresponding to the orchestra in the Lycurgus theater of about 330 B.C., that the size and position of this restricted area were determined by the "parascenia" and connecting walls which are assumed to have been grouped on and about the orchestra-terrace within the lifetime of Aeschylus, and finally that approximately these same arrangements were transferred to a slightly different site in the Sophoclean theater (some time between 460 and 430 B.C.) and reappeared about 330 B.C. in the theater "completed" by Lycurgus. To these propositions, until new evidence can be produced to the contrary, I can pledge full allegiance.

P. 66, ll. 3–6. These additional entrances are required for the correct understanding of the anecdote in Cicero, *De Senectute*, XVIII, 63 f.; cf. Flickinger, *Philological Quarterly*, V (1926), 97–102. There are rear entrances also in the Thoricus theater; see Figures 70 and 86.

P. 66, ll. 17 and 28–30, and p. 68, ll. 2–6. But see p. 348, n. 1, above.

P. 67, n. 4. Miss Bieber, *Die Denkmäler zum Theaterwesen im Altertum* 18, improbably assigns them to the Hellenistic theater.

P. 68, ll. 21 f. In the drain which leads under the scene-buildings from the east end of the gutter (about the Lycurgus orchestra) Professor Heinrich Bulle and Dr. K. Lehmann-Hartleben have recently found a stone seat, bearing a brief inscription in letters belonging to the close of the fifth century. Since this seat is straight instead of curved, it would seem that at this period the seating arrangements at Athens were semi-polygonal in plan, not semi-circular, cf. *Journal of Hellenic Studies*, XLIV (1924), 271, and *Philological Quarterly*, V (1926), 108, n. Inasmuch as wooden bleachers (ἴκρια) are mentioned as late as Aristophanes' *Women at the Thesmophoria* (vs. 395; produced in 411 B.C.), perhaps the new discovery was one of the seats of honor in the front rows (προεδρία; see p. 69, above), while the mass of the audience continued to occupy ἴκρια.

P. 68, l. 25. The difference in the diameters of the orchestra-terrace and of the orchestra produces an apparent discrepancy with p. 65, l. 10, above. Cf. Bethe, *Hermes*, LIX (1924), 114.

P. 69, ll. 10 f. The irregularity in the east boundary of the auditorium is now seen to be due to the Odeum of Pericles, which has been recently

---

[1] Cf. *Philological Quarterly*, V (1926), 107 f., and n. 28.

excavated by Castriotis; cf. Ἀρχαιολογικὴ Ἐφημερίς 1922, pp. 25–38. For the adjoining Street of the Tripods, cf. Philadelpheus, Ἀρχ. Ἐφ. 1921, pp. 83 ff. and Welter, *Athenische Mittheilungen*, XLVII (1922), 72–77.

P. 69, l. 18. For the accuracy of this statement cf. Flickinger, "Some Problems in Scenic Antiquities," *Philological Quarterly*, V (1926), 102–5.

P. 70, ll. 26 f. The change was of course intended to facilitate the movements of the audience before and after the performances.

P. 70, l. 31 to p. 71, l. 6. From this situation von Gerkan argues that these columns were not designed to inclose panels but belonged to a late Hellenistic proscenium the top of which was meant as a stage for actors. He believes that this shift in function took place *ca.* 160 B.C. at Priene and contemporaneously in other Greek theaters, i.e., about a century earlier than Dörpfeld would grant. For the preceding periods he defends Dörpfeld's thesis that the Greek theater had no stage for actors (see p. 79, above). Cf. *Das Theater von Priene* (1921), 104, and 123–29, especially 124.[1] Allen has accepted these conclusions and finds confirmation for them in the fact that the intercolumnar spaces in the Hellenistic proscenium at Athens are unusually narrow, "too narrow," he thinks, "to have been intended for the insertion of panels"; cf. *California Publications*, VII (1923), 199 f. Whatever may prove true of theaters at Priene and elsewhere, I am unable to accept a stage at Athens until the rebuilding in connection with Nero's visit in 67 A.D.

P. 90, n. 1. It should be remembered, as stated on p. 69, that this particular seat belongs to the Lycurgus theater in the next century. The inscription was not cut upon it until the first century B.C.; previously the inscription must have been painted, or no need of one was felt until the chairs of other dignitaries were inscribed, cf. Dörpfeld, *Das griechische Theater*, pp. 46 f. Of course, there can be no doubt where the priest of Dionysus sat in the Athenian theater.

P. 91, n. 3. The scholiast on verse 149 of Aristophanes' *Knights* states that in theatrical usage ἀναβαίνειν and καταβαίνειν had acquired the technical meanings of "go on" and "go off" and that this had arisen "from ancient practice." This interpretation has been adopted by many modern authorities who have difficulty, however, in discovering the source of the "ancient practice." Allen, "The Greek Theater of the Fifth Century before Christ," *California Publications*, VII (1919), 36 ff., derives it from the upward slope of the parodi leading to the orchestra-terrace in the earliest period of the Athenian theater.

P. 92, l. 10. With some plausibility Ridgeway assigns the *Rhesus* to the period of Euripides' residence in Macedonia at the close of his life; cf. *Classical Quarterly*, XX (1926), 1–19.

[1] See also p. 352, below, *addendum* to pp. 113 f.

P. 92, n. 2.   Professor Navarre, also, *Revue des Études Anciennes*, XXIV (1922), 172, says that for a quarter of a century he has never ceased to protest against the conception that the proscenium in the Lycurgus and Hellenistic theaters was *un decor, non une scène*.   He satirically adds *en son pays même M. Dörpfeld a cessé, semble t-il, d'être profête*, citing Fensterbush (1912), Fiechter (1914), Petersen (1915), Frickenhaus (1917), and Miss Bieber (1920).   *Pour tous ces savants, le proskénion est une scène.*   However, von Gerkan (1921) marks a reaction in the other direction; see *addenda* to p. 70, ll. 31 ff. (above) and to pp. 113 f. (below).

P. 98, ll. 9f.   Cf. Fensterbush, "Σκηνή bei Pollux," *Hermes* LX (1925), 112, and Flickinger, "Some Problems in Scenic Antiquities," *Philological Quarterly*, V (1926), 101f.

P. 100, ll. 26 f.   Unless the anecdote in Athenaeus, p. 631F, is modernized, ὑποσκήνιον is there used with reference to the first-story room of the Hellenistic theater.   Antigenidas is mentioned in the Delian Victors'-List for 265 B.C.

P. 101, n. 2.   Dyer also called attention to what he called "Plutarch's superiority to topographical minutiae"; *Journal of Hellenic Studies*, XXVIII (1908), 252, n. 4.

P. 102, n. 1.   Miss Bieber, *Die Denkmäler zum Theaterwesen im Altertum* pp. 62 f., explains καταβάς in terms of certain African theaters (built in the second century A.D.), in which steps descended into the stage from the somewhat higher floor-level of the *scaenae frons*.

P. 106, ll. 13 ff.   See Figure 87; the camera stood on the steps descending from behind the proscenium and faced the opening in the center of the orchestra.

Pp. 111–13.   New dates for the history of the Ephesus theater have been proposed by von Gerkan, *Das Theater von Priene* (1921), 90–93, and Hörmann, "Die römische Bühnenfront zu Ephesos," *Jahrbuch d. arch. Instituts*, XXXVIII–XXXIX (1923–24), 275–345.   They assign the first stone building, possibly including a marble proscenium, to 274 B.C., the seven θυρώματα to *ca.* 150 B.C., the Roman rebuilding to 66 A.D., and the third story of the proscenium (i.e., the fourth story of the scene-buildings) to *ca.* 150 A.D.

Pp. 113 f.   Further light has been thrown on the Priene theater by Armin von Gerkan's profusely illustrated *Das Theater von Priene* (1921). He assigns the Hellenistic structure (Fig. 83)[1] to about 300 B.C. and with Dörpfeld interprets its proscenium as a background, not a stage.   He suggests, somewhat improbably, that the origin of the proscenium in Greek theaters is to be sought in the field of Peloponnesian comedy (p. 126). The Graeco-Roman rebuilding (Fig. 84)[1] of the Priene theater he places at about 160 B.C., and maintains that this was the period when a stage was

[1] Figs. 83 f. reproduce Plates 36 and 35 respectively in von Gerkan's book.

FIG. 83.—Reconstruction of the Hellenistic Theater at Priene According to von Gerkan

See p. 352, n.

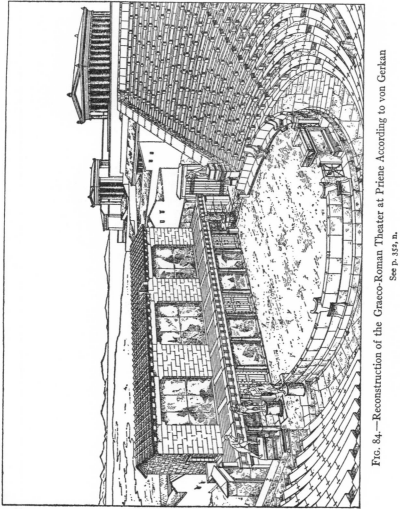

FIG. 84.—Reconstruction of the Graeco-Roman Theater at Priene According to von Gerkan

See p. 352, n.

introduced into Greek theaters under the influence of comedy as produced in Southern Italy (pp. 128 f.). He believes that alongside of the formal, state performances at Athens and elsewhere, which were choral by origin and so were best adapted to presentation in an orchestra, there must always have existed non-choral popular performances which made no pretense of artistic excellence but were very attractive to the masses, and that they were probably presented outside of the state theater and on rude stages. With the gradual shrinking of the dramatic chorus the existence of such performances facilitated the introduction of a staged type of theater from Magna Graecia in the middle of the second century. [See p. 381, below.]

Pp. 114 f. Cf. Athenaeus, p. 622C: οἱ δὲ φαλλοφόροι . . . . παρέρχονται οἱ μὲν ἐκ παρόδου, οἱ δὲ κατὰ μέσας τὰς θύρας.

P. 116, ll. 4–9. This was the method followed at Corinth in the rebuilding *ca.* 25 B.C. to 25 A.D.; cf. *American Journal of Archaeology*, XXIX (1925), 381–97. "This alteration was accomplished by removing some of the lower rows of seats and by cutting back the slope of the hill into the living rock to form a wall nearly three meters high, which would protect the spectators from the savage beasts and would, at the same time, provide much more space for the arena," *op. cit.*, pp. 387 f. Upon this wall was painted a polychrome figure with life-size combatants. One scene (Fig. 85)[1] represents the lower part of a composition in which a gladiator was poised as if to hurl a spear at a lion which is violently rushing away. Such a decorative device seems to be paralleled only upon a similar wall surrounding the arena of the amphitheater at Pompeii. Another wall rises on top of the first, set back three meters from its edge, thus leaving a suitable space for the accommodation of dignitaries (προεδρία; see pp. 69 and 350, *addendum* to p. 68, ll. 21 f., above).

P. 124, ll. 7 ff. and 29 f. Cf. Goodell, *Athenian Tragedy* (1920), p. 63: "But our personal suffering, while it may be idealized into a work of art that will give the right pleasure to others, cannot be so re-presented to us. Our pain will be so keen as to overpower the pleasure." Phrynichus had not learned this dramatic law.

P. 134, ll. 30 f. The following line in a Hellenistic tragedy dealing with Moses:

ὁρῶ δὲ ταύτας ἑπτὰ παρθένους τινάς

may perhaps be taken as referring to a chorus, thus affording some support to the evidence of the Cyrenaic wall-painting; cf. Kappelmacher, "Zur Tragödie der hellenistischer Zeit," *Wiener Studien*, XLIV (1925), 76.

P. 136, l. 15. Cf. Goodell, *op. cit.*, p. 77: "A Greek tragedy could not

[1] Fig. 85 is the same as *American Journal of Archaeology*, XXIX (1925), 385, Fig. 4, but was taken from a photograph kindly furnished by Professor T. Leslie Shear, who was in charge of the recent excavations at Corinth and wrote the report quoted above.

Fig. 85.—Part of Gladiatorial Scene Painted upon Wall Surrounding the Orchestra of the Graeco-Roman Theater at Corinth

See p. 354, n.

FIG. 86.—Ramp Leading to Rear Entrance of the Theater at Thoricus

See p. 357, n.

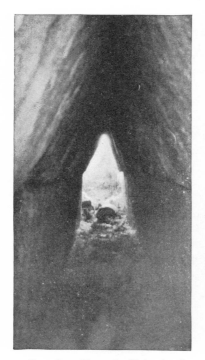

FIG. 87.—Charon's Stairs in the Theater at Eretria.

See pp. 352, *addendum* to p. 106, ll. 13 ff., and 357, n.

FIG. 88.—Columns from the Pro scenium of the Theater at Oropus.

See p. 357, n.

exist without a chorus, the historic beginning and ever the heart of drama to the Greeks. A unified group of participants in the action—fifty, twelve, finally fifteen—had to be provided, whether the story naturally called for them or not. The first business of the playwright was to shape the story so that it would call for them."

P. 138, 32 f. "The division of the comic chorus into hostile groups and the entire solidarity of the tragic chorus, together with its complete loyalty to the hero, are additional evidence of the impossibility of deriving both tragedy and comedy from the same ritual," D. C. Stuart, "The Origin of Greek Tragedy in the Light of Dramatic Technique," *Transactions American Philological Association*, XLVII (1916), 198, n. 23.

Pp. 141 f. For a second chorus in Roman tragedy, cf. *Classical Journal*, XIII (1918), 561 f. (Frank).

Pp. 147, ll. 15 ff. Cf. Gay, *The Beggar's Opera*, III, 13: "Let us retire, my dear Lucy, and indulge our sorrows; the noisy crew, you see, are coming upon us."

P. 148, ll. 22–25. See p. 351, *addendum* to p. 92, l. 10.

P. 152, ll. 12 f. Cf. Mrs. R. C. Bosanquet, *Days in Attica* (1914), p. 152: "Sometimes the interruptions [of the chorus] seem to introduce an element of commonplace—as for instance in the *Oedipus* of Sophocles [vss. 1297–1306] when the king appears with blood streaming from the empty eye-sockets, and the chorus can strike no deeper note than the cry—

    'Alas, unhappy man! I would have held
    Some converse with thee, but thy looks affright me;
    I cannot bear to speak with thee.' "

But the Greek text has been condensed in translation in a way which is, I think, unfair to the playwright.

P. 163, l. 4. The next step beyond the lyric duet between chorus and coryphaeus would be one between chorus and actor, such as Aeschylus' *Suppliants*, verses 843–903. This passage and verses 347 ff. and 736 ff., together with *Persians*, verses 256 ff. and 694 ff., are in the epirrhematic form (see p. 41, above) in which Kranz, "Die Urform der attischen Tragödie und Komödie," *Neue Jahrbücher für das klassische Altertum*, XLIII (1919), 145 ff., recognizes the first germ of dramatic action in both tragedy and comedy. For the latter there is nothing new about this doctrine (see p. 42, above). The tragic passages cited show types in the course of development, since the replies of the actor must originally have been in lyric meter, then in the primitive trochaic tetrameter (see pp. 22 and 45, above), and finally in iambics.

P. 169, l. 15. Rupprecht defends the variant reading ἐν μέσῳ (not μόνῳ) τῷ Θαμύριδι as the correct text in *Sophoclis Vita*, 5, cf. *Philologus*, LXXVI (1920), 213 ff. This would change the point of the anecdote.

P. 172, n.   Cf. Harrison, *Classical Quarterly*, XVIII (1924), 210.

P. 188, ll. 10 ff.   Cf. Prescott, "The Doubling of Rôles in Roman Comedy," *Classical Philology*, XVIII (1923), 23–34.

P. 192, ll. 19–21.   According to Stahl, in the dramas of Thespis there was only one episode (*Zwischenakt*), flanked on either side, of course, by the entrance song and exit song of the chorus; cf. *Rheinisches Museum für Philologie*, LXIX (1914), 592, n. 3.

Pp. 193 f.   Cf. Holzapfel, *Kennt die griechische Tragödie eine Akteinteilung?* (1914).

P. 196, ll. 9 ff.   By the terms of the alliance which followed the Peace of Nicias Spartan ambassadors were required to attend the City Dionysia in Athens every year for the purpose of renewing the compact; cf. Thucydides v. 23. 1.

P. 199, ll. 29–32.   It has now been established that the number of comic poets at the City Dionysia was reduced from five to three in 427 or 426 B.C.; cf. Dittmer, *Fragments of Athenian Comic Didascaliae Found in Rome* (1923), pp. 4 n. and 42 f. See pp. 359 f., below, *addendum* to p. 330.

P. 202, l. 23.   According to Plato's *Symposium* (223D), Socrates forced Aristophanes and Agathon to admit that "the same man might understand how to compose comedy and tragedy"; but Ion of Chios, who began to exhibit tragedies in 451 B.C. and was defeated by Euripides in 428 B.C., is the only known example.   He dabbled in a dozen forms of literature.

P. 204, ll. 34 ff.   The custom of attaching posters to the door of the theater to attract an audience by representing either the characters in the play or one of the most interesting scenes is said to date from the second half of the first century B.C.; cf. Horace *Satires* ii. 7. 96–100, and Holzknecht, *Philological Quarterly*, II (1923), 268.   In Elizabethan times a player or even the whole troupe, prior to the performance, would visit the principal places in the town, a rough equivalent of the προαγών.   Even as late as the seventeenth century playbills, designed to be posted about town or on the theater door, did not contain the names of actors or characters.   When shorthand writers were employed to take down plays at the theater, they apparently had no means of discovering a character's name unless it were mentioned in the text.   Cf. *ibid.*, pp. 272 and 277.

P. 205, l. 1.   For the Odeum of Pericles see pp. 350 f., above, *addendum* to p. 69, ll. 10 f.

P. 208, ll. 15 f.   Cf. Key, *The Introduction of Characters by Name in Greek and Roman Comedy* (1923).

P. 211, l. 36.   Cf. Austin, "The Significant Name in Terence," *University of Illinois Studies in Language and Literature*, VII (1921), No. 4, (130 pp.).

Pp. 225 f. David Belasco's *The Return of Peter Grimm* also observes the Greek rules. In this instance, however, the ghost's speeches, though heard by the audience, are thought of as being inaudible to the other characters on the stage but unconsciously affecting their thoughts and conduct.

P. 226, l. 35. Possibly at first by a single parodus, see p. 346.

P. 228, l. 26. See p. 348, n. 1, above.

P. 230, l. 2. Possibly only one parodus during part of this period; see p. 346, above.

P. 235, ll. 8 ff. Petersen, *Die attische Tragödie als Bild- und Bühnenkunst* (1915), p. 561, stages this scene in terms of upper and lower parodi, which he very improbably claims for the fifth-century theater.

P. 236, l. 1. See also Figure 88[1] and p. 351, above, *addendum* to p. 70, l. 31.

P. 236, ll. 15 f. See p. 348, n. 1, above.

P. 255, ll. 8 ff. Cf. Hoernle, *The Problem of the Agamemnon* (1921) and Mrs. R. C. Bosanquet, *Days in Attica* (1914), p. 60.

P. 241, ll. 21 ff. "In Racine and Corneille, on the contrary, the commonest location of the action is a palace; it is what takes place out of doors that must be narrated," cf. Goodell, *Athenian Tragedy*, p. 81.

P. 248, l. 11. Cf. Goodell, *op. cit.*, p. 89: "Discreet silence about distances and anything like a city plan leaves all inconvenient details floating in ideal space."

P. 249, ll. 3–5. A slighter instance occurs in Aescyhlus' *Eumenides*, cf. Goodell, *op. cit.*, p. 85: "The ancient image of the goddess was in fact in the temple, as everybody knew; but since dramatic necessity required it to be outside, outside it was, that the play might go on. And the temple itself is henceforth ignored and so disappears from the play."

P. 266, ll. 7 ff. There was the possibility, however, of a great difference between a personage's apparent character at the beginning of the play and that which was gradually revealed in the course of the dramatic action as his soul's history was unrolled bit by bit and stripped of its false glamor. This unveiling process commended itself to Sophocles in his *Oedipus the King* no less than to Ibsen in *Rosmersholm*. Cf. also A. T. Murray, "Plot and Character in Greek Tragedy," *Transactions American Philological Association*, XLVII (1916), 51 ff.

P. 267, ll. 14 ff. An opposite opinion was held by Goodell, *op. cit.*, p. 191: "Here, in a play extraordinarily rich in dramatic material of every kind, is a group of characters portrayed with a vigor and directness never surpassed, exhibiting a fullness of individuality that the greatest actors would find inexhaustible."

---

[1] Figs. 86–88 are from photographs taken by the author.

P. 272, ll. 23 ff.   Cf. Mrs. Bosanquet, *op. cit.*, pp. 153 f.: "Apart from the fact that the play was given once only and had therefore all the excitement of a first night added to that of the 'positively last performance,' there was also this keen, critical instinct to be satisfied.   Every Athenian was an art critic.   His verdict was a serious matter to himself and others.   What the Athenians approved or condemned would be in the same measure approved or condemned throughout Greece. . . . . The career of the poet must have been an exciting one under this régime.   Within a few hours of the production of his play its reputation throughout the Greek world was fixed."

P. 277, ll. 2–5.   Cf. Kent, *Philological Quarterly*, II (1923), 166, § 15.

P. 277, ll. 31 ff.   Such a statement is challenged by Gomme, "The Position of Women in Athens in the Fifth and Fourth Centuries," *Classical Philology*, XX (1925), 1–25.   In my judgment he carries his contention too far.   Lysias (*Adv. Simonem* 6) tells of Athenian women who lived so modestly that they were ashamed of being seen by the members of their household (τῶν οἰκείων).   For the inscriptional evidence, cf. *American Journal of Archaeology*, XXIII (1919), 73.

P. 278, ll. 33 ff.   A similar protective attitude toward a slave who is afterwards shown to have been free born appears in Plautus, *Captives* vss. 991 f.; cf. Flickinger, *Classical Weekly*, XVIII (1925), 167 f.

Pp. 282 f.   Cf. Goodell, *op. cit.*, p. 164: "Modern plays tend to abbreviate this final stage.   Modern audiences—perhaps because it is late in the evening—get impatient to leave after the struggle is decided; they are less interested in seeing results fully set forth.   The Athenians, on the other hand, liked a longer and fuller *telos*."

P. 284, n.   Cf. also Bickford, *Soliloquy in Ancient Comedy* (1922) and Law, *Studies in the Songs of Plautine Comedy* (1922).

Pp. 284 f.   Cf. Norwood, *Greek Tragedy*, pp. 66 f.: "The Elizabethan theater accepted precisely this contrivance of the eccyclema.   In our texts of *Henry VI* (Part II, Act III, scene 2) we read this stage-direction: 'The folding-doors of an inner chamber are thrown open, and Gloucester is discovered dead in his bed: Warwick and others standing by it.'   Instead of all this, the old direction merely says: 'Bed put forth.'   In another early drama we find the amusing instruction: 'Enter So-and-So in Bed.'   The aesthetic objection to the eccyclema has no force whatever."

P. 285, n. 2.   Figure 74 has been redrawn since the first edition in order to include the parascenia and their doors.   I am indebted to my friend, Mr. Thomas E. Tallmadge, of the American Institute of Architects, for the new drawing.

P. 294, l. 4.   Homer also was not above employing similar artifices; cf. Throop, *Washington University Studies*, XII (1924), 91–93.

P. 295, ll. 33 ff.   Some would interpret Euripides' use of the *deus ex machina* in terms of his alleged rationalistic propaganda. That is to say, accepting the presuppositions of the plot chosen for dramatic treatment he sought to develop the incidents in a perfectly natural and logical way to a finale which could only be transformed to the traditional ending by a divine interposition. Thus, at verse 1625 of his *Orestes*, we have reached a conclusion which was the inevitable outcome of Orestes' circumstances, character, and adventures. Only a deity could reconcile him to his estranged relatives and subjects and restore his fortunes. According to this view, the patent divergence between tradition and the actualities of existence would convince all who were capable of being convinced that the popular theology and its tales must be revamped or abandoned. This device would be particularly effective if a god should be required to impose his authority in a fashion which would not measure up to the best standards of human morality and conduct.

Pp. 298 ff. Cf. Spring, "A Study of Exposition in Greek Tragedy," *Harvard Studies*, XXVIII (1917), 135 ff., Stuart, "Foreshadowing and Suspense in the Euripidean Prologue," *Studies in Philology* (University of North Carolina), XV (1918), 295 ff., and Flint, *The Use of Myths to Create Suspense in Extant Greek Tragedy* (1922).

P. 303, ll. 17 ff. Stuart, *op. cit.*, p. 306, "amends" Murray's statement: "There is a secret and the playwright aims at this sort of excitement. We are told once in unequivocal words, with nothing to cast doubt on them, exactly what will happen (*Hippolytus*). But generally we are told what thing we may hope or fear will happen. Or we are told what will happen and we find that it does not happen with the expected result (Orestes and Electra condemned to death). Or we are told how it will happen and find that it does not happen in this way (*Ion*)."

P. 309, ll. 5–9. Professor Knapp maintains that "in the extant remains of Greek and Roman drama the practice here ridiculed is characteristic of tragedy rather than of comedy. . . . . I feel sure that in the passages cited . . . . we are dealing with allusions to the contemporary Roman stage"; cf. *Classical Philology*, XIV (1919), 49 f. Similarly, Fraenkel suggests that Plautine monodies were likewise derived from Roman tragedy; cf. *Plautinisches im Plautus* (1922), pp. 321–73.

P. 313, l. 21. It has been denied that Aeschylus ever used unconscious irony, but cf. *Libation-Bearers*, vss. 668–73 and 854 and Throop, *op. cit.*, pp. 97 ff.

P. 330, l. 8. Another such inscription, of which three fragments were formerly in Rome (two of them now lost), has previously been omitted from mention in this book for the reason that its proper restoration and interpretation had not been made out. The riddle has now been solved by Dittmer, *The Fragments of Athenian Didascaliae Found in Rome* (1923). The original document, when complete, must have covered nearly 500 sq. ft. of wall space. Each line contained 72–76 letters, embracing three items, and in all nearly 1,800 plays were listed. Körte suggested that the inscription once occupied the wall of one of the great imperial libraries at Rome. It recorded in chronological order, according to the date of their first exhibition, the name and dramatic career of all the comic poets who had produced comedies in either of the annual competitions at Athens. Under each poet's name, were listed by title all the plays which he had brought out, arranged according to their success, the victories first, then the seconds, thirds, fourths, and finally the fifths. Under each rank the plays produced at each festival, first the City Dionysia and then the Lenaea, were listed in separate groups, the arrangement of plays for each festival-group being chronological. It is clear that the document was a rearrangement of material contained in the comic Didascaliae from the introduction of comedy into each festival (486 and *ca.* 442 B.C. respectively) until 278 B.C. or even later. See also p. 356, above, *addendum* to p. 199, ll. 29–32.

P. 330, 35 ff. Körte, *Berliner philologische Wochenschrift*, XXXVIII (1918), 783–91, is undoubtedly correct in considering these two hypotheses as fragments from the περιοχαὶ τῶν Μενάνδρου δραμάτων prepared by Sellius, whom he would assign to the close of the first century A.D.

P. 332, ll. 14 f. According to the Preface to Hesychius' *Lexicon*, the modern system of alphabetizing words in a list was first employed by Diogenianus (second century A.D.).

P. 332, ll. 32 f. Geissler, however, *Chronologie der altattischen Komödie* (1925), p. 25, n. 5, favors the alphabetical interpretation of the numeral for Cratinus' *Dionysalexandros*. It is significant that he does not attempt to apply this system to Aristophanes' *Birds*. Though this play falls within the period of his discussion, he does not even mention its numeral. Menander's *Imbrians* falls outside his subject but its numeral must be taken into account before anyone can wisely hazard an opinion as to any of the others. It is absolutely fatal to an alphabetical interpretation.

ADDITIONAL NOTES TO THIRD EDITION

At the moment of going to press, the official summary of Dörpfeld's new investigations at the southwest corner of the *cavea* in the Athenian theater (see p. 341, l. 36, above) has been received; cf. *Arch. Anzeiger, Beiblatt zum Jahrb. d. arch. Inst.* XL (1925; actually 1926), 311–13. Here Dörpfeld distinguishes three sets of foundations, which he assigns to the close of the sixth, fifth, and fourth centuries respectively. His conclusions apparently harmonize with the positions advocated in the present volume.

A fortunate delay in the presswork enables me to refer to Dr. Dörpfeld's "Das Theater von Priene und die griechische Bühne," of which he has been kind enough to send me the advance sheets from *Athenische Mittheilungen* XLIX (1924; actually 1926), 50–101. He demolishes von Gerkan's contention that the Priene theater had a stage in the later Hellenistic period, and rejects (p. 90) the argument drawn from the absence of devices (to hold πίνακες) on the columns of the Hellenistic proscenium at Athens (see p. 351, above). At Priene he assigns the auditorium and scene-building (with wooden proscenium) to 350–300 B.C., the stone proscenium (with wooden episcenium) to 250–200 B.C., the stone episcenium with θυρώματα to 200–150 B.C., and the Roman stage to the second century A.D. From Dr. Leonardos and Professor von Gaertringen he has secured new opinions as to the age of the inscriptions at Oropus, and he now distributes parts of this theater as follows: the stone proscenium with its πίνακες to shortly after 200 B.C., the stone episcenium with its θυρώματα to about 150 B.C., and the marble seats of honor in the orchestra (a sure proof that the performances still took place on that level) to about 100 B.C. At Athens he recognizes more of the auditorium as belonging to the fifth century than he had previously thought (p. 89), and places the Periclean orchestra in an intermediate position between the sixth-century orchestra-terrace and the Lycurgus orchestra. He even hints that the Nero theater may have had no stage (!), and so persists in the opinion that theatrical references in Pollux and Plutarch are to be interpreted in terms of stageless theaters; if the Nero theater had a stage, then these authors still wrote in terms based upon their knowledge (derived from books!) that the earlier theaters had had no stage (pp. 98-100). The conclusions in this last sentence I cannot indorse, and as to these points I much prefer the positions advocated in the present volume. The article constitutes a valuable restatement of Dörpfeld's views, which he has materially strengthened in several particulars.

NOTES TO FOURTH EDITION

Pp. 65, 342, and 348, n. 2. In *Philologische Wochenschrift* XLIII (1923), 442 f., Dörpfeld threw doubt upon his original contention that stones B and C (see Fig. 32, above) belonged to the same circle and determined the position of the early orchestra-terrace. After repeated examination of these fragments I am now reluctantly constrained to accept this contention. With the waning of belief in these landmarks scholars have felt free to propose reconstructions of the early fifth-century theater in Athens, relying more upon literary evidence and theoretical considerations than upon the archaeological remains. For example, in "Die baugeschichtliche Entwicklung des athenischen Dionysostheaters im V. Jh.," *Philologus* LXXXV (1930), 229–42, Fensterbusch followed Bethe in assigning the shift of the orchestra to about 500 B.C., an impossibly early date, and suggested that this structure was in alignment with the sixth-century temple of Dionysus Eleuthereus. He maintained that a slight reorientation in the theater was made also in the period of about sixty-five years ending with the "completion" of the theater by Lycurgus in the fourth century, in order to align it with the new temple which was erected about 415 B.C. See also addendum to pp. 346–50, below.

Pp. 72, 81, 98, 117, and 361. All these references but the last represent Dörpfeld as assigning a high Graeco-Roman stage to the Athenian theater in the time of Nero. The article cited on p. 361 indicates his later tendency to deny a stage of any height to the Nero theater, and he has now elaborated this view in "Das Proskenion des Kaisers Nero im Dionysos-Theater von Athen," *Mélanges Navarre* (Toulouse: Édouard Privat, 1935), pp. 159–67. I continue to hold my own view, however, which was also Dörpfeld's first opinion, that this theater had a low stage. See p. 72, above.

Pp. 106, 352, and 354. Another example of "Charon's steps" has been found in the interesting remains of the theater at Philippi; see Fig. 89[1] and cf. *Bulletin de correspondance hellénique* LII (1928), 74–124. This theater was built about the middle of the fourth century B.C. with an orchestra in the form of a complete circle. It was reconstructed after the beginning of the Christian Era, when a Roman stage was built partly impinging upon the orchestra, which was then paved; in the center a place was left for the erection of an altar (θυμέλη). Steps were removed from the bottom of the cavea, which was thus transformed into a sort of pit; see pp. 111–16, above.

[1] The photograph was taken August 10, 1935, and is reproduced by permission of the Marine Photo Service of Colchester, England.

Fig. 89.—The Theater at Philippi

See p. 362, n. 1

About the second century A.D. the Roman proscenium was removed and the full orb of its circle restored to the orchestra, which henceforth was used primarily as an arena. A subterranean passage leading into the orchestra is clearly seen in Fig. 89 and has been assigned to this final period as affording better access to the orchestral arena for beasts and combatants. I venture to suggest, however, that this is but a modification of an earlier passage for actors such as is found at Eretria.

P. 115, Fig. 63. For mechanical reasons it is not feasible to replace this figure, which is now antequated. For later and more accurate drawings cf. Armin von Gerkan, *Das Theater von Priene* (Leipzig: F. Schmidt, 1921).

Pp. 199 f. Maidment believes that the increase in the number of comedies presented at the annual festivals from three to five coincided with the abandonment of the synchoregia; cf. *Classical Quarterly* XXIX (1935), 9. See next addendum.

P. 271. Maidment makes it seem probable that the choregic system was restored about 394 B.C.; cf. "The Later Comic Chorus," *Classical Quarterly* XXIX (1935), 1–24, especially pp. 4 and 8 f.

Pp. 244 and 247. Groh ignored my analysis of these scenes in attempting to find arguments for a raised stage in the *Ajax;* cf. "De Scaena Sophoclis," *Mélanges Navarre*, pp. 245–47.

Pp. 342–46. Allen's theories are now quite definitely placed *hors de combat* by more recent developments; see below.

Pp. 346–50. My theories were elaborated, with the aid of some suggestions from Fensterbusch's article (see above), in "The Theater of Aeschylus," *Transactions of the American Philological Association* LXI (1930), 80–110, but require a slight restatement in view of the latest developments. I believe that what became the parascenium in more developed theaters was the core of the earliest structure, appearing at the east margin of the orchestra in Aeschylus' *Suppliants*, was duplicated at the west margin with a connecting "parapet" between the two in the *Seven against Thebes*, etc. There was only one parodus (from the west) until after the construction of Pericles' Odeum about 441 B.C., and originally there were doors in the front wall of the parascenia, the central doors being relatively late. I have recently applied these suggestions to the *Peace* in "The Staging of Aristophanes' *Pax*," *Mélanges Navarre* (Toulouse: Édouard Privat, 1935), pp. 191–206.

P. 361. Dörpfeld has now assigned the republication of the Athenian theater to Fiechter, who gives a brief summary of recent results in *Archäologischer Anzeiger, Beiblatt zum Jahrbuch d. arch. Instituts* XLIX (1934), 543 f. He believes the oldest portion of the scene-building to be the long hall, with its retaining walls to the north and east, just north of the old temple of Dionysus. This complex of walls replaced the foundations of an older *Spielplatz* to which fragment B (see Figs. 32 f., above) belongs—

not, however, as a part of the old orchestra itself, but only as a portion of the supporting walls for the terrace.   The old orchestra was therefore smaller than Dörpfeld at first reported—about twenty meters, or sixty-five feet, seven inches in diameter; contrast pp. 65, 242, and 248, above—and lay opposite the opening for a door which may still be seen in the north wall of the long hall.   In the Phaedrus theater he differentiates three periods: (*a*) brick pits for the Roman curtain; (*b*) the relief in front of the stage belonging to the second century A.D. and here re-used; and (*c*) the steps leading up to the stage (*bema*).   These opinions are not altogether acceptable to me unless they can be supported by suitable evidence, but do not greatly affect the theater in which the fifth-century playwrights performed.   I shall reserve criticism, however, until Fiechter fulfils his promise of full publication at an early date in the series in which monographs dealing with the theaters at Oropus, Oeniadae and Neupleuron, Sicyon, and Megalopolis have already appeared (Stuttgart: W. Kohlhammer, 1930–31).

I cannot conclude without calling attention to the important and beautifully illustrated volume by Bulle, Lehmann-Hartleben, etc. entitled *Untersuchungen an griechischen Theatern* (Munich: R. Oldenbourg, 1928.)

INDEXES

INDEX OF PASSAGES

(Boldface figures refer to the pages of this volume. Works which are known to us only by title or short fragments are indicated by an asterisk.)

GENERAL INDEX